'The Caucasus is where European ar
interact: David Hunt's anthology is
world of pagan heroics and primeval n
speaking reader. The translations are both inventive and meticulous
(sourced from Russian-language versions) in rendering the extraordinary
folk poetry of the many nations of the Caucasus. Essential reading not only
for folklorists, but for anyone seeking an insight into the cultures of the
Caucasus.'

DONALD RAYFIELD
Queen Mary, University of London

'David Hunt's book has brought into the light some of the hidden treasures
of the Caucasus, a region that has been largely unknown in the West except
for its recent turmoil and wars. Hunt has given translations of a wide
selection of folklore, representing every portion of this complex and diverse
region. He has given us tales of great wealth and variety, all in fluid prose.
This is a major contribution not only to the study of the Caucasus, but also
to world folklore.'

JOHN COLARUSSO
McMaster University

Legends of the Caucasus

DAVID HUNT

SAQI

Grateful thanks are due to Professor Suyunova Nasipkhan, Professor Uzdiat Bashirovna Dalgat, Tanzilya Mussayevna Khajieva and Meri Khukhunaishvili-Tsiklauri for their help with anthropological and other details, to Anna Pilkington for her help with translation difficulties and to Laurence Hunt for correcting the texts.

ISBN 978-0-86356-473-4

First published 2012 by Saqi Books

© 2012 David Hunt

A full CIP record for this book is available from the British Library.

A full CIP record for this book is available from the Library of Congress.

Manufactured in Lebanon

SAQI
26 Westbourne Grove, London W2 5RH
www.saqibooks.com

Contents

Introduction

The Caucasus has an extremely rich folk literature – one that includes myths, legends, anecdotes and proverbs – which is almost unknown among English speakers. One hundred of their most interesting legends have been selected from the nearly one thousand that are available and translated into English for the first time here.

One of the reasons that the Caucasus has such a rich store of folk literature is that the bulk of the languages spoken in the mountainous and countryside regions had no alphabet until the early years of the twentieth century, and so nearly all communication was oral. All knowledge, including the classical history, literature and music of the people was retained in the collective memory, particularly of those who specialised in memorising and passing on their knowledge to the next generation. Naturally, the quantity of information is limited, but the quality is undeniable. Georgia differs in that it has had an alphabet for many centuries, although many of those living in the Georgian mountain regions did not know or use their alphabet. In other parts of the Caucasus there were educated people who could use the Arabic or Russian alphabets, although not for writing the many local languages. The Adyges acquired a written language around 1920, the Chechens in 1938 after an earlier attempt to use the Latin alphabet, the Tabasarans in 1932, the Balkars in 1924 (Narody Kavkaza 1960). However, the collectors of folklore had begun work about forty years before then, throughout the late nineteenth century.

Among the early collectors were Vazha-Pshavela and V. Nizharadze in Georgia in the 1880s, Ch. Akhriev in Ingushetia in the 1870s, P. Ostryakov and S. A. Urusbiev in Balkaria in the 1880s (Virsaladze 1973, 6; Dalgat 1972, 33; Khajieva & Ortabayeva 1994, 8). Even after the development of alphabets, there were many older people who still retained the oral culture, which was then available for recording by enthusiastic scholars. Even now, there are frequent expeditions into the mountains to collect folk material of various kinds, including stories, songs and proverbs. Some of the earliest published legends appeared informally in such publications as the newspaper *Kavkaz* in the 1840s, but between 1870 and 1880 special journals were launched specifically to record folklore and related subjects: these included the 'Collection of Information about the Caucasus Mountain People' (SSKG), the 'Collection of Information about the Terek Province' (SSTO), and the 'Collection of Materials for the Description of Places and Tribes in the Caucasus' (SMOMPK).[1] In the absence of alphabets for recording the texts in the original languages, with Georgian being the exception, the language of these publications was generally Russian. Since nearly all of the early collectors were Russian scholars, the language of their texts was of a good standard. When the collections were made by local people, they often had been educated in Russia, so again the quality of the translations into Russian was good. Examples were the Balkar collections by the well-educated princely family of Urusbiev, the Ingush and Chechen collections of B. Dalgat in the late 1800s, and those of E. B. Virsaladze in the first half of the twentieth century. All of the legends in this book were translated from the Russian texts.

The question might be asked: what are the differences between oral literature and written literature, and do they matter? There are several answers to this: perhaps one of the most profound differences being that written literature is usually a private transfer of information from the page to the reader, whereas oral literature involves at least two people, or more often one public performer and many listeners; in other words it is a public as opposed to a private performance. Therefore the oral material is more likely to be influenced by public scrutiny than the written material would be.

Another very important difference is that the written literature is fixed for eternity, whereas the oral literature changes over time. Firstly, the content depends on the memory of the performer, who tends to remember certain details at the expense of others. Secondly, the content is passed from one generation to the next, with consequent changes according to memory and inclination. And thirdly, and perhaps most importantly, the performer edits his or her performance according to the audience. In the case of a large public performance the performer is probably paid, and whoever is footing the bill will want to be pleased with the subject matter. For instance, a feudal prince might not want to hear a story about a peasant rebellion against the feudal authorities; or a rich merchant might not want to hear about the dishonest or miserly behaviour of merchants. Even in a private or family storytelling session, the narrator will probably orientate the narration according to the age and status of the audience. These dynamic influences will gradually alter the legend as it is universally perceived.

---

1   Respectively, 'Sbornik svedeniy o kavkazskikh gortsakh, Sbornik svedeniy o terskoy oblasti' and 'Sbornik materialov dlya opisaniya mestnostey i plemen Kavkaza'.

The other important difference is the proportion of the population involved in the transmission of the story or legend. Whereas written stories are generally transmitted by specialist authors or journalists, everybody can transmit oral literature, although large or important gatherings were usually entertained by specialists, who in medieval times were known as minstrels.

*

Legends have been chosen for this book as one of the most interesting genres of folk literature, since they tend to include matters that are especially important to the narrators and listeners, and consequently they are valuable for the study of past culture. Legends often have a strong local interest, and have a meaning and importance that is more immediate to their intended audience – compared with the folk narratives such as anecdotes and folk tales, which are composed for pure entertainment. Many of the latter consist of motifs and tale types that are internationally recognised and are listed in the international indexes.[1]

The characteristics that define a legend as opposed to other genres have been defined by Katharine Briggs (Briggs 1970, A Vol. 1; 1). Whereas tales are told 'for edification, delight or amusement, folk legend was once believed to be true'. The narrator of a legend 'is telling something that he expects to be received as fact, generally with the corroborative detail of person, time or place'. (Briggs 1971, B Vol. 1: viii). Of course, such a classification cannot be 'set in stone', since the beliefs of both the narrator and the audience change with time: what was believed at one time and one place would not apply to another time and place. The criteria that were mostly used for choosing the legends to be included in this book were: (1) that the name of the person or place was included in the text of the legend; and (2) that if any supernatural or magic elements were included, these could be concepts that were once believed to be true.

*

The legends here have been classified according to subjects that were of particular importance to the people who lived in the Caucasus up until the

---

1   See Antti Aarne, *The Types of the Folktale*, trs. by Stith Thompson (FF Communications No. 184, Helsinki, 1981) and Thompson, Stith, *Motif-Index of Folk-Literature*, 6 vols (Indiana University Press, Bloomington & Indianapolis, 1955).

end of the nineteenth century, when many of these legends were collected. This particularly applied to those living in the mountains rather than in the towns. Analysis of the body of Caucasus legends shows that they could be divided into three main categories: military matters, mainly the business of the men, in protecting their own lives and that of their families and their homes; food matters and protection against the ever-present risk of famine; and family matters, which dealt with everything that affected the family and the home, including religion.

In the first chapter are four examples of legends about well-known historical figures who were politically important in their time: the Nogay Khan Edige, the military leader Tamerlane from the East, known locally as Lame Temir or Lame Timur, and the early Georgian king and founder of Tbilisi, Vakhtang Gorgasali.

The next two chapters include legends in which the heroes fight against oppression, either by external foreign invaders or by real or aspiring internal feudal authorities. In the Caucasus a man was prepared to be a warrior as well as a provider of food. The Caucasus mountain man owned weapons and knew how to use them. This was partly because, living in a remote area, he could not rely on the protection of government agencies: to protect him and his family and community from foreign invaders, from other ethnic groups, from feudal overlords or from those striving to be so, or even from his neighbours. Moreover, in places where the feudal powers were strong, they might call him into service, or alternatively he might be in conflict with them. Chapter 2 deals with the subject of 'resistance to foreign invaders': respectively the armies of Tamerlane, of the Persian Nadir Shah and of the Russian Tsar. Chapter 3 on feudal oppression deals with various cases: in some the folk hero escapes unharmed, in some he is killed by his feudal lord, while others describe how the feudal lord is killed, resulting in freedom for the previously downtrodden population.

The rustling of animals was a favourite sport among many young men, and this subject is covered in Chapter 4. This sport particularly involved the stealing of horses, but it could also apply to the stealing of sheep or cattle for food (e.g., Byhan 1936).

While the theme of warriors is dealt with in Chapters 2 and 3, there are also legends about exceptionally gifted warriors, some of which are included in Chapter 5. The theme of blood revenge is also prominent in Caucasus legends, and this is closely connected with family honour. This is a very complicated subject, and can be viewed from various perspectives.

From the point of view of the blood enemy himself, there is the view that the dead live on, but in a parallel world. The spirit of the slain man not only requires blood revenge, but if he is not satisfied with his family in this respect he may become a most powerful ghostly enemy, with superhuman powers. The spirit of the unavenged slain man is likely to be more dangerous to his own family than to the family of his slayer. This danger, together with the requirements of family honour, encourages the living members of the family to exact blood revenge. This subject is discussed at length by B. Dalgat (Dalgat 2004, 102ff). The prospect of blood revenge acts as a deterrent to casual or premeditated crimes in a community that is not controlled by government in the form of a police force. This subject is further discussed in Chapter 9, on family and personal honour.

In societies where the supply of food is not assured, the obtaining of food is also of vital importance. In the mountains there were three means of obtaining food: hunting, animal rearing and agriculture, although the latter is not practicable in some of the mountain districts. This collection includes legends associated with each of these three food sources. Chapter 6 contains legends about hunting, which is a dangerous occupation in the high mountains, both from the point of view of food shortage caused by lack of hunting success, and of the dangers associated with the craggy terrain. This is not mere mountaineering; it involves following the animals wherever they lead, and recovering carcasses from dangerous terrain. Chapter 7 deals with the rearing of animals, which in the high mountains mostly means sheep or goats. This chapter about shepherds includes some examples of Cyclops legends. There are many variants of the Cyclops legend in the Caucasus, and one of the few common factors in these legends is that the giant (Cyclops) is a shepherd, as he was in *The Odyssey*. This is discussed in more detail in the relevant chapter. The theme of the importance of agriculture is included in Chapter 8 on abundance.

The last four chapters all deal with familial and religious matters, which are intertwined. These include Chapter 9 on family and personal honour, Chapter 10 on relations within the family, Chapter 11 on religion and relations with the dead, and Chapter 12 on Prometheus legends. Family and personal honour are linked, since the family is so important in the Caucasus that any personal shortcomings reflect on the family itself. Family honour is very strongly linked to such things as hospitality, the chastity of women and girls, the courage of men in battle and respect for the dead. Most of these themes are included in the legends presented here. The chapter on relations within the family continues with this theme, contrasting the personal relations within the family and relations with outsiders. In the Caucasus, religion is closely connected to relations with dead ancestors, as B. Dalgat shows (B. Dalgat 2004). The more recently deceased ancestors must be kept happy by memorial feasts and sacrifices of food by the family, but after the family members' personal memories of the dead have faded, some of the more prominent of the dead ancestors gradually acquire a 'saintly' status, with the introduction of sacrifices that take place in sanctuaries dedicated to that ancestor. This especially applies to 'clan' ancestors, when a family has multiplied and extended sufficiently to have formed a local clan. The last section, on Prometheus legends, is included with this group of legends on family matters because the family is symbolised by the central point of the home, which is the hearth with its fire, and so the acquisition of fire is of central importance. A second reason for its inclusion is that the core of the Prometheus legend is theomachy, the conflict between God (a god or gods) and men, and therefore these legends have a religious connotation. Variants of legends containing Prometheus motifs are widespread in the Caucasus, and the relevant chapter discusses what the core of the Prometheus legend is.

It is clear that there is a considerable amount of overlapping of themes, especially in these last four chapters. Since the aboriginal religions were partly based on respect for family ancestors, and the material centre of such a religion was the family hearth, the concepts of religion, family honour and relations between members of the family are closely linked, together with the Prometheus legends as explained above.

*

Many of the legends in this collection are in the form of songs or poems, or in some cases, such as the historical epic of 'Edige', it is a mixture of prose and poetry, with prose being used to move the action along, but poetry (song) providing descriptions of scenes and of people's thoughts and feelings.

Various scholars have studied the structures of epic songs. For instance, Lord (1981, 4) states 'oral epic song is narrative poetry composed in a manner evolved over many generations by singers of tales who did not know how to write; it consists of the building of metrical lines and half lines by means of formulas and formulaic expressions and of the building of songs by the use of themes'.

Clearly, the oral performer must capture and retain the interest of his or her audience. This requirement determines the structure and style of the performance. 'His manner of composition differs from that used by the writer in that the oral poet makes no conscious effort to break the traditional phrases and incidents; he is forced by the rapidity of composition in performance to use these traditional elements' (Jousse 1925, quoted in Lord 1981, 4). In other words, the legends were not memorised 'word for word'; the performance is impromptu, and in order to sing it in a poetic form the singer makes use of formulae that through experience he knows will fit in with the metre of the poetry.

The general development of the legends tends to follow the same route as the Homeric poems. These began as oral songs. Again, quoting Lord (1981): 'There is now no doubt that the composer of the Homeric poems was an oral poet. The proof is to be found in the poems themselves; and it is proper, logical and necessary that this should be so' (Lord 1981, 141). On being recorded in writing, the musical accompaniment was lost, and they became poems. With later translation, the poetry was transformed to prose. This established the typical pattern of the transformation of epic literature: song to poetry to prose.

The logical conclusion of the above is that for many or most prose renderings there was probably an earlier sung version of the legend, which has probably been lost. This does not necessarily mean that the songs in this collection are older than the prose works, but that for each prose legend there was probably an earlier sung form of it. In many ways this makes the songs more interesting, since they are more likely to include archaic elements. The structure of most of these legends shows that they were intended for oral presentation, and the poetic form, even if not accompanied by music, lends itself to a dramatic public performance.

In view of this, it is interesting to consider the legend of Edige, in which the action is presented in prose, while the thoughts and feelings of the main actors are presented in verse. This may be compared with the character of many of the recent *prose* publications of folk material. One rule-of-thumb for assessing whether folk material is genuine is that the action moves on without the distraction of descriptions of scenes or of the characters' emotions; if the latter are present, then the text has probably been reworked by the author or compiler of the book. It is clear that the verse passages of Edige would be inappropriate if rendered as prose, and this is a further indication of the genuine folk origin of this version of the Edige legend.

It may seem that most of the legends appear to concentrate on men's affairs and less on women's interests. Of course, this is partly because in the mountain environment relations with people and powers outside the family were mainly controlled by men. However, within the family the women played a key role, and a substantial number of the legends in the last group, which deals with family relations and hospitality to guests, together with the section on abundance of food, include women. In the section on military matters there are several women warriors. In the chapter on warriors there is a woman who performs blood revenge in the absence of other male relatives; and another legend includes an extremely strong woman who beats the enemy's champion in single combat, overcoming his experienced military tactics by sheer strength.

A word needs to be said about the choice of legends included in this book, and why the legends from certain ethnic groups are more prominent than others. The only considerations in selecting the legends for inclusion were availability, interest, originality and relevance to the theme of the chapter in which it was included. Absolutely no consideration whatever was given to politics or to the inter-ethnic conflicts and rivalries of the various Caucasus groups. Many legends that may be without doubt interesting have not been included because the texts were not available in the Russian language. Many legends that were available simply didn't fit in with the scheme of this book. And since the hundred legends in this book were chosen from about one thousand available, when several covered the same ground it was necessary to select those of sufficient difference to interest the reader. Bearing in mind the above restrictions, an attempt was made to include legends from as diverse a range of ethnic groups as possible.

I

Historical–Political Legends

It is no exaggeration to say that the epic saga of Edige is one of the world's cultural treasures. For the Turkish people of West Asia in general, and for the Nogay people in particular, it is a national epic that can be compared with the West European Arthurian romances, the English Beowulf and the Finnish Kalevala.

The saga of Edige deals with real historical characters and events that took place at the turn of the fifteenth century. Since that time the plot has diverged somewhat from the actual recorded history.

There follows some information about the actual people and places mentioned. Much of this information was obtained from Karl Reichl's outstanding book *Edige: A Karakalpak Oral Epic*. Reichl's book gives the complete recorded text and a translation of a version of the Edige epic recorded among the Karakalpak people; these and other ethnic groups were once part of the Nogay Horde and, according to Reichl, versions of the Edige epic have been recorded among the Nogay, Kazakh, Karakalpak, Tatar and Bashkir in their native tongues (Reichl 2007, 32).

The saga of Edige is an epic biography of a leader of the Nogay Horde of western Asia. It describes his humble beginnings and his rise to power, which included the overthrow of the previous leader, Khan Tokhtamysh. Although the background facts are political and historical, the story deals more particularly with Edige's human and familial relations. The Nogay Horde was formed from the remnants of the Golden Horde, which disintegrated after the defeat of Khan Tokhtamysh.

KHAN TOKHTAMYSH AND THE GOLDEN HORDE

Khan Tokhtamysh was of Mongolian origin, descended from Chingis Khan himself via his fourth son Jochi, although the details of his descent are uncertain. He was the last Khan of the Golden Horde, whose domains extended from the Crimea in the West to near Lake Balkash in the East.

Besides the territory of present-day Kazakhstan and Uzbekistan, they also controlled Southern Russia and the Ukraine. According to one account, the epithet 'golden' was coined by envoys from the West who were struck by the magnificence of the gold decorations on the dwelling of the khan (Reichl 2007, 22). An alternative explanation is that the various Hordes used colours to signify the cardinal directions: black for north, blue for east, red for south, white for west and golden for central (Internet: Nationmaster Encyclopedia: Golden-Horde). Although the leaders of the Golden Horde were of Mongolian origin, the majority of the population was of Turkic origin, with Turkic influence gradually increasing, and by the fourteenth century the language of the Golden Horde was Kipchak Turkic. These Turkic people were usually referred to in Russian epics as 'Polovtsy'. Khan Tokhtamysh's military campaigns included the sacking of Moscow in 1382, an invasion of Persia in 1385, and an invasion in 1387 of Transoxiana, which was the domain of Timur, his former ally.

The Golden Horde began its decline with the Black Death and a serious defeat by Russian forces at the Battle of Kulikovo Polye in 1380; and Tokhtamysh was conclusively defeated by his former ally Timur (Tamerlane) at the River Terek in the North Caucasus in 1395, with a further defeat at the Battle of Vorskla River by Edige and Khan Temir Qutlugh in 1399. He was finally killed during the winter of 1406–1407 by Tokhtamysh's successor, Khan Shadi Beg. In the Battle of Vorskla River, the Khan of the Golden Horde, Temir Qutlugh, was killed and he was succeeded by Shadi Beg. However, Edige wielded the real power in the Golden Horde as emir. During the fifteenth century the Golden Horde gradually disintegrated into various groups, one of which was the Nogay Horde, of which Edige is considered to be the founder. Edige himself was a Nogay, and the name Nogay is taken from a previous powerful emir of the Golden Horde. Historical sources say that Edige was killed in 1419 by Qadir Berdi, a son of Tokhtamysh.

One of the most important historical characters that appears in the epic is Timur the Lame (Tamerlane or Temir), named here as Khan Shatemir. He and Tokhtamysh had been allies until the two came to clash over their rival territorial ambitions in Persia and the Persian Empire. Tamerlane emerged as the eventual winner. Tokhtamysh's overwhelming defeat at the Battle of the Vorskla River was conducted by Tamerlane's forces under the command of Edige and Khan Temir Qutlugh.

The capital of the Golden Horde was established on the River Volga at Saray Batu, also known as Old Saray. It is thought that it was located on what is now the Akhtuba Channel of the Lower Volga near the present village of Selitryannoye, about 120 km north of Astrakhan. The capital was later moved upstream to New Saray (Saray Berke), which was possibly on the same channel, about 55 km south of Volgograd.

1. Edige *(Nogay)*

A certain poor shepherd used to graze his sheep on the steppe. One day he came across the skull of a man. After turning it over with his stick, the shepherd noticed an inscription on the skull's forehead.

The shepherd was illiterate. Putting the skull on his stick, he brought it into the *aul* and showed it to a certain literate man. The inscription ran: 'Before death I killed ten thousand men, after death I will kill only forty.'

The shepherd was surprised. He brought the skull home and smashed it into little bits with a hammer. Then, after turning them into flour, he wrapped it in a rag and gave it to his wife for safe-keeping. He gave it to her but did not tell her where the flour came from.

In an hour when there was nobody at home, the shepherd's daughter opened the chest where they kept the little bundle and unwrapped it. On seeing the white flour, the girl tasted it with her tongue and she became pregnant.

Her time came, and she gave birth to a boy, to whom they gave the name of Barkaya.

The boy grew very fast and soon became more intelligent and stronger than all of his contemporaries.

The years passed. And a khan was the ruler in that region. And one night he had a dream: in it he was riding on his favourite racehorse, and suddenly forty savage dogs surrounded him. After dividing up into two groups with twenty in each, the dogs rushed at the khan from two directions, intending to throw him from his saddle and tear him to pieces.

Upon waking, the khan related his dream to his viziers and demanded that they explain its meaning. But the viziers were incapable of interpreting the khan's dream. And the khan sent his heralds to go through all his khanate: whoever could explain the mystery of the dream would receive from the ruler all that he wanted.

But not a single man was able to undertake the task. This news even reached the boy Barkaya. And he presented himself before the khan.

'Allow me to try, my khan!'

'Try!' commanded the khan.

Barkaya said, 'You have forty viziers. And they have divided themselves in half, into two parties. Each of them is negotiating with your wife to kill you and set another on the throne. Each party wants to have their own man as ruler.'

'You are lying, son of a dog!' the khan snarled threateningly. 'I will hang you!'

'If you don't believe me, order your wife to be watched at night. You will see, Khan, how after midnight your viziers come to her.'

The khan did not believe it. But he decided to make sure. After midnight a series of viziers drifted to the khan's wife's bedroom. For a long time they were whispering with her about how they would kill the khan and about whom to set on the throne.

The khan and his men seized the plotters, and in the morning all forty of the viziers were hanged. And so the words inscribed on the forehead of the skull came true.

The khan was grateful to the boy Barkaya and asked him to become his chief vizier. But Barkaya would not agree. He went away to the banks of their mother-river Edil'.

And Barkaya became a mighty man. He lived alone in the open air, hunted in the forest and fished in the River Edil'. His body was covered with hair, and long hair grew on his head. His beard covered all his chest. And people accordingly gave him the nickname 'Baba-tu'kles Shashly Aziz', which means 'Shaggy-haired Grandfather, Hairy Aziz'.

One day, when Baba-tu'kles Shashly Aziz, that is Barkaya, was catching fish with a net at dawn on Lake Sekerli, nine white swans came flying in and sat on the shore. Barkaya hadn't time to blink his eyes before the swans flapped their wings, threw off their swan attire and turned into beautiful girls.

The fisherman returned to the shore and crept up to the girls without being spotted. Their beauty dazzled Barkaya. He fell passionately in love with one of them.

And when the girls, after leaving their swan's attire on the shore, rushed into the lake and started bathing, Barkaya surreptitiously stole the clothes of the beauty he had fallen in love with.

After enjoying a good bathe, the girls came out on to the shore and started dressing, but one of them could not find her clothes. Her girlfriends changed once more into white swans and flew away, while she, shedding bitter tears, was left on the shore. And now Barkaya came out of the thicket and told her of his passionate love. He asked her to become his wife, promising in return to give her back her swan's attire. There was nothing else for it, so the girl said, 'All right, I agree to become your wife. However, you must permit me to visit my elder sisters once a week.'

'All right,' said Barkaya, 'I agree to that.' And they began living together. Barkaya would catch fish and hunt for goats. And his wife would dry the fish and the meat.

Time passed, and his swan-wife became pregnant. One day, after returning to his cabin from fishing, Barkaya could not find his wife. A child's crying could be heard from the cabin. Going inside, he saw a newborn boy. But his wife had disappeared. Barkaya rushed to the place where he hid his wife's swan's clothing. The clothes were not in their place. And now Barkaya realised that his wife had abandoned him forever.

What was he to do? Taking the infant, Barkaya set off to the *aul*. He called his son Kutly-Kaya.

Kutly-Kaya grew up as an inquisitive, clever boy. From his early years the father took his son hunting, and Kutly-Kaya became a passionate hunter. He was especially fond of hunting with a falcon. At home he would occupy himself with breeding hunting falcons of various sorts. And with time, Kutly-Kaya's falcons became the best in the khanate.

The fame of Kutly-Kaya's falcons reached Khan Tokhtamysh, who was also a lover of hunting with falcons. And Khan Tokhtamysh made Kutly-Kaya his chief falconer.

Kutly-Kaya bred an outstanding type of hunting falcon. And there were no better falcons than those of Tokhtamysh, not just in the whole land but also in the neighbouring khanates. The other khans very much envied Tokhtamysh.

One day a certain neighbouring khan asked Tokhtamysh for one of his outstanding breed of falcon. But Tokhtamysh flatly refused. Then the khan persuaded Kutly-Kaya to sell him one of the two eggs, and to tell Tokhtamysh that the falcon was getting old and therefore this year it had laid only one egg.

Kutly-Kaya sold one of the special falcon eggs to the khan. From that egg there hatched a young falcon, which with time turned into a famous falcon.

And that khan came riding as a guest to Tokhtamysh with his young falcon. They went out hunting. And the falcon of the neighbouring khan was superior to Tokhtamysh's falcon in every way.

And then Tokhtamysh asked, 'Where did you get that falcon? After all, such falcons are bred only at my place!' But the neighbouring khan remained silent.

So they sat down to have a rest. They each drank several bowls of strong *kumys* ... and the neighbouring khan's tongue was loosened. He decided to make Tokhtamysh angry, in revenge for refusing him. And the neighbour confessed that he had asked for and obtained one egg from Kutly-Kaya.

Tokhtamysh grew terribly angry. On returning home, he decided to hang his falconer. But Kutly-Kaya had fled.

For many years Kutly-Kaya lived in the forest, feeding himself on game. And one day he met a daughter of the *albasly*. And she was a girl of indescribable beauty. Kutly-Kaya told her of his wish to marry her. The *albasly* girl agreed to become Kutly-Kaya's wife, but on the condition that he should not look at her armpits or at her feet when she was undressing. He accepted these conditions and took the *albasly* girl as his wife.

The days passed. One day, when the daughter of the *albasly* was undressing, overwhelming curiosity overcame Kutly-Kaya and he looked at her armpit. He saw that there she had an opening through which her innards could be seen. He glanced at her feet and was shocked: her feet were birds' feet.

The *albasly*'s daughter sensed Kutly-Kaya's gaze and she said, 'You have not kept your word, and our life together has come to an end. From this minute you are not my husband and I am not your wife. I am expecting a baby. On such-and-such a day our baby will be born. If it is a daughter then I will take her with me; if it is a son I will leave him under this tree. Come and take him.' The *albasly*'s daughter spoke thus and left.

On the appointed day Kutly-Kaya came to the specified place and saw that a boy had been left under the tree. The child was crying furiously. Not knowing what to feed him or comfort him with, the father brought him to his dog, who had recently given birth to pups.

Kutly-Kaya gave his son the name of Edige. For some time the infant fed on the dog's milk, but the day came when the dog no longer let him suckle.

Having landed in a desperate situation, Kutly-Kaya secretly came to the *aul* and gave his son to a certain horse-herd friend of his to rear. He himself went off into the forest once again, fearing the retribution of Tokhtamysh. And Edige grew up among the sons of the horse-herd.

Edige distinguished himself among the boys by being exceptionally quick on the uptake, and by his bravery and strength. Often he invented new and interesting games. And whenever he fought with the other boys, it happened that whatever part he grasped, it would be torn from that boy's body.

And somebody found out that Edige was the son not of the horse-herd but of Kutly-Kaya, who was hiding from Khan Tokhtamysh, and reported it to the khan.

The khan immediately summoned the horse-herd. 'Do you have Kutly-Kaya's son at your home?' he asked threateningly.

'I have!' replied the horse-herd.

'Bring him to me at once, I must hang him!'

The distraught horse-herd returned home and said to his wife, 'We have nine children. Kutly-Kaya has an only son Edige. And it is evident that he will become a famous *bogatyr*, he is the very image of his father. Let us give one of our own sons into Tokhtamysh's hands, and we will keep Edige.'

The wife agreed with her husband. And the father brought one of his own sons to Tokhtamysh.

'Is this Kutly-Kaya's son?' asked the khan.

'Yes!' the horse-herd replied firmly.

That same day Khan Tokhtamysh ordered the horse-herd's son to be hanged.

Fearing exposure, the horse-herd and his wife decided to give Edige another name. And they called him Kubugul, which means 'son of a *bogatyr*'. They called him that because truly he was the son of the *bogatyr* Kutly-Kaya.

Years passed. The sons of the horse-herd were pasturing Khan Tokhtamysh's herds of horses. And Kubugul started grazing the calves of a certain *bey*.

At that time Tokhtamysh, wishing to glorify himself, ordered a big cart to be built. The wheels of that cart were made of pure gold, and other parts of gold and silver.

The khan gathered the people together and commanded they evaluate the worth of that wagon. But nobody dared to express an estimate of how much such a large golden cart would cost.

Then Tokhtamysh set two men on the cart and sent it travelling: perhaps somebody would appraise it. They travelled on the golden cart all over the khanate. But nobody was able to determine the value of the cart. They rode and rode and saw the calves being pastured. The boy cow-herd had taken off his trousers and was dealing with a call of nature while at the same time having a bite to eat.

'Perhaps we shall find out the value of the cart from him?' one of the men asked.

'But just what can we ask from him? Look what he is doing.' They decided to summon him all the same. 'Ey, boy, come here!'

'Come yourselves, I am busy!' he replied. 'Can't you see?'

The men rode up to him. 'What are you doing, boy?'

'I am sending what is necessary into my belly, and what is unnecessary I am expelling.'

'Can one really do that?'

'If it is necessary, one can do it.'

'And what is this?' asked the men, pointing to the cart.

'It is a cart!'

'And how much would it cost?'

'If there is a crop failure in the khanate for two or three years, the value of that cart will be a piece of bread!' replied the boy.

The men took the boy for an idiot and returned to Khan Tokhtamysh. They related everything; after which, Tokhtamysh immediately ordered that the strange boy be brought to him.

'What are you occupied with, boy?' asked the khan.

'I live and work at a certain *bey*'s place. What can an orphan like me do?'

'Work for me!' offered Tokhtamysh.

'But just what would I do?'

'What do you do for that *bey*?'

'I pasture calves.'

'Then pasture calves for me.'

'No, I will not pasture calves for you!' the boy retorted decisively.

'Then pasture cows!'

'No, I will not pasture cows either ...'

'Then pasture sheep ...' persisted the khan.

'No. It is better that I go back to my calves!' said the boy, and he got ready to leave.

'Stop,' Tokhtamysh urged him. 'Maybe you will agree to pasture a herd of horses?'

'I agree to pasture a herd of horses!' replied the boy.

'And what are you called?' asked the khan.

'Kubugul!'

The khan had nine horse-herds. Kubugul was taken as the tenth. Once every ten days all of the horse-herds appeared before Khan Tokhtamysh. They reported to him about their business. They called in one at a time. The khan, sitting arrogantly, would answer their greetings with a barely perceptible nod. But each time he saw the tenth horse-herd, Kubugul, for some reason he was inwardly put on his guard and even, without knowing why, he would half-rise from his seat and greet Kubugul with a bow.

This strange behaviour of Tokhtamysh was noticed by his wife. 'Why is it that every time that Kubugul comes in, you rise a little from your seat? Are you afraid of him?' asked his wife.

'No,' replied the khan. 'I do not budge from the seat.'

The next time the occasion approached for the reception of the horse-herds, the khan's wife, without Tokhtamysh noticing, pinned the hem of his shirt to the cushion on which he sat. Until Kubugul entered the room, Khan Tokhtamysh sat majestically, without moving. But as soon as Kubugul went in and gave the khan his *salam*, the latter instinctively half-rose and bowed to him. But somebody was pulling the khan by the hem of his shirt. Tokhtamysh turned and saw that he had risen a little and pulled his cushion behind him. The khan lifted his head and was met by his wife's gaze.

'Well?' said the khan's wife.

'You are right ...' he answered. From that moment, thinking of Kubugul gave the khan no peace. When the next occasion arose for the coming of the horse-herds, Tokhtamysh told his wife to ferment some milk. Taking the bowl with the thick fermented milk, the khan drew a cross on its surface with his finger and silently gave it to Kubugul. The latter, also silently, got out his *kinzhal* and stirred the milk with it, then picked up the bowl, drank it to the bottom, returned the bowl to the khan and went out.

'Did you understand anything?' the khan asked his wife.

'What is there here to understand?' she answered. 'You gave him the bowl, he drank it up and left.'

'No, a big meaning is hidden in this,' said Tokhtamysh. 'By placing the cross, I wanted it to say: If you are planning anything against me, then I will quarter you.'

'And what was his response?' asked the khan's wife.

'He answered, "If you will quarter me, then I will destroy your khanate by the force of my *kinzhal*, just like this *prostokvasha*, and I will take it into my hands just as I am drinking up this bowlful." Without doubt we must find out the origin of this Kubugul,' Khan Tokhtamysh decided firmly. 'I have a hunch that he is not a simple horse-herder. There is the seed of something terrible for me lying inside him. Without doubt he must be killed.'

Tokhtamysh called all of the horse-herders to him and asked them from whom Kubugul was descended: what was his family, who were his ancestors?

But nobody could answer these questions. Then the khan, thoroughly scared by all of his growing and inexplicable terror before Kubugul, ordered him to be arrested and locked in the adjacent half of his *kibitka*. In his own half Tokhtamysh gathered all the honoured old men, the well-known *yuyraus* of all the land, and the famous *bogatyrs* of the various tribes, in order to learn from them the origin of Kubugul, and then to hang him.

Khan Tokhtamysh,
He slaughtered a mare, he poured out honey,
He made the singers gather,
He caused a fleecy tent to be raised,
He caused the old men of rank to gather
On a high hill,
He has a tall horse under him,
He has a golden whip,
He has everything that we can see, made of gold,
He has hairs sticking out on his cheek,
My khan began his song:
'Bogatyr Bolat Minsky,[1]
The origin of Kubugul –
Do you know it?' the khan asked.
'The origin of Kubugul
I do not know, my khan,
I am unable to offer counsel,' he replied.
'Bogatyr Nogay Yuzsky,
The origin of Kubugul –
Do you know it?' the khan asked.
'The origin of Kubugul
I do not know, my khan,
I am unable to offer counsel,' he replied.

---

1   Min is the name of a Nogay tribe. Later, after the names of the *bogatyrs*, is cited the name of the Nogay tribe to which the *bogatyr* belonged.

'Bogatyr Bugan Khiryuvsky,
The origin of Kubugul –
Do you know it?' the khan asked.
'The origin of Kubugul
I do not know, my khan,
I am unable to offer counsel,' he replied.
'Bogatyr Kasay Naymansky,
The origin of Kubugul –
Do you know it?' the khan asked.
'The origin of Kubugul
I do not know, my khan,
I am unable to offer counsel,' he replied.
'Bogatyr Nukay Isun'sky,
The origin of Kubugul –
Do you know it?' the khan asked.
'The origin of Kubugul
I do not know, my khan,
I am unable to offer counsel,' he replied.
'From your chest, which is like a blue[1] house,
Bogatyr Yanmukhambet,
Son of Tolush Buyrabassky,
The origin of Kubugul –
Do you know it?' the khan asked.
'The origin of Kubugul
I do not know, my khan,
I am unable to offer counsel,' he replied.
'Bogatyr Kuba Kypchaksky,
The origin of Kubugul –
Do you know it?' the khan asked.
'The origin of Kubugul
I do not know, my khan,
I am unable to offer counsel,' he replied.
'Bogatyr Kara-Bais Kanglinsky,
The origin of Kubugul –
Do you know it?' the khan asked.

---

1   In the ancient Nogay language, the word 'blue' (pale blue) means big and strong, so he is
     complimenting Nukay Isun'sky's large physique.

'The origin of Kubugul
I do not know, my khan,
I am unable to offer counsel,' he replied.
'Kara-Khoja Argynsky,
The origin of Kubugul –
Do you know it?' the khan asked.
'The origin of Kubugul
I do not know, my khan,
I am unable to offer counsel,' he replied.
'Bogatyr Uzun-Aydar Kongratsky,
The origin of Kubugul –
Do you know it?' the khan asked.
'The origin of Kubugul
I do not know, my khan,
I am unable to offer counsel,' he replied.
'Slu-Mambet Shirinsky,
The origin of Kubugul –
Do you know it?' the khan asked.
'The origin of Kubugul
I do not know, my khan,
I am unable to offer counsel,' he replied.
'Mannka-Yuyrau Mangytsky,
The origin of Kubugul –
Do you know it?' the khan asked.
'The origin of Kubugul
I do not know, my khan,
I am unable to offer counsel,' he replied.
'Son of Keneges Ker-Yanbay,
Most outstanding counsellor, Bey Yanbay,
Of a lush place, you are the grass.
Of a grey mare, in my famous herd
Of horses, you are the milk
You are my *nart*, and a robber.
But now, today,
Son of Keneges Ker-Yanbay,
You are my right-hand man for advice,
The origin of Kubugul –
Do you know it?' the khan asked.

Like a female camel, the mother of a slain young camel,
Crying and keening,
Yanbay then began to sing.
Like a mare, the mother of a slain foal,
Pitifully starting to neigh,
Yanbay then began to sing.
'I am a singer and once again as a singer,
I raise my *kibitka* on a place with feather-grass.
My uncle is the Kara-*yuyrau*,
While he is coming,
I will entertain you.
My uncle the Kara-*yuyrau*,
When he comes,
I will stand, bowing to him,
Laying my hands on my chest, bending my knees,
And putting my sword under my knees.
Having lived a hundred years and eighty besides,
And with rocking molar teeth –
Such today is my uncle, the Kara-*yuyrau*.
Just who will know then, if not he?'
After making the shafts from a red pine,
After making the shaft-bow with decorated designs,
After making the wheels out of silver,
After making the body of the cart strong,
After harnessing six black horses,
After tethering seven bay-horses along its sides,[1]
And in front of them all
Making a grey horse start to pull,
They rode out to Sybra-*yuyrau*.
Sybra had not the strength
To clamber on to the cart,
And not the heart to sit on a horse.
After winding ropes

---

[1]   Note from Sikaliev: for a distant journey one horse is not enough for a Nogay. In addition, they would take a spare horse without a rider, which they would lead on one side, having fastened its bridle to the saddle under the horseman. The 'seven bay horses' means that they sent a whole suite of seven horsemen to collect the old singer. Spare horses meant they had set out on a distant journey.

Around his jaws,
After putting his teeth
In a row with silken thread,[1]
After tying up his waist
With a sash,
After putting a stout stick
Under his arms,
And taking a sacred oath from him
That he would not tell a lie,
And setting him
In a large golden carriage,
They brought Sybra-*yuyrau*.
The khan gave a seat to this Sybra
Among the honoured guests.
'O Sybra, most aged *yuyrau*,
Well then, sing to us,' he was told.
Sybra the *yuyrau* made a wry face,
He began stirring,
And tried to sing.
But his mouth did not open,
His tongue did not bend.
On seeing that, Tokhtamysh
Gave him three *tostakays* of honey.
And when Sybra had drunk up the honey,
When the honey had gone down to his kidneys,
And after the kidneys had swollen with the honey,
After wriggling his teeth and nose,
Sybra began singing.
'Ay, Tokhtamysh, ay, my child,
I will tell what I myself have seen:
Beneath the moon there is a certain lake,
If you gallop around it on horses, you will not encompass it.
And growing in its middle
There is sedge and willow.
If you are bored and only amusing yourself,
You cannot shoot down the wild boar you are chasing.

---

1   To make him look better, for cosmetic reasons.

There is willow growing
Along its shores, straight, like on a street.
You have an abundance of wealth,
Who is there who would not wish to achieve the same?
In your gathering there is one man,
Nobody can compare with him.
And you, my child,
You are persecuting Kubugul.
Ay, Tokhtamysh, ay, child,
Of the old khans there were thirty,
Of the new khans there were fifteen,
Of them added together
There were forty-five khans.
I have seen them myself.
I am an old man who has outlived them.
As for the descent of Kubugul,
It would appear he surpasses them all.
The one who wore a cap with a golden crown,
Under the name of Alshangir
Was a masterful khan.
I have seen him myself.
I am an old man who has outlived him.
As for the descent of Kubugul,
It would appear he surpasses him too.
When Khan Sain appeared,
I saw him myself.
I am an old man who has outlived him.
As for the descent of Kubugul,
It would appear he surpasses him too.
The man who plundered the universe,
Khan Kutay,
Who turned into a pig
And left this world.
I have seen him myself.
I am an old man who has outlived him.
As for the descent of Kubugul,
It would appear he surpasses him too.
When advancing on the enemy, making them tremble,

The great ruler Khan Berke,
I have seen him myself.
I am an old man who has outlived him.
As for the descent of Kubugul,
It would appear he surpasses him too.
Khan Janibek, with a *burka* of gold,
Everything he was covered with was golden,
Whenever you looked, in his yard
Thousands of *argamaks* were tethered.
I have seen him myself.
I am an old man who has outlived him.
As for the descent of Kubugul,
It would appear he surpasses him too.
Khan Dinibek was a man
With a golden *tebyonki* on his saddle.
I have seen him myself.
I am an old man who has outlived him.
As for the descent of Kubugul,
It would appear he surpasses him too.
I have seen Berdibek,
Who with a stroke would cut through the neck of a *nar*,
As for the descent of Kubugul,
It would appear he surpasses him too.
I have seen Khan Uzbek,
With the golden straps of his stirrups,
With a golden saddle-cloth,
With a golden saddle-bow,
With the golden tips of his reins,
With his under-tail saddle strap of pure gold.
I have seen him myself.
I am an old man who has outlived him.
As for the descent of Kubugul,
It would appear he surpasses him too.
The khan under the name of Shagan,
Like a hen-quail, like a wolf,
Only yesterday
On the earth with the title of "Kalmyk".
I have seen him myself.

I am an old man who has outlived him.
As for the descent of Kubugul,
It would appear he surpasses him too.
Out of meadowsweet, growing in the valley of Tutam,
You used to make hoops for *kibitkas* and bows.
Your father was Toykozha,
And Toykozha's son was you, Tokhtamysh.
Only in recent days,
Barefooted and with uncovered head,
You were fit for nothing, grazing calves,
The time arrived, and you became khan.
Now I see you too.
I know that you will kill me.
If you kill me – what have I lost?
I will set out to the world beyond the grave,
I will enter the house of paradise.
In an honoured place of paradise
I will spend my time.
When Kubugul was living with you,
You did not allow him to be among the people,
You did not consider him as a *bogatyr*,
You scoffed at him as you wished.
But on this very day
Your best days have passed.
But now, my khan,
Why are you asking me about Kubugul?
He is the furthest of those sons,
He is the closest of these sons,[1]
He stands in the middle, with a fleshy neck,[2]
As for the descent of Kubugul with the eagle's nose,
It would appear he surpasses you too!
After climbing up the ridge, I look,
No way do I find your pedigree,
Kubugul, my son!

---

1   Note from Sikaliev: the singer Sybra is hinting to the Khan Tokhtamysh that although Edige, the
    leader of the Nogay tribes, serves the khan, and is close to him, he is also inaccessible to the khan.
2   Note from Nasipkhan Suyunova: this means a 'strong neck'. Other variants of the epic have
    'neck of a bull', or 'with the withers of a horse'.

After climbing up the hill, I look,
No way do I find your father's house,
Kubugul, my son!'
Then Edige himself began to sing.
'Edige will put in a word – the man will speak out,
The man who says his prayers will speak himself:[1]
After climbing up the ridge, you look,
Why are you looking for my pedigree?
After climbing up the hill, you look,
Why are you looking for my father's house?
Ey, *aksakal, aksakal,*
"Son, son," you are sitting and saying it,
It is not I who am your son.
When you say, "Son, son," it does not hit the mark.
If only you said "Edige,
The man who says his prayers, my son" –
Would that be out of place?
When they said "*Assalam aleykum,*"
And asked, "Who are you?"
"I am a *kopeyek,*" I would answer.
When they asked, "Who are you?"
"I am a Kuraysh," I would answer.
"I myself am the only child
Born of Aziz," I would say.
I trace my descent
From Abubekir Syddyk,
I become like a ray of the sun,
Ey, Tokhtamysh!
Your father was Toykozha.
The son of Toykozha, Tokhtamysh,
Do not boast of your descent from Alshangir,
So what, if your descent is from Alshangir?
A devout man was Makhmun Keremet,
The son of Keremet was Angshibay,
The son of Angshibay was Birperie,
The son of Birperie was Barkaya,

---

1   That is, a respectable, religious man.

The son of Barkaya was the one you knew:
Kutly-Kaya. I am his son!'
At that same time, at that same hour
Sybra spoke and sang:
'Ay, Tokhtamysh, ay, child!
Dried-up grass has no taste,
A dried-up shin-bone has no fat,
A word spoken by an old man is not given credit.
If the dried-up grass had taste,
If a dried-up shin-bone had fat,
If an old man has a conscience,
If a word spoken by an old man is given credit,
Ay, child,
You will recklessly persecute
Kubugul this very day.'
At that same time, at that same hour
Sybra spoke and sang:
'He is the furthest one of those sons,
He is the closest one of these sons,[1]
He stands in the middle, with the eagle's nose.
If one looks at Kubugul –
It is as if he was created from the rays of the sun,
With long arms, for stretching the bow,
Kubugul will be a marksman in shooting.
He has lean cheeks and fine lips.
Kubugul will be silver-tongued.
On this day do not humiliate Kubugul
While naming him Kubugul.[2]
While priding yourself on your strength, do not use force on him.
But if you do humiliate Kubugul, and
Priding yourself on your strength, you use violence,
In the first year, like an eagle owl,

---

1   Note from Sikaliev: the singer Sybra is hinting to the Khan Tokhtamysh that although Edige, the leader of the Nogay tribes, serves the khan, i.e., is close to him, he is also inaccessible to the khan, i.e., is far from him.

2   Note from Nasipkhan Suyunova: as explained earlier, the name Kubugul means 'son of a *batyr*'. So, basically these two lines mean: do not be a dissembler, a hypocrite, by giving him a respectful name at the same time as humiliating him.

Kubugul will turn up on the open steppe.
And while one more year passes,
He will select a pole for catching fine horses,
Out of a willow growing on the sand.
Your numerous herds of horses
Kubugul will start driving before him.
And he will cause your *nart*, who is pursuing him,
To take sand in his mouth from the earth.
What your people have collected in spoonfuls
Kubugul will collect in ladlefuls,
After separating you from your land,
Kubugul will enjoy all your blessings,
He will make your eyes go red like the *kuralay*'s,
He will make your neck stretch out like the heron's.
Kubugul will take away by force
Your throne of yellow gold with the curved head.
With his golden sleeves up to his elbows,
When he speaks,
Each word is equal to a thousand gold coins,
Your beautiful Kanike,
Your fair Kozike,
Kubugul will make his prize.
Kubugul will drive off into the bare steppe,
The father of nine heroes,
The master of numerous *narts*,
Kubugul will banish to the naked steppe –
You yourself, Tokhtamysh.
It would appear that Kubugul will stand on
The tub of honey,
It would appear that Kubugul will escape,
Getting out through the opening of the chimney!
Why should I keep on talking,
If all I have said is fated to come true?

In the naked steppe, in the waterless desert,
At the end of it all, it would appear,
Kubugul will clean up all your riches!'

Sybra the *yuyrau* had led Tokhtamysh to understand that Kubugul's descent surpassed the high birth of all the khans, and he asked the khan not to persecute him. But it was a gamble, to entertain the hopes of the crafty Tokhtamysh. That is why Sybra the *yuyrau* notified Edige that it was necessary to escape through the upper opening of the *kibitka*.

Edige immediately made use of the advice and climbed out of the *kibitka* as Sybra had told him. His nine comrades, the nine horse-herders, also helped him to escape. In the yard they got ready horses for their flight, and cut halfway through the stirrup straps and saddle-girths of the khan's saddled horses.

And when Edige, after sitting on a horse, had galloped away, the khan's men, who jumped up in order to pursue him, were unable to sit on their horses, for the stirrup straps and the saddle-girths snapped, and the men and saddles fell to the ground.

Then Tokhtamysh himself began to sing.
'Ey, you nine young heroes, you nine heroes,
All nine of you set off in pursuit,
First deceive Edige with kind words,
Then bring him closer to yourselves.
Deceive him and bring him closer to yourselves,
After bringing him closer, take off his head!'

But there was no possibility of getting Edige back: he could not be overtaken. Then Khan Tokhtamysh grew angry at Sybra the *yuyrau,* with the words: 'What have you done?'

Finally, Tokhtamysh decided to send Yanbay after Edige, to bring him back at any price. And now Yanbay rode off along Edige's tracks, caught him up and addressed him with a song:

'Come back, dear man, why don't you come back,
Turn around and cross the Edil'.
Choose your native land from among many lands,
After fastening a small ringing bell
To a large male camel,[1]

---

1   Note from Sikaliev: a large male camel with a bell on its neck is a symbol of a high-status dignitary. Here Tokhtamysh is promising to make Edige a powerful dignitary in order to

Your khan-master is calling you,
So come back!
Stoop, and make obeisance
To the beautiful *kibitka* with a high door.[1]
The khan, your master,
Gives you honey
In a fine Chinese bowl – so drink!
The khan, your master,
Gives you a fur coat
With golden skirts and sleeves – put it on!
The khan, your master,
Is giving you a racehorse
With a gilded *burka*,
With a horse-covering of gold,
With golden *tebyonki*,
With golden spurs,
And a saddle-bow of gold,
With gold-tipped reins,
With its ears pricked up like pikes,
Combing his fringe like a girl,
Counting his steps when he walks,
Of a superb Arab breed – mount it!
The khan, your master,
Gives you a sabre, and an axe with a golden handle,
So fasten it to your belt!
The khan, your master,
Gives you a white gerfalcon
With a long tail – so fondle it!
He gives you an armed force,
Picked out from his warriors,
So become the chief of the force!
The khan, your master,
Gives you a chain-mail shirt,

---

entice him back (to kill him).

1   Note from Nasipkhan Suyunova: this refers to the *kibitka* of Tokhtamysh. Here the expression
'high door' has the sense of 'majestic' or 'grand'; in reality the top of the door of the khan's
kibitka is made especially low, so that everybody who enters bows as a sign of respect. The low
door prevents anybody from forgetting to do this.

There are not one of its links
Among a thousand *kyzyls*,[1]
It is worth more than
The value of the khan's cattle
It is beyond the capability of
A thousand craftsmen with the hammer.
He gives it – so put it on!
The khan, your master,
Has chosen the best of his many lands,
He gives you, a young hero,
The whole land together with
A beautiful girl,
So become the master of the land!
After separating out one of his mares,
He gives you a mare from them,
Tether her, and then drink her *kumys*!
Of his unbounded lands,
He has divided off some,
And gives you land – so rule it!'
'Edige will now speak, the young hero will speak,
The man who says his prayers will himself speak:
After I choose my native land among many lands,
After he has fastened a small ringing bell
To a large male camel,
Although the khan, my master,
Calls me, I will not go,
Since I myself have moved away from his land.
I will not stoop and make obeisance
To the beautiful *kibitka* with a high door,
Since the crown of my head has become unlucky.
The khan, my master,
Even though he gives me honey
In a fine Chinese bowl – I will not drink it,
Since my lips are bloody.
The khan, my master,

---

1   In the ancient Nogay language *kyzyl* (red flower) means the south. In this case it refers to a
    person from the Caucasus. The ancient Nogays called the Caucasus Mountains 'Kafkyzyl' or
    'Kafkazyl', which means 'South Kaf Mountains'.

Although he gives me a fur coat
With golden skirts and sleeves – I will not put it on,
Since my shoulders have become unlucky.
The khan, my master,
Even if giving me a racehorse
With a gilded *burka*,
With a horse-covering of gold,
With golden *tebyonki*,
With golden spurs,
And its saddle-bow of gold,
With gold-tipped reins,
With his ears pricked up like pikes,
Combing his fringe like a girl,
Counting his steps when he walks,
Although of a superb Arab breed – I will not mount it,
Since my buttocks became unlucky.
Although the khan, my master,
Gives me an axe with a golden handle,
And a sabre – I will not attach it,
If my waist has become bent![1]
Although the khan, my master,
Has a white gerfalcon with a long tail,
And he actually gives it to me – I will not fondle it,
Since I myself have become unlucky.
After dividing up his mares,
He will give me a mare from them,
But when she is tethered, I will not drink her *kumys*
Since my mouth has become unlucky.
Although he gives me a chain-mail shirt,
White, with a golden collar,
Though there is not one of its links
Among a thousand *kyzyls,*
Though worth more than
The value of the khan's cattle,
Though beyond the capability of

---

1   Note from Sikaliev: a bent waist refers to a man in a subjugated humiliating position, in
continual fear, since Edige is no longer trusted. From then on, there can be no mutual trust
between the khan and Edige.

A thousand craftsmen with hammers,
And a damask-steel coat – I will not put it on,
Since all of my body has become unlucky.
The khan, my master,
Having selected the best of his many lands,
Although he gives me a beautiful girl,
I will not take them,
Since I myself have become bad for him.
Even if he gives me an armed force,
Picked out from his warriors,
I will not become the chief of the force.
Even if he gives me land, after dividing it up,
I will not rule it,
Since my head has become unlucky!
Son of Keneges, Kyor-Yanbay,
The khan's counsellor, the dog Yanbay,
Disappear and go back, Yanbay!
For the one who gives you a horse, you are the son,
For the one who gives you food, you are the slave.
Go back, Yanbay, go back,
After you return, find your house, Yanbay.
Without pulling your tongue, I will cut it off,
To your palate I will apply
A burning hot willow.
After pulling out your tongue, I will cut it off,
Without cutting your body, I will take out your gallbladder.
Since I have sat on my horse like a man,
Since I have set out, after choosing the road,
I will not turn back, like a woman,
I will not utter words of insult
With my own lips.
I am not going to boast any further,
But if you will compel me to boast,
I will say to you:
There lived in the past a man, Shingiz,
Who had an arrow of twelve spans,
And I compare myself
With Shingiz.

I am a tree taller than a pine,
If a storm comes suddenly, I will not falter.
Ey, you nine young men of Tokhtamysh,
Think about my words!
My whip will strike you on the neck,
The blood will run down your bosom,
You will not endure
My playing with you.
I – it is I myself
While saying "I", and relying on my strength,
I am a young *bogatyr*!
I will not light the fire of my enemies,
I will not extinguish the fire of my friends.
Your mouth – is a round wicker aperture,
Of what interest are your lying words to me?
Now I am setting off,
I will go to Khan Shatemir,
If Shatemir extends his hand to me,
If Kuday-Allah offers victory,
Then Tokhtamysh with the broken teeth,
And those like Tokhtamysh
With the vague wishy-washy tongue of the khans,
I will lay beneath my feet
And make a laughing stock of them.'
Edige will speak – the man will speak,
The devout man himself will say,
'My nine are my guard,
For my mighty body,
Ay, my nine friends, my nine,
Limping, like a *drofa*,
Yielding their turn, my nine,
Jumping up, like an eagle[1]
Guarding me, my nine,

---

1   Note from Sikaliev: limping – pretending to be wounded, crippled and weak, with the aim
     of deceiving an arrogant enemy into a position that is convenient for himself, in order to
     attack him unexpectedly; yielding their turn – avoiding a direct engagement when it is
     disadvantageous, to behave judiciously; jumping up – before taking off an eagle jumps up in
     the air, runs and opens its wings. Like the eagle, a *bogatyr* prepares himself to attack an enemy.

A wild carrot[1] growing in the earth
Is nourishing meat for you, my nine.
If you fancy meat, shoot a gazelle,
If you are persistent, you will achieve your goal.
When the time is ripe, then I will remove
From Tokhtamysh, Nogaystan with all its people,
After stirring it up, like a wave,
I will place it on our Mother-river Edil',
As Saraychuk,[2]
So that it should pass to your sons and grandsons,
May it be nourishment for you, my nine!
The luxuriant-haired daughters of rich men,
With the hairs on the back of their heads unplaited,[3]
And whose faces the people have not seen,
Let them be booty for you, my nine!
Ey, my nine friends, my nine,
I will become a guide for my nine,
If your horses die, I will replace them,
If you remain alive,
You will be dressed in black sable-fur coats.
But if you die,
After washing you well, I will bury you in white shrouds.
If we are successful, I will do that,
But if, by the will of Kuday, we are unsuccessful,
Then just what shall I do?'

---

1   Note from Nasipkhan Suyunova: the wild carrot is a perennial plant whose leaves are similar
    to the leafy top of a cultivated carrot.
2   Note from Nasipkhan Suyunova: 'Saraychuk', or 'Saraychik' was founded on the lower reaches
    of the River Volga in the tenth to eleventh centuries. In the thirteenth to fourteenth centuries
    it became a big trading and cultural centre linking Europe and China. From 1391 this town
    was the capital of the Nogay Horde, but in 1395 the town was destroyed by Tamerlane. Later,
    around 1430–1440 AD, it was restored, and from the second half of that century it became
    the political centre of the Nogay Horde, and the headquarters of the khans of the Nogay
    Horde. The epic saga of Edige was composed during the life of Edige himself, in the first half
    of the fifteenth century.
3   Note from Robert Chenciner: girls do not usually wear their hair like this until puberty.
    Plaited hair might also be connected with work, so unplaited hair means that you do not
    work, i.e., you are rich, and also that the rich girls do not walk about in public, and if they go
    anywhere it is in a Nogay covered cart, again because they are rich. The luxuriant hair also
    might refer to rich girls who have leisure to wash and comb their hair.

Some time later, when Edige and his nine friends had taken the road to Shatemir, they met a snake with nine heads and one tail.

'A snake, a snake!' his friends shouted to Edige.

'Kill it!' said Edige.

The nine young fellows rushed and cut off all nine heads of the snake. Some time later they came across a snake with one head and nine tails.

'A snake, a snake!' his friends shouted to Edige.

'Kill it!' said Edige.

While the young heroes turned here and there, the snake quickly vanished into its nest before the young fellows had time to kill it.

Then Edige said, 'You yourselves saw: you quickly dealt with the snake with nine heads and one tail. But the snake with one head and nine tails you were unable to kill – where the head passed through, all nine tails passed too. In that case, then we too must choose a leader for ourselves.' They elected Edige as their chief. Edige and his nine friends gave their oath that they would not desert each other in any kind of trouble.

In that way they arrived at Khan Shatemir's place. They spent a little time with him.

One day Edige took his nine friends hunting. It was March. Taking advantage of Edige's absence, Kabarty-Alyp Batyr, with one thousand warriors, came to Khan Shatemir and demanded his daughter in marriage. Khan Shatemir became frightened and told his daughter, 'My child, I cannot fight with him. I do not have the forces. Whatever happens, go to him. If it becomes completely unbearable for you, may God send Edige to meet you.'

'All right,' his daughter assented, 'there is no other way out. I will go with him. But how shall I recognise Edige?'

Her father answered her: 'Edige is this kind of man: all his clothes are white, but he never soils his white clothes. He sits on the ground without putting anything under him. But if however he has nothing, he lays his knout or whip under him. And when he performs *namaz*, he takes out his *kinzhal* and sticks it into the ground in front of him. If he slaughters an animal on his own, Edige does not soil his clothes with a single drop of the animal's blood. He is as neat as that.'

Kabarty-Alyp carried off Shatemir's daughter. Edige and his nine friends, while returning from their hunting, reached one of Shatemir's herds. Edige went up and saw the numerous tracks of horses' hooves on the ground. Then Edige asked one of the herdsmen, 'What sort of tracks are those?'

'Kabarty-Alyp has carried off Shatemir's daughter!'

'When?'

'This night.'

And Edige proposed to his nine friends: 'We will not go to Khan Shatemir now, but we will follow this track.' Edige's nine friends agreed to follow the track of Kabarty-Alyp Batyr.

They set off. After several days they saw an army in front of them. Then Edige said, 'You remain here, and I will approach them. I will try to get fixed up as a cook there. I will leave food for you, burying it beneath the hearth.'

Edige approached Alyp. Alyp asked him, 'Who are you? Where is your journey taking you?'

'Ey, I am looking for some kind of work for myself,' replied Edige.

'And what can you do?' Alyp grew interested.

'I am a cook. I alone can slaughter a mare for your army, skin it, butcher it, cook it and feed your men.'

'Then I will take you!' said Kabarty-Alyp.

Thus the days passed: Edige prepared food for the whole army; and for his companions who were following the army he left food buried under the hearth. His friends later procured it and ate it.

A week passed. Usually Kabarty-Alyp went for seven days without sleeping, and for the seven following days he slept, without waking. Edige worked for Alyp, while Khan Shatemir's daughter, Alyp's captive, was attentively observing the cook. She noticed that he conducted himself just as Edige would. And one day the girl said to the cook, 'Tell me, are you Edige?'

'No, I am not Edige!' replied the cook. 'Why do you ask that?' The girl repeated her father's words. 'In that case, I really am Edige,' said the cook. 'What are we going to do now? This giant will not die from a man's blow. Apparently he has a vulnerable place where his soul is kept. You are his wife. You find out from him where his soul is to be found: caress him and charm him, then he will tell.'

The time was approaching when the giant was due to go to sleep for a week. The horses had to be watered. They all went to the river and wanted to unharness the carts and settle down to rest. Edige told the giant, 'Here is what we need to water them, but there is no feed, and nowhere to pasture the horses. Wouldn't it be better to go a little farther from the river but closer to the pastures? And the horses can be driven to the watering place.'

'Spoken truly!' Alyp agreed.

They rode off to a grassy place, unharnessed the carts, set up the *kibitkas* and lit their fires. Edige prepared the food and fed the whole army. After a hearty meal the warriors drove all the horses to the river to be watered. Around the cart there remained only Alyp, Edige and Shatemir's daughter. Shatemir's daughter had already had a talk with Alyp. 'However much I am struck,' Alyp told her, 'nothing will happen to me. However, if I am shot under the arm once, I will die. And if I am shot a second time, I will revive.' Shatemir's daughter conveyed all this to Edige.

When just the three of them were left, Alyp lay down and slept with the sleep of a giant. Edige sat on his horse, rode some distance away and shouted to Shatemir's daughter, 'You raise his arm so that I can hit his armpit.'

The giant's wife lifted Alyp's arm, and Edige shot his arrow into that place which lay unprotected by his chain-mail shirt. But as soon as the arrow had penetrated Alyp's armpit, the enormous giant flinched and rose to his feet. After looking around with bleary eyes, he saw the rider directly in front of him and, with one leap he overtook him, seizing Edige's horse by the tail. Edige struck his *argamak* with all his might, but no matter how he tried, the horse could not move away from Alyp. Then Edige pulled out his *kinzhal* and with one slash he cut off the tail of his own horse. The huge giant crashed to the ground with the tail in his hand, and gave up the ghost.

Edige sat Alyp's captive girl on his horse and they galloped off to the place where the warriors had driven the horses for watering. They rode up and saw that Alyp's army had divided into two parts. One half declared themselves to be Edige's army, while the other half was Alyp's army, and the two parties were fighting against each other. 'Ey, which side is standing for Edige?' Edige asked.

'This one here!' they answered him.

'Stop fighting and go your separate ways,' shouted Edige.

The army obeyed and went away. Edige went up to the five hundred warriors who were fighting for Alyp and said, 'From today you are free men. Each of you is your own master. Go to your homes!'

The warriors dispersed joyfully. And Edige came riding to Khan Shatemir with Alyp's girl captive. The khan was delighted with the release of his daughter and told Edige, 'I will give you half of my khanate!'

'No, I do not need your khanate!' replied Edige.

'Then marry my daughter, become my son-in-law!' suggested Shatemir.

And Edige married Shatemir's daughter, and remained living at his palace. After some time Edige's wife gave birth to a son. They called the boy Nuradin. Edige lived for many years with Khan Shatemir. Nuradin grew up and became a *jigit*.

One day Nuradin had a quarrel with one of his companions. And the latter said to him, 'Don't demonstrate your strength and courage to me, but to Khan Tokhtamysh, who drove your father Edige out of his native land.'

Nuradin came running to his father: 'Let us take revenge on Khan Tokhtamysh, for mocking you and driving you from your native place.'

Then Edige asked Khan Shatemir for his help. The khan gave him only a few warriors. But nevertheless Edige decided to go forward against Tokhtamysh.

They reached the khanate of Tokhtamysh. Khan Tokhtamysh, sitting on the roof of his multiple-storied palace, was already expecting Edige to appear. And Edige, approaching close to Tokhtamysh's herds of horses and cattle and flocks of sheep, kindled a big fire in the night and drove his small army past the fire. Being cloaked in the darkness, the riders were turning around and once more going past the fire. And so it went on all night. Tokhtamysh's shepherds and horse-herds saw it and reported to the khan that for the whole night an uncountable enemy army had gone past, and the flow of unknown horsemen did not stop until the very morning.

When Tokhtamysh, who had been awaiting the return of Edige anxiously, heard that, he was frightened to death. He had not expected Edige to appear with such a large army, and so had not assembled a big army himself.

Not knowing what to do, Tokhtamysh sent against Edige his own scanty armed force, which Edige smashed without any particular trouble. Some of Tokhtamysh's soldiers ran away, while the rest joined Edige and Nuradin.

Then Tokhtyamysh realised that the only escape for him was to hide. And he decided to escape from the khanate. Nuradin asked his father, 'Permit me to pursue Tokhtamysh and to deal with him!'

'Go,' said Edige, 'only bring me his head.'

'All right,' answered Nuradin, 'Only, Father, I ask you urgently, give me Tokhtamysh's daughters as wives.'

'May it be so,' said Edige. 'I agree, dear son, Tokhtamysh's daughters will go to you, and his wife I will take for myself.'

And meanwhile Tokhtamysh, getting ready to leave his khanate, sang plaintively:

'Today is the day when a khan is fleeing, and his *beys* are pursuing him,
A day when the khan has landed in trouble,
A day when a golden throne has come into decline,
A day when horses have fallen and saddles have broken,

A day when iron bits have snapped,
And the reins have hung down in men's hands,
A day when the khan's wives arrayed themselves in black,
And loaded up their pack on a black camel,
And harnessed the cart with a shaft of limewood,
Saying, "Our time has come to this,"
Keening, they howl.
A day when they filled up their nostrils with dust,
Treading on the earth with bare feet,
With their heads uncovered,
They were moving home,
Walking on one side and driving a pair of horses.
A day when, with eyes filled with tears,
With nostrils stuffed with dust,
In the naked steppe
The khan's wives whiled away their days.
My open, infinite land,
My open, unbounded native land,
The land where, in a white *beshmet*,
My father became a son-in-law.
The land where, in a white covering,
My mother became a daughter-in-law,
The land where, with their tails streaming in the wind,
Innumerable herds of horses grazed.
The land where, pouring out the yellow honey,
The people would gather at the *sabantoy*.[1]
A warm land, where the bushes would burn,
A land where a foal became a mare,
A land where a calf changed into a cow.
A young camel-calf shedding its hair

---

[1] Note from Nasipkhan Suyunova: the word 'saban' here signifies 'plough', 'plough-lands',
a 'spring crop'; and 'toy' means festivities and a holiday. So it refers to a traditional spring
festival. Among the Nogays, as among other Turkish peoples, the origins of the celebration
of Sabantoy go back to deep antiquity and are connected with an agrarian cult. Formerly
the Sabantoy was celebrated in honour of the start of spring work in the fields, but later in
honour of their completion. Probably the original aim of the ceremony was the winning over
of the spirits of fertility in order to favour a good harvest in the coming year. Incidentally, the
Kuban Nogays and the Nogays of Turkey and also other Turkish peoples even now carry on
this ancient holiday.

Became a male camel, like a crag.
A land where a lamb left in the steppe
With time turned into a thousand sheep.
My Edil', my Ten!¹
Your grass is sugar, and your water is sherbet,
My land!
Today an unhappy khan
Goes away to be a cossack,
Are you wishing a happy journey
To the khan your master?'

Khan Tokhtamysh fled and hid himself in the thick reeds on the shore of a lake. Suddenly out from under his feet a lapwing darted and, rising into the air, called pitifully. Then Tokhtamysh, addressing the lapwing, sang:

'At this time, at this hour,
Khan Tokhtamysh on this day
Sings, saying this:
Ey, you lapwing, you lapwing,
With sturdy wings,
With a soft neck,
With a horny beak for a mouth,
Do not call, lapwing-bird,
Now I have no subjects
To take your eggs.
Do not worry, you wildfowl,
You were the master of the lake,
I was the master of the land.
Nuradin, the son of Edige,
Has parted you from the lake,
He has parted me from the land.
May Kuday not let his wishes be fulfilled.
With a sabre hanging at his belt,
After turning yellow,² let him go away and become a cossack.
Do not buzz, you pale blue wasp,

---

1   The Edil' is the River Volga, the Ten is the River Don.
2   Turning yellow here means growing old.

You will lose your strength when
Edige's son comes with his many forces.

Do not become choppy, dear mother Edil',
When winter comes, you too will become like stone.
Do not rise, you brown dust,
Heavy rain will fall, and you will settle.
Do not beat, you muscular heart,
I will sing once, and you will calm down.
Calm down, you *savrasy* racehorse,
I will gallop all night, and you will grow weak.
The comrade who is near me
Whispers to someone.
As trouble overtakes me,
He abandons me and leaves.
To unknown young men
How can I confide my secrets?
How will I saddle an unbroken horse
If he is not tamed?
Behind me, without falling behind,
Nuradin is overtaking me.
May his blood be spilled,
May his dreams not come true!
I am a khan and the son of a khan,
I will not give myself up alive.
By the will of Allah
My death has come,
Today, even though
I fall through the earth, I will not escape.'

Khan Tokhtamysh hid himself. Nuradin, the son of Edige, caught Yanbay.
Then Yanbay began begging Nuradin, 'Do not kill me, I will guide you to
Khan Tokhtamysh!'

'Guide me!' said Nuradin.

Yanbay used a trick to bring Khan Tokhtamysh out of the reeds and
straight to Nuradin. Nuradin said to Tokhtamysh, 'I do not want to kill
an unarmed man. Take your weapons. You are old enough to be my father.
I yield to you the right to shoot first. Here I stand before you. So shoot!'

Tokhtamysh took his bow in his hands and shot his arrow at Nuradin, but did not hit him. Nuradin rushed at the khan and chopped off his head with a sabre.

Nuradin had only just got ready to return to his father when Yanbay said, 'Permit me to inform your father of this joyful news.'

'Go!' Nuradin permitted him.

Yanbay galloped off not to Edige but to the two daughters of Tokhtamysh. 'Nuradin has killed your father Tokhtamysh,' Yanbay told them, 'and he himself will show up here right away. Most likely he will make you his concubines. But now you must fasten small pillows to your bellies and pretend to be pregnant. If he asks what befell you, you reply, "Whatever happened, it was all according to the will of your father Edige." Then Nuradin will either kill his father or drive him away.'

The daughters of Tokhtamysh did what Yanbay told them. Shah Nuradin returned to his father. He gave him the head of Tokhtamysh. Then he set off to the daughters of Tokhtamysh. 'Ey, what happened to you?' he asked, when he saw the girls with big bellies.

'Nothing would have happened to us if it had not been for your father,' the girls replied.

Then Nuradin grew furious at his father and demanded that Edige should leave immediately. And then Edige sang:

'Edige will speak, the man will speak,
The man who says his prayers himself will sing:
On a holy Thursday
I was born into the world.
After opening my eyes,
I saw good deeds.
Truth served me as an example,
I would imitate a ray of the sun,
Taking the wise book in my hands,
I would give praise to the Creator.
Taking an Arab book in my hands:
"The words of learned men
I will speak myself," I used to say.
Not trusting in heaven above,
Not trusting in the earth below,

After meeting with Kydyr-Ilyas[1]
In the raging sea,
For forty days I asked the Creator.
In these requests,
Ey, Nuradin, my son,
I was asking the Creator only for you.
In order to give you opportunities
I spent my time kneeling
In humble obeisance
To khans like Tokhtamysh,
To khans like Shatemir.
When a favourable hour came for me,
I myself dealt simultaneously
With five hundred enemies.'
Edige's son Shah Nuradin will himself speak:
'My father, when I saw you
Setting spurs to the dark-red *argamak*,
I set out on my way.
On the summit of a high ridge
In the district of Ezeshik and Boz-Eshik,
I then caught up with some men.
In the upper reaches of the Irtysh is a dark forest,
I overtook Tokhtamysh there.
After overtaking him, what did I do?
I took off his head,
To give you a present.
As a talisman, I hung it around my neck.'
Edige will speak, the man will speak,
The man who says his prayers himself will speak:
'When they told me that you had been born,
I slaughtered some fat mares,
And when you had grown up,
I slaughtered some choice mares.
I ordered your face to be washed
With fragrant scents,

---

1   In folklore Kydyr-Ilyas was an ancient wanderer who would come to the aid of lost travellers
and people who had landed in a difficult situation.

I ordered your body to be enrobed
With the strap of a long sabre.
When they asked "Out of what
Should Nuradin's cradle be made?"
I ordered them to make a birch cradle.
When they asked "Out of what
should Nuradin's mattress be made?"
Thinking velvet to be coarse,
Beneath you they spread a silk cloth.
I created you out of nothing,
After making *murzas* into your friends,
I made you into a gentleman.
You were my nestling – I made you into an eagle,
You were a wolf-cub – I made you into a wolf.
Like a kite, I watched over you,
Like a birch arrow, I straightened you up.
In the years of his old age
You are persecuting your old father.
Ey – Nuradin, my son who is like a *murza*,
What have I done for you to banish me?'
Edige will say, the man will speak,
The man who says his prayers himself will speak:
'Out of my eighteen sons,
The one who galloped straight, leaving all behind,
When one needed to give
Yellow gold,[1] cut into pieces,
He was the one who gave it in its entirety,
Like a *murza*, my son.
May everything be looted,[2]
Ey – Nuradin, my son,
What have I done for you to banish me?
If I burn up the grassy steppe,

---

1   In days before minted coinage, money could be carried in the form of sheets of silver or gold, and pieces cut from them as required (hence the name of the Russian currency, the ruble, from the word 'rubit', to cut).

2   Note from Nasipkhan Suyunova: these were the words of a father in despair: telling his son Nuradin that he had given him everything, but if he did not value this wealth, then let it all be plundered (in other words, it was a curse).

Where will you graze your cattle?
If I kill the black falcon,
What bird will you caress?
If I kill the black *argamak*,
What racehorse will you saddle?
In your old father's senior years,
With his eyes reddened like an antelope,
With his hair turned grey like a white swan,
With his neck stretched out like a heron's,
You are persecuting him,
Ey – Nuradin, like a *murza*, my son,
When you start out, where will you find happiness?'
The Murza Shah Nuradin,
The son of Edige, will speak:
'If you set fire to the grassy steppe,
I will select the best of its herbs and browse them.
If you kill the black falcon,
Out of the birds I will caress the gerfalcon.
If you kill the black *argamak*,
I will saddle a *tulpar*.
If I am persecuting my old father,
With his reddened eyes like an antelope,
With his hair turned grey like a white swan,
With his neck stretched out like a heron's,
If I go three times around Beytulla,[1]
The beloved house of Allah,
I will ask forgiveness of the Creator,
I will cleanse myself of my sins.'
Edige will say, the man will speak,
The man who says his prayers himself will speak:
'When the snow storm was blowing,
Wasn't I a shelter
Of reed fencing for you,
My son like a *murza*?
When, like rain, the arrows were falling,

---

1   The Beytulla, or Baytu-llah, the 'House of Allah', refers to the Kaaba in Mecca, around which pilgrims of the Hajj are supposed to circle seven times.

Wasn't I a damask-steel shield
For the back of your head, my son?
If one collects steel shields from everywhere,
And from Khiva and Bukhara,
You will not find a gramme of bronze in them.
Wasn't I actually like that?
Wasn't I a black falcon,
With a glorious pedigree,
With an infallible spurt of speed,
My son?
But if you do persecute me,
I will fly from you.
May every one of your enemies
Fly before you, like I do!'

Thus Edige harnessed a white horse to carry him away, abandoning the land. After selecting for himself a secluded place, he began whiling away his days in solitude.

There were four brothers living then in the khanate. And they had only one goat. They shared the goat among themselves. Each brother owned one leg of the goat. But one leg was lame and wrapped in a rag. The youngest brother got this leg. One day the goat with the lame leg stepped on a fire. The rag started burning. The goat ran off through the hayfield of a certain *bey* and started a fire. The *bey* to whom the burning field belonged seized the youngest brother, as the owner of the burning leg, and brought him to court, to Khan Nuradin.

Nuradin heard the *bey's* plea and imposed a large fine on the poor man. He was required to bring a large sum of money at once. Upset, the poor man went off to wander. And in a certain out-of-the-way place he ran across an old man. The young man told him of his trouble.

'Ey, my child!' said the old man, 'I will give you one piece of advice, if you do not betray me.'

'No, I will not give you away!' swore the young man.

'Then it is this,' continued the old man. 'Go to Khan Nuradin and say, "A just verdict evaded the judge, and one word was left unspoken by us: if the goat had not had three healthy legs, my lame leg would have been totally unable to reach either the fire or the hay. Why was the fine imposed only on me alone? It is unfair." Say that to Nuradin, and you will save yourself.'

The young man went to Nuradin and told him what the old man had taught him.

'Why didn't you say that straight away?' Nuradin was exasperated. 'Somebody instructed you. Just who was he?'

'No, nobody instructed me. I thought of it myself. But then I simply forgot it.'

'Don't lie,' said Nuradin. 'You did not think up such an idea. Who was he? If you do not say, I will hang you.'

'A certain old man in the steppe,' confessed the young man.

Nuradin set off at once to the old man and saw before him his father Edige. There and then Nuradin asked his father to return home. 'If you will carry me on your back, I will consent,' said Edige.

Nuradin set his father on his back, and from the weight his feet sank into the ground up to his knees. Dragging his feet out of the earth with difficulty, Nuradin brought his father home with great effort. The father and son were reconciled, and they began living in harmony, knowing no strife.

But at this time Tokhtamysh's son Kadyrberdi was growing up. In order to take revenge on Nuradin for the death of his father, Kadyrberdi had collected a small army and invaded Nuradin's property. He came, and near the Lake Sekerli he seized Yanbay, who was hunting. 'Aha,' said Kadyrberdi, 'you are working for my enemy. You are also my enemy. Now I shall kill you.'

'I implore you, hear me out!' Yanbay begged, falling on his knees. 'Isn't it Shah Nuradin that you need? Right away I will bring him unarmed into your hands. For by means of weapons you will never defeat him. He has great strength!'

'Go and bring Nuradin!' Kadyrberdi ordered. Yanbay ran straight to Nuradin.

'Ey, what are you running for?' Nuradin asked him.

'How could I not run!' exclaimed Yanbay. 'There at Lake Sekerli there are so many game birds that they are eating one another.'

And Nuradin was a passionate hunter. On a hunt he would forget everything in the world. 'There are countless multitudes of game birds there!' Yanbay was pressing Nuradin. 'Hurry up! No weapons are needed. It is only a stone's throw to the lake. And at the lake it all literally crawls into one's hands. Only hurry! There is an incredible, unprecedented accumulation of all kinds of game birds, all kinds of animals. You can just grasp them with your hand. We might already be too late ...'

Aroused by the sincere excitement of Yanbay, who kept on pressing him, and pleased by the closeness of the lake, Nuradin ran after Yanbay, without taking any kind of weapon with him.

But as he approached the lake, and came out from behind the trees on to the grass, he saw the tents of Kadyrberdi and realised that he had fallen into a trap. But it was too late to turn back. And to run fearfully was worse than death. Nuradin headed straight into Kadyrberdi's tent, to his deadly enemy.

Kadyrberdi at once ordered Nuradin to be seized and forced to sit on a chair on which two sharp spikes were pointing upwards. As Nuradin sat on the chair, the sharp spikes went right through his thighs. The blood spurted. But Nuradin did not reveal his suffering to his enemy. On the contrary, he smiled and, taking the sharp ends of the spikes that were sticking out of his thighs in his hands, he looked straight into Kadyrberdi's eyes.

And Kadyrberdi spoke:
'My large-eyed bay racehorse
Who used to gallop playfully,
Who would jump over an obstacle on its path,
And after jumping over, falling directly on to his feet,
Just where did you put it, Nuradin?
My hatchet with the fringe,[1]
Just where did you put it, Nuradin?
My six carts travelling
Over the mountain ridges,
All six with money,
The ten carts leaving my house,
All ten with money,
Just where did you put them, Nuradin?
The large *kibitka* with the ornament,
The beautiful *kibitka* with the twelve corners,
Its threshold of steel with a gold covering,
The cover of its smoke-hole – silk within,
And brocade on the outside,
The side supports covered with braid,
The cover of the roof of petalled braid,
Which a skewbald white-browed male camel,
Straining himself with the exertion,

---

1   Note from Sikaliev: a mark of distinction, the high status of its owner.

Did not manage to shift by one step:
The twelve-sided *kibitka*
Just where did you put it, Nuradin?
The white iron coat
Left from my father:
There are not one of its links
Among a thousand Caucasus men.
It is worth more than
The khan's cattle,
It is beyond the capability of
A thousand craftsmen with the hammer:
Just where have you put it, Nuradin?
The beautiful Kanyke,
The fair Kozike,
They kill with their beauty the man who sees them,
When they speak, they speak like men,
Just where have you them, Nuradin?
From the very start there were forty-five khans,
My father Tokhtamysh,
Who was the master of the rich land,
Was the youngest of the forty-five khans,
Just where have you put him, Nuradin?'
Nuradin, the son of Edige will speak:
'Your large-eyed bay racehorse
Who used to gallop playfully,
Who would jump over an obstacle on its path,
And after jumping over, would fall directly on to his feet,
On the day when Allah allowed me,
I saddled it myself, after making it a trophy.
Your hatchet with the fringe
On the day when Allah allowed me,
I fastened it on my slim waist.
The six carts travelling
Over the mountain ridges,
All six with money,
The ten carts leaving your house,
All ten with money,
On the day when Allah allowed me, I made them my booty.

The large *kibitka* with the ornament,
The beautiful *kibitka* with the twelve corners,
Its threshold of steel with a gold covering,
The cover of its smoke-hole – silk within,
And brocade on the outside,
The side supports covered with braid,
The cover of the roof of petalled braid,
Which a skewbald white-browed male camel,
Straining itself with the effort,
Did not manage to shift by one step:
I left on the open steppe
The twelve-sided *kibitka,*
After committing it to the flames,
So that my thirsting one should return,
So that my lost one should find the road!¹
The white iron coat
Left from your father:
There are not one of its links
Among a thousand Caucasus men,
It is worth more than
The khan's cattle,
It is beyond the capability of
A thousand craftsmen with the hammer.
On the day when Allah allowed me,
I put it on myself, after making it a trophy!
Your beautiful sister Kanyke,
Your fair sister Kozike,
Who kill with their beauty the man who sees them,
When they speak, they speak like men,
On the day when Allah allowed me,
I took them for my wives!
From the very start there were forty-five khans,
Your father Tokhtamysh,
Who was the master of the rich land,
The youngest of the forty-five khans:

---

1   Note from Sikaliev: this means that the speaker was a beacon on the endless steppe, able to
     quench the thirst of those suffering from thirst, and lighting the way for those who were lost.

On the summit of a steep ridge,
I caught him up, overthrowing all who were in my way,
After overtaking him, what did I do?
I cut off his head.
Fearing not to keep my word, which I gave to my father,
I hung it around my neck like a medallion, and returned.
I am a big black cloud,
I will not clear away
Without coming down on you as rain!
I am more bitter than the salt of the white sea,
You can pour in sugar in cartloads,
But you will not sweeten me.
I am harder than hardwood,
Until I reach the clouds, I will not break.[1]
I am the lightning, which strikes with thunder,
I am a brightly burning light in the sky,
In my anger I am damask-steel that breaks.[2]
Accompanied by sixty *nukyers*
I am a *murza*, who selects *narts*!
To the *nukyers* accompanying me,
I am a *murza*
Who pays wages above the standard rate!
Without asking about their fathers,[3] I will not take *nukyers*,
I will not give cattle without first learning their pedigree,
When I give – I will not stop
At one thousand five hundred pieces of red gold.
I will not extinguish the fires of my friends,
I will not kindle the fires of my enemies.

---

1   Note from Sikaliev: the shorter the spear, the more difficult it is to overcome an enemy. The Nogay *bogatyrs* boast that their spears are so strong and long that they can touch the clouds, but it is not easy to break them.

2   Note from Sikaliev: damask-steel (*bulat*) does not bend but only breaks if bent. So the Nogay *bogatyr* is not a coward before the enemy – he does not bend or yield; either he will overcome the enemy or die, i.e., break like steel.

3   Note from Sikaliev: according to the deep conviction of Nogay *bogatyrs*, genuine fearless *bogatyrs* can only be reared by working people. The social origin is the most important. Warriors born to families of the rich or of princes will retreat at the critical moment; while a man springing from the working masses will defend his people to the last. Therefore any Nogay *bogatyr*, the hero of an epos, selects for himself a companion after asking about his birth and tribe, about his father and grandfather.

I was born black from my mother,
However much you wash me with soap, I will not grow white.
Shah Nuradin, the son of Edige –
It is I!
Am I less than any of you
Khans with your red plaits?
Not only through my thigh, but even through my nose
You can stick a sharp spike, but I will not blink!
My long arrows or my wide bow
I do not have in my hands.
But now if only I had in my hands
My long arrows and my wide bow,
Kadyrberdi with the red plaits,
Young Sultan,
I would now send you
Along that same road, along which I sent
Your father, the Khan Tokhtamysh!'

Kadyrberdi was observing, with unconcealed delight and with envy, his captive Nuradin, who was uttering these words proudly, after laying his hands on the bloodied ends of the sharp spikes that had penetrated his thighs.

The young Kadyrberdi was struck by the firmness of will of Nuradin in bearing his suffering, by his pride, and by his disdain towards death and towards him himself, in whose hands he was.

Kadyrberdi had also been fascinated by the eloquence of his worthy enemy. For all of that, Kadyrberdi forgave Nuradin for the blood of his slain father.

As soon as Nuradin had finished his song, Kadyrberdi extended his hand to him as a mark of friendship and offered to forget the past, and to live in peace. Nuradin agreed, but demanded that Yanbay should be killed, which was done. After Yanbay's death Kadyrberdi and Nuradin were completely reconciled and started living as two khans – as neighbours, and as brothers-in-law.

❧

The epic poem Edige, one of the most popular in the Nogay epos, was recorded by me in the *aul* of Ikon-Khalk (the former *aul* of Tokhtamish), in the Adyge-Khabl' region of Karachayevo-Cherkessia in August 1958 from the renowned singer of the Kuban Nogays, Kumukov Haji-Iskhak Juma-Ali uly.

Haji-Iskhak Kumukov (1888–1966) was a Nogay. He acquired this poem in 1905 from the well-known Nogay singer Arslan Shaban uly (1858–1912) in the *aul* of Kangly near the town of Mineral'nye Vody. The word-for-word translation of this variant of the poem was performed by me at the request of Academic V. M. Zhirmunsky, and was then sent to him in Leningrad. V. M. Zhirmunsky spoke warmly about the variant of the poem presented here, in his book *Tyurksky geroichesky epos*, (Nauka 1974, Leningrad, 354, 383).

Ashim Imam-Mazem uly Sikaliev (Sheykaliev)

2. The Ditch of Temir the Lame *(Ingush)*

Introduction

In the year 1386 Temir (Timur, Tamerlane) seized and laid waste Tiflis (now Tbilisi), and then passed through parts of the South and North Caucasus. In 1395 he began a campaign against Tokhtamysh, the Khan of the Golden Horde, which culminated in a great battle in the valley of the River Terek. This was described by the Arab historian Sherif-ad-Din Ali Yezdi.[1] In accordance with their military tradition, Temir ordered a place to be chosen for a fortified camp and the large army to be arranged there. A moat was dug around the camp, stakes were hammered in, trench-shields were set up, and beyond this trench was dug a second one, an external ditch. Tokhtamysh's army was unable to withstand the charge of Temir's army, and they turned and fled. Tokhtamysh abandoned his camp, which was then looted. After that Temir passed through various parts of the Caucasus, during which time campaigns did not always go his way, with armies suffering considerable losses from the guerrilla tactics of the mountain men. One such encounter is described in 'Partu Patima', in the next section on 'Resistance to Foreign Invaders'.

In Sherif-ad-Din Ali Yezdi's description of Temir's campaign, he also

---

1   M. Brosset, 'Additions et éclaircissements a l'histoire de la Géorgie', St Petersburg, 1851, 387.

mentions Timur's son, Miran-Shah, who supposedly fell from his horse and broke his arm in one of the battles.[1]

Part of the legacy of Temir's campaign is the naming of a crossing of the Sunzha River not far from present-day Grozny; it is called Kopyr-Aksak-Timur, or the Bridge of Lame Timur.[2] The ditch that passes through all of Chechnya is called Timur's Ditch. Incidentally, judging by the folk traditions, the ditch of Tamerlane formerly stretched the length of the Caucasus chain, from Derbent and the Caspian Sea to the Black Sea and through the lands of the Cherkess. In 1886 V. Miller noted that in some parts of the North Caucasus 'traces of ditches can be seen, formerly stretching an enormous distance.' According to him, traces of a ditch are very noticeable in various places in Chechnya, beyond the Argun, near the Vozdvizhen fortification, in Little Chechnya and on the Terek. Miller also saw traces of this ditch in Kabarda along the road from Kotlyarev to the town of Nal'chik.[3]

In this legend it states that Temir's missing son was bought by a man named Barkim. Barkim also figures in a number of other Vaynakh (Chechen or Ingush) legends. In some of these he is named as a Kumyk, a tribe speaking a Turkish language, which was also the language of Temir and his people. According to U. B. Dalgat, there is a tradition[4] that 'Barkim was one of the retainers of Tamerlane. In the Caucasus some kind of discord took place between him and the conqueror. Then Barkim, in order to escape the threat hanging over him, fled from Timyr's camp in the night. For greater safety he kidnapped and carried off Timyr's son with him. He did this because he knew that Timyr would try to search him (Barkim) out, but was unable to cause him any harm on account of his son, who was a hostage. Barkim fled into Ingushetia, into the Galgay community.' This tradition accords with the statement in the legend included below, that 'Barkim had sworn at the time of his purchase that he was going to keep watch on him as if he had been his own son. Temir's son, in his turn, also gave an oath to Barkim that he would live with him until Barkim told him "Go home".' But Temir's son galloped away from him on the *turpal* horse.

---

1   M. Brosset, op. cit., 389.

2   SSTO, Issue I, 1892, 257.

3   V. Miller, 'Kavkazskie legendy', *Trudy etnograficheskovo otdela imp. Obschestva lyubiteley estestvoznaniya, antropologii i etnografii*. Book VII, Moscow, 1886, 48.

4   The tradition was recorded by I. Dakhkilgov from Haji-Bekar Bankhayev (the Bankhayevs are also a branch of the Barkinkhoys); it has not appeared in print. According to another contemporary variant, Barkim descended from the Kazikumyks, i.e., the Laks.

There are various other traditions about Tamerlane in the Caucasus. The Digorians, for example, call the Pole Star Akhsak-Temir (which means Lame Temir). In 1882 V. Miller managed to record an interesting mythological legend which includes some historical truth. Akhsak Temir is characterised as a wicked man who walked through the sky with the *aeds*, and strongly oppressed seven simpleton brothers living on the earth. He killed their foster child who had been taken from a *vodyanoy* (Donbyotar), on whom he was dependent, to be educated. The *vodyanoy* taught the brothers how to go about killing Akhsak-Temir with his help, and Akhsak-Temir stopped going to the water, but sat down in the middle of the sky instead and posted two stallions as guards; and the brothers turned into seven stars, the Great Bear, who vainly chase after Akhsak-Temir.[1]

There are other legends about Tamerlane in Ossetia and Kabarda, in particular about the ditches that are attributed to him. In an Ossete legend the ditches were dug by slaves who followed behind, so that the army did not stray from the road. In a Kabardan legend his army was so numerous that the path they trod became a deep and wide ditch. In the Abkhaz legend 'The Black Candles', in the chapter entitled 'Family and Personal Honour', the ditches were dug by a magic spirit so that Temir's horses could drink clean water on their campaign. In both this legend and the Kabardan one, Tamerlane was resident in Derbent and his daughter had been magically abducted, either to Anapa on the Black Sea coast in the Abkhaz legend, or Istanbul in the Kabardan legend.

From the Galgay Gorge to Little Kabarda there runs a ditch which, as the Chechens tell it, reaches the Caspian and Black Seas; it was produced by Temir the Lame for the purpose of searching for his lost son; but in the tradition it is not said that Temir was a khan, but that he was the son of a man with a mediocre position ... he could recognise a magnetic sword – reflecting the belief that a hard sword should be magnetic. The question is, could he really distinguish a *turpul* from an ordinary horse? According to the beliefs of the mountain people, a man who could recognise a *turpul* horse and a magnetic sword was one who had been endowed with supernatural strength, or who spoke a foreign language, or who was a sheikh. A *turpul* horse was an exceptional or heroic horse, sometimes winged.

1   V. Miller, *Osetinskie etyudy*. Ch. 2, 'Uch. Zap. Imp. Mosk. Un-ta', Issue II, Moscow, 1882, 300.

Temir's father was a sheep-breeder, which is why from his young years Temir was trained in that same kind of farming. One day, when Temir was pasturing the sheep, he caught a hare and sent it into his flock, supposing that the hare was a young goat. While returning home with the flock, Temir showed his father the hare, which he had taken for a kid.

'Well, just catch that kid for me,' his father told him.

Temir made several swift and skilful leaps, caught the hare and handed it to his father. 'Ey,' thought the father, 'with such adroitness and speed he will not stay living with me for long,' and he broke his son's leg. They say that it was from that time that Temir became lame.

A fellow villager of Temir was some kind of blacksmith, who lived at the end of the *aul*. One day Temir was sitting in that blacksmith's smithy, and at some point the blacksmith leaned his head on the handle of his hammer and went to sleep. Temir noticed some little insect come out of the blacksmith's nostrils, head down along the hammer handle on to the anvil and then into a vessel filled with water. After some time the insect returned to the blacksmith's nostrils. 'Uff!' said the blacksmith, waking up. 'What a dream I have just had!'

'Just what did you see in your dream?' Temir asked him. 'Tell me.'

'Just imagine it yourself, I dreamed that I was setting out along a narrow ridge of mountain towards an iron hill, and from there into the sea, but what I saw at the bottom of the sea! Oh, it was an extraordinary wonder!'

'Well, just what did you see there?' Temir asked him.

'I saw gold and silver,' the blacksmith went on, 'and there would have been enough of these valuable metals for the whole world.'

Temir immediately interpreted that dream for himself; he recognised that beneath the smithy there was a treasure, and he said to the blacksmith, 'Transfer your smithy to another place. After all, for you it does not matter where it is; but for me, a lame man, it is more convenient to live at the end of the *aul*.'

The blacksmith agreed to Temir's proposal and transferred his smithy to another place, while Temir began building a house in that place. As Temir began building the foundation, he found whole piles of silver and gold. Temir concealed his wealth from everybody.

At that very time Temir's son went missing and could not be found anywhere; as the consequence of which Temir, without sparing his wealth, undertook the building of an enormous ditch. For that he engaged a great number of people, thinking that the workers would spread the word throughout the world, of the reason for that work, and that probably word would reach his son if he were alive, and perhaps he would come running to him.

Subsequently it turned out that his son had been bought by Barkim. Barkim had sworn at the time of his purchase that he was going to keep watch on him as if he were his own son. Temir's son, in his turn, also gave an oath to Barkim that he would live with him until Barkim told him 'Go home'.

Temir's son secretly possessed the ability to recognise a magnetic sword and a *turpul* horse. One day, when he and Barkim were riding together, they found the skull of a horse. Temir's son, stopping near the skull, said, 'They killed you, horse, because they probably did not recognise your supernatural strength and that you were a *turpul*.'

'Can you really distinguish a *turpul* from an ordinary horse?' Barkim asked him.

'Yes, I can recognise a horse of that kind and distinguish a magnetic sword from an ordinary one,' replied Temir's son.

'All right,' said Barkim, 'we will set off on the most handsome horses and with the best weapons, and wait on the high road for a man who has such a horse and a magnetic sword.'

They stood on the highway and observed each person who passed. At last they spotted several men with loaded horses. As soon as Temir's son saw them he said, 'That one there, who is riding last, his horse is a *turpul* and his sword is magnetic.' When the travellers came up level with them, Barkim and Temir's son stopped the man who was riding last and offered him in exchange for his horse a fine horse with a silver harness, and in exchange for his sword, a sabre mounted with gold and silver.

The traveller was surprised by the offer, even taking it as mockery, and said to them, 'Don't laugh at my horse and my sword, and don't make me lag behind my companions.' Barkim and Temir's son assured him that they seriously wanted to exchange the horse and sword with him; naturally the man did not know the merits of his horse and sword, and he exchanged happily.

Temir's son released the horse with three mares into the mountains to free pasture. At the end of the year he caught one of the mares and slaughtered her, but looking at her bone marrow he said that it was necessary for the horse that he had acquired to graze freely some more, and with these words he again sent him to pasture with the other two mares.

At the end of the following year he caught a mare, slaughtered her and found that his horse still needed to graze on free pasture. After another year Temir's son also slaughtered the third mare; from her muscles he judged that it was now possible to ride on the horse that he had acquired.

One day Temir's son and Barkim set off to a certain public horse race, at which the very best riders gathered. In this contest Temir's son distinguished himself, both by his boldness and by the speed of his horse. When he had made the last circuit, Barkim said to him, 'That's enough. You distinguished yourself by coming first in this race, and now go off to your own home.' As soon as Barkim uttered those words, Temir's son galloped off in the direction where, so he had heard, his father was building a ditch. Barkim realised that he had made a blunder by forgetting his oath given to Temir's son, namely that the latter would live with him until he told him 'Go home'.

Barkim sent some of his men in pursuit. But, on seeing that he was already nearly being overtaken by a rider sitting on a grey horse, Temir's son directed his horse over stony ground. Then the man who had been catching up dropped behind. But another rider, whose horse had a white patch on his brow, was gaining on him. Temir's son began galloping towards the sun, and that rider lagged behind him too. A little later a third rider began gaining on him. This time Temir's son directed his horse into the wind, after which the third rider also began lagging behind him.

The last rider, on seeing that his pursuit of Temir's son was in vain, shouted to him: 'Stop for a short time and answer my questions.' Temir's son stopped and turned towards him. The rider asked, 'Why was it that when one of us, sitting on a grey horse, nearly caught up with you, you started galloping on stony ground?'

'It is because a grey horse has weak hoofs, and it is not in a condition to gallop over stones, while for mine it is all the same, since it is a *turpul*.'

'And why did you head towards the sun when one of us, sitting on a horse with a white patch on his brow, had nearly caught you up?'

'Because a horse with a white patch on his brow has thinner bones, and the sun's rays heat its brain: the result is that the horse becomes weaker and cannot gallop as mine does.'

'Why did you direct your horse into the wind when I was catching you up?'

'Because your horse's tail and mane are too thick, so the wind affects the strength of your horse, while for mine it is all the same.'

After that the rider returned the way he had come, while Temir's son rode on his way towards his father. He arrived in the night at the camp of his father, who was all this time still constructing the ditch. He went softly into one of the cabins and hung up his magnetic sword. All of the swords that were in the cabin were drawn towards Temir's son's sword. After hanging up the sword, he went out, unsaddled his horse and released it among his father's horses. As soon as these horses were joined by Temir's son's horse, they began neighing.

Although Temir realised (since he was a sheikh) that his son had arrived in the camp, he did not tell anybody. However, early in the morning he gathered his retainers and gave them a bag of gold, for them to carry it through the camp and show to each man for his appraisal. Temir's retainers carried the bag through the camp showing it to everybody. Some said that the gold was an everlasting piece of bread, others said that with the gold one could achieve everything that the heart of man could wish for. In other words, each one valued the gold differently.

When the bag of gold had been shown to everybody in the camp, Temir's retainers presented themselves to him and related the opinion of each one. Temir asked, 'Did you ask everybody about the value of the gold?'

'Everybody,' the messengers replied, 'except for one young man who arrived last night and lay down to sleep not far from the tents, after covering himself with his *burka*.'

'Go away and ask that young man what he values the sack at.'

They went off to the young man and asked him how he valued the gold. The young man answered with an ironic smile that it was not worth a piece of bread. That answer seemed ridiculous to Temir's retainers, and they went back guffawing and conveyed to Temir what they had heard from the young man.

'Yes,' said Temir, 'that young man speaks the truth. The bag of gold, which you showed him for evaluation, is not worth a piece of bread, because without gold a man can manage, but without bread he is unable to live. Only my son could give an answer like that. Bring that young man to me.'

The retainers brought the young man to Temir, who recognised him as his son, and the young man recognised Temir as his father. Temir learned from his son that he had been with Barkim, and he moved with his army against him. Barkim was obliged to escape from Dyattakho into the Galgay Gorge, where he founded the present *aul* of Ozik. Subsequently Barkim also left that *aul* and moved to the Shuan Gorge, where he built the *aul* of Makale, and from there he moved to the Kistin Gorge where, between the present *auls* of Lyazhg and Obbono, he founded a new *aul*. After that Barkim left that *aul* too, crossed into the Jerakhov Gorge on the left bank of the River Terek and built the present *aul* of Chmi. It was there that he actually died.

ॐ

This Ingush legend was recorded by Ch. Akhriev and first published by him in 1875. It was published in U. B. Dalgat, *Geroichesky epos chechentsev i ingushey*, Nauka, Moscow, 1972, 400–403.

3. Vakhtang Gorgasali *(Georgian)*

Introduction

Vakhtang Gorgasali (442–502 AD, from Gorgasali, 'Wolf's head') died in the year 502. He was a king of the Kartli region of Georgia. He was killed in one of the battles with the Persians. The activities of Vakhtang I were directed towards the unification of Georgia and the centralisation of power, which also meant a weakening of the arbitrary rule of the feudal lords and the servants of the Church. This made him popular with the folk. Simultaneously he conducted a long struggle with Sassanid Iran for the independence of Kartli. The name of Vakhtang is extraordinarily popular in folklore, particularly Georgian folklore. A cycle of songs and traditions about him has been preserved (see Sikharulidze, I, 53–62, 181–190; see also the Russian translation of one of them, *Poesia Gruzii*, 1949, 21). It is interesting that after the ploughman was banished from the land, although he was guilty, 'plenty' and the 'harvest' also left the land. According to E. B. Virsaladze, the concept that prosperity can abandon a house along with a particular man, animal or even thing is very widespread in Georgia (Virsaladze 1973, 30).

To this day, a ploughman is traditionally called *gutnisdeda*, which means 'mother of the plough', preserving a matriarchal slant.

On that land which is seen from the Bochorma Mountain[1] there lived the Georgian King Vakhtang Gorgasali. The mountain, on which his palace stood, towers right there, all cut and rutted. Its ruins are preserved even today. A little lower down can be seen the ruins of the royal watch tower and fortress of Ujarma, around which there was formerly a town.[2] That mountain was an impregnable stronghold. At what a height the remains of towers and churches are standing around here! From here our king ruled both Kartli and Kakheti.[3] He was a powerful king and so blessed that he could hear the ringing of the church bells in heaven.[4] About this the song says:

'King Vakhtang was beloved of God,
He used to hear the church bells ringing from heaven.'

He erected many churches, and the town of Tbilisi was built by him. But his wife turned out to have an evil nature, and one day he himself was unfaithful to his word, and therefore a bad end awaited him. He ascended the throne when only fourteen years old. Not even a little time had passed before a certain king attacked his land.

'Let us not ruin the people, but we ourselves measure our strength against each other,' that alien king said to him.

It would have been a disgrace for any hero to back down when he was summoned to a duel, and Gorgasali went out to battle. His retainers began to whisper in the king's ear, 'That one is an experienced and renowned warrior. The victory will remain with him. If you do not manage to cheat him, our land will be ruined.'

The king would not agree to this, but in the end he decided to break his word and, when they went out to the place of battle, he shouted to his

---

1 Bochorma is a mountain above the River Iori, 60 km from Tbilisi. On this mountain even now there stands a magnificently preserved fortress with a high fortified rampart, walls and castle ruins. The first reports about it come from the first quarter of the tenth century.
2 Ujarma was a former fortress town on the right bank of the River Iori in the Sagarejo region of Georgia. The walls and towers date from the fourth to sixth centuries, when Ujarma was one of the most important towns in Georgia.
3 Kartli was the most ancient province of Eastern Georgia, and in antique sources it was called Iberia. Kakheti was one of the most ancient provinces of Georgia, separated at the time of the feudal break-up of Georgia into an independent unit and once more united with Kartli in the eighteenth century by Irakli II.
4 In the words of the text recorded by Z. Gulisashvili, 'according to the beliefs of the people, every day in heaven the bells are sounded three times, but only saintly people hear them'.

adversary, 'It is not honourable for a hero to come out to battle with such a numerous suite.'

The poor fellow, so they say, looked around, and as he did so Gorgasali plunged an arrow into his neck.

One day Gorgasali set out on an expedition to India, and left his wife in the palace on that mountain. Down below in the valley, there happened to live a ploughman from Javakheti.[1] He was a blessed man, he would plough and sow and then gather a great harvest.

The royal wife was gazing at him from above while he was ploughing. She did not safeguard her honest reputation, and she tempted the ploughman. Since there was nowhere for them to meet, at nights the ploughman would cut the cliff, so as to climb up steps to the top of the mountain. Those holes and grooves that can still be seen on the cliff are the handiwork of that ploughman.

On that night when he finished cutting the cliff he climbed up to the queen. Gorgasali paid a visit from India and caught the ploughman with the queen. This is how the ploughman answered him:

'By day I was tilling the land with my plough,
By night I was cutting out the cliff,
At midnight I met with my beloved –
Not very tall, with the face of the sun.
Honour and conscience I have forgotten.
May God help the murderer!
May God be a help to the one
Who deprives me of life!'

Gorgasali did not deprive the ploughman of his life, but he sent him out of his sight into Javakheti. All the abundance of Kartli and Kakheti went away with him, so they say. And for a long time nothing would grow among us, whereas in Javakheti the harvest was like the sea. After that a man was sent after the ploughman; they wanted him to come back, but he did not want to. He merely sent several handfuls of wheat. That seed was scattered on the fields, so they say, and from that year abundance returned to Kartli and Kakheti, although in Javakheti the harvest was twice as much.

---

1   Javakheti is a province in Southern Georgia.

The king was good-hearted and forgave his wife. But now his wife betrayed him once again. A huge army invaded our land, one could not see light on the Samgori Field[1] for their great multitude. And they approached Ujarma. Gorgasali repulsed them cruelly. By day he would defeat them in the field, and by night he would return to his castle, surrounded by the impregnable fortress.

Behind his back the queen came to an agreement with the king of the infidels: 'If you take me as a wife, I will help you kill my husband. In the night I will give his horse plenty of salt, and in the morning, when he starts to cross the river on his horse, the horse will bend his head and start drinking water. The king will pull the horse by the bridle and raise him on his hind legs. Meanwhile you take cover on the other bank of the river, and at that instant you plunge an arrow under his arm. Otherwise you will not kill him. From head to foot he is sheathed in armour.'

The queen put into effect this criminal conspiracy, and on the next day the mortally wounded king was carried into the castle hall. After two days that renowned king gave up the ghost. Moreover the king of the infidels sent her to follow in his footsteps: 'You had no mercy on your husband, such a conspicuous hero! Should I, then, expect loyalty from you?!' said he.

He ordered her to be tied to the tail of Gorgasali's horse, and that horse smashed her to pieces.

ৡ

This Georgian legend was recorded just before 1885 by Z. Gulisashvili from the words of Chimia, aged eighty. It was published in E. B. Virsaladze, *Gruzinskie narodnye predaniya i legendy*, Nauka, Moscow, 1973, 157–159.

4. Where the Name of Metekhi Came From *(Georgian)*

Introduction

For the Georgians, there is a series of traditional episodes to this tale: the reproach hurled at the hero, calling him to take vengeance for the outraged

---

1   The Samgori Field is the Valley of Samgori, adjoining Tbilisi.

honour of his family, the compulsion of the mother to tell the truth, the invulnerability of the hero.

Under the name of Metekhi is a well-known series of fortresses, churches and villages in Georgia. One of the churches, built in the thirteenth century, is in Tbilisi, in the narrowest part of the Gorge of the Mtkvari, where the statue of Vakhtang Gorgasali has now been placed. The village of Metekhi, with the remains of a fortress and church (twelfth to thirteenth century), is located higher up the Mtkvari, 150 km from Tbilisi. The Tsilkani Church (fourth to ninth centuries) was located near Mtskheta in the Gorge of the Aragvi, and was repeatedly rebuilt. The Sioni Church (eleventh century) is located in Tbilisi. Ertatsminda is a church built at the turn of the thirteenth century. Samtavisi is a cross-domed church built in 1030, 30 km from Gori. Mention of the churches built earlier than the time described is an anachronism.

Gorgasali was still only a few years old when Os Bogatar invaded Kartli, kidnapped Vakhtang's sister and took her for himself as a concubine. For the time being their mother hid this from Vakhtang. But one chance happening brought it all to light. One day Vakhtang was playing amongst his fellows and for some reason gave a box on the ears to one of his play-mates. The one who had been hit shouted at him in a fit of temper, 'What are you swinging your fists for here? If you are such a hero, go and rescue your sister from Os Bogatar, who keeps her as a concubine.'

These words so upset Gorgasali that he hurried back home, came to his mother, laid his head on her lap and asked, 'Dear mother, let me try your breast for one last time, to say goodbye to childhood.'

His mother got out her breast. Now Gorgasali squeezed her nipple in his teeth and said, 'Tell me right now, where is my sister, otherwise I will bite off your nipple.'

His mother would have refused, but Vakhtang would not give up, and in the end she told him everything in detail. Lastly she told him, 'For the time being I concealed all this from you, my son, but now you have grown up and I am relying on you to help both your sister and all Kartli.'

After that Vakhtang began diligently to get ready for an expedition; he gathered an army and secretly sent a communication to his sister about his intentions. His sister wrote in response, 'My dear brother, Bogatar is a giant. He has deprived many *palavans* of their lives, and it would be better to give up your plans. But if you really will not give up the idea, I tell you that it is possible to kill Bogatar only by inflicting a wound under his arm, since he is always encased in armour.'

As soon as Vakhtang had gathered his army, he sent an express messenger to Bogatar and called him out to battle. Bogatar was blazing with anger. He collected the Ossetians and went against Vakhtang, who was standing with his army at the place where the Metekhi Church now stands. Bogatar came and stood on the other bank of the Mtkvari. Vakhtang flung at him a battle challenge. Bogatar extracted from him an oath that he would not begin shooting arrows at him while he was crossing the river.

He rode his horse into the river, the horse was cutting through the waves, but Vakhtang did not take his eyes from the self-assured Os, who was only slightly curbing his horse. Now Vakhtang seized his chance. He saw the uncovered part beneath his arm, and instantly shot an arrow, and so accurately that the mortally wounded Bogatar fell from his horse and was carried away by the waves of the Mtkvari.

The Ossetian army wavered. Vakhtang pursued them closely, invaded Ossetia, subjugated it and freed his sister. As a mark of repentance for the violation of his oath, Vakhtang erected five churches: Tsilkani in the east, Sioni in the south, Ertatsminda in the west and Samtavisi in the north. And in the centre, the Church of Metekhi, which means 'Me vtekhe', meaning 'I violated' (the oath).

That is what the people say.

ஒ

This Georgian legend was first published in 1902 in Georgian. According to E. B. Virsaladze, it carries traces of literary polishing. It was published in E. B. Virsaladze, *Gruzinskie narodnye predaniya i legendy*, Nauka, Moscow, 1973, 160–161.

II

Resistance to Foreign Invaders

This section contains three legends associated with three of the most devastating invasions of the Caucasus region. It must be noted that there have been many other invasions of parts of the Caucasus, but these three probably had a more far-reaching effect, and were also sufficiently recent for a legend to be composed and still remembered. These were firstly the Mongol and Tatar (Turk) invasions of the thirteenth and fourteenth centuries. Later came the Persian invasions of the eighteenth century, especially under Nadir-Shah. Finally there was the long period of resistance to the expansion of the Russian Empire, especially in the nineteenth century. The most prominent hero of that latter resistance was the Imam Shamil', who conducted the resistance as a holy war.

The first legend, 'Partu Patima', describes how a Lak girl warrior-hero fought against a detachment of Timur's (Tamerlane's) army and won. Timur's army roamed throughout the Caucasus, but legends concerning him seem to be especially common in the eastern Caucasus: present-day Daghestan, Chechnya and Ingushetia. It was in a great battle on the banks of the River Terek that Timur defeated Tokhtamysh, the leader of the Mongol Golden Horde. The latter was based on some of the remnants of Chingis Khan's Mongols, and also included many absorbed Turkish groups. In these regions there are numerous legends about Timur, including one in the previous section, 'The Ditch of Temir the Lame'. There is a tradition of female warriors, the Amazons, in regions that include the Black Sea and the Caspian Sea, and there is much literature dealing with the female warriors of the region, starting with Herodotus. The subject is also discussed by U. B. Dalgat (Dalgat 1972, 234–246).

The second legend, 'Murtazali', deals with a battle against the Persian conqueror Nadir-Shah, in which Nadir-Shah's army was defeated by the mountain men. Because of Daghestan's location, north of the powerful nation of Persia and on the coast of the Caspian Sea, in the past Persia often considered Daghestan to be part of Persia, or at least its empire. The Tats and Mountain Jews of Daghestan are also thought to be of Persian origin, since they speak dialects that are considered to originate in Persia (Bezhanov 1993,

75

150; Kukullu 1974, 3). The compiler of a book of Lak songs (Khalilov 1983) wrote a detailed account of the situation leading up to the battle and the battle itself, and this is presented as an introduction at the start of the legend. It was very rare for Nadir-Shah to be defeated, and the mountain people are justifiably proud of their performance. There are many Caucasus legends that name Nadir-Shah or his generals, and they all involve the violence and conflict occasioned by Nadir-Shah's military campaigns in Daghestan. Some of these were cruel 'punishment campaigns', especially in the more accessible lowland parts of Daghestan, after the murder of Nadir-Shah's brother, Ibrahim Khan, by the Lezgs. In spite of early successes, Nadir-Shah was unable to overcome the Lezgs and others who had retreated into the dense forests and mountains; eventually a unified Daghestan army came forward and defeated Nadir-Shah. There are some legends, especially from Daghestan, in which resistance to Nadir-Shah's armies is depicted. For example, there is a Dargva legend in which a girl from Kala-Koreysh takes revenge for the loss of her seven brothers by killing the shah's brother (Abakarova 1999, 107–109); there is another, 'The Muchalis', in which the Kubachi people take advantage of their reputation for metalwork to make the shah think they are much better armed than they really are, by arranging pitchers on their roofs in such a way as to appear like cannons (ibid, 120–123); and another Dargva legend that describes how the shah is overcome by a prolonged spell of bad weather near Kubachi (ibid, 151).

The third legend presented here, 'Shamil', is one of very many that have been recorded about the 'Murid Wars' against Russian imperialism. In the Caucasus, and especially in Daghestan, the Muslim people fought what they considered a holy war against the Christian Russians, although the underlying causes on both sides were mainly political. The conflict has been described in detail by various authors, including Lesley Blanch, and it can only be summarised here (Blanch 1960).

Russia had been actively working at expanding its empire to the south, with especially strong efforts during the reign of Catherine the Great. For a long time there had been confrontation between Persia and Russia in the Caspian Sea region, and towards the end of the eighteenth century the Russians had moved into the Caucasus, for imperial reasons and on the pretext of a request from the Christian Georgians for protection against the Persians. The Caucasus mountain people, especially those living in the North Caucasus, began resisting the Russian expansion. The first notable leader was Sheikh Mansur, who was eventually taken prisoner by the Russians and exiled to northern Russia. After 1800 'Muridism' started becoming a strong religious force against the Russian occupation, and at first it was led by Khazi Mullah in their holy war, or *Ghazavat*. Shamil' himself was born in Ghimri, in northeast Daghestan, and this mountain *aul* was later defended by him and Khazi Mullah against the Russians. Ghimri was almost surrounded by bare steep rock faces and there was only one approach, by a precipitous track around the rock face, with a sheer drop below. However, the Russians managed to haul their cannons over the almost impassable mountains behind the *aul* and eventually take the *aul* with enormous losses on both sides. Only two *murid*s survived, one of whom was Shamil', who literally leapt over the heads of the line of Russian soldiers who were trying to kill him. The legend presented here describes the final surrender of Shamil' in his stronghold of Gunib in the year 1859, after nearly thirty years as imam. In the final Russian assault, one of Shamil''s *naibs* had accepted a bribe to allow the Russians to enter his fortification. Finally he surrendered for the sake of the children. Shamil' was well treated in captivity by the Tsar Alexander II.

5. Partu Patima *(Lak)*

Introduction
According to Kh. Khalilov (1983, 235–236), from the beginning of the thirteenth century the Mongols repeatedly invaded Daghestan. The invasions of the Tatar-Mongols during the time of Tokhtamish and Timur were especially cruel. In February 1395, after subjugating and laying waste the coastal region of Daghestan, Timur broke through into the North Caucasus and in the same year routed the Golden Horde. On his journey back, Timur fell upon the population living between the Terek and the Sulak. 'He passed through the locality of Tarki and reached the locality of Ushkujan, dispatched soldiers in various directions to make raids, while he himself stayed in that area until his troops arrived from the surrounding places with looted goods. The region of Kazikumuk-Luk and the army of Aukhar (the Avars) had the custom of fighting with infidels (i.e., non-Muslims) each year for a month. Timur thought he would help them. But this time, changing their custom, they rose to the aid of the infidels and did the opposite to what was hoped of them. Timur selected five hundred fully armed cavalry with which he made a raid on them and began driving them before him. Meanwhile the *shamkhal*, Mubashshir Bakhadur, who was their leader, by virtue of his

efforts and courage, was taken and his head brought to his majesty ... The victorious army took the locality of Ushkujan, made a raid on his province and built a hill of its slain ...' ('Sbornik materialov otnosyaschikhsya k istorii zolotoy ordy', from *Collection of materials relating to the history of the Golden horde*, II. Collected by V. G. Tizengauzen, extracted from Persian literature, publ. AN SSSR, Moscow-Leningrad, 1941).

Little is preserved among the people concerning Partu Patima, the heroine of the battles with Timur's hordes. In 1957 Khalil Khalilov recorded two prose legends about Partu Patima. Reference to the existence of the heroine of the bloody battles with Timur is found in a pre-revolutionary ethnographic collection: 'The Laks have their kind of Joan of Arc – Partu Patima, who once saved her native region from the invasion of the Mongols. As witness to her feat there is also a tombstone, which attracts during the summer many pilgrims, mainly women: they consider her as a saintly maiden,' writes Said Gabiev in a paper, 'Laki, ikh proshloye i byt', 'The Laks, their past and their way of life', in the thirty-sixth issue of SMOMPK, 1905.

The valley between the villages of Khuna and Khura is called Partuvalu. Old people related that Partu Patima was buried here. The grave has been levelled.

The young men who had gathered near the cemetery
Had drawn their Egyptian sabres, and were brandishing them.
They were throwing clubs the length of a *chchantiaku*.
They were dressed in chain-mail shirts and holding shields,
On their heads they wore spiked helmets.
Their *kinzhals* struck against the shields with a clang,
When they brushed against the mail shirts, they bent,
And from those dressed in spiked helmets the sparks were flying,
Their horses were rearing up.
While the young men were competing,
Partu Patima walked past.
'Although a girl should not say "*Salam*",
All the same I say to you, "*Salam*, young men!"
You are brandishing your *kinzhals*, is the enemy actually close?
You are brandishing your sabres, is war actually drawing near?
You have put on your mail shirts, are you ready for a campaign?
The spiked helmets on your heads – are you preparing to go far?'

'*Va alaykum salam*, Partu Patima,
For the mother who bore you, may there be paradise!
Take the copper pitcher off your shoulder
And give us a drink of the cold water.'
'If you want me to take the pitcher off my shoulder,
If you want to have a drink of the cold water,
Give me a curved Egyptian sabre,
I want to show what a girl can do.'
After hearing such words,
The *aul's* young men were surprised.
They looked at one another, dumbfounded,
Not knowing what to say to Partu Patima.
Time was passing ... And when some time had passed,
One young man rode out in front,
Making the horse dance beneath him,
And he asked Patima with a taunt:
'Is it possible, Patima, that you are speaking seriously?
Will you kill a man by slashing with a sabre?
Will you kill a horse by throwing a club at him?
Will you kill a man by striking him with a *kinzhal*?
Is the word of a virgin the word of a man?'
'Young neighbour, you are sitting proudly before me,
Rocking arrogantly in your saddle,
While speaking with me, you consider yourself a hero.
You are chuckling because I am a girl.
Give me the horse that is under you,
Give me the golden spiked helmet you are wearing,
Give me the mail shirt of thick iron to cover my body.
Give me the curved Egyptian sabre to prove my strength.'
'The horse that is under me is the horse of a hero,
The spiked helmet on my head is the helmet of a *bogatyr*,
The mail shirt on my body is the shirt of a lion,
The Egyptian blade in my hands is the blade of a brave man.'
'Good young hero, sitting on your horse,
Daring *bogatyr* with a spiked helmet on your head,
Genuine lion with a mail shirt on your body,
Get ready to demonstrate your manliness!'
Thus spoke the girl, and she went away.

And the dumbfounded young men remained in their place.
Time was passing ... And when a little time had passed,
A man appeared like lightning.
The black horse beneath him was skipping friskily,
The spiked helmet on his head was shining brightly,
On his raised sabre the sun was sparkling,
The *jigit* was dressed in a chain-mail shirt.
'*Salam alaykum*, ey, famous heroes,
Can I now say, "*Salam!*" to you?
Now there shall be no more boastful speeches!
And there shall be no more arrogance in your words!'
'*Va alaykum salam*, daughter of famous parents,
Why shouldn't we accept a hero's greeting?
Va alaykum salam, Partu Patima,
Forgive us for our offensive words.'
Partu Patima did not say a word,
And underneath her a lion was dancing – her black horse.
Dextrously she brandished her sabre.
High in the sky flew her spear.
'We ask you, we beg you, Partu Patima,
We have only seen you going for water,
Toiling while tying up sheaves in the field.
Tell us, where and when did you learn men's business –
And to wield the Egyptian sabre so skilfully?'
And again Patima said not a word.
Inserting her curved Egyptian sabre in its sheath,
She jumped nimbly from her horse
And went up to the *jigit* who was questioning her.
'Young man, let you and I measure our strength,
We will test the strength of our Egyptian sabres,
We will fly up into the sky on our lion-steeds,
We will try to cut pieces off the sun!'
The broad-shouldered *jigit* came out of the ranks.
He was taking deep breaths in his mighty chest,
He was holding a big spear in his mighty hands,
And holding a shield the size of a large copper basin.
A smile twinkled on the face of the youth,
Sparks were flashing from his black eyes,

And his horse, lowering its proud head,
Drew a track on the ground with his hoof.
Now the two heroes came together in single combat.
They were two veritable lions, like *narts*.
Their mighty horses reared on their hind legs,
Like two steep mountain slopes.
The young man was slashing with his huge Egyptian sabre,
But the blade was bending, hardly touching the girl's shield.
And the young man slashed again and again.
The girl was deftly parrying the blows with her sabre.
'Now it is my turn,' said the girl.
She swung her steel Egyptian sabre,
Striking the young man's shield, her sabre bent
And knocked the big sabre from the young man's hands.
And his sabre plunged straight into the ground.
The young man's handsome face went pale,
He hung his head, looking at the ground.
Leaning down from his horse, he tried to pull out
The Egyptian sabre thrust into the turf.
But suddenly the heroine stooped to the ground
And pulled the sabre from the earth without getting off her horse.
But her helmet started rolling over the ground,
Her black plaits spreading out across her shoulders.
When the young man picked up and gave her the helmet,
The girl gave him his Egyptian blade.
The girl was sitting on her black horse,
But the distressed young man climbed off his.
He sat down on a stone that was just alongside.
Clasping his head with both hands,
He sighed deeply, it was wretched for him.
'I ask you, I beg you, Partu Patima,
Forgive me for my conceitedness,
Now I have seen who is the genuine warrior,
Who is the renowned hero who deserves to boast.'
'I ask you, my beloved neighbour,
Do not hang your head so low.
It also happens that the donkey grasps the wolf in fright,
And after all it happens with us too.'

*

When Patima returned home,
Her old mother was standing on the roof,
She was shaking a wooden sieve, sifting the grain,
And from time to time chasing away the chickens.
'Oy, I am ashamed how you're dressed before the *aul's* folk.
Where is a girl seen going out on the street like that?
Now how can I go out in public?
Why did you put on your dead brother's armour?'
'Don't be ashamed, Mother, on account of my dress,
All my girlfriends are the same as I am.
Go out, Mother, go out among the people,
The daughters of the others are the same as I am.'

*

One day a neighbour woman came
To Patima's home, sent by a young man,
In her hands she was holding a shred of paper,
After learning by heart what she had to say:
'No matter how shameful it is for me,
I have come to you with a message.
He is very comely with a figure like a plane tree,
He is the very best among the young men.'
'Salikhat, neighbour, about whom are you speaking?
Who has a dream in his heart about marriage?'
'I am speaking, my dear daughter, about Ahmed,
The *nart* has a dream in his heart about marriage.
Make him joyful, my dear daughter, he is suffering,
Being consumed by the fire of passionate love,
He raves about you even in his sleep.
He is sinking in the abyss of his deep love:
"Greetings, light of my heart, which is burning with fire,
Limitless respect to you, heart of my body,
I have a certain anguish, which only you can cure.
It is my burning love. You are the cause of it."'

*

The noonday sun stood at its zenith,
When a messenger appeared on a horse,
The *bashlyk* he wore was fluttering like a banner,
He had galloped to Kumukh with alarming news.
His steed was all covered with foam,
The messenger himself was wet with sweat,
He headed directly to the great Shamkhal
To inform him that Tamerlane himself was on his way.
Time was passing ... And when some time had passed,
The public criers started assembling the people.
Messengers set off to the small *auls*
To sound an urgent summons to the Lak heroes.
From all directions the heroes poured in,
They gathered in Kumukh, to stand against the enemy.
The women and children came with provisions,
So as to inspire the glorious warriors.
After putting the mail-shirt on her well-built body,
And putting a golden helmet on her head,
With her horse dancing like a fire
Partu Patima appeared all of a sudden.
'*Salam alaykum*, glorious heroes,
Standing against the enemy, to defend our fatherland!'
'*Va, alaykum salam*, good young hero,
Among the very boldest, a lioness!'
In one hand Patima held a banner,
Which fluttered in all directions like the waves.
In the other hand she held an Egyptian blade,
Shining like a flame in the sun.
The girl-lioness stood at the head of the group,
Like a falcon in front of eagles.
The girl's black horse was walking and dancing,
As if it was proud of its rider.
Time was passing ... And when some time had passed,
The enemy army appeared in the distance.
Their criers began shouting,
They raised the alarm in all of their troops.

*

A messenger galloped off to Lame Timur,
To tell him a small detachment of Laks was coming.
When the messenger imparted the news,
Timur smiled arrogantly.
Then the messenger went up very close to him
And whispered something in his ear.
Timur opened wide his narrow eyes
And said with surprise,
'I have passed through many lands, taken towns,
Conquered lands, captured kings,
But never have I seen an army with a girl at its head,
Ready to fight against my renowned soldiers ...'
The two armies met,
Like two fiery rocks striking each other,
The field of battle grew red with blood,
The *maydan* was covered with the heads of heroes.
The blades bent, one striking against the other,
The horses grew tired, one galloping against the other,
And the heroes grew tired in single combat, (not yielding to one another),
But the Mongols were confused and struck dumb.
Timur led his best troops into the battle,
The battle was flaring up over the wide plain.
The Lak heroes darted into the fray,
Like falcons attacking crows ...
The warriors stood up in rows,
And the single combat contests began.
The first to come out was a Mongol by the name of Tugay,
The Lak youth Ahmed went out to meet him.
Tugay was taller and his horse was bigger,
He struck and sliced through the Lak youth.
Then Partu Patima rushed towards him,
Raising her excited horse on his hind legs.
Her blade of the best steel was bending,
As an ear of corn would bend in the wind,
The horse, restlessly dancing under Partu Patima,
Would himself speak of his rider's horsemanship.

Tugay struck with his sabre,
Patima skilfully parried the stroke.
Patima slashed with her Egyptian steel blade,
Her hated enemy's head fell from his shoulders.
Then yet another Mongol came forward,
All the gathered Mongols began to shout:
'Hurrah! To the veritable eagle, Tugay's elder brother,
Going to catch the Lak partridge!'
All of a sudden Patima made a spurt,
The lion-horse leapt beneath her,
The blood poured from her enemy's shoulder,
He winced and fell from his horse.
'Hurrah!' rang out, like thunder,
As the Lak side rejoiced,
Groans resounded on the enemy side,
As Patima rode proudly past before their eyes.
After winding her plaits around her helmet,
After rolling her sleeves up to her elbow
After making her Egyptian sabre whistle,
The lioness threw herself into the thick of their enemies.
She slashed to the right, an enemy's head flew off,
She slashed to the left, she wounded a horse,
'Hurrah, young men!' she issued the cry.
'Hurrah!' shouted the heroes, rushing at the enemy.
Time was passing ... And when some time had passed,
The enemy soldiers started taking flight.
Left on the field was a mountain of corpses,
Some on foot, others on horses, save their heads.
On hearing the news of his men's defeat,
Lame Timur grew agitated
And started cursing all those around him.
He issued an order to his *nazir*:
'Take your soldiers, both foot and mounted,
Catch that girl alive and bring her to me,
If you want to keep your head on your shoulders,
If you want to command respect where my power reaches ...'
All the Lak youths surrounded her,
Like stars around the moon,

And Patima was among the heroes,
Like the new moon among the stars.
'Gather up, you heroes, the wounded and the slain,
Those who gave their lives for the fatherland.
Bring here my beloved Ahmed,
I will shed tears from my hawk's eyes.'
Patima's eyes that had never wept tears
Shed tears in streams on seeing Ahmed,
The lioness Patima had never shouted '*Vav-shav*'.[1]
But here she shouted '*Vav-shav*' and fell on the corpse.
'I would carry him home, but the way is far,
I would bury him here, but I'll be reproached!
What can we do, young men, offer your advice?
How can I keep my heart in my breast?'
Ahmed's brother came out in front,
Hot tears pouring from his black eyes:
'How do you want to act with your lion?
Oy, why didn't I die his death,
If only your lion's heart had not suffered!'
'Let us go, heroes, we will return home,
We heroes have shining faces,[2]
Let's go, young men, to our native home.
From today our native land has been raised high!'
The sun set, night came,
And the heroes wended their way.
The ranks of this small detachment had thinned out,
Like the teeth in the mouth thin out.

This poetic story about Partu Patima was recorded in 1938 in Kumukh from the words of ninety-year-old J. Khaydakova, by the teacher S. Khaydakovy, now a Kandidat of Philological Studies, an employee of the Institute of Linguistics of the ANSSSR. It was first published in 1954 in the almanac 'Dusshivu' in the Lak language and in a poetic translation of S. Lipkin into

---

1   A Lak expression of grief or sorrow.
2   A Lak expression, meaning that they have done their duty conscientiously.

the Russian language in 'Dagestanskaya Pravda', No. 159, August 1954. This version was translated from Kh. Khalilov, *Lakskie epicheskie pesni*, Dagestan Filial AN SSSR, Makhachkala, 1983, 125–136.

6. Murtazali *(Lak)*

Notes from Kh. Khalilov (1983, 235–236)
The song about Murtazali reflects the struggle of Daghestan against foreign invaders in the eighteenth century. The mountain men of Daghestan more than once raised an insurrection against the Iranian yoke in the eighteenth century. The first big uprising took place in 1707 among the Avars of the Jaro-Belokansky free communities.[1] Agitation later arose in Kaytag in 1710. In 1738 the Jaro-Belokansky free communities rose once more and killed Ibrahim-Khan, the brother of Nadir-Shah.

In 1741 Nadir-Shah undertook a campaign against the 'Lezgs' (i.e., the Daghestan people) in order to avenge his brother's death. The cruelty of the Iranian invaders, who were well organised and trained and armed with artillery, was unprecedented. Traditions are preserved in Daghestan about *shahkhirman* (the shah's threshing). At Nadir's command, in many places women nursing babies and young children were herded together on to the square for the threshing and were then trampled by horses. After a bloody massacre in South Daghestan, Nadir-Shah moved into the mountains in 1742. The Lezgs, Tabasarans and Dargvas withdrew into Kumukh and remained stubbornly opposed to the shah. However, the Kazikumukh militia, hastily gathered by Surkhay-Khan, was unable to resist the enormous onslaught of the shah's troops. The khan ordered Murtazali to cross Turchidag into Andalal urgently, while he himself began covering the retreat of the cavalry headed by Murtazali. However, the Iranian troops broke into Kumukh, and Surkhay-Khan found himself surrounded and was obliged to surrender to the enemy. The very next day the shah pursued Murtazali's cavalry into the mountains.

When the Iranian hordes approached Mount Turchidag, numerous detachments of men from Andalal, Khunzakh and Laks, Lezgs and Dargvas were lying in wait for the invaders. The night before the battle the mountain

---

[1]   The 'free communities' were those not controlled by feudal powers.

men, making use of local knowledge of the terrain, surreptitiously went up to the grazing horses of the Persians, slew the guards and some of the horses and a larger part they drove away. The shah could not make up his mind to pursue the enemy at night in unfamiliar territory. And at dawn the united forces of the mountain men attacked the Persians from all sides. The rear of the enemy was struck by the rebelling Kazikumukhs and the inhabitants of the local villages. In order to inspire terror in the enemy the women were dressed up in men's costume and on the slopes of the mountains stone posts were set up, which from a distance looked like detachments of warriors.

The basic forces of Nadir-Shah were thrown back by Murtazali's cavalry. The Iranian soldiers fled in panic. The mountain men pursued them as far as Derbent.

In the fighting near Chokh a large number of detachments and warriors took part. This battle, which was unprecedented in the history of the mountain men, became the theme of many epic songs of the Avars and Laks.

In the Lak song the main emphasis is on Murtazali and his feats. Besides that, the song emphasises the communal character of the struggle of the mountain men against the Iranian invaders. As the song shows, taking part in this battle were Avars, Akushins, Kaytags, Kyurins, Kumyks and Laks.

Listen, friends, I will tell you a story
About our grandfathers, about times past.
I will make the deeds of heroes known to you all,
I will recall the names of the *narts*
Who defeated the Kajar[1] army.
I will tell the story of Murtazali,
And of Nadir-Shah, who roared through the whole world ...
After sending men to Stambul to order guns,
And buying flintlocks in the Crimea,
After ordering steel sabres in Egypt,
And buying ordnance in Tiflis,
After collecting Kajars from Iran,
And collecting horses from Arabia,
With *zhazails* shooting downwards,
And howitzers shooting upwards,

---

1   A Turkish-speaking tribe in southern Iran.

With banners with golden tips on their poles,
Having an army dressed in silver,
After wishing to become a god and master of the world,
And deciding to break the spirit of Daghestan,
Nadir-Shah went on a campaign with his Kajars.
And he said, 'I will do *shahkhirman* in the small *auls*.
I will take Surkhay-Khan prisoner.'
After seizing Sheki and taking Shirvan,
After assembling troops from Teheran and Tabriz,
Nadir-Shah approached Tiflis.
The Tiflis khan submitted to him
The well-known towns of Baku and Salyan,
Hearing that he was coming, they started trembling,
The important towns of Gyanzha and Baku,
On hearing that he was coming, surrendered to him.
Nakhichevan and Yerevan he took by force.
In renowned Tiflis, the chief of towns,
He executed the town's heads, he killed them,
And those who were fair of face he took captive and led away.
Shikh-Alikhan,[1] on hearing about it, barred his strong iron gates.
The Khan of Kuba, which had iron gates, he took prisoner,
First taking from him his robe embroidered with silver.
They began shooting with the cannons from Tiflis,
Shaking the earth's mountains.
After galvanising their steel bodies
The Kazikumukh people went out at the alarm.
The Lak heroes felt the power
Of Nadir-Shah's Kajars going to do *shahkhirman* in the mountains,
Sending the Afghan soldiers down on them,
He did *shahkhirman* in the small *auls*.
Sending those Iranian troops,
He went into battle everywhere.
Numerous enemy soldiers, like grains of sand,
Moved into the mountains like ants.
The roads they travelled poured with blood,
And the conquered lands were sown with bones.

---

1   A Derbent governor.

Nadir-Shah's Kajars drove on,
Taking captives in Georgia and Daghestan.
He marched to Arali near Khosrekh.
He joined the battle at Arali near Khosrekh,
Trampling with their hoofs the small children.
When the soldiers settled on Mount Kukma,
Kurban went out with a steel mace.
When the army entered Khosrekh,
Ahmed came out to meet them with his long bayonet.
When the army of Nadir-Shah reached Kuli,
Chupan came out with an arquebus in his hands.
When the Kajars reached the Kumukh fields,
Gazi-Kacha himself went out ahead of his bold men.
Nadir-Shah sent a letter to Kazi-Kumukh,
To Surkhay-Khan, demanding that he should give himself up.
Why wouldn't Surkhay-Khan surrender,
When Nadir-Shah's Kajars showed themselves so strong?
The mother of Surkhay's children, Gaji-Ayshat,
Went away to the mountains with the small children.
The Iranian soldiers were brought into the town,
And Surkhay-Khan was made prisoner in Kumukh.
Nadir-Shah settled down on Mount Turchidag,
In the valley of Megeb he pitched his tents.
In the homes of Kumukh were laments for the dead,
The neighbouring *auls* were looted.
They started setting fire to the homes in the *auls*,
The clouds of smoke rose into the sky.
The Kajar soldiers started shooting
Pood-weight missiles[1] from their cannons,
Making the valleys and gorges shake,
And making the big mountains shudder.
In Daghestan, in a region of rich springs,
The water stopped when the Kajars came.
On Turchidag they pitched as many tents
As there are stars in a clear sky.
On Turchidag, which is covered with flowers,

---

1   *Pood* = 16.38 kg.

The grass could not be seen for the tents.
Through the small *auls* the call went up,
Calling the famous heroes to war.
'Whoever wants victory over our country's foes,
Let him come to the valley of Sogratl.'
Like the streams of water after a thunderstorm,
Young men began thronging – the Lak warriors,
The Avars and Kyurins came as armed groups,
Akusha people, Kumyks; Kaytags and Dargvas
Came, like springs flowing into a river.
Let Murtazali's mother die,[1]
He uttered a speech hotter than fire:
'Heroes, we have joined together to fight.
We are ready to take revenge on the enemy
Today, you demonstrate on the field
That the courage of our fathers is still alive.
The one who dies today, his name will live forever.
Those who are wounded today will be highly honoured.
Today we have to destroy the enemy,
We have to liberate our fatherland.
After all, real heroes die in battle,
While young mothers die in labour.
Even if the water, flowing down, starts to flow backwards,
We will not retreat, we will only go forwards!
Even if the dead rise out of their graves,
We will not expose our backs to the enemy's bullets!
Even if the sun rises up in the west,
We will not lay down our weapons while the enemy is alive!
In the cruel battle with the hated enemy
Either we will die or be victorious in this holy war!'
So swore those gathered there,[2]
Calling on the mountains, the land and the heavens to witness.
Time was passing ... And when some time had passed,
One detachment appeared out of Sogratl'

---

1 Distinctive praise for the hero, implying his mother could rest content for her hero-son would not shame her by cowardice.
2 It was customary to swear, calling inanimate objects as witness. This custom is preserved among the Laks even to the present day.

With green banners in their hands.
In this detachment they all had identical weapons,
In this detachment they all had identical clothes,
In this detachment they all had identical horses,
The leader of the detachment had a black horse.
This small detachment went on and on,
Like lightning from the sky,
As Murtazali went out, on his prancing black horse,
After him went the Kumukh men
Making the mountains shake by shooting with their guns.
Time was passing ... And when some time had passed,
A cloud of dust appeared from Khunzakh.
They reached Udaniv near Chokh.
A shot thundered in the valley of Obokh.
Sabres clashed on the fields of Megeb.
The call rang out: 'Geyta, Hurrah!' and they rushed at the enemy,
As wolves rush on a flock of sheep.
The armies came together, rivers of blood flowed,
A humming set in, in the mountain valleys.
It was not a snowstorm, bringing avalanches,
Nor was it thunder accompanying a thunderstorm.
It was the bullets sent by the heroes
And covering their enemies, like hoar-frost.
They poured handfuls of powder into their guns,
Then inserted a bullet and squeezed,
The sparks flew out of the Tsudakhar flint,
The lead bullets flew out with the fire.
'May your mother die, Murtazali,
You were like a hawk in a flock of partridges!
You went in from one side and came out the other,
You went in from this side, you did your business.'
The Kajar's Nadir-Shah started asking:
'I ask you, I ask you, Armless Surkhay,[1]
Where does this small detachment come from?
Do you know who is on the black horse?'

---

[1] Surkhay's arm was crippled in single combat with his seven brothers; accordingly he was known as Cholak-Surkhay, or Armless Surkhay.

'That is a small detachment of true heroes,
The rider on the black horse is my Murtazali,
May your right hand fall off, Murtazali, my son,
Who started the battle without my permission.'
'May your own hand fall off, Armless Surkhay,' said Nadir-Shah,
'For giving yourself as captive to me, when you have such a son.
I would like to have a son like your son Murtazali,
Let Daghestan and Gurzhistan be yours, Surkhay,
If only I had a son such as your Murtazali.
I would settle down in Mecca and Medina.'
Time was passing ... And when some time had passed,
The Kajar troops started making their getaway ...
When the armies met and rivers of blood flowed,
That small detachment had gained the upper hand,
And numerous enemy soldiers began running away,
Armless Surkhay-Khan began to shout:
'I ask you, I ask, son Murtazali,
I was obliged to surrender as a prisoner to the enemy.
If you can, try not to let
The Kajar soldiers escape.'
'Don't shout from on high, my father Surkhay,
My right arm is completely paralysed.'
'If your right arm is paralysed,
We will call the doctors and we will cure it.'
'Don't shout from on high, my father Surkhay,
In my eyes is bloody sweat the colour of jasper.'
'If in your eyes the bloody sweat is the colour of jasper,
I will find doctors, I will make them cure it.'
'Don't shout from on high, my father Surkhay,
The blade of my Egyptian sabre has bent.'
'If the blade of your Egyptian sabre has bent,
I will send you a damascened one with a golden handle.'
'Don't shout from on high, my father Surkhay,
The lips of my black horse are covered with hoar-frost.'
'If the lips of your black horse are covered with hoar-frost,
I will send you a war horse of a bay colour.
Try, my son Murtazali,

Not to kill those three *kizilbashis*.'[1]
As Murtazali slashed with his sabre,
On each field where they sow one *dachu*, he was killing ten,
On each field where they sow ten, he was killing a hundred.
The sabre in Murtazali's hands
Seemed like lightning from a blue sky.
Time was passing ... And when some time had passed,
Murtazali started shouting:
'My lion's arms are paralysed!'
'If your lion's arms are paralysed,
The detachment standing behind is well matched with you.'
Once again Murtazali shouted out:
'My silk shirt is full of blood!'
'All right, if your silk shirt is full of blood,
The Kajar soldiers have started running away,
Like sheep being chased by a wolf,
Like partridges pursued by an eagle.'
Again Murtazali shouted out:
'My bay-coloured war horse has slowed down!'
'If your bay-coloured war horse has slowed down,
The Kajar soldiers have begun running away after all,
Like jackals pursued by hounds,
Like cranes frightened by an eagle,
Like flocks attacked by a lion.'
On Turchidag where there was not even a pebble,
Whole mountains of corpses lay.
In the valleys where not even a drop of water is found,
Rivers of Kajar blood were running.
Then the Kajars' Nadir-Shah started shouting:
'May you perish, my great army!
After all, it's not the whole world standing firm before you.
May your homes burn down, Kajar soldiers,
How has this youth inspired fear in you?
Why have you started flying from this youth?'
The *kizilbashis* started shouting:
'Don't speak, don't tell us, Kajar's Nadir-Shah,

---

[1]   Soldiers of Nadir-Shah who wore red headgear.

His eyes are like lakes,
And his arms are like posts,
Nothing can be seen for the steam from his mouth,
He cannot be seen for the fire from his horse's hoofs,
While he himself kills one, his horse is killing ten.
We entreat you, master of our heads,
Ask him to let us return to Iran.
By God, he is taking our souls like Azrail.
His lightning-sabre is smiting twenty men each time.
You ask Murtazali,
After all, a noble hero must listen to a request.
Ask him not to block the road to our native land,
May he let us go to our native Khorosan.'
The Kajar army began begging for mercy.
The Kajars' Nadir-Shah began entreating.
He started humbly appealing, entreating:
'I ask you, I beg you, Murtazali,
If you need gold, we will give you gold,
If you need silver, we will give you silver,
If you need prisoners, we will give you prisoners.
Let us leave for our homes in Khorosan.'
'Why should I want gold from you?
Gold I will get with a sharp blade.
Why should I want silver from you?
Silver I will get with fire from a gun.
Why should I need prisoners acquired without labour?
Prisoners I will drive in by giving rein to my horse.
I will let you go home, to your native region,
After making a hole in your heart with my gun.
Very well, I will let you go to Khorosan.
After marking this date on my dark-blue sabre,
I will drive you before me to that Khorosan,
Holding you by the *cherkeska* and striking your backs with my sabre.'
With their sabres that small detachment drove forward,
The soldiers famous throughout the world.
And sent them to Khorosan,
After marking that date on the blade of the blue sabre,
After making them repent with the barrel of a gun.

ॐ

This variant was recorded by Kh. Khalilov in 1962 from the words of
Ibrahimov Musa, aged seventy-two, inhabitant of the *aul* of Khanar of
the Lak region. It was published in Kh. Khalilov, *Lakskie epicheskie pesni*,
Dagestan Filial AN SSSR, Makhachkala, 1983, 136–146.

7. Shamil' *(Dargva)*

Introduction

There are a few things to note in this account about Shamil' and the Caucasus
War. Amuzgi sabres come from the village of Amuzgi, well known for the
making of steel blades and situated in the Dargva region of Daghestan, a
region famous for its metalwork. *Naibs* were the chosen officers of Shamil''s
army. There were a hundred *naibs*, his highest-ranking officers, then lower-
ranking *naibs* who numbered about a thousand. They obtained this rank, as
bodyguard or special troops, only by rigorous testing in loyalty and strength.
They were required to remain unmarried. They wore the Caucasian tunic,
or *cherkeska*, the ordinary fighting men (*murids*) in brown, and the *naibs* in
black. The latter were fanatically devoted leaders who had taken a special
oath. In peace or war they vowed by the sacred ten-fold oath to live and
die for Shamil'. Temir-Khan-Shura was the former name of the present
Daghestan town of Buynaksk. The stronghold of Gunib, on a desolate rock
plateau, had been considered unassailable before the introduction of long-
range guns. It stood alone, isolated from the surrounding mountains, rising
sheer from the valleys below, a thousand or more feet high. The summit was
hollowed out like a deep shell, covered with grass, which afforded excellent
pasture for sheep and horses, and protected from enemy fire by high rock
scarps edging it all around. It had fresh-water springs, and places where fruit
and grain could be grown. There were even seams of coal, suitable for fuel.

For a long time the mountain men were writing
    The song of the Amuzgi sabres.
This song was mingled in the mountains
With the whistle of bullets and the ringing of blades.

For a long time the Tsar fought with the hero,
Who had been born among the crags,
And was unable to tame him,
For he was the people's hero.
Shamil' rose up for freedom,
He called the mountain men from their *saklyas*
And said, 'Better to fall on the field of battle
Than to live in bondage to the tsar.
Well, what does it matter that we are few,
For we are in the right, we will stand up for
The starkness of the mountains, and our life in the mountains,
Which is destined for freedom.'
But letters flew to the tsar,
From Levasha and Temir-Khan-Shura,
From the governor-general at Tiflis,
From all those who did not love Shamil'.
In the letters were wishes and promises
To take the hero of the mountains alive.
To deliver the Imam Shamil' alive
To the crafty white tsar,
And they found the means to take him.
The tsarina had suggested to them:
'Where the soldiers and army
Have not the strength to overcome the enemy,
There is always gold and riches,
With which one can give bribes.'
The white tsar was crafty,
But the tsarina turned out to be more cunning.
She sent gold and riches
To traitors. She knew that
The poor mountain men were also exhausted
By the never-ending wars.
And there is a thirst among the weak
For the ringing sound of gold and wealth.
The army indeed moved towards the fortress,
To the last refuge of the imam,
One could not count them, as one can't count
The grass on an Alpine meadow.

They kept coming, in their hundreds and thousands,
Those sent by the white tsar.
Gunib, the *aul* on a high mountain,
The stronghold of all the strongholds,
Was surrounded by the soldiers of the tsar,
The traitors had helped them.
May the curses on their heads
Remain in the memory of the people.
After selling out their lives for coins,
They betrayed the hero of the 'Land of Mountains'.
At midnight, with the help of ropes
And ladders woven from hemp,
One on the shoulders of another,
The enemies climbed into the fortress.
Shamil', not knowing about the betrayal,
Calmly went out at dawn
In order to perform his prayer,
And to wash his feet and face.
Suddenly he pricked up his ears and saw
That they were surrounded by the enemy.
After performing his prayer at the evil hour,
The imam hailed his faithful *naibs*.
He pulled his sword 'Bazalay'[1] from its sheath,
It was double-sided and sharp.
Behind his belt he thrust his flintlock
And Shamil' was ready to fight with the enemies.
'Ey, wake up, whoever is sleeping,
Get up, whoever is awake,
We have been betrayed by unworthy people,
So we will die worthily in battle!'
In the front went the Imam Shamil',
He had made up his mind
To fight to the end,
But the children barred his way,
His children entreated him:
'Imam, concerning your bravery

---

1   His pet name for his sword.

The crags have composed an immortal song,
Think, in this evil hour,
Whether you will win renown
By forgetting about us and the future of the mountains,
You will embitter our pitiless enemy?
And he, without mercy
Will massacre us too, together with you!
So think about it and decide,
Imam, we are subject to your will,
And let your greatness serve
For the future of the "Land of the Mountains".
Shamil' thought about this and hung his head,
He threw off his military equipment,
And took his *papakha* from his head,
Compressing it in his hand, he submitted to them.
It is not easy for a soldier to lay down his arms.
And was it easy for the imam?
But he was also sensible, in that
Life was more dear to him,
He did not want life to be extinguished in the mountains,
He wanted his children to carry on his work.
No, his enemies did not take him prisoner,
He laid down his arms for the sake of the children,
For the sake of those in whose hands will remain
These mountains, which were dear to him;
For the sake of those in whose hearts
Will remain the curses on those who,
Through greed, and forgetting their native land,
Betrayed the mountains and the imam.

This Dargva legend was published in Fatima Abakarova, *Darginskie skazki*, Kavkazsky Dom, Tbilisi, 1999, 123–126.

III

Resistance to Feudal Oppression

The words 'feudal' and 'feudalism' tend to arouse strong feelings among us these days, with our sense of freedom and equality, but it is often argued that the system originally developed to satisfy a need: for mutual local protection against the threat of invasion, or impositions from others outside the local community. This protection for the small family or clan was obtained at a price: the offer of services in return for shelter or support. Such an arrangement should have been mutually beneficial, but clearly the feudal lords were in a stronger position than their dependants, and it was their frequent abuse of the system that led to the types of conflict recorded in these legends.

The feudal system was strong in parts of the Caucasus in the past, especially in the plains regions, where it was easier for a feudal authority to maintain control. In the mountainous districts, where transport was more difficult, the feudal system, if present at all, was harder to maintain, and the mountain people were generally more independent, living in free communities.

Where the feudal system was fairly strongly developed, such as in the plains regions of Kabarda and Cherkessia, there were generally up to five social strata. At the top were the princes and their families: in the Adyge language the *pshis*, in Tatar *beks* or *bys* (*beys, bays*). The second layer was the ancient nobles, the *uorks*, whom the Tatars and Russians called *usdens* or *uzdens*. The third included the freed men, freed from the relation of serfs to the *pshis* and *uorks*, but still under the authority of their former masters regarding military service. The people of this layer were in effect new nobles. The fourth layer consisted of the freed men of these new nobles. The fifth consisted of the vassals or serfs, who were subdivided into those engaged in agriculture and those who were engaged in menial work for the superior classes (Klaproth 1814; 314).

A somewhat idealistic description of a mutually beneficial system among the Cherkessian princes in the late nineteenth century was given by a member of a local princely family: 'The traditions of the mountain land gave the prince many rights, but also many duties. To everyone who asked for help he owed advice and aid, protection and charity' (Tuganoff 1936, 37).

An alternative description was given by Yu. M. Sokolov in 1936 (Sokolov 1936, 634, 635). It must be borne in mind that his description was published during the Stalinist era of the Soviet Union and there was clearly a strong bias. It was also written some time after the feudal system had ceased to exist. However, much of this description also accords with that of Klaproth (op. cit. 314–315).

The subjects of Kabarda were, to all intents and purposes, slaves and tributaries of one or another of the *pshis*. Within their dominions (principality) the *pshis* possessed unlimited power (administrative, judicial and military). By customary right (the *adat,* or unwritten customary code), the *pshis* could appropriate any Kabardan man's goods, wife or daughter, so long as they did not belong to an *uork* of the first two ranks. If a *pshi* had been killed by an *uork* of the lower ranks, then the murderer and his nearest male relatives were liable to be executed, their property confiscated, and their family turned into slaves. The luxury with which the *pshis* surrounded themselves proclaimed itself not so much in the structures and furnishings of the houses, which were usually modest, so much as in their dress, in their equipment and in their expeditions: when they stepped out they were surrounded by a huge retinue of *uorks*. Moreover, they strictly observed the rule of disposition of the riders according to the rank of their nobility. Every mounted Kabardan, on meeting a *pshi*, was obliged to turn around and accompany the *pshi* until released by him. The *pshis* strictly guarded the purity of their blood, and a marriage was contracted only within their own estate, or with children of the Nogay Khans. The Muslim clergy energetically supported the idea of the 'chosen' status of the *pshi* among the illiterate masses, reinforcing the slave code of obedience of the *karakhalks* or lower classes to the high-born 'sun-like' class. The heyday of the power of the *pshis* was the seventeenth, eighteenth and early nineteenth centuries. The subjugation of Kabarda by Russia weakened the importance of the *pshis*, after promoting the *uorks*. This depended not only on the fact that many *pshis* were killed in the war[1] or escaped to Turkey, but also that the *pshis* were deprived of the possibility of extracting payment from the neighbouring peoples and performing raids. The abolition of serfdom in 1867, and also

---

1   The Caucasus War, which ended in about 1865, in which Russia conquered the Caucasus.

the slow but sure penetration of capitalism, set the two basic classes, the landowners and the peasants, against each other.

The *uorks*, besides the inherited titles, could also reach that estate through war exploits or on the basis of the special favour of the *pshis*, and also as immigrants from the corresponding estate of other Adyge tribes. These *uorks* were the chief buttress of the *pshi* and his real physical power. The material interest of the *uorks* was because part of the war loot of the prince and part of the *kalym* (dowry) went to him. The second-rank *uorks* lived without exception in the prince's settlement (Sokolov, 1936).

The first legend, 'The Batyr Khuchulav', is popular throughout Daghestan, and describes how a local outlaw hero was tricked into coming to a town controlled by a feudal prince, who proceeded to kill him; but the hero managed to take the feudal lord's two young sons with him. The Lak song, 'Davdi of Balkhar', also deals with the poisoning of one of the feudal lord's retainers, after he has appeared to be showing an interest in one of the lord's wives. The next two Georgian legends, 'The Battle of the Gorges' and 'The Sword of Mamuka Kalundauri', both deal with the resistance of an army of local mountain men against an army of the feudal lord's retainers. The people living in high mountain regions were generally reluctant to submit to the control of feudal lords. 'The Death of the Areshidzes' commemorates the elimination of the ruling feudal family by the inhabitants of a Georgian village – in this case the entire village cooperated in the fight for freedom. 'Lom-Edalbi' describes the attempt of a feudal lord to appropriate the sweetheart of a local hero, and the hero's successful resistance. The Ingush legend 'About Tkhobya-Erda' describes how a Georgian feudal prince demanded to be given the wife of a local Ingush man; in return the Ingush man demanded that the Georgian prince should leave the area and take his Georgian people with him. This bargain had far-reaching consequences on the religion of the region, as Christianity departed with the Georgians. 'The Death of Napkha Kyagua' describes the resistance of a local Abkhaz man to the slave raids by the neighbouring feudal Adyge princes from across the mountains. Finally, the legend 'Kapsog Goshteliani', which was narrated by one of his descendants, describes how a powerful Georgian prince tried to sell into slavery a subject whom he disliked. On the way to Turkey the hero escaped.

8. The Batyr Khuchulav *(Lak)*

Notes from Kh. Khalilov

The Avar epic song about Khochbar is diffused through Daghestan, among the Avars, Laks and Dargvas. Among the Laks it is current under various names: 'Khuchbar', 'Yarttaschiyal Omakhan', 'Batyr Khuchulav'. This song also exists among the Rutuls, but here it has changed into a prose legend without the name of the chief hero. Among the Ingush and Chechens the song about Khochbar is popular under the name of 'Song about Bakhadala Khushpar'.

An invitation came from the Yartaschi[1] Nutsal[2]
To appear at a wedding the next evening.
'They have come from the Khunzakh Nutsal to invite me.
Should I go or not, my old mother?'
'There's no need, don't go, my beloved son,
The Khunzakh Nutsal is tricking you.'
'Truly, I will go, my old mother,
A *batyr* would go where he was invited.
Never in my life has my courage failed,
It cannot fail me, although I am married.'
'If you won't stay but must go, my beloved son,
Take a black horse as a gift to Omakhan,
Take a damascened sabre to Omakhan's brother,
Take a flintlock gun as a gift to his son,
Take some muslin to Omakhan's daughter,
Take a ring as a gift to his wife,
Take a Georgian bull to the *aul's jamaat*.'
He chose a restless horse and sat on it,
He chose shining arms and put them on,
He took a black horse as a gift for Omakhan,
He took a damascened sword for Omakhan's brother,
He took a flintlock gun as a gift for his son,
He took some muslin for Omakhan's daughter,

---

1   The Lak name for Khunzakh.
2   The title of a feudal lord.

He took a ring for Omakhan's wife,
He drove a bull for the *aul's jamaat*.
And Batyr Khuchulav set off.
When he reached the Yartaschi fields,
The red flowers had become black,
Riding, he came to Upper Khunzakh.
'*Asalamu aleykum*, brave Khunzakh men!'
'*Va aleykum salam*, wolf who devours the sheep!'
Without waiting for him to hand over the black horse,
They cut off its mane and tail and sent it into the mountains.
Without waiting for him to hand over the flintlock,
After leaving him the butt they took away the barrel.
Without waiting for him to hand over the ring,
They cut off his finger and took it by force.
'We will help him off his horse,' said the young folk,
And they bound his hands with a chain of blue iron.
'We will help,' said the old men,
And on his feet they put a block of rotten wood.
'I would see how these Yartaschi men would seize me,
If only I had my damascened steel sabre at my belt!'
They brought the damascened steel sabre,
Broke it in two and threw it at his feet.
'I do not reproach them for that,
After all, you[1] chopped the heads of young Yartaschi men.
See if these Yartaschi men would seize me,
If I had my Stambul flintlock on my shoulder!'
They brought the Stambul flintlock,
Broke the butt and threw it at his feet.
'I do not reproach them for that,
After all, you have shot through a thousand heads.
See if these Yartaschi men would seize me,
If I had my black horse next to me!'
They brought his young black horse.
They led it out on to the *godekan* and slaughtered it before everyone.
'I do not reproach them for that,
After all, thousands of heads of cattle were trampled by you.'

---

1   'You' refers to the sabre that has just been broken, then the gun, the horse, etc.

They fettered his body with iron in nine places,
The Upper Khunzakh men set him in prison.
Time was passing ... And when some time had passed,
The Khunzakh town crier started summoning the people:
'Bring firewood, whoever has lost a son,
Bring kerosene, whoever has lost a brother,
Bring *kizyak*, whoever has lost a husband,
The wolf who devours the sheep we burn in the fire.'
Time was passing ... And when some time had passed,
The young Khunzakh men started shouting:
'Ey, get up, get up, Batyr Khuchulav,
The Khunzakh Nutsal calls you.'
Pushing their gun-butts into his back,
They took him to the Khunzakh *godekan*.
The Khunzakh youths were standing around.
The Khunzakh Nutsal began questioning:
'Tell us, I ask you, Batyr Khuchulav,
By how many men have you diminished the *aul*?'
'Who will count all those slain?
I have removed the heads of three hundred *nukyers*.'
'And besides, tell us, I ask you, Batyr Khuchulav,
By how many lambs have you diminished our flocks of sheep?'
'Who will count all the lambs taken away?
But I gave a hundred lambs each to the children of widows.'
'And once more tell us, I ask you, Batyr Khuchulav,
How many horses have you driven away from our herds?'
'Who will count all the horses driven away?
But I assigned ten each to all the small *auls*.'
'I ask you, I request you, Batyr Khuchulav,
The fame of your singing is widespread,
The fame of your *chagana* is widespread,
Cheer us up too with one of your songs.
They speak everywhere of your dances,
Dance, do a caper around the fire.'
'I will not refuse to sing,
But let my silver *chagana* be brought,
And let my fingers be untied from the ivory,
If just to loosen a little the fetters on my lion's hands.

And I will not refuse to dance for you,
If my feet are freed from this block of rotten tree-stump.'
The young people said, 'Let us untie him!'
The old men said, 'No, we won't untie him!'
The young people won – they untied him.
They brought him his silver *chagana*.
And Khuchulav started singing in the Khunzakh *godekan*:
'You young women standing on the roofs,
Who are you staring at? By whom were your husbands killed?
You brave Khunzakh men, standing around me,
Who are you staring at? By whom were your fathers killed?
You Khunzakh women, standing around me,
Who are you mourning for? By whom were your sons killed?'
The sounds of the *zurna* and drum were heard.
While dancing around the fire,
Batyr Khuchulav began advancing forward.
He looked around with his lion's eyes,
His heart was telling him he would not escape.
At the feet of the Nutsal stood his two piglets,[1]
The *batyr* grabbed them and threw himself into the fire.
'Aman!' the Khunzakh Nutsal started begging,
'I ask you, I beg you, Batyr Khuchulav,
We did not kindle the fire in order to burn you.
We kindled the fire for your amusement.
Throw out here those children of the sun.'
'Get lost, get lost, base Omakhan,
I knew that you were an ignoble man.'
'Once more, I ask you, Batyr Khuchulav,
I will hand over to you my power as a khan,
Throw out here those children of the sun.'
'Get lost, get lost, base Omakhan,
I knew that you were a shabby man.'
Time was passing ... And when some time had passed,
Those piglets began whimpering.
'Wait a little, don't whimper, piglets,
My lion's eye has still not flickered.

---

1   His children.

Wait a little, don't whimper, piglets,
My lion's moustache has still not singed.'
Time was passing ... And when some time had passed,
The powers started leaving his sweet body,
The fingers started shrinking out of the ivory.
Let the Nutsal's wife proclaim mourning clothes,
Let my old mother arrange a celebration.
Let the Nutsal's wife dress in black,
Let my beloved wife dress in red.
Into the Nutsal's house they will carry two corpses,
Into the *batyr*'s house – the body of an orphan.

ə❧

This Lak song was recorded by Kh. Khalilov in 1957 in the settlement of Gamiyakh of the Novolak region from the words of Abdulkadyrov Abdulkadyr. It was published in Kh. Khalilov, *Lakskie epicheskie pesni*, Dagestan Filial AN SSSR, Makhachkala, 1983, 146–151.

The Lak variants of the song about Khochbar were first recorded by Ali Kayayevy in 1932 in the settlement of Mukar of the Lak region from the words of Kunbuttayev Muhammed, and in 1934 in the settlement of Balkhar of the Akusha region from the words of Aysha Bagandova, and in the settlement of Shali of the Charodi region from the words of Budutsov Kurban. There are three variants of this song in the manuscript archive of the Institute of History, Language and Literature, Makhachkala, Daghestan.

9. Davdi of Balkhar *(Lak)*

Notes from Kh. Khalilov
According to the Lak traditions, Davdi of Balkhar served the last Kazikumukh khan Aglar-Khan as a judge, and enjoyed the respect of the people for his clear intelligence. Davdi was attracted to one of Aglar's wives. They made their declarations only with glances and with a nod of the head. The khan's *nukyers*, spotting some kind of prearranged signs given to Davdi, reported it to the khan. The cruel and hot-tempered Aglar-Khan became furious: Davdi was poisoned while being entertained at a banquet.

Knowing that according to the custom of the mountain men a man does not refuse a request from a woman, the khan makes Zaza and Shamay pour out a goblet of poison for Davdi. The poisoned Davdi regrets the fact that when Zaza and Shamay offered him the goblet, he did not have the sense to pay them off with the flintlock and the horse. The love of the folk towards their hero in this variant is shown in the address of Davdi to the Tabakhlu women and their reply to him. From that dialogue it is clear that the khan had used the same means to take care of other men who had crossed him.

Aglar of Kumukh
Sent a letter to Balkhar
Requiring proud Davdi of Balkhar
To come to Kumukh.
'Don't go,' said my wife.
'Oya!' my mother began wailing.
I was obliged to visit
A scorched Lakia.
I sat on my black horse,
Like a hawk on the hand,
The black horse dashed on his way
Like water over a plain.
The black horse was neighing
While I was singing songs.
For an hour we were riding
Over the Unchukatl' Fields.
Into the khan's gates
Where men can ride mounted,[1]
You go in there too, Davdi,
Sitting mounted on your horse.
'*Asalamum aleykum*,
Aglarkhan of Kumukh!'
'*Va aleykum vasalam*,
Proud Davdi of Balkhar!
Climb off your black horse,
Give your horse to the *nukyers*,

[1]   The gates being so high that one can ride directly into the yard.

Ascend to the balcony, Davdi,
Quench your thirst with *machcha*.'
'May good come to you!'
Aglar said.
'And the same to you,'
Said Zaza as she filled the pitcher.
The carved pitcher, which was filled
Only for dear friends,
Zaza filled for me,
After pouring in poison.
From that bane
My insides started burning.
The pitcher filled by Zaza
Proved to be strong poison.
When the khan said to me,
'May good come to you,'
After quickly throwing it up from my shoulders,
I could not hand over my flintlock.[1]
And when Zaza
Said 'The same to you,'
Having taken the saddle from my horse,
I could not quickly hand over the black horse.
Zal[2] gave me death,
When the khan poured in poison.
Oy, Allah, I am dying of poison
From the pitcher filled by Zaza,
It would have been better if I had not come to Lakia!
It would have been better if I had stayed in Balkharakh!
It would have been better if I had not drunk the *machcha*,
But had drunk strong *buza* instead!
I ask you, Haji Butta,
Hold the stirrups of my horse,
In my sweet body
There is absolutely no strength left.
I ask you, khan's *nukyer*,

---

1   It appears as if there is something missing from the song: perhaps this and the horse had been
    intended as gifts to mollify the khan.
2   The Laks call God 'Zal', although they also use the word 'Allah'.

Lift me into the saddle.
My eyes, like black grapes,
Have already started to go blind.
Then I turned and headed
For my own *aul,*
After laying my head on the saddle,
With a terrible pain in my belly.
May you become weak with loss of blood,
This Tabakhlu Mazukur.[1]
You have become endless,
Like the *maydan* of Gudu.
There is never enough moisture here,
On the Tabakhlu Mazukur, but
From the drops of sweat falling from me,
Lakes have formed.
I have in my mouth thirty iron teeth,
Like those of an *azhdakha,*
But they spilled out into the mane of the horse
While I was riding through Okhli.
My black horse that outstrips
All the Akusha horses,
If you carry me there alive,
Let the barley you are given be *halal.*
You golden-winged falcon
Flying over me,
Won't you fly there,
To the *aul* of Balkhar?
If you are thinking of flying there,
Ask the Balkhar elders,
Let them send a wooden horse.[2]
You deft young hawk,
Hovering in the air:
Won't you fly there,
To my native *aul*?
If you fly there,

---

1   Davdi is cursing the plain for taking so long to traverse.
2   A stretcher for carrying a corpse. Male corpses are covered with a black *burka* in the mountains.

To my native *aul*,
Ask the young Balkhar people
To prepare a guest room.
They carry the stretcher from *aul* to *aul*,
Heavier than a stone of lead.
In every *aul* the funeral lament
Is blacker than a black raven.
I ask you by God, brothers,
Do not rock the stretcher –
My sweet body that is on it
Is already burned up with poison.
I ask you, my old mother,
Do not lift my *burka*.
My sweet body beneath the *burka*,
Let nobody see it grown black.
I had a young wife
From the beauties of Balkhar,
From this day may she be
Halal to the man who wishes for her.
Let my young life drain away,
I only pity my mother,
She will go blind with tears.
My young wife, say "Oya!"
After turning to Kumukh:
"May stone rain fall
On the home of the khan!"
My own mother, shout,
When going out to the riverbank:
"My young golden hawk
Has been carried away by the flood!"
I ask you by God, *aul's dibir*,
Leave chinks among the gravestones:
When my young wife goes for water,
May I hear the knocking of her *bashmaks*.
God-loving young people of the *aul*,
Strew a thin layer of earth on my grave
So that I can hear my black horse neighing
When he is going to be watered.

ஐ

This Lak song was first recorded by Ali Kayayevy in 1930 in three variants from the words of Muhammed Gaziev, inhabitant of the *aul* of Viltaschi of the Lak region; from Davud Shamkhalov, inhabitant of the *aul* of Kuli of the Kuli region; and from Kadi Charakayev, inhabitant of the settlement of Balkhar of the Levashi region. It was published in Kh. Khalilov, *Lakskie epicheskie pesni*, Dagestan Filial AN SSSR, Makhachkala, 1983, 184–189.

10. The Battle of the Gorges *(Georgian)*

Introduction

The inhabitants of a certain gorge constituted a family and tribal union. Squabbles used to break out among the various unions, about pastures and so on. This legend is about the union of the free men of the gorges of Upper Svaneti, who did not know the yoke of serfdom, against the common enemy, the nobles and princes of Lower Svaneti, who were continually threatening the freedom of the free inhabitants of Upper Svaneti.

In the old days there was conflict between the inhabitants of the Svaneti gorges. Podaant Puta was the leader of Mulakh.[1] Above the Ugviri[2] Pass the leader was Kipiani[3] of Gukari.[4] Ugviri and Mulakh were united in battle. The loot belonged to the Ugviri men, and the glory to the Mulakh men.

Gigo Galpkhani was surrounded by enemies from Lower Svaneti. That was Ber Gelovani with his soldiers. Gigo Galpkhani dressed in a goatskin and, in the guise of a shepherd, penetrated the army of Ber Gelovani.

Ber Gelovani was conferring with his followers. They were deliberating about how to trap Gigo Galpkhani and destroy him.

Gigo Galpkhani returned to his place, took two *sapalne* of wine, and took an ox. At the gates of 'Our Saviour' of Mulakh he tied up the ox as a gift,

---

1   A village community in free Svaneti.
2   A village on a mountain pass in Svaneti.
3   Kipiani and Gelovani are princely families.
4   Gukari is a village in Svaneti.

and sacrificed the wine to Our Saviour. He himself went to his kinsfolk and stayed there until morning.

In the morning the headman of Mulakh, Puta of the Podany, saw the ox tied to the gates of the church and the wineskin of wine on the ground. He was surprised: 'Whose hand did this?'

The inhabitants of Mulakh gathered. Gigo appeared before them and appealed for help: 'Ber Gelovani has laid siege to me with his army. He has treachery in his heart. I ask you, help me against Ber Gelovani.'

They sent a messenger to Kipiani. The armies joined up and moved towards Choluri.[1] Near Choluri they set up a camp on a wide clearing. They sent a messenger to Ber Gelovani: 'Go back again, and leave Gigo Galpkhani alone, otherwise your expedition will not end well.'

Ber Gelovani answered them, 'I am not afraid of Svaneti dogs.' He sent the messenger back.

Three times mediators were sent to him with an offer of peace, and three times he sent them back.

After that, during the dark evening, the Svaneti men went and spread peas on the shingle along the riverbank. The next day they slung their gleaming guns over their shoulders and began to gather the peas and eat them.

Ber Gelovani looked out from his camp and was amazed. 'What kind of marvel are you collecting up and chewing?'

'We are actually gathering the river shingle and small pebbles, and now we are chewing and eating them, so that our enemy's rifles will not overcome us. Now we will deal with you, we will massacre you all.'

Ber Gelovani's soldiers became frightened and scattered, some to the east and some to the west.

The Svaneti men gave chase to the disordered army and annihilated it.

ﺩﮟ

This Georgian legend was recorded by E. B. Virsaladze in 1951 from the words of B. L. Iosseliani in the village of Mulakhi, Svaneti. It was published in E. B. Virsaladze, *Gruzinskie narodnye predaniya i legendy*, Nauka, Moscow, 1973, 206–207.

---

1   Choluri is the name of a locality.

11. The Sword of Mamuka Kalundauri[1] *(Georgian)*

Introduction

The Zurab Eristavi was one of the prominent feudal lords, the Lord of the Aragvi Gorge (seventeenth century). He was well known for his repeated attempts to enslave the free mountain men of Eastern Georgia (among them the Khevsurs, Pshavs, Mtiulis and Gudamakari men). The family lair of the Aragvi Eristavis, the fortress of Ananuri, even now towers on the bank of the Aragvi 70 km from Tbilisi.

According to the Khevsurs, some folk heroes contain an element of divinity. This appears in various forms, but mainly in that of light emanating from the hero.

More than once the Zurab Eristavi invaded Khevsureti. One day he gathered an army for battle with the Khevsurs. The only thing he saw in Khevsureti was trouble. He passed Pkhituri,[2] went through Osauri, and led his troops up towards Mount Roshki.[3] Zurab was confident of victory. In a song of that time they say:

'The cranes flew to Pkhita, tired from the long road;
In Roshki the towers began groaning, in Blo[4] the house roofs began trembling.
They were afraid, they sensed that in Sadzele an ice avalanche was coming!
Zurab sat proudly on Mount Roshki, the sunlight hid itself.'

The Khevsurs gathered in Sana:[5] 'These places belong to us.'

Zurab had decided to assess the tribute from the Khevsurs in the same way as he was accustomed to do with others. Not many were able to hold out against him: he was a powerful warrior. Among the Khevsurs only Martia Misliauri, Berdia Mamukauri, Khirchla Baburauli and Khosharauli were able to repulse Zurab and his warriors. Nobody else was equal to him.

---

1   Mamuka Kalundauri was the hero of a cycle of heroic songs and traditions of Khevsureti in the seventeenth century.
2   Pkhituri is a mountain pass in Khevsureti, and Pkhita is its abbreviation.
3   Roshki and Sadzele are mountain peaks in Khevsureti.
4   Blo is a settlement in Khevsureti.
5   Sana is the Gudani sanctuary on the Sana Mountain.

But in this campaign, in the struggle with Zurab, Mamuka Kalundauri became famous.

As it happened, this Kalundauri, from a family from Guro, was sitting oblivious to what was going on, digging up *khipkhola* in the field. They say that Kalundauri's sword had been blessed from on high. On a day when Kalundauri could expect victory, his sword came out of its sheath by itself, thus letting its owner know that victory was coming.

No matter where Kalundauri was, he would immediately sense that his sword was stirring in its sheath. It was the same on that day: while digging up *khipkhola* in the field, he sensed something and went home. He glanced at the sword hanging high on a post in his home, and saw that it had come halfway out of its sheath. 'What has happened and where, and who is in need of help? Where must I go?' thought Kalundauri. He went out and shouted to his neighbour Bachakauri, 'What is happening, Bachaka? My sword has come halfway out of its nest! Where and who needs my help? Where is my sword calling me to?'

'That I do not know, Kalundauri. The Khevsurs were saying that Zurab's soldiers have invaded Khevsureti.'

'Well then, who indeed is in need of my help, if not they?' said Kalundauri. 'We are familiar with Zurab's habits. He will not leave one stone unturned from the Khevsur villages, unless they have help and very quickly.'

'Be careful. Zurab is cunning, he might kill you!'

'What will be will be,' answered Kalundauri. 'It seems to me that the victory will remain with me. I would not expect victory if my sword was not starting to burst out of its sheath.'

He returned and went back into his house, ascended into the *ketkho*, put on his chain-mail shirt, took his weapons, buckled on his sword, put it back in its sheath and said, 'All right, my sword, now show me what business you are good for!'

Mamuka went off, and after him other inhabitants of the neighbouring mountains.

When he ascended Mount Borbalo,[1] he took in all Khevsureti at a glance, and saw at once the Khevsur army and Zurab's army near Sana. He raced there headlong.

God's grace was on Mamuka. Setting out on an expedition, a shaft of light preceded him like a star. This time too, a ray of light was moving before him.

---

1   Borbalo is a mountain peak on the border of Khevsureti.

Zurab looked, saw Kalundauri walking at the foot of the mountain, and was unable to stand firm. Losing his head, he rushed towards the Khevsurs: 'What kind of man is that coming towards us, with a star going before him?'

'We do not know what sort of man he is,' answered the Khevsurs.

Zurab gathered up his army. He said to them, 'That man does not bring us any good. We will get away from here at once.' He collected his army and escaped, together with his soldiers.

But Kalundauri quickly caught up with Zurab's army, at the foot of the mountain Bekeni,[1] by the river. Zurab himself got away, he slipped away, but Kalundauri overtook his troops by the river and rushed at them with the sword in his hand. He killed one, then a second, then a third. He killed twelve at one time. When he had struck the twelfth with his sword, so that the body of the dead man stood in the river upside down, news reached the Lord God about the massacre of so many men.

At this point Mamuka put his sword back in its sheath and appealed to God: 'Do not be angry with me! I am not going to kill any more!'

(In Khevsureti the old warriors follow this rule even now. If during hand-to-hand fighting a man killed by the sword stands upside down, one is not allowed to continue the battle. Such a battle is not pleasing to God.)

Kalundauri put his sword back in its sheath and told those of Zurab's soldiers left alive, 'Farewell. A good journey to you! The Lord told us not to kill you.' And right there and then he set up a *samani*, saying, 'After my death, if a traveller passes by here and does not drink up three horns of vodka, giving a blessing, then may all the sins committed by my sword, and all the blood shed by it, fall on him.'

Then it was also said:

'The men of the district came down from the mountains,
A ray of sunshine followed Mamuka Kalundauri.
At the mountain of Bekeni he overtook Zurab's soldiers and hacked them
    to pieces,
On returning from there, he set up a *samani* of stone.
Let every young man who steps on our land act according to Mamuka's
    wish.'

---

1   Bekeni is a mountain in Khevsureti.

This Georgian legend was self-recorded by V. M. Kalundauri in 1914 in the village of Chimga, of the Arkhoti Gorge. It was published in E. B. Virsaladze, *Gruzinskie narodnye predaniya i legendy*, Nauka, Moscow, 1973, 208–210.

12. The Death of the Areshidzes *(Georgian)*

Aru[1] – to Areshidze,[2]
The army – to Japaridze,[3]
If they annihilate the masters,
All will go to the Lobzhanidzes.[4]

In the past, as you know, the custom was: on the night of the wedding the newly-wed bride, the 'queen', was taken away to the master. It was for that reason that among us the 'king and queen' used not to be seated together.[5] They found themselves separated, and if the master wished it, the woman was in his power.

One inhabitant of the village of Gebi, Zviad Lobzhanidze, did not want to get married. 'Why don't you take a wife?' they used to ask Zviad.

'What, bring one and present her to the master?'

A man has to be steadfast,
Not squirming with fear.
Bring your wives,
Lead them off to the master,
You yourselves have become like women,
It's time to cover yourselves with women's shawls!

The time had come to teach the princes and noblemen some sense. They began arguing and discussing: 'What can we do?' they asked.

---

1   A sound similar to hallooing or whooping. On the night of the summer solstice, when it was usual to light bonfires and jump through them, they would shout 'Aru-ru to the devils!' in an attempt to banish them.
2   Areshidze was the surname of the princes of Racha.
3   Japaridze is a noble Racha surname, famous for heroism in battle.
4   Lobzhanidze is the surname of mountain people of the village of Gebi (in the mountain area of Racha, at the upper reaches of the River Rioni).
5   In Georgia newlyweds are referred to as 'kings' and 'queens'.

There were three Areshidze brothers, the Gebi overlords. Their fortress was called Devtsikhe, or Fortress of the Devs. Their steward went by the name Gagnia. Zviad Lobzhanidze said, 'We will arrange a feast. We will invite Gagnia, win him over, and with his help we will annihilate all the Areshidzes.'

The Gebi inhabitants agreed.
They invited Gagnia to a feast,
They entertained him with wine and bread.
Gagnia's head started ringing.
Now the inhabitants of Gebi told him all,
They demanded a terrible oath.

Gagnia said, 'I will lure the Areshidzes to hunt in the neighbourhood of Gebi; on the bridge of Tsinchala,[1] you massacre them. Arrange an ambush in the piers of that bridge, and when the Areshidzes step on to the bridge, you shower them with arrows. But do not be too hasty, do not hit me.'

The steward went to Areshidze. The prince asked him, 'What is new in the countryside?'

'There are many animals in the forest, *batono*. We have to go hunting.'

'I had a bad dream and I fear to go hunting,' Areshidze told him.

'A dream, that is nothing.'

'I was showered with arrows in my dream, I was swimming in blood.'

'That is a sign of a great hunt.'

'That is good, but the dream is weighing me down.'

The steward persuaded him, and he took two of the Areshidze brothers hunting.

They had only just stepped on to the Tsinchala Bridge when the Gebi inhabitants showered them with arrows. They killed one brother outright, but the other jumped into the river.

Into the whirlpool of the Rioni he leapt,
Asking God for help.

They chased after him, but the prince swam well, and quickly cut through the water. They shot arrows at him, but not one of them hit him. Swimming,

---

1   Tsinchala is a bridge across the River Rioni at the village of Gebi.

the prince reached Gebi. The women at the Church of Matskhovari noticed him and informed the old man Gulitad Gavasheli. (The rest of the men had collected at the bridge.)

That old man had been an outstanding marksman in his youth, but now he was lying sick on a wicker *chelti*. 'What has happened, why are the people running along the bank?' asked the old man.

'Thus and thus, it is Areshidze, he has run away from our men.'

'Lift me up on the stretcher and carry me to the bank. Give me my bow and arrows.'

They carried him to the bank, the old man stretched the bow, shot an arrow and killed the prince.

The third Areshidze brother learned what had happened. He wanted to cross the Rioni, to go into the settlement. The Gebi inhabitants demolished the bridge, so that there was no access for the prince.

A certain old woman rode down to the riverbank on a horse. The master asked her, 'Carry me across the river.'

The old woman sat him on the saddle in front of her. When they had gone in sufficiently deep, she clasped him in her arms and threw herself into the water with him. They were both drowned.

Such was the old woman's last will: 'When I die, each year put on a memorial dinner for me.' And in truth, so it has been observed since early times. In the old days we used to put on three memorial dinners: to the Father, to the Son and to the Holy Ghost. And among us we put on also a fourth dinner, as a memorial to the soul of that old woman.

That is how the village of Gebi gained its freedom.

This Georgian legend was recorded by E. B. Virsaladze in 1960 from the words of P. Lobzhanidze in the village of Gebi. It was published in E. B. Virsaladze, *Gruzinskie narodnye predaniya i legendy*, Nauka, Moscow, 1973, 215–217.

13. Lom-Edalbi[1] *(Ingush)*

In past times, when people used to be taken captive,[2] there lived a certain *padchakh* in the Khamkhoy *shakhar*.[3] He was very rich: his sheep and cattle were grazing on all the neighbouring mountains. He seized the Tsoroy *shakhar*[4] and held sway over it, for he had a vast and strong army. His bed was spread with swan's down fifteen *loktey* thick.

One day a slave made his bed and the king lay down to sleep, sighing loudly. In the morning the bed was found to have a thickness of three *loktey*. His slave, surprised at this, asked his *padchakh*, 'My formidable and great *padchakh*! What sort of miracle is this? At night the bed was fifteen *loktey* thick, but now it is three *loktey*. What can this mean?'

'My devoted slave, I rule the Khamkhoy and Tsoroy *shakhar*s, and I have many riches. Even people who are not under my rule respect this. But what is the use of these riches and this sovereignty if there is nobody to meet me in the evening, and to send me on my way with a kind word in the morning. In the Metskhal *shakhar*, in the *aul* of Erzi,[5] lives the sister of seven brothers, the radiant beauty Misalmat. In manhood, strength and honour, there is nobody to compare with her brothers. Their horses can outstrip beasts of prey; they can catch flying falcons. Misalmat compares in beauty with the sun and the moon. When she goes out in the daytime, nobody is able to look at her; even the sun hides behind the clouds, considering her to be more beautiful than he is. At night, when she looks out of her tower window, the mountains light up and the moon hides itself. In their delight at her beauty, the mountain streams sing melodies. I have thought many times about how to get possession of her. Burdened with these thoughts, my body reduced the thickness of the bed from fifteen *loktey* to three. My slave, you have to go to the Metskhal *shakhar* with my commission and say to her brothers, "Give me your sister voluntarily, or else I will apply the force of a *padchakh* and take her from you."'

The slave saddled his long-sided Cherkess horse and set out to search for the seven brothers. He rode out in the morning and, when the sun was declining towards sunset, he reached the mountain of Khulakhoy. As he

---

1   The first part of his name, Lom, means 'lion'.
2   They were sold as slaves, usually either to the Turks or Persians.
3   A settled area in the upper reaches of the River Assa.
4   One of the branches of the Ingush, who live in the eastern part of Mount Ingushetia.
5   A complex of towers in the Aramkhi Gorge (from Ingush 'eagle').

rode into Khyuli, they were arranging races there. They were shooting at a target with bows, and people were betting among themselves.

'*Assalam-aleikum*, you splendid young fellows, not distinguishing between day and night! Will you accept a guest who is not being pursued from behind, nor has he baseness in his heart?' asked the *padchakh*'s slave.

'*Va aleikum-salam*, unknown guest from a distant place! If there is a chase behind you, we are also men to repel it; and we will be such hosts as even to receive a man with baseness in his heart. Have a rest, and let your swift-footed Cherkess horse rest too,' answered a young man like a stretched bowstring; his face, like the bright moon, radiated light on a dark night.

'Thank you, I am in a hurry. I have an urgent mission. Who can show me the way to Erzi, where the radiant beauty Misalmat, sister of seven brothers, lives?' asked the guest.

'In the Metskhal *shakhar* anybody is ready to give service to a guest,' and the brave Lom-Edalbi quickly saddled his horse.

The guest did not speak of the reason for his trip, and the brave Lom-Edalbi did not question him.[1] They rode to Erzi.

'*Assalam-aleikum!*'

'*Va aleikum-salam*! Welcome, guests from a distant place. Dismount and go inside,' the seven brothers greeted them.

'And our best wishes to you! We are not going to enter. We have business with you.'

'We can speak about business in the house; so why do you not go in? After all, your guest is our guest,' the eldest of the brothers reproached Lom-Edalbi. They quickly seated the guests, they slaughtered a ram, and the seven brothers and Lom-Edalbi began to entertain the slave. Thus, three nights in succession they slaughtered rams, but the guest did not speak about the reason for his coming, and the hosts did not question him.

The third night passed, and the eldest brother asked, 'Three days and three nights have passed since you came riding here, but the purpose of your coming is still not known to us. Now tell us why you have come.'

'Splendid young men! For three days and three nights I could not bring myself to tell you, but now I am obliged to do so. I do not dare to tell you, but if I do not tell you I fear the *padchakh*. I have come to inform you that the powerful *padchakh* asks you to give him voluntarily the radiant beauty

---

1   According to the custom of the Vaynakhs, as also with other mountain people of the Caucasus, guests are not questioned about the purpose of their visit. But they do question him after three days.

Misalmat, competing in beauty with the sun and the moon. If you do not give her voluntarily, then the *padchakh* will take her by force.' So spoke the guest.

After some time the brave Lom-Edalbi answered him, 'Guest, for three days and three nights you have said nothing about why you have come. If only you had said it at once, then you would have received a worthy answer from us. You did not speak because of cowardice, and your *padchakh* is equally cowardly. We will not give Misalmat voluntarily. Let your *padchakh* try to take her by force,' said Lom-Edalbi, who loved Misalmat.

The brothers sat down to a banquet, not thinking of the danger. In the morning Misalmat went out to milk the cow and she saw from the tower window a triple ring of the *padchakh's* warriors surrounding the fortress. She had not had time to tell her brothers about it when Lom-Edalbi forced his way into the ranks of the warriors and joined battle. He struck with his sword to the right, and he cleared a space on which one could build a village! He struck to the left, and he cleared a space on which one could build a tower. He fought with the *padchakh's* warriors until the shining golden sun had set. Lom-Edalbi did not let the girl's brothers join in the battle. Finally, the *padchakh's* warriors conceded to him, both in strength and in bravery. Then their leader shouted, 'Who can do so, save yourselves!'

The warriors took to their heels, and when they were passing the Khulakhoy Mountain the brave Lom-Edalbi flung his sword after them. The sword sliced off the mountain like a saw. This sliced-off mountain stands even to this day. It looks as if two huge giants have sawn it off. After routing the *padchakh's* army, Lom-Edalbi married the radiant Misalmat, who competed in beauty with the sun and the moon.

They began living happily.

This Ingush legend was recorded in 1962 by A. U. Malsagov from the words of B. Aldaganov in the town of Grozny. It was published in A. O. Malsagov, *Skazki i legendy Ingushey i Chechentsev*, Nauka, Moscow, 1983, 320–322.

14. Tkobya-Erda *(Ingush)*

Introduction

This is one of several versions of the same legend, dealing with the same people: the Ingush and the Georgians. However, Klaproth recorded a story containing the same motifs and referring to the Cherkess (Adyges). The tradition was that in their country there once resided Frengi or Europeans, to whom they were themselves in some measure subject. One of their (Cherkess) princes, as they relate, had a very beautiful wife, whose charms made such an impression on the ruler of the Frengi during a visit, that he demanded her for himself. The Cherkess prince made some excuse to gain time, and consulted with his family on how he should act. At length he consented to give her up, on condition that the Frankish prince would promise to comply with his request. He himself took his wife to the enamoured Frank, who swore to grant his petition; on which the Cherkess required the cession of the country occupied by the Frengi ... The Kabardans still have a proverb, which seems to allude to it, which is: *For this land we gave our wives* (Klaproth 1814, 314).

A certain mountain man related the following.
   'When I was still a little boy, a certain decrepit old woman lived in our village. One day, when she was lying in the sun warming herself, I and other kids began throwing pebbles at her. The old woman grew angry and said, "May you be under the patronage of the infidels." We fell to thinking about what that meant, and I proceeded to question her.

"'When I was still a little girl," she answered, "in the place where Tkobya-Erda is now, there lived the people of a certain prince. They were peace-loving and strong. At the time a certain man was living there. His wife was so beautiful that people spoke of nothing else but her beauty. That man was a great friend of the prince. They so respected each other that they even gave their oath not to refuse, if one of them asked the other for something. One day the prince said to that man, 'Everybody says that your wife is a real beauty, give her to me as a present!'

On hearing such a thing, the man lapsed into great sorrow. He did not know how to act. Not to fulfil the prince's request by giving away his wife meant breaking his given oath,[1] but he did not have the strength to give his beloved wife to another man. The man came home and told his wife about the prince's request. She heard him out and answered, 'Don't be so upset. I shall teach you how to act. You tell the prince this: "I will give you my wife, since you ask her of me, but you must also fulfil what I am going to ask of you. After obtaining my wife, you leave here with all of your people, and give me your word that you will never again return here."'

That man actually said all this to the prince. The prince himself was unable to decline the beauty, and therefore he gave the required word, which he was obliged to fulfil. He collected all his people, took the other's wife and voluntarily left those parts."'

This is the story from a certain Galgay mountain person, who at the time was 140 years of age (narrator's explanation). This Ingush tradition was recorded in 1892 by B. Dalgat from the words of Daniil Kotiev, who heard it from Temurko Vedigov, an inhabitant of the village of Srkhokhi; who, in his turn, heard it from a hundred-year-old mountain Galgay man. It was published in U. B. Dalgat, *Geroichesky epos chechentsev i ingushey*, Nauka, Moscow, 1972, 368–369.

15. The Death of Napkha Kyagua *(Abkhaz)*

On many occasions Napkha Kyagua and his fellow villagers repulsed the predatory raids of princes. More than once they punished greedy people who had robbed the peasants. It was not only in Abkhazia that they had heard of Napkha Kyagua. They knew him even in the Northern Caucasus. Kyagua was feared and hated by the princes and the nobles. But the peasants called him 'heart and mainstay'.

Napkha Kyagua died as befits a real hero. Not far away from Napkha Kyagua there was living a poor widow, who had two teenage sons. One day they set off into the mountains to look for their buffaloes. The boys did not return.

---

1   An oath at that time was considered sacred, not like now (the narrator's explanation).

At that time, princes and nobles were engaged in the theft of children; they sold them into slavery. The widow feared this terrible calamity. She came to Kyagua and related what had happened. He promised to search for them. Slinging his gun over his shoulder, Napkha Kyagua set off into the mountains. He searched the forests and the ravines, but he did not find the boys.

Beyond the pass lived Prince Khaamit Mazlou. He traded in children. Everybody knew about it; Napkha Kyagua also knew, and for that reason he also crossed the pass.

In a certain *aul* Napkha Kyagua asked for hospitality, in the *saklya* of somebody he did not know. When the mountain-dweller found out that his guest was the fearless Napkha Kyagua, about whom such great fame had spread, he organised a feast and invited the distinguished people of the *aul*.

Khaamit Mazlou also appeared at the feast. He looked with curiosity at the stocky and thickset Kyagua and sat down at the table smiling. Kyagua coldly examined the prince. During the feast, they sat for a long time in silence. Then Khaamit could not restrain himself, and he asked, 'For what good purpose, Kyagua, have you come to us? And moreover alone ...'

'I do not need a guide,' answered Kyagua. 'Instead of him I have a trust-worthy gun. And I was led here by the tracks of the missing boys. There are two of them. They disappeared from my village and have turned up here: I know who has them.'

Khaamit did not like these words. 'All right,' he said. 'I will give you the boys, but in return ... in return I will take revenge on you in the near future.'

To this Napkha Kyagua answered, 'Khaamit, you ought not to speak like that. After all I am a guest in your *aul*. But since you have made up your mind, I agree. Attack, when I am no longer here, in two weeks, on Wednesday. Then the livestock and the horses will be home in my village, and there will be something for you to profit by. Only beware that you do not touch my wife.'

'And what will happen if I take your wife away too?'

'Then I will grow angry.'

'How will you grow angry, Kyagua?'

'I will kill you, Khaamit Mazlou!'

'Good, we shall see!' Kyagua collected the boys and returned to his native village.

On the appointed day, Napkha Kyagua and his fellow villagers waited for the raid. But more than a week passed beyond the end of the agreed time, and Khaamit Mazlou and his henchmen did not appear. Napkha Kyagua and his friends decided that Khaamit had changed his mind about attacking them. They all went about their own affairs. Napkha Kyagua and his relatives, Symsym Ucha and Myshv, set off to graze their livestock on Mamdzyshka.

But now, around evening, Symsym noticed the glow of a fire in the direction of their village. He informed Napkha Kyagua. He realised at once that it was their village burning, and that Khaamit Mazlou had set fire to it. Kyagua hastened into the mountains. He gathered a detachment of herdsmen and settled himself with them in the gorge of the River Gegi, in a place where Mazlou had to pass.

At dawn, when the prince entered the gorge with his captives and his looted goods, Napkha Kyagua shouted, 'Listen, you cheat! You broke the agreement, you have behaved like a bandit. But you will have to return your loot, otherwise – death!'

Khaamit knew that he could not slip away out of this gorge, but nevertheless he was hoping for good fortune. Anger and spite tormented him. Not having the strength to contain the anger that had overcome him, he shouted to Kyagua, 'I will give you back your goods and that of your neighbours, but I am going to take your wife all the same!'

'In that case, Khaamit, then you try shooting at me first!' Khaamit fired. 'You shoot badly, Khaamit!' Kyagua began to laugh. 'Now thrust your whip into the earth.'

Mazlou thrust it into the earth, and Kyagua, with his bullet, sliced off the loop fastened to the handle of the whip. 'Even now, you will not give me back my wife?'

'No!'

'Why don't you have a look at your navel?!' Mazlou inclined his head, and Kyagua's bullet felled him, hitting him directly on his navel.

Napkha Kyagua and the herdsmen slew the bandits, leaving only one of them alive. Kyagua shouted to him, 'I will give you your life! Be off to your own people, and tell them how ingloriously Khaamit died.'

'All right,' he answered. 'But first, allow me to collect a gun from one of those who have fallen here. The road home is long, and the journey is dangerous.' Kyagua permitted him to do so. Then he, with a flattering voice, turned to Kyagua: 'I have no way of thanking you for the kindness you have shown. But to make up for it, I will tell you a surprising dream which I had yesterday.' But when Kyagua, lowering his gun, leaned on it and began to listen, the villain quickly aimed, fired and mortally wounded him. While his comrades bustled about Kyagua, the murderer escaped.

Feeling the approach of death, Kyagua turned to those around him: 'That worthless fellow is not worth vengeance. I have succeeded in punishing the main culprit. That will break villains like him of the habit of robbing and humiliating the people. What was in my power, I did. I die with a clear conscience. It is your duty to lighten my wife's grief, as a widow.'

ə♦

No details of the narration are available for this Abkhaz legend, which was published in Kh. S. Bgazhba, *Abkhazskie skazki*, Alashara, Sukhumi, 1985, 299–301.

16. Kapsog Goshteliani *(Georgian)*

The Dadeshkeliani[1] were powerful princes, and the Goshteliani[2] were *vargi*.[3] There was enmity between them. Otar Dadeshkeliani had the idea of taking Kapsog Goshteliani prisoner.

One day Fust Otar's people fell on Kapsog when he was on the road. They tied him up and delivered him to Dadeshkeliani's court.

Fust Otar asked his followers, 'Who will undertake to take Kapsog to Turkey and sell him into slavery there?'

Murza Kalabetshi came forward: 'Fust Otar, trust me to do it. Just provide a detachment of forty men.'

Then Kapsog said to the *fust*, 'If Murza can sell me, let my house and farmstead remain with him, for his good fortune. But if not, let his house and farmstead stay with my people.'

Kapsog was carried to Turkey in chains. They reached the ridge of Tsitskhvari.[4] It was dark. Now they settled themselves in a camp for the night. They lit a fire. The men had grown tired on the journey. Murza said to his detachment, 'You can all sleep peacefully. I will guard Kapsog myself.'

---

1 The family of the ruling princes of Svaneti.
2 The Goshteliani and Kalabetshi were noble families in Svaneti.
3 Minor nobility in Svaneti.
4 A mountain range in Svaneti.

It was way beyond midnight. Murza Kalabetshi was sitting at the fire, leaning on his Lezg sword, thrust into the ground in front of him. At last even he was overcome with drowsiness. Kapsog took advantage of the moment. He somehow contrived to grasp with his teeth a hot charred log, threw it over behind his back and burned the ropes with which his hands were tied. After that he broke the iron chains on his legs. But he did not get up, he held his breath. After resting, Kapsog all of a sudden jumped to his feet, seized the sword of the dozing Murza and chopped off his head. Jumping off to one side, Kapsog began shouting in a loud voice: 'It is time to get yourself up, Murza! Kapsog has run away.'

The members of the detachment took alarm, they looked at Murza, and his head was lying by the fire. They all panicked, not knowing where to go. They simply could not make up their minds to pursue Kapsog.

But meanwhile Kapsog made for the palace of the ruling prince. He burst into the yard of Fust Otar, selected the best steed in the stable, jumped on it and began shouting in a loud voice: 'Fust Otar, come into the yard! Murza Kalabetshi has come riding, and he has brought you the profit money for Goshteliani.'

When he heard this, the *fust* shouted to him from the house, 'I know, you are Kapsog Goshteliani, I recognise your voice! Wait, I will reward you generously.'

'I do not need your gift. I have already picked out your best steed for myself. Later I will settle accounts with you for it.'

Kapsog galloped to his own place, rode up to his tower and shouted, 'My mother, open the door to me!'

His mother woke up and began lamenting and weeping. 'Alas, may God serve you the same way as he did the one who is not with me, and who used to call me "Mother"!'

'My mother! It is I, your son, open the door to me!'

'I don't believe it, the one who called me "Mother" has been taken far away.'

'Believe me, my mother, I am your son.'

'If you are my son then, all right, thrust your hand in the door.'

Kapsog tried, but his powerful hands would not pass through the narrow crack. 'My mother, you ought to know the thickness of my hands!'

Then his mother believed him and she opened the door. Kapsog rushed towards her. His mother recognised him, cried out, and fell on her knees before him. Her son embraced her, covered her forehead with kisses and told her of everything.

ॐ

This Georgian legend was recorded by E. B. Virsaladze in 1951 from the words of A. S. Goshteliani in the village of Mestia, Svaneti. It was published in E. B. Virsaladze, *Gruzinskie narodnye predaniya i legendy*, Nauka, Moscow, 1973, 204–206.

IV

Rustling, Stealing of Animals

The rustling or stealing of other people's animals has long been a traditional pastime of the young men in the Caucasus, as it is among other horse-riding populations, such as the North-American Indians (for example, Neihardt 1961, 75). Byhan says that the Cherkess (Adyges) had 'a solid reputation as thieves', 'like the Mingrelians' (Megrelis) (Byhan 1936, 138). He also stated that the (Cherkess) 'men, when not at war, preferred to spend their time in hunting or pillage' (ibid, 148). However, it is clear from the Balkar, Ingush and Lak examples below that the stealing of animals, especially of horses, was prevalent throughout the Caucasus. For instance, Klaproth states that 'hunting, war and marauding are deemed by the Ingush the most reputable employments of youth; and they rob as much for the sake of honour as from necessity' (Klaproth 1814, 344).

The first legend, 'Sosuruk and Akbilek', is one of the Balkar Nart sagas,[1] and its hero, Sosuruk, is one of the most prominent heroes of this group. It is clear from the legend that his main occupation is the rustling of horses from their traditional enemies, the *emegens*. As is stated in the legend and in its introduction, the hero was born from a stone, and so could not perform the sexual requirements of marriage. In the legends about Sosuruk his stony origin gives him great strength, though he is not completely invincible. In some variants the stone is evidently iron ore, so that his birth from the ore is likened to the production of iron and steel; in this case one small part of his leg remains unhardened, and so provides a point of weakness, like the heel of Achilles. This legend offers one of the many explanations for the twin peaks of Mount Elbrus, which is not only the highest mountain in the Caucasus (and Europe), but also a very prominent landmark and the subject of many legends. On seeing the twin peaks of Elbrus for the first time one is supposed to make a wish.

---

[1]   The Nart sagas describe the legendary exploits of heroes of an idealised past era, similar to the Western European Arthurian romances. Each ethnic group of the Caucasus, including the Balkars, have their own distinctive versions of these.

The second legend, 'Soska Solsa and Gorzhay', also has a hero whose life is evidently dedicated to stealing, including the rustling of animals. Soska Solsa is the Chechen-Ingush name of the same Nart hero as Sosuruk of the previous legend. In this case, instead of stealing livestock from enemies, he and his band steal from neighbours. A special interest in this legend is that the owner of the flocks is completely confident in the efficacy of his sacrifices to the saint, in this case the thunder god Seli. This legend contains a common Caucasus theme of theomachy, the disrespect and conflict with a god, gods or God. This legend contains themes of religion and also of family honour.

The third legend, 'Ashtotur and Prince Batok', also deals with an animal rustler's disrespect for a god. The owner of these animals has also asked for protection from a god, but unlike in the previous legend, in this case the god is strong enough to take effective revenge, and makes the rebel first repent and then die.

'The Farmstead of Ssurdu' is an example of how the feudal authorities not only undertook rustling raids against neighbours, in this case into Georgia, but also conscripted their feudal dependents to take part in the raids. If these men returned alive from the raid they might reap some material reward for their service, but in many cases, as in this legend, the only reward was death in a foreign land.

'The Song of Shagumilav Ilyas' is evidently based on a relatively recent horse-rustler, since he acquired local approval by stealing them from the Russian military, evidently during the nineteenth century, and probably during or soon after the Murid Wars. Clearly the clergy approved, or at least expected to receive a share of the loot.

'The Tomb of Beksultan Borogan' describes a fight with cattle-rustlers that resulted in the deaths of most of the participants, including finally the owner of the animals. It is an indication of the desperation, both of the thieves and of the owners of the flocks.

17. Sosuruk and Akbilek *(Balkar)*

Introduction
According to legend, Sosuruk's 'mother' Satanay (or in this legend Kyrs-Biyche) was standing on one side of the river in front of (or behind) a large

stone, while the shepherd Sozuk lusted after her from the other side of the river. Sozuk's seed (sometimes in the form of an arrow) flew across the river and landed in the stone, which consequently became pregnant. After nine months the stone split open and Sosuruk was born. Because Sosuruk was born from a stone, and despite being very strong and brave, he was unable to perform the functions of a married man, as is stated in this legend.

Kyrs-Biyche, having become the foster mother of Sosuruk, brought him up to be brave, upright and patient; and she taught him to run, to shoot and to fight.

In her *aul* there lived a beautiful girl, Akbilek.
The whole land of the Narts used to speak of her beauty.
She was not only beautiful, but also powerful.
She could even wrestle with a bullock, grasping him by the horns.
Akbilek was the daughter of a Nart *peliuan* by the name of Ekizhurek,
Who set out alone for battle with his enemies
And perished in an unequal battle, after killing a hundred men.
Kyrs-Biyche married Sosuruk to Akbilek and made Akbilek her daughter-in-law. But they say that Sosuruk was not able to live with her, because he was the son of a stone, while she was the daughter of a human.

One day Sosuruk was riding for a long time.
After swimming across the River Kyrk-Suu,[1] which nobody could overcome,

He found himself among the *emegens*,[2]
And saw a huge herd of *emegen* horses.

Outwitting them, he gave the *emegens* drink,
Feeding them with henbane, he deprived them of reason.

After beheading seventy *emegens*,
He drove away their herd. When he drew near his fortress,

---

1   The River Kyrk-Suu is an epic toponym.
2   An *emegen* is a member of a race of multi-headed monsters, a traditional enemy of the Balkar and Karachay Narts.

Night had set in, and the river was raging.
Sosuruk kept on walking a long time in the dark, not finding a ford.
When she heard the neighing of the horses,
Akbilek climbed onto the roof of the fortress.
Baring her hand, she stretched it out towards the river.

The light radiating from her hand lit up the river,
Enabling Sosuruk to find the ford.

Taking the herd across, he drove it into the fortress.
That is how they lived for several years.

But one day Sosuruk, in front of his wife
Boasted about what a *jigit* he was.

His wife Akbilek decided to teach him a lesson.
'Never mind, I will show you who you really are,
Then you will realise that all you do you owe to me,' she thought.

The next day Sosuruk, as always, set off on a *zhortuuul*.
When he brought in the livestock
And the herd of horses to the bank of the river,

Akbilek, climbing onto the roof of the fortress,
Uncovered her hand and lit up the nocturnal river.

When Sosuruk, after driving the herd into the river,
Had swum to its middle,
Akbilek withdrew her hand.

Pitch darkness set in at once,
The livestock and the horses strayed from the ford and drowned.

Sosuruk, too, drowned with the animals,
And his corpse they only found later on.

After Sosuruk's death, Akbilek lived alone.
One day Akbilek met the Nart Yoryuzmek.

And Yoryuzmek was a ladies' man,
He was a fearless and manly Nart.

In the month of Khychauman[1] he always rode out of his home,
In this month he would set off on a *zhortuuul*.

Once, when he was riding in the month of Khychauman,
He met with a group of people.

There the rain overtook him,
Yoryuzmek dismounted from his horse.

When the rain started, Akbilek approached that place,
Because of the rain she hid under Yoryuzmek's *burka*.

They say that then Yoryuzmek seduced Akbilek. After that Akbilek herself
   became angry at Sosuruk, because he had not lived with her like a husband
   does with a wife,

She took a shovel and went straight
From there to the grave of Sosuruk.
In her anger she began scattering his grave.

But Yoryuzmek came after her and stopped her.
That is why Sosuruk's grave became twin-headed.[2]

This Balkar legend was recorded by S. O. Shakhmurzayev from the words
of Amiy Bashiev, born 1873, of the village of Kichmalka in 1965. It was pub-
lished in T. M. Khajieva & R. A-K. Ortabayeva, *Narty*, Nauka, Moscow,
1994, 388–390.

---

1   Khychauman is the month of May in the folk calendar of the Balkars and Karachays.
2   According to the testimony of S. O. Shakhmurzayev, who recorded this legend, the narrator
     told him that Sosuruk was buried at the summit of Elbrus and that it became twin-peaked
     after this act of Akbilek.

18. Soska Solsa and Gorzhay *(Chechen-Ingush)*

This happened a long time ago. The Orkhustoys[1] were sitting; and among them was Soska Solsa. They were debating: was there a region where they had not been and had not plundered? While they were having this conversation, a certain widow[2] was coming back from the river with water. She unintentionally overheard the conversation of the Orkhustoys. The Orkhustoys also spotted her. 'She is probably laughing at our self-confidence! Go and find out, Batoko Shertuko: perhaps she knows a land where we have not been and have not plundered?'

Batoko Shertuko went to the widow to ask her. 'I am a widow and an orphan. If my answer is not pleasing, the Orkhustoys could insult me. Who will stand up for me?'

'Do not be afraid, speak!' said the Orkhustoys.

'Beyond seven mountains, Gorzhay's flock is grazing, and the Orkhustoys have not attacked that flock!'

'We must set out!' they all said together.

The Orkhustoys set off on their way. Now they crossed the seventh mountain and saw Gorzhay's enormous flock. 'It is shameful and unworthy to behave so secretively!' said Soska Solsa. 'We must let Gorzhay know that the Orkhustoys are getting ready to fall on his flock.[3] Let him prepare himself!' They sent the message to Gorzhay.

'How can they attack a flock from which sacrifices are dedicated to God? It would be sacrilege! I don't believe you. Something must have happened among them,' said Gorzhay to the messenger, and he sent him back.

'How on earth can we make him believe that we want to make an attack, in order that he should raise the alarm?' said Soska Solsa. 'Only his daughter-in-law, the wife of his youngest son, can convince him. She goes for the water of the spring from which Gorzhay himself drinks water. If she tells

---

1   Strictly speaking, one ought to write 'Orkhustkhoy', since in Ingush if one is speaking about a member of some community, the ending is usually added: in the singular 'kho', but in the plural 'khoy'. Thus, in the singular they say 'Orkhustkho' and in the plural 'Orkhustkhoy'; Orshtokho (Karabulak), Orshtokhoy; Jerakho, Jerakhoy; Nasyrkho, Nasyrkhoy and so on (Note of Ch. Akhriev). The Orkhustoys also feature in the legends 'How the Orstkhoys Won Back the Land', 'How the Nart-Orstkhoys Vanished from the Earth' and 'Batoko Shertuko' in this book.

2   The widow plays the role of the wise woman (like Zherbaba, the old wise woman of the Ingush legends and tales).

3   This is the ancient epic etiquette, by which an enemy is warned about an attack.

him, then he will surely believe her. Which of you is capable of enticing a woman?' asked Soska Solsa.

'I can!' said one of the Orkhustoys by the name of Takhshako.[1]

Takhshako set out early in the morning, towards the time of *namaz*, to the spring from which Gorzhay took his water. When he arrived, Gorzhay's favourite daughter-in-law was already there. He dragged her off and tore her dress a little. Returning, Takhshako said to her, 'Tell your father-in-law that the Orkhustoys have come, including Soska Solsa, to drive away his white flock,' and he threatened that if she said nothing, then he would spread the word that he had had intimate relations with her. He said that he would wait for an answer from her.

'Today one of the Orkhustoys disgraced me. Here is the proof, my torn dress. He asked that you prepare for an attack on your white flock,' she told Gorzhay.

'A woman always remains shameless! I look at you as at a woman who has lost her shame. How can they attack my flock, which I have dedicated with gratitude to my creator, to God and the high saints? When I bring a sacrifice, I do not begrudge my best ram. Surely somebody's greedy self-interest is at the heart of this?' Gorzhay did not believe his daughter-in-law.

The daughter-in-law went back to the spring where Takhshako was waiting for her, and told him, 'I told my father-in-law about the Orkhustoys' intention to attack his flock, but he did not believe me.'

Takhshako went back to his people. 'Well, what have you managed to do?' the Orkhustoys asked.

'I waited for Gorzhay's favourite daughter at the spring, and when she appeared, I seized her, tore her dress a little and ordered her to tell her father-in-law about our intentions. She came back and said that Gorzhay did not believe her.'

'How can we call Gorzhay out to answer an emergency?' said the Orkhustoys. They set off to the shepherds for advice.

'The only way is to kill Gorzhay's favourite bird,[2] which sits on his tower,' said the shepherds.

Then Soska Solsa addressed the Orkhustoys with the following question: 'Which of you knows how to shoot best of all?'

---

1   Takhshako is not mentioned in other legends. Takhshako as a name is met very rarely among the Ingush.

2   It is possible that the bird is an attribute of some pagan god, as for example the hoopoe of the goddess Tusholi.

'I can!' said one of the Orkhustoys by the name of Oruzbi. When it was barely light, Oruzbi set out to Gorzhay's house and killed his favourite bird. Gorzhay got up early and saw his favourite bird in the yard. 'Evidently, they don't want to leave me in peace!'

After saddling his horse and mounting it, he raised the alarm. He appealed to the sky with the following words: 'The Orkhustoys have come to drive away my white flock, from which I always brought the best ram to God and the great saints. You saints stand up for me!'

His entreaty was heard by Seli (the thunder god). After that a storm arose, a thunderstorm, and all of the inhabitants gave chase to the Orkhustoys. Those of the Orkhustoys who were best at shooting went last.

'We must go a little more slowly, let Seli catch up, and I will squeeze the side of that saint!' said Soska Solsa. And truly, Seli caught up with them, and Soska Solsa seized the saint and broke one of his ribs.[1] The storm subsided. The saint stopped pursuing the Orkhustoys, and the sky cleared. As it became clear, the Orkhustoys let Gorzhay catch them up. Soska Solsa seized Gorzhay, tied him up and sat him on his horse back to front, and then sent him into the field for the fun of the people.[2]

The Orkhustoys returned home with Gorzhay's flock.

This Chechen-Ingush legend was recorded by Ch. Akhriev in 1875. It was published in U. B. Dalgat, *Geroichesky epos chechentsev i ingushey*, Nauka, Moscow, 1972, 310–311.

---

1   This is the second case (after the ancient myth 'The Birth of Sela Sata') of Soska Solsa overcoming the supreme pagan god Sela.

2   Such a way of riding (face to tail) is a symbol of his shame and humiliation. According to an ancient custom of the mountain people of the Caucasus and Daghestan, after committing adultery a woman would be sat on a black donkey, back to front, and showered with stones (see SSKG, 1874, Issue VII, 35). It is quite possible that connected with this custom is the conduct of the well-known Ossetian Nart Uryzmag, after he had admitted an incestuous marriage to his own sister. In the legend 'How Uryzmag Married his Sister' (SSKG, Issue V, 1871, 15) the hero voluntarily sits on a donkey facing the tail and rides past the Narts three times, evidently as a mark of self-abasement for the act committed.

19. Ashtotur and Prince Batok *(Balkar)*

Alchagir of the Gazayev clan
Had an uncle through his mother – Akhmat.
He used to drive livestock away from people and sell them in distant regions.
One day Akhmat came to Alchagir and asked him for animals.

But Alchagir did not give him anything.
Then Akhmat, growing angry, set off to Prince Batok:
'Alchagir gives me nothing from his livestock,' he said,
'He does not recognise me as his relative,' he said.

'And just how can I help you?' Batok asked him.
'This is what you can do, Batok:
The Gazayevs have a big herd of horses,
Let us ride and drive away that herd.'

Prince Batok and Akhmat began driving away the Gazayev herd.
While driving the herd, Prince Batok and Akhmat
Had ridden as far as the saddle of Mystyl
When Alchagir, looking out of his shed, saw them.

'One of them is our Akhmat *altynly*,[1] oy, oy ...
And the leader is Prince Batok, may his blood be spilled!
Ashtotur, I ask you to protect my herd, oy, oy ...
By the name of Teyri, I beg for your help!'

While driving the herd, they had ridden as far as the Atdan Tyushyuuchyu.[2]
Akhmat said, 'Batok, we have ridden to the Atdan Tyushyuuchyu,
If we do not dismount from our horses here, we will not pass this place
    alive,
We must dismount and pay respect to Ashtotur.'

'Oy, Akhmat, may you give up your soul!
You will not make me get off my horse for Ashtotur!'

---

1   'Altynly' is a gun. 'Akhmat *altynly*' means 'Akhmat with a gun'.
2   A place where they dismount from a horse.

Lashing his horse, he rode up to Ashtotur's stone,
And thus he addressed him: 'Ashtotur, if you are a real man, come out here!'

'I do not think your sword chops better than my *kinzhal*,
That your arrows pierce deeper than my arrows!
If you are a real man, why don't you come out here!'
After saying this, he began driving the herd from there.

Batok drove the herd across the stone of Ashtotur,
After lashing the stone with his whip, he jeered at the stone:
'I am driving away your herd,
If you are a real man, come out here!' he said.

And then from under the stone a wasp flew out,
He began circling above Prince Batok.
The wasp, flying up, stung Prince Batok on the tip of his nose,
The nose of Batok was covered with a deep wound.

From Batok's nose black worms began tumbling.
'Akhmat, why has this happened to me?' asked Batok, oy, oy ...
'Batok, it is Ashtotur who has punished you,
Turn back and pay your respects to him,' replied Akhmat.

Batok, deserting the herd, prostrated himself before Ashtotur:
'Forgive me, I was wrong!' he was entreating the stone for a long time:
'I will bring you as a sacrifice black-eared white oxen,
And their calves I will present to you.'

The prince left the herd there, riding past Kapchagay,
He reached his home and at once gave up his soul to God.

ﻊﺩ

This Balkar legendary song was communicated privately by Tanzilya
Khajieva in 2003.

20. The Farmstead of Ssurdu *(Lak)*

Introduction

There was a time when the feudal authorities of Daghestan undertook raids against the neighbouring peoples. They used to perform raids on neighbouring Georgia particularly often. This was reflected in distinctive epic works, in the so-called 'songs about raids'. It was not only their own armed men who took part in the raids organised by the feudal authorities, but also levies collected for this purpose, and even representatives of other nationalities. In the organisation of raids on the Christian folk of the Caucasus a special role was played by the local Muslim priesthood, who were doggedly sowing enmity towards the infidels among the mountain folk. By including the masses in the campaigns, often by force, the feudal powers saw a means of distracting them from an anti-feudal struggle. The raids brought easy loot and cheap slaves. As for the ordinary people who were duped into becoming involved, they gained nothing but sacrificed themselves.

When we were baking
    Bread for the wedding,
The envoy of the khan told us,
'Get ready for a campaign!'
'If we put on the harness
And we give him a horse,
Can the khan's envoy
Leave us the bridegroom?
If with our kerchiefs in our hands
We go on our knees,
Won't our Magomed-Khan
Agree to our request?'[1]
After putting the harness on the horse,
We gave him the fine horse.
By God, the khan's envoy
Did not leave us our bridegroom!
With our kerchiefs in our hands

---

1   In the mountains, a woman's request after she has removed her headscarf is considered to be sacred and must be fulfilled.

We went on our knees,
But our Magomed-Khan
Did not heed our request ...

*

When I was weeding in the green field,
My old mother, weeping
Started calling me.
I thought, what could have happened,
At the call I glanced around.
And I saw, walking,
A group of armed men.
My falcon's horse
Was in the middle of them,
His silver-white weapons
Were fastened to his saddle.
'I ask you, tell me,
Soldiers in the detachment,
Where have they left
My red-flag bearer?'[1]
'Your red-flag bearer was left there.
He was caught by
A nasty Aznaur bullet.
He has sent you
A big greeting
So that you will not forget him
While you are alive.'
'Did you hear, my mother,
The news from Georgia:
My young falcon
Was left there, so they say.
He was caught by
A nasty Aznaur bullet.
I ask you, my mother,
Don't tell me, "Get married,"

---

1   The red flag was inserted by the singer during Soviet times.

Otherwise I will run away
With the crazy people into the mountains.
I ask you, my mother,
Don't tell me that once more
I shall find a lover.
Or I will throw myself over a cliff,
And find death for myself.
My mother, spread out
A silken bed,
I will throw on to the bed
All the hundred parts of my body.
Lay down, my mother,
A downy pillow,
I will lay my black plaits on it.
In the morning I will go
To the Ssurdu farmstead,
I will look in the direction of Georgia
And weep bitter tears.
In the evening I will come
Into our hateful *aul*,
I will squat in the corner of the house
And sigh bitterly.
All those who have gone on an expedition
Have acquired great loot,
But for my beloved fiancé,
There is only a bed under the snow.
All those who have gone to Georgia
Have brought back prisoners,
But my beloved acquired
A bullet of blue lead in his head.
My falcon had
Long legs,
Let them, there in Georgia,
Use them instead of a bridge.
The shoulders he had were broad,
May my mother die,
Let them there, in Georgia
Use them as buttresses of the bridge.

My falcon had
Long hair,
Let the women of Georgia
Cut them off for plaits.
His fingers were long,
May your sisters die,[1]
Let those priests
Cut them off for pencils.
The sweet body
Of my beloved fiancé,
To which tree
Have the wolves dragged it?
The hawk's eyes
Of my young falcon,
Have the ravens started pecking them,
After sitting on his head?'

ॐ

This Lak legendary song was recorded by Ali Kayayevy in 1930 in the settlement of Tturchi of the Lak region of Daghestan from the words of Magomedova Udrida. This song was published in Kh. Khalilov, *Lakskie epicheskie pesni*, Dagestan Filial AN SSSR, Makhachkala, 1983, 160–163.

21. The Song of Shagumilav Ilyas *(Lak)*

Introduction

Emphasised here is the self-interest of the representatives of Islam. They demand half of the loot for themselves. In the folklore of the Laks it is a rare phenomenon when in a single song the khan and the tsarist autocracy are placed on the same level. In this respect 'The Song of Shagumilav Ilyas' is important.

---

1   Meaning it would be better for your sisters to die than for you to die – i.e., they are offering to sacrifice themselves for him.

'Give me mother, my arms,
I am going to the *kadi*.
Is there any sin, I will ask,
In my stealing the khan's wealth?
Give me, father, the young horse.
I am going to the mullah.
I will ask what the *chiri* will be,
For one who inflicted harm on the Russian soldiers.'
His mother gave him his arms,
His father brought the horse,
And through the extensive Vitskhi fields
He went to the *kadi*.
And to the *kadi* he related
What he had stolen from the khan:
'I sold the cauldron in Akusha,
And the black horses in Balkharakh.'
In the Koran the *kadi* found
An excuse for me:
'On the one who sold the khan's cauldron,
There is no sin,' said he.
'I will write in the book of *chiri*,
If you give half of what
You received for the cauldron
In which soup was cooked for the soldiers.'
The black-coloured horses of the khan
Who carried goods to the Russians –
He said, 'One could sell them
If the *zakat* goes with them.
Whoever caused harm to the Russian soldiers,
It will be a big *chiri* for him,' he said.
'All that was acquired as loot
Needs to be shared between us.'
They called the mullah,
They gathered the *muduns*,
And all they needed they took from me,
And they began to pray.
I left them praying.
May they share what they took from me!

While I headed for Kumukh
To drive away the khan's black horse.

ನ♥

This Lak legendary song was recorded in 1936 in the settlement of Kurkli of
the Lak region of Daghestan by the teacher Abdulmejid Magomedov from
the words of Omakay Abdurahman. It was published in Kh. Khalilov, *Lakskie
epicheskie pesni*, Dagestan Filial AN SSSR, Makhachkala, 1983, 189–190.

22. The Tomb of Beksultan Borogan *(Chechen-Ingush)*

Not so long ago, when the Kabardans were occupying the neighbour-
hood of Nasran, there lived a maiden descended from the family of
the Akhlov princes.[1] Her ancestors lived on the right bank of the River
Sunzha. That locality was called Gazyey Kauv (which means 'country estate
of Kaziy'). Not far from the named country estate there is a large *kurgan*
(Iy-Iiy Boarz),[2] raised, according to tradition, by that same Prince Akhlov.
A little farther away, to the north of that *kurgan*, there is a spring named
Suv-Khast in a dried-up riverbed.[3] Above that spring there is a stone, and on
the stone a bowl-shaped depression in which, so they say, the prince's wife
used to put the soap when she was washing linen.

Beksultan Borogan lived in the place where the village of Yandyr is now.[4]
He was in love with Prince Akhlov's daughter, and moreover the princess
was not indifferent to him. Beksultan usually went to sleep after hobbling his
horse and laying the saddle beneath his head and spreading his *burka* under-
neath him, in that same place where now there is the mausoleum of Boroga-
Kash (Boroga's grave).[5] In that place he used to pasture his cattle and watch

1 This family is encountered quite often in the epos of the Ingush.
2 This name means 'maiden's *kurgan*'; this *kurgan* really exists.
3 Suv-Khast, in Ingush, means 'the princess's spring' (in this case the wife of a prince); this
   spring is still well known today.
4 This village is at the confluence of the Small and Great Yandyrka Rivers, tributaries of the
   Sunzha, to the northeast of Nazran (note of B. Dalgat).
5 This is near Nazran. The Ingush consider this place sacred. On the mausoleum are the
   following three inscriptions (in Arabic): 'Imazis Sultaniya', 'Bek-Sultan Khuddadov', 'Here
   lies the dust of the deceased people, and between them there is neither light nor moisture'.

them, so that a gang of *abreks* would not fall on them at any time and drive them away. The princess often would go out to the Iy-Iiy Boarz Kurgan and look at Beksultan, and Beksultan at her, and thus they would feast their eyes on one another. Not far from the *stanitsa* of Karabulak there was the *kurgan* of Iaysni-Iuna-Boarz,[1] where Beksultan's brother used to graze his calves.[2]

One day, from the direction where the *uzdens* of the Zhogishevs lived, a gang of Chechen horsemen came out and headed towards Beksultan, with the aim of driving off his cattle and horses. But Beksultan did not lose his presence of mind, and he began shooting his gun at his enemies. His brother, the herdsman of the calves, also began shooting. Both of them and their people were fighting, they conquered and chased their enemies with their drawn swords in their hands. When they had killed them all except one man, Beksultan chased that man. This last one said to him, 'Don't chase me! If you receive a wound from a bullet from my gun, you will certainly die, because my gun is one of the Pyasi-Lach guns.'

But Beksultan said, 'Until I kill you all, I will not return home,' and he continued pursuing him. Then the Chechen fired his gun and killed Beksultan. In that same place (near the village of Yandyr) where Beksultan used to sleep, the princess built the mausoleum of Boroga-Kash, which exists even now. For this she conveyed the stones on mules from Tbilisi. When the chapel was ready, and Beksultan's body had been transferred to it, the princess placed the handle of a *kinzhal* on Beksultan's chest, and she herself leaned on the sharp end and thus ended her life. Her body was laid alongside the body of Beksultan.

Such is the old men's tradition about Boroga-Kash.

This Chechen-Ingush tradition was recorded by B. Dalgat in 1892 from the words of Isup Nauruzov-Azhigov in the village of Plievskoy. It was published in U. B. Dalgat, *Geroichesky epos chechentsev i ingushey*, Nauka, Moscow, 1972, 373–374.

For a description of Boroga-Kash see, for example, P. I. Golvinsky, SSTO, Issue I, 1878, 248; L. Semyonov, 'Mavzoley Boroga-Kash', IINIIK, Issue I, Vladikavkaz, 1928, 1–18.

1   Iaysni-Iuna-Boarz (in Ingush Insin Iuna-Boarz) means 'the kurgan of the herder of calves'. The name of Beksultan's namesake was 'herder of calves' (note of B. Dalgat).

2   Karabulak is not far from Nazran, to the northeast, on the left bank of the River Sunzha; it stands at approximately three kilometres from the village of Yandyr. Karabulak, in the Ingush language is Ildarkha-Gala. A *stanitsa* is a large Cossack village.

V

Warriors, Including Blood Revenge

This chapter contains a small sample of seven warrior legends. Three of them include blood revenge, which is an aspect of family honour. In a community where there is no supreme authority to maintain law and order, the chief sanction against serious crimes, including murder, was the fear of revenge – in particular blood revenge – by the victim's family. Family honour required the shedding of 'blood for blood', even if the man whose life repaid the blood debt was personally innocent. If the actual murderer could not be punished, then it was sufficient to punish another member of his family, since the family was considered to be an integral unit, with collective responsibility. Clearly, an orphan who had no family, such as Aydemir-Khan in the first legend, remained totally unprotected by such a sanction, and so could be ill-treated or killed without risk of retribution.

An example of internal compared with external family relations can be seen from an incident related by Baddeley.[1] 'A son shot his old father in my presence for having verbally insulted him. He stood calmly by to reload his weapon while the death rattle sounded ... All others present passed by the dying man indifferently, uttering no regrets, making no attempt even to move him out of the way. I called upon the chief elder, to whom I had boasted the superiority of our laws, to punish the murderer. He laughed at my fervency and said, "Why, what would you do?" To which I replied, "Put him to a still worse death." "So that is your vaunted justice!" cried he. "Yet he is not your father or mine, but that man's! There stand his brothers; pray, what business is it of ours?" It was purely a family affair.'

One aspect of the personal honour of a warrior was of course not to show any fear, and that applied even when the warrior knew or suspected he was going to his death, such as Aydemir suspected at the end of the legend 'Aydemir-Khan', when he was being lured into a trap without his trusted horse or his weapons.

---

1   J. F. Baddeley, 'The Rugged Flanks of Caucasus', Vol. 1, 173–174; quoting from Steder, 'Tagebuch einer Reise die im Jahr 1781 von der Gränzfestung Mosdok nach dem inner Caucasus unternommen worde', St Petersburg & Leipzig, 1797.

The more epic type of warrior legend, such as the first two examples about Andemyrkan, was generally composed for presentation to an audience. It must be remembered that the narrator was probably paid for his presentation. He might have been commissioned by the relatives or descendants of the hero of the epic, or perhaps by wealthier people, who often had a personal interest in the material. Inevitably this interest and the fact that they were paying the narrator influenced the material that he presented. Historical accuracy was therefore rarely the first priority. The same legend may well have been presented differently by the same narrator on different occasions, depending on the audience. The functions of the narrator in presenting a description of a warrior's exploits in a recent battle are described in the appendix to this book.

THE KABARDAN HERO, ANDEMYRKAN

Aydemir-Khan, who was more usually called Andemyrkan, was the hero of a cycle of heroic tales among the people of Kabarda, and also an Ubykh variant, given below. Two of the tales are included here. It is not known whether Andemyrkan was a historical figure, although the legends are probably based on a real person. Andemyrkan was basically a type of Robin Hood figure, a friend of the weak who made enemies among the proud princes (*pshis*). In the example here he had been stolen by a giant bird while still a baby, and brought up as an orphan by the prince who had found him. In other versions he was the illegitimate son of a prince and a slave woman, and the story of a hero being found as a baby in a bird's nest sounds like a typical way of explaining the existence of an illegitimate baby – an alternative to 'finding it under a gooseberry bush'. As explained in Chapter 10 on family relations, an orphan was in a dangerous position unless adopted into a family, but it helped if the orphan was a strong hero, a *bogatyr*, as Andemyrkan was, so that he could fend for himself. Inevitably such a hero, especially if somewhat arrogant as Andemyrkan was, attracted the envy or hatred of powerful rivals, and eventually Andemyrkan was murdered. Because he was so strong, the murderers only succeeded in killing him by treachery, by inviting him to go on an outing without his trusted horse or his sword.

As described above, and in the introduction to this book, the narrators of these epic sagas were often paid or rewarded for their oral performance by rich nobles. In legends where the hero was actually in conflict with some of the princes and nobles, the narrator often needed to be diplomatic in his portrayal of a hero such as Andemyrkan, especially since he was stronger and bolder than the princes of his own era and was then killed by their dishonourable treachery.

23. Aydemir-Khan *(Ubykh)*

Introduction

There are several versions of his name: Aydemirkan, Ademirkan, Andemyrkan, Antemyrkan, Aydemarkan. The 'khan' ending of the hero's name, which means a chief, instead of 'kan', which means a foster son, also suggests a separation of the tale from its roots. The identity of the Kazaks is not certain, but there is a strong possibility that it refers to the Cossacks, who were basically roving bands, many of whom led a martial existence.

Once the wife of a certain *bey* gave birth to a baby boy. A month later she set off to the sea to wash linen. When the mother, together with other young women, was washing her linen and her baby was sleeping not far away, a large bird, a black eagle, came down from the sky all of a sudden, snatched up the sleeping baby and carried him away in the direction of the sea. The parents realised that there was nothing they could do, and they declined to search for the baby.

As for the bird, it set off with its burden for a land that lay on the other side of the sea, landed there and wanted to eat up his prey. Exactly at this time a certain *bey* with his armed followers was returning from an expedition. He saw the eagle landing with his prey in his claws and he ordered, 'Have a look and see what that bird has brought!'

There and then ten horsemen set off at a gallop to the place where the bird had landed with the baby. On approaching, the people scared it off and it flew away. The baby himself was left lying on the ground. When they saw that he was alive, the horsemen carried him to the *bey*. The *bey* said, 'We will take the baby and bring him up.' And so they went back home with the baby.

The bird had seriously wounded the baby in the belly. The wound was treated, and it closed over. They named the baby Aydemir. The *bey* brought up the boy, and while the boy was growing up he accompanied the *bey* everywhere. Gradually the youth turned into a man. When the *bey* went away on an expedition, Aydemir fought the enemy better than anyone.

One day the *bey* decided to make war on the land of the Kazaks, and for that he collected all the men of his country. Before starting out, he summoned the three most intelligent people in his land and stationed them in various houses, so as to question each one individually.

The *bey* turned to the first one: 'We are setting out on an expedition. Pick out from my soldiers the one who could be placed in front of the armed force with our standard in his hands.'

The first wise man answered, 'There is only one who is suitable to be at the head of the armed force with the standard in his hands. That is Aydemir, the bravest one!'

The *bey* turned to the second one: 'When we get to the place where the *bey* of the Kazaks is, and we take his fortress, name the one who must be the first to penetrate into the fortress and hoist our standard there.'

That man answered, 'There is nobody braver than Aydemir! It is he who ought to hoist our standard on the fortress!'

The *bey* turned to the third wise man: 'When we have defeated the army that is in the fortress, we will kill the *bey* of the Kazaks, and we will carry all the property away from the fortress and then burn it down, not leaving anything of value in it. We will then start off on the return journey and, if they begin pursuing us, who do you think ought to cover our withdrawal and delay the pursuers?'[1]

The sage answered, 'Only Aydemir is capable of doing what you say.'

The *bey* said, 'If that is the case, then from today you shall begin calling him Aydemir-Khan.'

After this the army started on its way. Under the leadership of Aydemir the armed force penetrated into the land of the Kazaks. When they were preparing for the assault on the fortress where the *bey* of the Kazaks was, the soldiers said, 'Aydemir, take the standard, enter the fortress and hoist it up!'

---

1   An Adyge war party was composed of infantry and cavalry. The function of the horse-soldiers included forming patrols that roamed about the foot soldiers during their advance; to follow them into battles, protect their rear, defend it while retreating and carry the dead and wounded from the battlefields to their kinsmen (Mufti, 1972).

Aydemir took the standard, and the soldiers advanced on the fortress and took possession of it. Aydemir hoisted their standard over the subjugated fortress. After that they killed the Kazak *bey*. When, after taking everything that could be carried away, the troops got ready for the return journey, they told Aydemir, 'Aydemir, cover us and, if they begin pursuing us, do not let any of them through, kill them all!'

And Aydemir, covering their withdrawal, killed all the Kazaks pursuing the army, leaving none alive. Thus they left the land of the Kazaks and returned to their own.

After their return the *bey* began to feel envy towards Aydemir. One day, while coming back by the seashore, Aydemir saw a herd of horses entering the sea from the reeds and swimming away. Riding up to the place from where the herd had gone into the sea, he found there three newly-born foals. Aydemir-Khan led them away with him. When the foals had grown a little, the *bey* took the two most handsome ones, while Aydemir kept the weakest one for himself and reared it. When he rode out on it, all the dwellers in the land feasted their eyes on Aydemir-Khan, they all loved him so much, and this vexed the *bey* even more; it reinforced his envy, and he had the urge to kill the universal favourite.

The *bey* had a son-in-law. When Aydemir was a guest of this son-in-law, he often used to canter along the seashore. Every time he did so, the horse that he had reared, while walking along the seashore, would strive to enter the water. One day, while on the shore, Aydemir had the thought: we shall see where he makes for. And he went into the water. After swimming across the sea, they found themselves on the shore of some unknown country. Stepping on to land, Aydemir said to himself, 'We shall see where the horse makes for.' And he let go of the reins.

The horse set off directly to a village. A certain woman was washing her head, when her daughter, sitting next to her, saw a rider emerge from the sea. She said, 'Dear mother, a horseman has emerged from the sea and is heading for us.'

Her mother looked up and said, 'Ach, my daughter, the rider heading towards us resembles your brothers, and the horse under him is similar to one of your father's horses!'

While they were conversing, the rider rode into their yard. He declared himself as a guest. The horse was led away to the stable, and the horseman was invited into the guest chamber. After several days the hosts began saying, 'Is it possible that this is the one the bird carried off as a baby! He looks like our child ...'

In order to make sure, they brought clothes and linen, saying, 'Put this on ...'

Their guest began undressing, and while he was putting on the clothes, the hosts observed him through the keyhole. They saw the wound that the bird had left on his belly. Now it became clear to them that this really was their child.

The mother beckoned to their guest and asked, 'Where are you from? What family do you come from?'

The guest answered, 'They call me "the boy brought by the bird". I have been living in a certain country where I had no parents. I don't know myself where I was born.'

The elderly woman told him, 'When we were washing our linen on the seashore, a large bird carried you off. This is your native land. I am your mother, this girl is your sister, and your brothers themselves will soon come.'

The guest was overjoyed. In the evening the brothers returned, and they were also extremely glad.

Several days passed, and the guest wanted to go back again. He said, 'I have not been drinking the local water, I am going back to where I have been drinking it.'

They replied, 'Since you do not want to stay, what can we do?' And they gave him a horse, better than the one on which he had come; a horse capable of overcoming any obstacle in his path. 'If you are killed in the country that you are going back to, this horse will bring us your corpse,' thus they spoke when saying goodbye.

Aydemir sat in the saddle, plunged into the sea and swam his horse across it. He went back to live with the man where he was living before he had swum away.

But the *bey* kept on seeking an opportunity to kill Aydemir. Since he felt fear in his presence, the *bey* did not know what to do, and he fell to thinking. The man who was giving refuge to Aydemir was, after all, his son-in-law. One evening he summoned his son-in-law. When he was leaving, the *bey* said to him, 'Either you give me your eyes[1] or you give me your life!'

'My eyes I cannot give you,' answered his son-in-law, 'but if you want my life, take it.'

---

1   An enigmatic formula: 'your eyes' means 'your guest'.

'Your life I do not want,' retorted the *bey*, 'I need your eyes!'

'Since I cannot find a way to avoid it,' said the son-in-law, 'I will give you my eyes.'

'Tomorrow morning your guest should not sit on his horse, and let him not take his weapons with him,' said the *bey*. 'Set off together on the road, and I will be in an ambush.' With that they separated.

The next day the *bey*'s son-in-law said to his guest, 'So as to stretch our legs, you and I will go for a little walk!'

'All right,' answered his guest.

When they had just gone out the host said, 'Do not sit on your horse, let him have a rest. Leave your weapons too. We are not going to walk for long, we will soon return.'

Aydemir had some suspicions, but he gave no indication of them. However, he saddled his horse, secured the bit and shut him in the stable. They began walking. When they arrived at the ambush, the *bey*'s people seized and killed the hero. The horse, which he had shut in the stable, smashed the door, came running to the place of his master's death, carried away Aydemir-Khan's corpse and returned with him to his home country, where his parents committed him to the earth.

This is how Aydemir-Khan died, and it is the truth.

وف

There are no details available about the narration and recording of this Ubykh legend. It was published in N. Gelashvili, *Ubykh Folklore*, Kavkazsky Dom, Tbilisi, 1995, 65–69.

24. The Lament for Andemyrkan *(Kabardan)*

Introduction

The following lament *(gybza)* is a typical lament composed by a professional bard, a *geguako*, probably for a public performance, either at a funeral or on a festive occasion at table (Gutov, 2000).

I

When you have heard the voice of Andemyrkan, you have heard thunder.

The *pshis*[1] do not like his threatening speech.

Tlepsh held the handle of his sword,[2]

Aush-ger[3] touched the steel with his hand.

Andemyrkan does not know fear or terror.

His sword, so they say, is sharply ground.

He is like a bird when he is on his horse.

Like a thick fog when he is on the ground.

His strength is more than the strength of an ox.

He makes the *pshi* Aslanbek tremble.

He declares the Kan of Elmurza[4] to be an enemy.

He takes possession of riches without difficulty;

He bestows them, eclipsing the Narts with his generosity.

The arrows fly: the sleeve of his chain-mail shirt is his shield,

Their points spare his face.

Zheman-Sharyk's[5] flanks are often sweaty;

Albiche-Guasha[6] often weeps,

She grieves that Andemyrkan is often absent.

Like an eagle he looks into the distance of the steppe.

What has Andemyr's eye seen on the steppe?

It cannot hide from Zheman-Sharyk, it will not get away.

Enemies tremble at Andemyrkan's call,

They run apart, they rush about like sheep.

Your sword has reassured you, Andemyrkan!

---

1   The *pshis*, or feudal princes, relied on Amdemyrkan's help in battle, but were otherwise antagonistic towards him.

2   Tlepsh, who 'held the handle of his sword', was the legendary primordial blacksmith who taught the people the art of smelting and the forging of iron and steel.

3   Aush-ger is the local name of Saint George; the Kabardans were generally Christians until their forced conversion to Islam in the eighteenth to nineteenth centuries, but generally throughout the Caucasus the remnants of Christianity still live in their minds, and Saint George is the true patron of all Caucasians, his gallant aspect with his knightly ornament embodying all virtues of Caucasian chivalry.

4   The kan of Elmurza is not known. It is one of the obscure passages.

5   Zheman-Sharyk was the name of the hero's faithful legendary horse, which Andemyrkan had selected and reared in a remarkable way, as detailed in other legends of this cycle.

6   Albiche-Guasha was Andemyrkan's mistress, the suffix *guasha* meaning a lady of status.

II

The cushion of your saddle[1] was embroidered by the daughter of the
    Eristovy,[2]
His heart is bleeding: the horse without its rider!
Andemyrkan's spacious house is now in desolation,
It was able to contain an army, now it is going to ruin!
Because of you there are crosses on the graves of *giaours*.
From the mountains they brought deer for you as tribute.
From their gilded saddles you used to throw off brave men.
'It is not my habit,' you would say, 'to preserve arrows.'
The Braguny[3] in their covered carts would hide themselves from you.
The *karakhalks* would come to you to seek protection.
You would bestow saddles generously on youthful *uorks*,
When both Kabardas were galloping to Astrakhan.
At the division of spoils a large part went to you:
On top of the others' share was an extra *tavro*.[4]
You were harder than gold and marked by steel.
Your sword has reassured you, Andemyrkan!

III

May Tkha strike the *pshi* Kambolet, your friend!
He vowed eternal friendship, after breaking an arrow.[5]
He betrayed Andemyrkan to his enemies, for his death.
After saying, 'We will ride hunting for foxes,'
He took me to the most deserted place on earth.

---

1   The real basis of the first line of the second verse cannot be established. Baranov has an
    indication of a raid of Andemyrkan into Georgia, so the saddle cushion could have been
    stolen or given.
2   The Eristovy was the name of a noble Georgian family.
3   The Braguny was an ancient name of one of the Chechen tribes – there is still a settlement
    named Braguna.
4   The use of the word *tavro* in connection with the wounds that Andemyrkan inflicted on his
    murderers suggests their humiliation by him, as a *tavro* is a brand, a distinguishing mark of an
    owner burned on to horses or cattle.
5   'If two persons had quarrelled and wanted to reconcile, each of them journeyed to the temple
    [at Tatartup] taking with him a bow and arrow; and in that holy place each one held one side
    of the arrow and pledged his word not to deceive, harm or quarrel with the other; then they
    would break the arrow and return as two sincere friends' (Mufti, 1972).

In exchange for Zheman-Sharyk he gave me a nag,
My sword he substituted for an old chipped sabre;
He set me unarmed against a whole army.
Do not hasten to tie my hands, gold-bearded Kambolet!
Already I cut off your golden beard.
I cut off three fingers, now you will not forget me!
With the chipped sword I will put a *tavro* on your face!
I would still play a little with you, but the sword is short.
I would run races with you, but there is no Zheman-Sharyk.
'The unarmed man is wielding his sabre well!
Strike boldly, chop him up like firewood!'
Andemyrkan, who wields his sword well,
They shielded from the sun with the shadow of their swords.
Andemyrkan's blood runs into the gorge of the Cherek,
In the dark Cherek Gorge, in the Khu-u Ravine.
His lion's head is in the hands of Kambolet,
May Tkha strike Kambolet, his friend!
Your sword has reassured you, Andemyrkan!

In the notes to this lament it was written that there are eight records, one in the Kabardan language, in the XXV issue of SMOMPK.[1] In the Russian language the song is quoted in SSKG, Vol. VI.[2] The language of the lament is extremely archaic: many narrators, no longer understanding some of its words, gave place either to uninterpreted phrases or freely substituted one for another, altering the text. The translator in Sbornik Svedeniy o Kavkazskikh Gortsakh, back in 1872, in spite of all his efforts, was obliged, especially in the second part of the lament, to omit a series of lines, 'the meaning of which it was impossible to restore'. Several passages remain obscure.

The text was published in Yu. M. Sokolov, *Kabardinsky fol'klor*, Nauchno-Issledovatel'sky Institut Natsional'ny kul'tury, Moscow, 1936, 321–322.

---

1   SMOMPK is the 'Sbornik materialov dlya opisaniya mestnostey i plemen Kavkaza'. SSKG is the 'Sbornik svedeniya kavkazskikh gortsakh'.
2   SSKG is the 'Sbornik svedeniya kavkazskikh gortsakh'.

25. Cha and Cherbazh[1] *(Ingush)*

Introduction

This legend describes two brothers who were hunters, but they could also act as warriors when the occasion required it. It is interesting that they placed little value in being recognised as princes; what they wanted was their own land, which was in short supply in the Ingush regions.

In Erzi there lived two brothers, Cha and Cherbazh. One day they went hunting high up along the Ortskhoyev Gorge. They walked until dinner-time and killed only one hare. Cha left his younger brother to cook dinner, while he himself decided to hunt a little longer.

Cherbazh lit a fire, roasted the hare, lay down and dozed off. He dreamed that an old man came out of the forest and approached him. The old man was of pleasant appearance and dressed all in white like snow. He thrust his staff into Cherbazh's back and said, 'A gang of kidnappers is coming. Prepare your weapons and your powder.'

Cherbazh jumped up, but he did not see anybody. Deciding that it was a trick of the Devil, he fired into the air, lay down and went to sleep again. And once more the same old man approached him. He thrust his staff into Cherbazh's back and said, 'A gang of kidnappers is coming. Prepare your weapons and your powder.'

'What a miracle!' said Cherbazh in surprise on waking up. 'After all, there is not a soul around. May the wrath of God fall on the Devil.' He fired into the air, lay down once more and went to sleep.

The old man approached him for a third time. He thrust his staff into his back and said, 'I wish you well, you know, and I say to you: get ready for battle with a gang who are kidnapping people,' and he disappeared from sight again.

Cherbazh could not go to sleep any more, and he was thinking, 'What could this mean?'

Out of the forest came his elder brother bringing a *tur*. 'What was that shooting for? Has something happened?' asked he.

The younger brother told the elder one everything that he had dreamed,

---

1   Cherbazh means literally 'bear'; Cherbazh was the proposed original ancestor of the Ingush family of the Cherbizhevy, living at the settlement of Kazbeg on the Georgian Military Highway.

and what the old man had said. The younger brother then said 'Come here!', and when his brother came up to him, he lifted up his shirt. Between the shoulder blades he saw three marks.

'We have to do what the old man said. Get ready to fight with the gang,' said the elder brother.

They ate up part of the *tur*, had a good rest and got ready to move. The sun was declining towards evening. They saw, high up along the gorge of the Terek,[1] that a gang was moving. There, where the gorge was especially narrow, Cha and Cherbazh arranged two ambushes: one above and one below. If members of the gang ran above along the gorge, Cha would attack it; if below, Cherbazh would do so. Thus they annihilated the entire gang: only one man remained alive. They tore off his *papakha* and said, 'You should know why you were left alive. Relate it everywhere that we, Cha and Cherbazh, two brothers, annihilated the entire gang. If you do not tell it, we will reveal your *papakha* and disgrace you.'

That man related everything, and all of the people knew about it. This news reached the royal authorities, who had not known what to do with this gang. They invited Cha and Cherbazh and offered them any reward they fancied. 'We will give you a banner certifying that the men of your family are princes, and the women are princesses,' they said to them.

'We do not need anything. Indeed we are not slaves aspiring to become princes. If you want to give us anything, then give us land,' answered Cha and Cherbazh.

So then land was assigned to them in the place where Gveleti is now.[2] Cha and Cherbazh and their kin moved there to live.

ଵ

The legend was recorded by I. Dakhkil'gov in 1965 from the words of Mahomet Kurkiev, born in 1941, a native of Gveleti. M. Kurkiev heard it from his father. It was published in U. B. Dalgat, *Geroichesky epos chechentsev i ingushey*, Nauka, Moscow, 1972, 396–397.

---

1   The Gorge of the Terek, where the gang was spotted, refers to the Darial Gorge.
2   Gveleti is a village on the Georgian Military Highway, in Ingush 'Gilt'.

26. The Living Chain-mail *(Georgian)*

Introduction

This next legend bears a remarkable resemblance to the episode in the Gilgamesh epic where the hero loses the flower of immortality. In each case the hero loses the treasure while bathing. In each legend a serpent plays a part. While bathing, Gilgamesh loses the potential for immortality, whereas Torgva loses the potential for invincibility as a warrior – in other words, temporary immortality. The traditional armour of a warrior once consisted of overlapping 'scales' of leather or other material, somewhat reminiscent of the skin of a snake. In the Gilgamesh epic it is the snake that *takes away* permanent immortality from the hero, whereas in this legend it is the dragon that *gives* temporary immortality to the hero. The surface of water together with the surface of the earth (a boundary that is the abode of snakes that swim on the water and crawl in the dust) is a boundary between life and death – below it one is dead, above it one is alive.

Torgva was a famous hero of Khevsur heroic songs and traditions. He was a contemporary of King Irakli II, and was advanced thanks to personal merits and to links with the royal court: afterwards he started to oppress his fellow tribesmen. In some variants the birth of Torgva is accompanied by wonderful signs: out of the earth burst sheaves of sparks and clouds of oil. 'On his shoulder-blade was the mark of the cross, on the right the image of the sun, and on the left the horseshoe of the moon ...'

Torgva went hunting. At a certain place he fell through into an ice fissure. There happened to be a dragon there, and Torgva fell onto his back. Torgva was perishing with cold and hunger. The dragon felt sorry for him, he got his precious dragon-stone and let him lick it a little. It both warmed him and fed him. They became sworn brothers. That dragon made a gift to Torgva of war chain-mail, *begtari*. It had the following virtue: at the place where a stroke of a sword fell on it, or a bullet or an arrow hit it, all the loops of the chain-mail gathered and piled up in one place, and no weapon was able to hit its owner.

But in the very end the chain-mail vanished. And Torgva perished from the arrow of the Pshav Chota. Torgva's right hand was stained red.

It was also said that by gathering in one place, the iron loops of the chain-mail would throw a bullet back. Neither in the day nor at night would

Torgva take off the chain-mail, and his enemy would never have overcome him but for an unfortunate incident.

One day Torgva was bathing in a warm spring. During his bathe the river carried away the chain-mail which was lying on the bank, and a blood-enemy killed him.

Eight hunters descended through Andaki.[1]
Torgva descended too – a deer in the springtime.
He was striding sadly, the trace of tears could be seen on his face.
What have you done with your chain-mail, Torgva, given by your sworn brother?
I went off hunting, I was following game.
I went down into Archilo, I came across a warm spring.[2]
I went down to bathe, I threw off my chain-mail.
It was then that I lost it, I did not keep my eye on the damned thing.
And so my chain-mail floated away, like the waves of the river.
I sent out a search party for it, but nowhere did they find any trace of it.

I am coming from there. What could I do? That is why there are traces of tears on my face.

ॐ

This legend was recorded by T. Razikashvili, date and narrator not known. It was published in E. B. Virsaladze, *Gruzinsky okhotnichy mif i poeziya*, Nauka, Moscow, 1976, 288–289.

27. The Tradition of Bora Abayev *(Chechen-Ingush)*

Bora Abayev was a man of very large build: in a former time he had had a reputation as a *bogatyr*.

One day when he was riding on his *bogatyr* Arab horse, a great fire over-took him. In order to save himself from the fire, he put his horse into a

---

1   Andaki is a locality in Khevsureti.
2   In the locality of Archilo a warm spring really does gush, and it is called Torgva's Spring.

gallop. Suddenly a squeak sounded behind him; he looked around and saw crawling after him a large snake, which was unable to catch him up. Bora took pity on him and offered him the end of his whip, saying, 'Here you are, snake, hold the end of my whip, but really firmly.' The snake grasped the end of the whip, and Bora set spurs to his horse and sent him into a gallop. Thus he saved himself and the snake.

When they had ridden out into a safe place, Bora said, 'Well, snake, now you are in a safe place, and you can stay here. Let go of my whip and rest with God.' The snake let go of Bora's whip, but just would not become separated from him. When Bora turned around, the snake turned back, but as soon as he carried on riding, he crawled after him. And thus it was repeated all the way. At last Bora said, 'Evidently, snake, you want me to follow you. And so I will give you my word of honour that wherever you crawl, I will ride after you.'

He was obliged to follow the snake quite a long way. Finally they came to a den; the snake looked around at Bora and then crawled into the den, and some time later its tail could be seen in the den. Then Bora said to himself, 'Well, probably he has invited me here with a good motive! If the snake crawls out tail first, it means that he wishes a man well.'[1]

Certainly, the snake crawled out and brought out of his den a big suit of damask-steel armour. Bora said, 'No doubt, in gratitude for my saving you from the fire, you are making me a present of this armour. I give you my word not to give it away to anybody, and to make it my will that my heirs do the same.' After saying this, he put on the armour and rode off home. There is a tradition that that armour is with the Abayevs even to this day.

This Chechen–Ingush tradition was recorded by B. Dalgat in 1892 from the words of Ibrahim Darshkiev of the village of Nasyr-Kort. It was published in U. B. Dalgat, *Geroichesky epos chechentsev i ingushey*, Nauka, Moscow, 1972, 372–373.

---

1   This is a characteristic expression for explaining the world outlook of the people (note of B. Dalgat).

28. The Grandson of Kozash, and Germanch *(Chechen-Ingush)*

Introduction

This legend is based on the theme of blood revenge; not just for an individual, but for a whole family or clan. After working for the Cherkess prince for some time, the prince says he has come to love him like his own son. This feeling, even if formal adoption had not taken place (we do not know), makes his guardian-employer inclined to provide the young man with the means to obtain blood revenge. The legend shows Kozash in a positive light, but other legends portray him as a cruel tyrant, who made a coat of 'the beards and moustaches of well-known men' (U. B. Dalgat 1972, 389–390).

Close by the settlements of Dolaky and Kantyshy are two burial mounds. They are called the burial mounds of Kozash and Germanch. People say that Kozash used to live on the burial mound of Kozash, and Germanch on the burial mound of Germanch. They were at enmity with each other.

One day Germanch and his army made war on Kozash. Germanch was the victor and he exterminated even the children and extremely old people. Germanch decided to slaughter all of the descendants of Kozash, and therefore he put to death even pregnant women. The dwelling of Kozash was consigned to the flames. Having decided that Kozash was finished off, Germanch returned home.

But the lineage of Kozash had not ended. One of his daughters-in-law, being at this time in the mountains at her parents' place, was pregnant, and she gave birth there to a boy. When he had grown up, his mother told him everything.

The grandson of Kozash set off to Cherkessia to a certain prince, who offered him the choice of either pasturing his innumerable flocks of sheep and horses or receiving guests in the house. The grandson of Kozash agreed to the latter. He was attentive to the customs and manners of the Cherkess and he fulfilled his duties well.

In the prince's yard there grew a huge tree. Remembering his duty, the grandson of Kozash often used to grieve beneath this tree in his free time, and to cut the tree with his *kinzhal*. Many years passed, but he continued to cut at the tree. Finally it crashed down.

Then the prince asked the grandson of Kozash, 'For a long time I have been noticing that something is weighing you down. Tell me your trouble.'

The grandson of Kozash told him everything: about how they had killed his grandfather, father, cousins; about how he himself had remained alive: he told him about his blood duty, which it was essential to perform.

'I have come to love you like my own son,' said the prince, 'and I will give you a large army. I will keep on driving my horses over this fallen tree until it has turned to dust.'

When all of the prince's horses had been driven along the road across the tree, only half of it had turned to dust. The prince borrowed horses from his relatives and friends, and only then did the whole tree turn into dust. This is the kind of army that the prince gave to the grandson of Kozash!

By the burial mounds of Kozash and Germanch is to be found the 'hill from which the fallow deer have been driven'. At this hill the grandson of Kozash halted his army, while he himself set off to the place where Kozash had formerly lived. There were some mud huts, in which a few women were living. They told him everything.

'When midnight comes, look in the direction of the burial mound of Germanch and you will learn something,' said the grandson of Kozash.

At midnight he routed the army of Germanch. Not a single man was left alive, and the entire farmstead was consigned to the flames. Germanch himself was taken captive, tied up and given to the women living on the burial mound of Achamza.[1] They killed him by jabbing him with needles.

The grandson of Kozash gave his army back to the prince, and invited him home and organised a feast. The grandson of Kozash lived in peace and friendship with the Cherkess.

࿇

This Vaynakh legend was recorded by I. A. Dakhkilgov in 1966 from the words of M. Balkhayev at the Dolakhov School. It was published in A. O. Malsagov, *Skazki i legendy ingushey i chechentsev*, Nauka, Moscow, 1983, 319–320.

---

1   The Kurgan Achamza is a hill between the villages of Ekazhevo and Surkhokhi in Ingusheti.

29. The Abrek Sulumbek *(Ingush)*

Introduction

This legend also deals with blood revenge, but in this case the avenger, Sulumbek, and the culprit become reconciled, and Sulumbek had difficulty in persuading his relatives that family honour did not require blood to be spilled from the guilty man. The reconciling of blood feuds was often accomplished by payments of animals, such as is included in this legend. The procedure was also often concluded by the adoption of the guilty man into the slain man's family by the symbolic sucking at the breast of the head woman of the family. Baddeley has a description of such a reconciliation, following the family's solemn oath never to forgive the guilty man:

> [the man trying to effect a reconciliation went straight to the injured party and asked him] to become my sworn brother. He agreed, willingly, and sent for his wife that I might suck her breast, but I refused, gently, saying that we were both old and it was not seemly, though the custom. So we swore on the Koran instead. Then for a whole year I worked uninterruptedly for reconcilement, but the exasperation was so great that I hardly hoped to succeed. Eventually, however, Batal Hadji helping, the affair was arranged on the basis of the payment of 310 rubles cash, three horses, three cows, three sheep, and sixty rubles more as compensation for the widow, to be handed to her on her accepting Inal's brother, the guilty party, as her own son under oath. He, as our custom is in such cases, must go to the dead man's tomb with the cattle and the horses and wait there holding a white flag and imploring pardon out loud; and so he did, but the family forbade him under threat of death to touch the tomb (lying full length on it would be a necessary part of the performance) until all the negotiations, to the last detail, were ended.

(This quotation, together with other examples of the reconciliation of blood feuds, is given in Baddeley 1940, I, 261–263).

There lived, so they say, the bold *abrek* Sulumbek, son of Gorobozh.[1] They say that he was a friend of the *abrek* Zelimkhan of Kharachoy.

On one occasion Sulumbek's brother decided to steal oxen from a poor man. The night was dark, but the owner saw that his oxen were being taken away, and he fired a shot after the thief. The bullet hit its mark exactly, and Sulumbek's brother was killed.

Many times Sulumbek arranged an ambush in order to avenge his brother. He lost many a night, for the purpose of settling accounts with his blood enemy.

One night Sulumbek lay in wait for him at the bridge near the village of Sagopshi. In the middle of the night he heard the clatter of a horse's hoofs. Sulumbek prepared his weapon, came out from beneath the bridge and rode after his blood enemy. After some time he hailed him, 'You killed my brother, I am Sulumbek, son of Gorobozh. Prepare your arms, I am going to avenge my brother's blood.'

The rider continued on his way, as if he had not heard anything. Sulumbek once more shouted out the same thing. Silence. Even for a third time Sulumbek shouted to him. Then the rider dismounted, threw on the ground his arms, his pistol and his *kinzhal* and said, 'You are right, Sulumbek, it was I who killed your brother. But know that in this case there was no way that it was my fault. I did not kill him basely, for profit. Hear me out.' His blood enemy related everything that had happened, and he added, 'Now I declare you to be innocent of my blood, perform your revenge. I am fed up with hiding from you, who are continually arranging ambushes for me!'

Sulumbek realised that his blood enemy was not guilty. Being a real man, he said, 'I declare you to be not guilty of the blood of my brother. From today live in peace and fear nothing. Nobody will dare to reproach you with anything, since you are not guilty of anything.'

On the next day, many cattle and horses were driven into Sulumbek's yard. It was the blood pay-off. Sulumbek summoned his relatives and announced that he had forgiven the blood of his brother. He added, 'I do not sell human blood for money and livestock. I forgave the blood, and not in order to receive payment. Drive back the cattle and the horses!'

Thus he forgave the innocent man, and the people were grateful to him for that.

---

1   Sulumbek Gorovozhev, from the village of Yandyrek, was a comrade-in-arms of the well-known *abrek* Zelimkhan of Kharachoy, who established terror in the Imperial administration in the neighbourhood of Grozny from 1903 to 1913.

But one day, at a village assembly, one man reproached Sulumbek: 'You are not a man! Shame is lying upon you! Why do you not avenge the blood of your brother?'

Sulumbek said, 'I knew that at least one man would blame me for my act. However, do not think that your words will anger me and that I will go and kill an innocent man. My word is inviolable!'

The people at the assembly cursed that man and, even after that, Sulumbek did not betray his word. His relatives behaved the same way too.

ঌ

This Ingush legend was recorded by S. Gandaloyev in 1977 from the words of A. Kh. Akhmurziev in the village of Sagopshi. It was published in A. O. Malsagov, *Skazki i legendy ingushey i chechentsev*, Nauka, Moscow, 1983, 326.

30. The Sister of Seven Brothers *(Ingush)*

Introduction

The hero of this legend is a female warrior who performs the required blood revenge in the absence of any brothers to perform it. There are several Caucasus legends with this theme, sometimes ending with the death of the wounded but successful girl. Others end with her suicide, because she has nothing left to live for (i.e., without a family). In this present legend she remains alive, but as a confirmed spinster, having rejected her suitor for his breach of etiquette. It is also interesting that the girl is a good judge of horses, even of a horse that appears to be an 'unprepossessing thin nag'. This is another common theme in Caucasus legends, and is also contained in legends about the son of Tamerlane (see 'The Ditch of Temir the Lame').

The Maiden's Tower mentioned stands in the Assa Gorge in the Galgay community. The tower was built at such a height and with such difficulty of access that only an Alpinist could clamber up to it. The mountain people relate traditions to this day concerning this tower and the maiden who lived there. One of them can serve as a continuation of the legend:

The girl became wild. If anybody came to the tower, she locked herself in there. If somebody met her hunting in the forest, she would run away. People lived down beneath the crag on which the girl's tower stood. They used to sow millet but, so they say, the girl would urinate from above in such a way that the harvest was always ruined. Then the people conceived the idea: if she does not lose her maidenhood, there will be no life for us. Nobody had the courage to go to her. Finally one man made up his mind. He took some dried meat with him and went to her. When she saw him, the girl started running, and the man also began running, but in the other direction, as if running away from her. That made the girl interested, and then she caught him up. The man gave her a good feed of the dried salted meat, after which the girl acquired a great thirst. The man went down to the river with her and there deprived her of her maidenhood. After that the girl was no longer able to spoil the harvest. Some time later that man married her.

That tradition was recorded by I. Dakhkilgov and was not published until 1972 by U. B. Dalgat.

In a large strong tower there lived seven[1] brothers and a sister. The brothers used to go away for plunder or hunting, while the sister would look after the house.

Contemporary with them there lived strong and cruel Nogay princes.[2] And not much time had passed before the Nogays had killed all seven brothers one by one. No men were left to avenge their blood. The sister did not shed a single small tear. Taking the clothing of one of her beloved brothers and putting it on, she rolled up her long hair under a *papakha*, sat on her horse and set out to the land of the Cherkess. She was like an adolescent lad, on whose face a beard and moustache had not yet appeared.[3]

On arriving among the Cherkess the girl asked, 'Who in your land can give me one sheep for supper every day?'

'In that village lives a man by the name of Akhlo.[4] He can slaughter one sheep every day.'

---

1 The number 'seven' is an epic number.
2 The Nogays were a nomadic tribe of Turco-Mongolian origin.
3 A girl dressing in man's clothes gave her freedom to travel and to be seen among men.
4 The Ingush call that village 'Akhlo-Yurt'.

The girl rode off to him, said '*Assalam-aleykum*' and he replied '*Va aley-kum-salam*'. Then, after killing one sheep, he met his guest. Thus passed several days. Akhlo did not ask who she was, where she came from, or what her name was.[1]

One day, after sitting on their horses, the girl and Akhlo rode out into the steppe together. The village herd of horses was grazing at the edge of the village. They saw one unprepossessing thin nag, which had separated from the herd and was grazing in the place where all the village used to throw their dung. In that place the grass was taller and more lush. The girl said, 'Look, Akhlo! That is not an ordinary horse, it is a *turpal* (*bogatyr*) horse. If you will give your horse for that nag, will the owner give it to us?'

'Why wouldn't he! Certainly he will give it,' said Akhlo.

The girl chased the nag, and it ran into its owner's yard. Galloping in after it, the riders stopped at the house and, when the owner came out, Akhlo asked, 'Will you swap your horse for my horse? If you are willing, we will exchange.'

The owner was very content. Akhlo gave him his own horse, he himself sat on the nag and together with the girl he rode home.

And then the girl said, 'Keep this horse for three years on a halter in a stable where not a single ray of sun can penetrate.'[2]

She instructed Akhlo how to look after it, what food to give it, and from what spring to give it water. After saying all that was needed, and promising to come after three years, the girl rode away home.

For three years Akhlo looked after the *bogatyr* horse, as his guest had advised; but through the straw roof of the stable, through an opening which was the size of a needle, but which Akhlo had not noticed, a ray of the sun entered at noon. It kept on falling on the wide crupper of the horse.

Three years later, after putting on her brother's clothes and hiding her hair beneath her *papakha*, the girl came riding once more to Akhlo. After the greetings and questionings Akhlo said that he had looked after the horse

---

1   According to the ancient ethical rules of the mountain people, it was not done to ask an unknown traveller, a guest, who he was, where he was from or where he was going. Such questions might worry a man, if he was escaping from blood revenge or striving to perform it, going on a raid or returning from it.

2   According to the legends of the Vaynakhs a *bogatyr* horse requires special tending, in which it must be held in the dark, sometimes in a basement behind several doors, sometimes as many as nine of them. The segregation of the horse gave it protection from the 'evil eye'. The number nine is often used to represent 'a very large number'. In other cases, the number forty has the same connotation.

for three years, following her bidding. They went into the stable. As soon as they went in, the girl went up to the horse and put her finger on the position on its crupper where the sun's ray fell. Then she said, 'A sun's ray has been falling on this place. It is necessary to keep this horse for three more years.'

When Akhlo examined the roof carefully, he observed a chink the size of a needle. He trebled the roof, and the girl rode away. After three years she returned. She had a look at the horse and acknowledged that it was now at its full strength. Then she told Akhlo that it was time to get ready for a journey. The girl did not say where it was to, and Akhlo asked no questions. Crossing the Terek, and riding through sandy and stony lands, they reached a certain river. The Nogay lands began on its other bank.

'This is it. You stay on this bank, while I spend some time on the other bank, and then come back. After two days and two nights, you have a look at the river. If blood and foam are flowing along it,[1] you ride away from here with all your might, without looking back,' said the girl.

'All right,' said Akhlo, and he stayed there while the girl crossed the river.

Of the herds of horses which were roaming over the Nogay steppes, she rounded up three herds into one and began driving it. It is not within the powers of one man alone to control even one herd of horses; it needs to be driven by two or three men along the sides and by one man in the middle. But the *bogatyr* horse allowed her to gallop from one side of the herd to the other. By such means she alone dealt with the herd and drove it faster than the wind. The Nogays dashed after her in pursuit. Sitting as three on one horse, they were already almost catching her up. Driving the whole herd together, she galloped to meet them. From one of her arrows three of them fell, from one stroke of her sword, six of them fell. After defeating the servants of the Nogay prince, she drove the herd further.

At that time Akhlo had a look at the river from the bank. The water was carrying both blood and foam. And when he looked into the distance he saw a dust storm moving. As it continued to approach, he realised that it was a herd of horses galloping, and then that it was his friend and guest who was driving the herd. His heart did not allow him to leave. As the herd drew near the river, a second group of pursuers appeared in the distance. Wishing to help his guest, Akhlo had just readied himself to cross the river when the

---

1   This is a common epic passage of Vaynakh legends. Blood and foam on the water usually symbolise the danger that the hero is experiencing.

girl said, 'Do not leave your place. Otherwise I will shoot my arrows at you.'

Akhlo stayed in his place. Half of the herd had crossed the river, while the other half was just still crossing. Leaving the herd, the girl again galloped off to meet her pursuers. With her arrows and sword she wiped out all her enemies. No longer holding himself back, Akhlo went into the river and drove across the remaining horses of the stolen herd.

Thus, for the blood of each of her brothers, the girl put down sixty enemies and crossed over to this bank of the river. Driving the herd from two sides, they brought the horses into Akhlo's yard.

'All this herd is for you, in return for your companionship. These horses have such-and-such qualities,' said the girl and she informed him of all their merits. 'And now I am riding away. Farewell and be healthy.'

Leaving the *bogatyr* horse and sitting on her own horse, she rode off home. The happy Akhlo was left with the herds. But suddenly he remembered: after all, I simply did not ask what sort of a man he is, where he comes from and what is his name. I will not rest until I catch him up and question him.

After mounting the *bogatyr* horse, Akhlo rode off along the tracks left by the girl's horse. On the second day after noon he saw his guest in the distance. Akhlo did not have time to catch up before the girl rode into a yard. Akhlo saw the young man go into the house. The girl took off her brother's clothes and dressed in a woman's dress. Climbing up on to the very top floor, she shook down her hair into the wind and began combing it with a brass comb. The wind carried the long strands of her hair far away. When Akhlo rode up to the tower, he saw the girl above. 'How really beautiful you are!' he said to himself. Then he shouted to her, 'Send to me that young hero who rode into this yard.'

'Akhlo, that was not a young hero, it was me. You did not have enough quick-wittedness to ask me who I am, where I am from and what I am called. Your nobility left you when you saw the Nogay horses. If that had not happened, I could have become your wife. But now, ride back where you have come from.'

'No, of course not!' Akhlo began saying.

'Nothing will come of it, ride away,' said the girl firmly.

Grudgingly Akhlo began riding back home, but after riding a little way he came back and said, 'Marry me – I beg you!'

'Akhlo, go away! It will be better, otherwise I could resort to force.'

Knowing that he was unable to overcome the girl by force, he rode off home.

The girl remained living in her tower. It is in the Assa Gorge and is called the Maiden's Tower.

ॐ

This Ingush tradition was recorded by I. Dakhkilgov in 1967 from the words of Izmael Birikhanov of the village of Upper Achaluki. He heard it from his father Jabrail Birikhanov. It was published in U. B. Dalgat, *Geroichesky epos chechentsev i ingushey*, Nauka, Moscow, 1972, 374–377.

31. How the Orstkhoys Won Back the Land[1] *(Ingush)*

Introduction

Epic stories about strong women, who enter single combat with men, are widely distributed among the Orstkhoys, Ingush and Chechens. For example, there is also a well-known Chechen legend of approximately the same content, 'The Cherkess Ridges' (ChF, Vol. III, 1964, 115).

They tell that the lands over which the Rivers Fartang and Sunzha flow were occupied by the Cherkess. The Orstkhoys were continually disputing this land with them. The wars did not cease between the Cherkess and the Orstkhoys, they attacked one another, took people away into captivity and plundered them. Both sides became fed up with this protracted war. And then the Cherkess said to the Orstkhoys, 'Bring forward one of your fighters, and we also will put up one of ours. The land will remain with the side whose fighter wins. If, however, neither of the fighters wins, we shall fight, army against army, country against country.'

The Orstkhoys replied that they were willing. The armies of the Orstkhoys and the Cherkess stood up facing one another. 'Bring out your fighter,' said the Cherkess, and they brought forward their own warrior.

The Cherkess warrior was a very tall and heavy man. Not one Orstkhoy was confident that he could beat him. They began nominating one another.

---

[1]   Orstkhoy was the Ingush name of a tribe who obtained legendary prominence as the Nart-Orstkhoys.

Thus, a fighter did not come forward from the Orstkhoys, and the war was just on the point of flaring up. One old Orstkhoy man told them to call for his daughter-in-law. Any man would hardly reach the height of her armpits. 'Fight with this warrior,' the old man told her.

That woman went against the Cherkess warrior. The Cherkess fighter started laughing. He thought that it would be quite easy to beat that woman. He began with fighting tricks. But that Orstkhoy woman did not understand anything about fighters' methods; she went up and simply grasped the Cherkess fighter by his waist with her arms. She both grasped and lifted, she squeezed him with her arms, and his soul just departed.

The Cherkess became frightened and panicked. They all got up and left. Thus the Orstkhoys indeed won back the land.

The people asked the old man how he had found out that his daughter-in-law possessed such strength. Then the old man related, 'On one occasion I was sitting and looking out of the window, from boredom. My daughter-in-law was milking the buffalo. The buffalo stepped on the hem of her dress. Neither shouts nor blows could make the buffalo move from the place. My daughter-in-law crawled under the buffalo and, lifting it on her back, carried it across to another place. It was then that I realised that she was very strong.'

From that time the Orstkhoys lived on their own land.

This Ingush story was recorded by I. Dakhkil'gov in 1967 from the words of Khamid Galayev of the village of Arshty. Galayev heard this story from Mukhtar Daurbekov. It was published in U. B. Dalgat, *Geroichesky epos chechentsev i ingushey*, Nauka, Moscow, 1972, 395.

VI

Hunting

Hunting used to be an important economic activity and provide an extra source of food, especially in the high mountains, where it was difficult to grow crops, and in some places even rear sheep.

The uncertainties and dangers of hunting in the mountains led to dramatic stories and inevitably to dramatic legends. The uncertainties included the chance of not finding an animal to kill for food, which could have serious consequences within the hunter's family and community. In the high mountains, where a fall from a crag could result in the death of the hunter, there was the added uncertainty of whether the hunter would return alive at all. The mountain animals such as the Caucasian ibex and the mountain goat are sure-footed even on mountain crags where a hunter cannot go. Moreover, even if the hunter's arrow or bullet hit their mark, the animal might fall into a place from which its carcase was difficult to retrieve. Although bullets might be expendable, an arrow was a valuable item that might have taken more than an hour to make; it was therefore desirable to retrieve it, whether it had hit its mark or not.

A returning hunter would no doubt have had stories to tell, either about the drama of a successful hunt or a story about 'the one that got away'. The hunter may well have embellished these stories with some exaggeration and elements from his imagination. However, if the hunter did not return alive, the situation provided a vacuum into which the imagination of the community could project an explanation. The members of such a community would not have considered the possibility of 'chance': what a scientific person might call a 'chance accident' the mountain man would know had been caused by an agent. This agent might have been another person, an animal or a supernatural spirit, in any case acting out of malevolence. It is very unlikely that one would meet another person in the remote mountains. The legend below, of 'The Balkh Meadow', describes a case where an ill-disposed herd of animals was almost the reported cause of a hunter falling. However, the most likely agent would have been the 'Master of the Beasts' or the 'Mistress of the Beasts', the owner of the beasts.

The owner of the beasts was likened to a shepherd tending his or her flock. The shepherd is protective of the flock, and is only willing to give away animals to those that he or she favours. Moreover, there are some special animals that are favourites and are not willingly given away under any circumstances. These considerations go some way towards explaining the anger of the Master or Mistress: namely either that the hunter takes too many of the owner's animals or that he takes the special 'pet' animals. In either case this can explain the hunter's failure to obtain game, or explain his injury or death.

What about the explanation of apparent *good* luck in hunting? In localities where the animals are owned by a Mistress of the Beasts, there can be a sexual explanation. The mistress has a relationship with the hunter. So long as he is faithful to her, he is assured of hunting success. But woe betide him if he is unfaithful with an earthly woman – the vengeance of the Mistress is swift and sure, and the hunter will surely die. In Georgia, after the arrival of Christianity, the Mistress of the Beasts was replaced by Saint George, and an expression of good will towards him usually involved the lighting of candles and the recital of prayers.

The pagan or pre-Christian Master of the Beasts had daughters who could perform some of the functions of the Mistress of the Beasts, as shown in the first of these legends, 'Biyneger'. It is shown how Biyneger has taken many animals, including one of the Master's favourites; his daughter accordingly lures the hero into the high mountains by taking on the form of a white doe. It is well known in folklore that the killing of a white animal inevitably leads to the death of the hunter, but in this case the hero needs its milk or meat to cure his sick brother. The next legend, 'Dali is Giving Birth on the Crags', has the Mistress rewarding the hunter with hunting success in return for the favour that he has done her, but then she takes revenge for his spurning of her love, thus supporting the adage that 'hell hath no fury like a woman spurned'. In the next legend, 'Betkil', the hero, has evidently given away the Mistress's special love token and consequently is lured into the mountains, becomes stranded on a cliff and in desperation jumps to his death. This legend is re-enacted annually in Svaneti, Georgia, with the performance of the sacred round-dance, Samti Chishkash, attached to the spring festival of Agbaligral, in the last week of Shrove-tide (Virsaladze 1976, 63). The next legend, 'Dali and Amirani', describes the narrow escape of the hero from the Mistress. In this case there is a strong hint of the influence of Christianity, for which the idea of a goddess was unacceptable, so that the goddess was altered to a witch-like character, and her herding qualities and responsibilities were taken over by Saint George. In 'Tebru Kvartsikhsky Ivane' there is no supernatural agent mentioned, but the story possibly describes the effect of an earthquake, since the Caucasus is an earthquake zone, although some versions of the story imply the influence of the Mistress of the Beasts. The next legend, 'Azhveypsh', shows how the Master's daughter punishes the hunter for taking her pet animal, and then portrays the Master as a typical shepherd, herding his flock of deer. 'Azhveypsh's Daughter' gives a description of the tender attitude of the Master's daughter towards a hunter with whom she has a relationship. 'The Young Man and the Snow Leopard' is one of a cycle of Georgian legends that describe a battle between a hunter and the chief predator of the mountains, the snow leopard. It is probably significant that the song starts with the hunter shooting a *tur* (ibex) and that when he meets the snow leopard, the latter's 'eyes are full of God's rage'. The question is, was the hunter being punished in connection with the particular animals that he had killed? The final legend, 'The Balkh Meadow', describes how the animals themselves attempt and almost succeed in being the agent of a hunter's death.

Many of the legends quoted in this chapter are Georgian. This is because a very interesting and important collection and analysis of hunting legends was made by the famous Georgian folklorist Elena Virsaladze (Virsaladze 1976).

32. The Song about Biyneger *(Balkar)*

Oy, the most brave Biyneger, son of Gezokh,
There is no place in the mountains where he has not been.
His arrows always hit the target,
In the language of beasts and birds he converses like Apsaty.[1]

However much you tried, they did not let you rule an *aul*,
Both Teyri[2] and Apsaty took a dislike to you.
Biyneger, who does not burn in the fire,
Who is not pierced by arrows,

---

1   Apsaty was the pagan god of hunting, the protector of wild animals.
2   Teyri was the supreme god in the pagan pantheon of the Balkars and Karachays.

Who swims like a fish in raging rivers,
Who parts young deer from their mothers.
Oy, on the bank of the Chaynashkhi a huge *tur* appeared,
Prince Biyneger shot an arrow at him from the castle of Karchi.

The wounded *tur*, glancing towards the castle of Karchi and bleeding
    profusely,
Came running to Apsaty, who was counting his animals by the light of the
    moon.
Oy, weeping and sobbing he told
Apsaty all about Biyneger.

And Apsaty, knowing about all the hunters' weaknesses and secrets,
Began thinking how to punish Biyneger more terribly.
Biyneger, who has overcome all the mountains of the Caucasus,
However much you tried, they did not give you an *aul* to rule.

In Great Balkaria there was not found an *aul* for you to rule,
There was not found for you an honoured place at Gollu.[1]
They did not render due honours to a prince's son,
And he, in a fit of temper, went off to be a hunter.

You wounded Apsaty's favourite animal, Biyneger,
You cannot even conceive what punishment awaits you now.
Apsaty is bandaging up the *tur's* wound and casting a spell,
With malice and anger at Biyneger, his blood is boiling.

Summoning his children, he orders them,
'Take revenge on Biyneger, because he
Massacres the deer in the hollows, in the mountains,
He leaves no birds on the trees, in the forests.'

Once while hunting Biyneger had a bad dream:

---

1   Gollu is a large universal holiday which was celebrated on 22 March, on the day of the spring
     equinox, and was dedicated to the deity of fertility and the patron of warriors, Gollu (Gollu,
     as also Choppa, Ashtotur and some other pagan deities of the Balkars and Karachays, were
     multifunctional).

It seemed that his brother Omar fell ill with a terrible sickness,[1]
And that there was no kind of medicine or remedy for it
Except the milk of a white doe – only that would cure him.

In the fortress of Basiyat they gathered all the wise women.
Telling fortunes with haricot beans, they said this to Biyneger,
'Only the milk of a white doe will help Omar,
And only the *borzoi* of your mother's brother can catch it.'

When I came to my uncle's house, I swear by Teyri, they did not receive me
    as a guest,
It was not just their hound, but not even a puppy would they give me.
Addressing me, they spoke like this:

'Let a man who begs another's dog be the same kind of homeless dog as you,
    Biyneger!'[2]

'Oy, yes, Biyneger, the one who cursed you like that, let him, like you, be
gone,
The one who did not give you his dog, let him too become the very worst
dog!'
In ancient Balkaria, the *kaplans*[3] who would have caught a doe for you have
    disappeared,
There is not a man left in Baksan from whom you have not begged a
    wolfhound.[4]

Returning from there, you called in at the yard of the Kubadievy,
But the Kubadievy are faithful servants of Teyri.

---

1   The terrible sickness literally means 'dog's sickness', and referred to an incurable skin disease, such as leprosy or skin cancer. According to the narrator, Baydymat, the daughter of Apsaty, in fulfilling her father's order, sent down the sickness on Omar and arranged everything so as to destroy Biyneger. She even applied her magic to the family of his uncle so that they would not give him their dog.
2   Among the Balkars and Karachays it was not done to ask for somebody else's (a foreigner's) hunting dog. In a case of extreme necessity the hunter can only ask that the owner of the dog (or one of the men of the family) would go on the hunt with him, taking his hound with him. Biyneger is hunting all the time and hardly ever at home, hence a 'homeless dog'.
3   *Kaplan* means 'tiger'. Thus are called a breed of famous hunting dogs, which are bred in the Cherek Gorge.
4   It was considered that the inhabitants of the Baksan Gorge had the very best wolfhounds.

They greeted you like a genuine servant of Teyri,
From their hunting dogs they chose the best two for you.

My brother Omar, looking at me, cries:
'Think up something, catch the white doe.'
When I had prepared for the hunt, I swore to the old men of the *aul*,
'I will get my brother the healing milk of the doe.'

Without hurrying, I reached the stone of Botash.
Sitting down there, I lapsed into a long meditation.
Suddenly an old shepherd approached me, I held council with him.
On parting, he asked me as follows:

'Biyneger, whose arrows always hit their target,
I entreat you, by my grey beard –
Take care, on no account take aim at the white doe,[5]
No matter what, don't shoot an arrow at it.'

'If indeed you shoot an arrow at it, you will never return to your *aul*,
You will eternally yearn for your family and friends.'
I climbed from there to the little glade where the deer usually rest.
So as to observe the does, I selected a suitable place.

I sat there for a long time, but nothing happened.
Despite the difficulties, I climbed up Mount Dykhtau.
And there I encountered a three-legged golden-antlered white doe,
I would wish such a meeting only on my threefold enemy.

The doe's appearance startled me,
I had seen nothing more surprising in the world:
One of her legs was much longer than the other two,
Her antlers were sharp, like the ends of spits.

Her eyes, oy, were burning like stars,
Her radiant appearance dazzled my eyes.

---

5   To this day the belief exists among the Balkars and Karachays that a man who has raised his
hand against a white deer (doe) can expect imminent death.

I had only just taken aim when all was obscured by fog,
Instantly the doe standing before me vanished somewhere.

The doe galloped off from the mountains of Balkaria into Kholam,
From there she crossed into the Chegem and Baksan Mountains.
For three months I searched for my doe, but did not find her.
All these months I did not sit down even to eat.

And now at last I spotted my doe in the mountains of Great Baksan,
I began climbing up Elbrus after it.
The doe easily skipped across the eternal glaciers of Elbrus,
She flew up from one mountain terrace to another.
For long I roamed across the steep mountains of Great Baksan,
But no longer met there either a deer or a doe.
Worn out, I finally caught up with her.
Remaining faithful to the oath I gave to the old men,

I wanted to set my hounds on her, but they did not touch her,
I drew my arrow, but it did not go.
Again I began following her,
I was already convinced that I was chasing the white doe.

The doe, glancing from behind the twin-peaked crag,[1]
Uttered the following in its own deer language:[2]
'Prince of princes, Biyneger, what are you doing?
What do you think you are doing, tirelessly pursuing me?

If you are the one who makes all the wild animals and beasts weep,
I am the one who protects them from you.
Turn back, do not trouble yourself for nothing!
Then you will feel sorry, let me not be mistaken!'

'Who are you? I want to milk you,
By the name of Teyri, I entreat you, do not cheat me.
Who are you? Do not give me the slip, tell me who you are.

---

1   Mount Elbrus, the highest mountain in the Caucasus, is famous for its twin peaks; on first
    viewing them one should make a wish.
2   In some variants of this song the doe speaks with a human voice.

Why do you torment me, why do you conceal your name?

Who are you? A *shaytan* or a *jinn*,
Or the doe in milk that I am searching for?
In mountain *auls* my kinsfolk await me,
I ask you, heed my words:

My brother Omar is confined to his bed,
Without the milk of a white doe, he will not live.
If you are a deer, let me send an arrow at you,[1]
But if you are a doe in milk, allow me to milk you.

But if you are really a *shaytan* or a *jinn*,
Do not torment me further, let me continue on my way!'
The doe looked angrily at me
From behind the twin-peaked crag, and said this:
'To the end I will be true to the oath given to my father!
You poor fellow, however you tried, you could not even approach me:
If you are the brave hunter, the Prince Biyneger,
Then I am the daughter of Apsaty, the beautiful Baydymat.

You are ceaselessly pursuing me,
However much you eat, no way can you sate yourself with our meat.
But at last you have landed in my trap, and now I can go back to my castle,
And in conclusion I will offer you some 'good wishes':

May you be shrouded by a dense fog,
And may your brother Omar be cured.
May a bottomless abyss appear before you,
May impregnable crags, reaching above the clouds, rise behind you,

And at your sides may there be crags across which even a snake cannot crawl.
And may you spend many days of your life in this trap!'
Oy, just as soon as she had uttered this, I found myself among impregnable
    crags,

---

1   The ancient Balkars and Karachays believed that the meat of a white deer could cure all
    illnesses.

And in this trap I was fated to live for many days.

When my provisions had finished,
I was even reduced to eating the leather cover of my gun.
And I fed the *borzoi* with the flesh of my own calf,
For full fifteen days I was feeding him with my flesh.

As for Omar, he recovered and became healthy, as before.
After he had seen himself naked in a dream.
In the night, Biyneger, one of your hound dogs came running into your
    native *aul*, Basiyat,[1]
Howling shrilly, he ran into your brother's yard.

Omar, with a presentiment of misfortune, ordered his horse to be saddled,
After long searching he rode up to that immense crag.
On this crag that rose above the clouds, Omar saw his younger brother,
He tried to clamber up there, but all soaked in sweat he realised that he was
    unable to cope with this crag.

'Oy, just what has happened to you, Biyneger, my dear,
The messenger of misfortune you sent, one of your dogs, came dashing to me.
You landed in this trap on my account, after all.'
Realising that Biyneger would not get away from there, he began grieving
    beyond measure.
He ran to Byzyngi and Kholam searching for help,
He brought all the people to this crag.
In the *auls* everyone collected ropes,
On this day all festivities and celebrations were cancelled.

The inhabitants of Balkaria, Chegem and Baksan also came there,[2]
They too saw Biyneger on a ledge of the crag.
There is nothing they did not think of, to rescue Biyneger,
But when they saw the hopelessness of the matter, they returned to their
    auls.

---

1   The narrator has probably forgotten the episode in which it is told how Biyneger, before
    Apsaty's daughter cursed him, and sensing something bad, had sent one of his hounds to his
    brother. In some variants of this song the motif is given in detail.
2   Meaning the Cherek, Chegem and Baksan Gorges.

The terrible news also reached Biyneger's mother, Kyabakhan,
She came running to the foot of the crag, stretching out her hands to
    Biyneger she gave a shout:
'O my child, my darling Biyneger, I am your mother,
Coming here, I have seen what a disaster you are doomed to.

By my milk with which I fed you, I entreat you to do what I ask:
O my mountain eagle, have courage and jump down from the crag.'
'O my mother, my darling, I ask you not to grieve in vain,
O my mother, my darling, I cannot jump from here, after all life is so sweet.'

Meanwhile Biyneger's brother Omar stands steadfastly in his view,
But Biyneger does not heed even his entreaties.
And then he shouted, 'If you don't jump from there, this is what I will do:
I will make your wife my slave,

Your elder daughter I will sell to the East,
Your younger daughter I will sell to the West.'
'These threats of yours do not move me,
Do not speak to me about this any more.

In Babugey my beloved is living,
If only I could see her, I would have much to tell her about.
If only you let her know, she would come running here at once,
If there is any possibility at all to help me, she will find it.

If you bring her, I will do all she tells me,
If she too asks me to throw myself from the crag, I will do it.'
Biyneger's brother Omar approved of that,
He set off to her and informed her of everything:

'My sister-in-law who lives in Babugey, get up,
My brother Biyneger is craving to see you.'
After hearing it all, Biyneger's beloved began crying bitterly:
'I will also die there where Biyneger dies,' she swore.

She ran off to Biyneger, weeping and sobbing,
She ran there, after turning her legs into a horse,

She ran there, after turning her hands into whips,
She ran there, after turning her long thick hair into a *burka*.

Ey, who will order all the misfortunes on earth to be measured,
but who indeed can measure them?
Oy, Biyneger, like a bird your beloved is flying to you,
Like a lioness, she is rushing to you.
Burning and blazing, she came running to the crag where her Biyneger
  stood.

'O my Biyneger, I have come racing to you from my *aul*,
I have sworn to die together with you.
Prince of princes, my beloved, brave son of Gezokh,
Do not give your enemies cause to delight in your misfortune, my darling.

Oy, take yourself in hand, don't be afraid,
Jump down, don't let your body stay on the ledge of the crag,
If you don't jump, your corpse will become prey to black vultures,
And then your loving family and friends will be yet more distressed.

Oh, if only I could reach out to you ...
I pray you, fulfil my request today:
Bind up your eyes with the white shirt I sewed for you
And jump on to my white breast which you so loved.'

Taking off his shirt, Biyneger bound up his eyes,
Taking his gun by the barrel, he flung it to one side.
Gathering all his waning strength, he threw himself from the crag.
On that day he tested his bravery there,

If he climbed up the crag nimbly like an iron hook,
Then he fell from there and smashed himself, he fell to bits like *khychin
  zhummak*,[1]
Only a tuft of his forelock flew to his beloved.
The poor woman, pulling scissors from her belt, thrust them into her belly.

---

1   *Khychin* means 'pie', and *zhummak* means a lump or little ball; so here the meaning is 'filling
     for a round pie'.

It so happens, the castle of Apsaty stands very high,
This is how the brave son of Gezokh perished.

ॐ

This Balkar song was communicated privately by Tanzilya Khajieva., but
has also been published in T. M. Khajieva, 'Karachayevtsy i Balkartsy:
Yazyk, Etnografia, Arkheologia, Folklor', Seria Kavkaz: Narody i Kultury.
Part I. Moscow, 2001, 270–285.

33. Dali is Giving Birth in the Crags *(Georgian)*

Introduction
E. B. Virsaladze suggests that this song might also be connected with a cer-
emony of the ritual killing of a wolf (Virsaladze 1976, 102). Such a ritual is
described in detail by V. V. Bardavelidze (Bardavelidze 1957, 243).

Dali is giving birth in the crags,
She gives birth in the white crags ...
'You have dropped your baby,
You have dropped him from the rock face.'
Below, a wolf was lying in wait for him,
Below, the wolf seized him with his jaws,
He ran with him through the field below.
A hunter was walking by chance along the mountain ridge,
The hunter Mepisa was walking there.
The hunter Mepisa noticed it,
Along the mountain ridge, by chance, the hunter was walking,
Across the plain the wolf was running.
The hunter Mepisa was lying in wait for him,
Lying in wait in the proper place,
His gun rang out and it caught him right on the brow,
The hunter made him drop Dali's baby.
He picked up Dali's baby.
He thrust the wolf skin under his belt.

In the crags Dali was wailing,
The crags were wailing even louder.
The hunter Mepisa approached,
He approached the foot of the white crag.
'My mother, let down your plait to me!'
'May a mother's blessing be with you,
I have nobody who would call me mother.
The one who called me mother a beast has taken from me!'
'I am your child!'
'Who was your rescuer, then?'
'My rescuer was the hunter Mepisa.'
'I will offer him the choice of three things:
If he wants it, every day
We will give him a mountain goat;
Or else, then in September
We will make a present of nine *turs*,
Or else, then he will lie with me.'
'I do not dare to share your bed,
Make me a present of nine *turs*!'
She brought out the nine *turs* for him,
A golden-horned one she joined to them.
The hunter took aim at the golden-horned one,
That same one deflected the bullet
And sent it back at the hunter's forehead.
The hunter Mepisa she laid out on the ground!

This Georgian legend was recorded by Meri Gujejiani in 1936 from the words of David Margiani of the village of Muzhali in Upper Svaneti. It was published in E. B. Virsaladze, *Gruzinskie okhotnichy mif i poeziya*, Nauka, Moscow, 1976, 227–228.

34. Betkil *(Georgian)*

Mulakh-Muzhal assembled,
They were doing a round dance in harmony.
A white chamois leaped into the circle of dancers.
It jumped between Betken's thighs.[1]
Who would chase after it?
Who would chase after it – why, Betken.
In front was the chamois, behind it was Betken,
They were competing together on the way.
In front it was a road laid down by sleighs,
Behind, it came to be covered up.
They came to an absolutely bottomless cliff.
There Dali was waiting for him.
'My Betken, you have come in peace,
How are you keeping, how do you feel?
I gave you a memento,[2]
Where have you put it, you wretch, show me?'
'Your memento I have
Lying at the head of my bed.'
'As you have preserved it,
I will give you the same kind of return home!'
She left him only a handhold for his right hand,
She left him only a foothold for his right foot.
Betken hung from the cliff,
He sees no one to help.
A hunter was walking below ...
'Renowned hunter, look up at me:
Make sure you tell my mother:
Let her consecrate *rakhi* for me.
Be sure to tell my wife:
Let her not leave the children as orphans.
And tell my young friends:

---

1   In all of the variants of this song a prey animal jumps between the hero's thighs, which is
     evidently symbolic, as described by E. B. Virsaladze (1976, 114).
2   Evidently the hero has lost the goddess's memento or more likely given it to another woman,
     his sister-in-law Tamar, whom he blames for his plight; the anger of the goddess at being
     taken for granted by her supposed lover is the cause of his death.

Let them mention me in their prayers once a year.
May my sin fall on Tamar,
Tamar, my sister-in-law,
She let me go hunting in an impure state.
If she will remember me,
Let her adjust her headscarf a little,[1]
She will not be any the worse for it ...'
Betken, poor fellow, indeed jumped,
He perished, smashed up on the rocks.
Dali had avenged her shame,[2]
And may there be God's blessing on us!

This Georgian legend was recorded by M. Chikovani in 1953 in Upper
Svaneti. It was published in E. B. Virsaladze, *Gruzinskie okhotnichy mif i
poeziya*, Nauka, Moscow, 1976, 239–240.

35. Dali and Amirani[3] *(Georgian)*

Why Khazhoie Birds have Little Moustaches[4]

Introduction
Many of the motifs of this legend are considered to be very archaic and unique
(Virsaladze 1976, 331). It is a curious coincidence that the goddess Dali names
herself 'Dalila', as in the biblical story of Samson and Delilah. There is also an
inversion of the biblical long hair motif; in this case the woman renders the
strong-man hero weak by cutting off some of her own hair to bind the hero.

---

1   To adjust the scarf on the head to the right is considered, among the Svan women, a sign of
    mourning.
2   Generally a hunter would take care to go hunting only in a 'pure' state, as described by E. B.
    Virsaladze (1976, 132), and this is emphasised in this line.
3   Amirani is the hero of a Georgian epos; he was a Prometheus figure, and is portrayed in the
    legends 'The Chained Amirani', 'Amirani and the Herdsman', 'The Legend of the Return of
    the Fire' and 'Amiran' in chapter XII.
4   The khazhoie is a small bird, along the sides of whose beak little feathers stick out like a
    moustache.

The sun turned over and rose up. It went away. It went out. The moon had risen, but it could not be seen. It was not seen and it was seen. There was both no moon and a moon. At that time, whether it happened or did not happen, there lived a certain man. That man was a hunter. He lived in a large forest. That man had a dog. He called it Tapie. The dog was all white, and it had only one distinguishing mark: one ear flickered, just like a fire.

One day that man went hunting. He walked past many mountains and gorges, he killed many animals and returned home late. After that he did not go hunting for a long time. He had food, and what was the purpose of him roaming!

A long time later he again went into the forest. He was walking a great deal. His dog got tired. Towards night the man's eyes were goggling, they became huge like a pot, but in the same way as my enemy does not spend time here, so he was unable to find anything. During all this walking and searching it got dark. The man lay down in a meadow, while his dog sat down next to him and laid his paws on his head. It grew terribly dark.

Suddenly something similar to fire came out of the water, and it clambered up on to a stump right next to them. The man was very pleased, thinking it was a flame. He went towards it, saying that at least he could warm his hands. The hunter walked towards it, and the flame ran from him, and along the road it left little tongues of flame. The man nearly went out of his mind. In the end he got up close and saw that the flame was a woman's hair. When he touched it, the flame went out. The man kept walking, whether following the flame or following the hair. And the dog was following him. Thus the hunter and his dog approached a certain crag. On the summit of the crag a huge flame was burning. There was only one strange thing – it was not burning, nothing even was catching fire from it, nothing.

After that the flame silently descended. The man had a look and saw that the flame was the woman's hair, nothing else. And sitting up above on the crag was a woman, like the moon, smiling to him and calling:

'At last you have come to me, Amirani,
A man who grew up not by days but by hours.
Climb up, sit down on the crag,
I am tired, I will sleep a little.
Keep watch over me, stay awake next to me,
I am a weak woman, Dalila,

I am tired of running through the forest,
I am the lady of the beasts, Amirani.
I was searching for you, at last I found you,
Come, embrace me tightly, Amirani.'

Amirani was surprised. What is she saying, thought he, and he shouted to the woman:

'I will climb up, but what can I do?
My dog Tapie is with me.
I am looking and want to gaze upon you,
Your face is like a flowering rose.
Woman, tell me, on to this crag
Why have you climbed up, and how?
If you are the lady of the beasts, why do you fear them
And ask for help from Amirani?'

There was something in this that Amirani did not like, but on the other hand the woman was very pleasing to him. And again she shouted from above:

'Climb up, walk along the edge,
I will let down a ladder to you,
Soon I will let you go, do not fear,
Let your dog wait by the crag.
I am a woman, Dalila,
Day and night I walk through the forest,
I have been searching for you, and finally found you,
I am the lady of the beasts, Amirani.'

The hunter went up to the top. But down below the dog Tapie was crying, saying:

'Don't go, she will deceive you:
She will bind you to the edge of the cliff,
She will not let you take a breath, she will choke you,
With her hair she will bind you to the top of the crag.
You will be crying and shouting,
Saying, "What is this that has happened to me?"'

He did not listen to him, but went up above. He went, but the ladder vanished behind him. More and more. He went up on to the top, but the woman had disappeared somewhere, and he himself was left alone on the summit of the crag. It was now that the man realised what had happened to him, but now it was too late! Left down below, what on earth could the dog do to free his master? And moreover he happened to be fastened to the crag by the hair of that woman.

The thunder roars and the lightning flashes:

That is Tapie barking,
The rain is pouring like out of a pitcher:
That is Tapie weeping.

But there was absolutely no way to help him, the crag is immovable. In the end Tapie shouted to him:

'How are you doing, Amirani,
Perhaps your nails have grown,
Is idleness destroying you
Or are you grinding your teeth from hunger?'

Amirani shouted to him, moaning:

'If only I had seen!
You can see what a trap this crag is!
Help me, my dog Tapie.'

What could this dog do? In the evening he himself climbed on to the next crag. He was very hungry. Suddenly, right out of the blue, there flew a little khazhoie bird. The hungry Tapie was just grabbing it in his teeth, but the bird said to him:

'Dog Tapie, do not eat me,
I am not guilty of anything.
Let me go, I will free your master,
Here is my feather as a token!'

'All right,' said Tapie, and he let it go. The khazhoie bird flew up to the crag and began tearing the hairs with its beak. It had only just torn away the last hair when Amirani darted off and the crag collapsed. Moreover, at the same time the woman reappeared. The hairs were stuck in the beak of the frightened khazhoie bird. The woman cursed it for Amirani's escape and said:

'May you be useless, as a bird,
And obtain your sustenance with difficulty,
May he lure falcons with you:
The one whom you have freed, and allowed to fly away from me.'
Since that time the khazhoie bird was indeed left with a little moustache. But it is also useful for the catching of falcons. When they want to catch one, they place a trap in the crags. If it does not end up in the trap, the people say that today Dalila is passing by here on her way to the mountain Sakorie, plotting how she can catch Amirani again ...

This Georgian legend was recorded by M. Mzhavia in 1971 from the words of Antimoz and Ilya Koronadze of the village of Sakvavistke in Guria, Georgia. It was published in E. B. Virsaladze, *Gruzinskie okhotnichy mif i poeziya*, Nauka, Moscow, 1976, 257–259.

36. Kvartsikheli Tebru Ivane[1] *(Georgian)*

Introduction
Twenty-seven variants of this song have been recorded, in some of which the hero leaps from the crag either at the request of his beloved or more often through being unable to put up with her taunts. Elena Virsaladze writes: 'Although in some of the variants Kursha appears as an ordinary dog, and his master as an ordinary hunter, in the majority of the variants their description and the unusual nature of their death is connected with some kind of concealed meaning, sometimes not even understood by the performers themselves' (Virsaladze 1976, 53).

---

1   Kvartsikheli is from *kva*, meaning 'stone', and *tsikhe*, meaning 'tower'. The actual 'stone tower' is not far from the village of Gebi, Racha, Georgia.

There is a certain raven, and she lays two eggs. When the time comes, a raven nestling hatches out from one of them, and from the other a puppy dog who is called Kursha.[1] When the raven sees that the puppy is not like herself, she takes it and throws it out of the nest. Whoever finds it and rears it will obtain a wonderful hunting dog from it. No kind of animal will evade this dog. One such puppy was reared by Kvartsikheli Tebru Ivane.

Ivane used to go hunting with his Kursha, and would take with him a two-week supply of bread. One day he went hunting and sat down to rest on the summit of a mountain. Suddenly the ground began trembling and all around it collapsed. But Ivane and his Kursha were left unharmed on the summit. There was no longer a path. They remained just the two of them in that deserted place. There was no help to be seen, and it was impossible either to get down or to jump off. Their supply of food came to an end, and they grew hungry. In desperation Ivane shouted to Kursha:

'Bark good and loud, O unfortunate Kursha,
Black is the fate of your master.
Either a shepherd will hear us
Or a mountain hunter.
On the mountain I am hanging, caught up by my foot,
In *kalamany* of cowskin.'

Kursha began barking very loudly. But nobody came to their aid. When the hunger had become unendurable for them, Kursha signalled to his master to kill him and relieve his own hunger. Perhaps somebody will come after that and help you. Ivane refused at first, but life is sweet. When hunger began tormenting him he began to weep, said farewell to Kursha and slaughtered him. He struck fire, broke up his bow, lit a fire, roasted the meat and ate it.

Ivane's brother had seen that he had not returned home for a long time, and he went off to look for him. Finally he found his brother stuck on top of the mountain, and shouted to him:

'Ivane, Kvartsikheli Tebru,
O you, hunter of the mountains,

---

1   The name Kursha is from Georgian *Kur-shavi*, meaning 'black-eared', and is a common name for a dog.

Your arrows and bow
Make *devs* and *goliaths* dissolve with terror!'

Ivane answered:

'I have burnt my bow and my arrows,
I lit a fire with them.
I slaughtered Kursha and ate him,
Alas, I have taken that sin on my soul!'
'You must jump then, jump
You, born on an ill-fated day,'
his brother shouted to him.

Then Ivane said farewell to life, he jumped and was smashed to pieces, and a huge piece of the crag rolled after him. They laid the dead man on a litter. They carried him home and his brother addressed the sister-in-law with the lament:

When Ivane flew from the crag,
He was like a heavenly falcon.
The crag which crashed down on him,
Even a dev would not withstand,
Through the puddle of his spilled blood
A small boat would be able to sail.

This Georgian legend was first published in the journal 'Akakis Krebuli', 1889, No. 1, 21–22 (in Georgian). This text was translated from the Russian of E. B. Virsaladze, *Gruzinskie okhotnichy mif i poeziya*, Nauka, Moscow, 1976, 267–268.

37. Azhveypsh[1] *(Abkhaz)*

Introduction

E. B. Virsaladze writes about the motif of the Master of the Beasts 'feeding on the meat of the beasts, and after the meal they collect the bones into the skin of the beasts they have killed, and with a blow of a stick or a whip they bring it alive again. The hunters obtain, in the form of game, precisely those that have already been eaten once by the deities of the beasts. If, while they are eating, some bone of the animal goes missing, they replace it with wood.' And later: 'Based on such ideas, it is forbidden to throw away the bones of the beasts killed, nor to burn them or give them to the dogs to gnaw.' (Virsaladze 1976, 41).

Azhveypsh – or, as he is still called, Azhveypshaa – is the lord of the forests and mountains, the beasts and the birds; he is the patron of the hunt. Azhveypsh has a family: a married son by the name of Iuan, and an eternally youthful beautiful daughter. He also has a faithful servant, the swift-footed Shvakvaz.

Azhveypsh, although he is a real grey-beard, is nevertheless still a sturdy old man. All the beasts make up his flock; he pastures it like a good shepherd. He milks the females and distributes game amongst the hunters. To them are apportioned only those animals that Azhveypsh has eaten, but the remaining beasts of Azhveypsh's flock are invisible to hunters and therefore inaccessible. Only the game animals that have been eaten and resurrected by Azhveypsh can catch the eye of hunters, so that they can be killed by them.

Azhveypsh has his herdsmen. These are the white beasts; they herd the other animals. Hunters do not kill white beasts because they know that Azhveypsh will punish them for it. He will not give them any more game.

One day it happened that one hunter unintentionally fired at a white kid, and suddenly, from somewhere, there sounded the voice of a weeping girl: 'Mama, Mama, my little goat has been killed!' It was the voice of Azhveypsh's daughter. From that time that hunter knew no success. However much he wandered through the mountains and forests, no game at all caught his eye. That is how Azhveypsh punished!

---

[1]   Azhveypsh was the Abkhaz lord of the forests, protector of the beasts and birds and protector of the hunt.

With time, the master of the animals and the patron of the hunt became decrepit and deaf, and so he had to be spoken to loudly. By the instructions of Azhveypsh, the game is distributed amongst the hunters by his servant Shvakvaz. He also, like his lord, became old, and became a bit hard of hearing. Azhveypsh was just and kind. He wanted to share the game equally amongst all the hunters. He used to say, 'Give to the one that we have not given to!' But Shvakvaz thought he heard: 'Give to the one that we have given to!' So it happens that Shvakvaz does not give game to the one whom he should. Because of this, some hunters are always successful, but others can get nothing.

The only person for whom it turned out well to see Azhveypsh was the heroic hunter Akun-Ipa Khatazhukva. It happened like this.

One day, Akun-Ipa Khatazhukva set off hunting with some companions. On the way, he became separated from them and wandered off into a dense forest thicket. Suddenly a deer ran into him. The hunter fired at him and hit him in the side; he did not kill him but only wounded him. The deer hid in the thicket. Akun-Ipa Khatazhukva followed his trail. For a long time he tracked the wounded deer, and towards evening he approached a clearing on which he saw a big herd of deer, *turs* and chamois. A good-looking grey old man in a conical felt cap was milking one of the deer. The old man noticed the hunter and hailed him, 'Welcome! Go into my house. Just now I cannot leave the herd, otherwise they will disperse.' The hunter realised that this was Azhveypsh himself. The house was not big, but it was built of copper. Akun-Ipa Khatazhukva went into it.

Having milked the herd, Azkveypsh and Shvakvaz carried into the *asura* a large copper pot of milk. 'Hunter, you are tired and hungry,' said the master. 'Sit down and eat.' Azhveypsh gave his guest *akhartsvy*. Akun-Ipa Khatazhukva ate three spoonfuls and felt satisfied. Then Azhveypsh chose and cut up that very deer from his herd, which the hunter had shot at. They boiled the meat. The host gave his guest a shoulder blade. Khatazhukva took out his knife, cut off from the shoulder blade three slices of meat and ate them, but then he secretly inserted his knife between the meat and the bone of the shoulder blade.

After they had eaten, Azhveypsh gathered up the bones of the deer and the rest of the meat, laid them together in the skin and struck them with a whip. In the twinkling of an eye, the deer came to life: it jumped up and joined the herd.

Akun-Ipa spent the night in the house of Azhveypsh, and in the morning, after eating three spoonfuls of *akhartsvy* and feeling fully satisfied, he thanked the host for his hospitality and set out on his way. In the forest he met a deer and killed it. Soon Akun-Ipa Khatazhukva found his companions. They were waiting for him in a hunting glade. They brought the deer, dressed it and boiled the meat. For each one there was a large piece. Akun-Ipa took a shoulder for himself. He started to cut the meat from it, and suddenly discovered his knife. His companions were very surprised: how did Akun-Ipa's knife end up in the body of the deer? Then the fearless hunter related how he had been a guest of Azhveypsh and how he had inserted his knife between the meat and the bone of the deer's shoulder.

'So you see,' said Akun-Ipa in conclusion, 'our great magnificent Prince Azhveypsh sends us only those animals that he has himself cut up, eaten with his family or with guests, and then brought back to life for us simple mortals!'

ཨ

No narration and recording details are available for this Abkhaz legend, which was published in Kh. S. Bgazhba, *Abkhazskie skazki*, Alashara, Sukhumi, 1985, 16–18.

38. Azhveypsh's Daughter *(Abkhaz)*

The Lord of the Beasts and the Birds, the patron of the hunt and the forest, the old man Azhveypsh, has eternally young daughters. Their bodies are white like fresh milk, and their golden curls hang down to their ankles. They often make the acquaintance of unmarried hunters and become their lovers. The daughters of Azhveypsh generously endow their favoured ones with game.

It happened that the eldest daughter of Azhveypsh fell in love with a married hunter. They used to meet on flowery mountain meadows or in gorges. It used to happen that she did not let the hunter go, and he would spend the night with her in the forest. So that his wife would not have any suspicion, on such occasions he would bring home an especially large amount of game.

But one day Azhveypsh's daughter led her lover to the very kitchen garden, which adjoined the forest, and spent the night with him on the little balcony of the corn storehouse. The hunter's wife, having got up early in the morning, went into the kitchen garden and saw that side by side with her husband was sleeping a forest beauty. Her golden curls hung over to the very ground, and a gentle breeze was bathing the long silky locks in the dust.

Many different feelings blazed up in the heart of the offended woman, but generosity overcame them. She lifted up the golden hair of her rival, tied it up with her headscarf and carefully laid it on the bosom of Azhveypsh's daughter. Then she went away noiselessly.

Soon the forest beauty woke up and guessed whose kerchief had fastened her hair. She parted forever with her hunter and forbade her sisters ever to meet with married people.

No narration and recording details are available for this Abkhaz legend, which was published in Kh. S. Bgazhba, *Abkhazskie skazki*, Alashara, Sukhumi, 1985, 26–27.

39. The Young Man and the Snow Leopard *(Georgian)*

The beardless young man said,
  'I have toured the summits of the crags,
While hunting, I walked all over
The little mountain paths,
I came upon, on the summit of a crag
A herd of *jikhvis*.
I fired a shot from my gun at an old *jikhvi*,
His horns crashed down to the bottom of the gorge.
I came across a snow leopard lying down,
The time was midnight,
The snow leopard flew at me,
His eyes were full of God's rage.'[1]

---

1   This line suggests that the snow leopard's attack might have been a punishment by the Master of the Beasts for the killing of the *jikhvi* (Caucasian mountain ibex).

The snow leopard and the young man grappled,
Then the earth trembled.
They made the crags tumble down,
They broke the forest branches.
There was no time left for the young man
To struggle and strain,
He defended himself with his shield, but it did not shield him,
The mountain snow leopard was fast.
Like pincers, he tore up the hem
Of his iron chain-mail shirt.
At this point the young man finally grasped the handle of his sword,
Only after that did he strike with the *pranguli*,
The time came for him to collapse to the ground ...
The snow leopard hung down on the crag,
Staining the sand with his blood,
The young man himself lay down on the crag, breathing his last.
The blood, running down him
Was staining the sand a red colour ...
Who will bring themselves to tell his mother?
The seer fortune tellers are sitting by her ...
After all, our hunters do not use up
Their arrows for nothing.
The mother walked and wept, her eyes full of tears.
'My son met a snow leopard on his path,
An evil, accursed one.
For my son, with his sword in his hand, and for the snow leopard fighting
    with claws,
A sunny day has grown dark!
Neither was the snow leopard weak
Nor was my son a coward,
They have killed one another,
They did not cover themselves with shame.'

She was weeping and bandaging up the wounds
Inflicted by the snow leopard's claws.
'My son, you have not died, you are sleeping,
Weary with your heavy labour.
The hem of your chain-mail shirt,

Accursed thing, how it has been reduced to rags!
But you too turned out to be well matched to him,
Your sword has become worn out in the battle,
Nor did the snow leopard give you time,
Nor did you start waiting for him,
Nor did you manage to cover yourself
With the shield that was in your hands,
Nor did he cover up his paws –
His bones were hacked with your sword.
I will weep for you no more,
For such people as you, one does not weep.
Goodbye! The cross be above you.
So here is the door of the grave.
At least I brought up one son –
A fighter of snow leopards ...'

Now the snow leopard, and now her son
Appeared to the mother in her dream,
Now the snow leopard was stripping the chain-mail shirt from her son
    above his waist,
Now her son in his turn
Knocked the snow leopard from his feet,
These were the kind of dreams she was having.

She would wake up weeping.
Then she was thinking: without a mother
Not a single child would grow up, after all,
Maybe the snow leopard's mother
Is weeping more bitterly than I.
I will go, I will come to her,
And sympathise with her in her grief,
And she will tell me about her son,
And I will tell her about my own.
And I expect she is grieving
About the one mercilessly killed by the sword.'

ৰৈ

This Georgian legend was self-recorded by Vakhtang Razikashvili of the village of Chargali in Pshavi, Georgia. It was published in E. B. Virsaladze, *Gruzinskie okhotnichy mif i poeziya*, Nauka, Moscow, 1976, 306–308.

40. The Balkh Meadow *(Georgian)*

The mountain Chitkharo, which separates Svaneti from Racha, is full of *jikhvis*. Often the people from both Svaneti and Racha used to go there hunting, and they made common use of the pastures on this mountain. They say that on this mountain there are pastures on to which man's foot has never stepped; a certain meadow there is called the Balkh, such that the grass grows there winter and summer. The grass grows there up to a man's waist. The flocks of *jikhvis* on that meadow are innumerable. The only entrance to it is narrow and inaccessible. The foot of man has not trod there. There was, so they say, a certain renowned hunter. One day, quite accidentally, he landed up at the entrance to the Balkh Meadow. But then, as it happened, the *jikhvis* that graze there sensed the approach of the man by his scent, and with a hissing the whole flock rushed to the entrance, in order to throw the uninvited guest off into the abyss. Then they darted at the man, but the hunter managed to hide behind a crag and miraculously survived. They say there is a great variety of grasses on the Balkh Meadow.

This Georgian legend was recorded by O. Oniani in 1968 from the words of E. K. Chelidze of the village of Sasa in the Lentekhi Region, Lower Svaneti. It was published in E. B. Virsaladze, *Gruzinskie okhotnichy mif i poeziya*, Nauka, Moscow, 1976, 255–256.

VII

Legends About Shepherds, Including Cyclops Legends

Besides the hunting of wild animals discussed in the previous chapter, the rearing of sheep is another important source of food, and many of the mountain pastures are suitable for grazing sheep but not for agriculture.

This chapter contains two types of legends about shepherds: those without magic elements, and the Cyclops stories that often contain magic elements. The question might arise: why are Cyclops legends included in a chapter on shepherds? The answer is that when the Cyclops legends were studied and their motifs were listed, the cannibal giant was a shepherd in almost all of them. Perhaps the narrators were themselves shepherds. During long days and nights spent in the mountains with their sheep, mutual entertainment became very important for them, and the telling of tales and the playing of music were the most obvious means of amusement. Or perhaps the concept of the dangerous shepherd accords with the mother's warning in the first legend, 'Black-eyed Ashura', that:

'In the mountains the shepherds are wild,
And the dogs are drunk with whey,
Be careful with them.'

Or that of the similar warning of the mother to her daughter in the second legend, 'Udaman Alil':

'But do not go, my dear, into the high mountains.
There the dogs are drunk with whey.
And the shepherds behave wildly from the meat they eat.'

It is interesting how the playing of music and the interpretation of its message figures in several of these legends, a theme that also accords with the mountain environment of the shepherds, in which the conveying of messages to other distant shepherds is often important. In 'Black-eyed Ashura' the heroine's brother makes a musical instrument, a *chagana* from his sister's bones and hair, which then speaks to him of what has happened to her. In 'Udaman Alil' Udaman's mother-in-law hears the music of his distant pipe and then her daughter interprets the message that the music conveys. In 'Koloy Kant' the hero plays music on his home-made *zurna*, or shepherd's pipe, which conveys to his distant family the message that he is in trouble. The conveying of messages by music is a recurring theme in Caucasian folklore, and moreover it is known that the shepherds in real life do actually convey messages to friends or family in distant mountain pastures in this way (Khajieva 2003). The third legend, 'Seska Solsa and the Wolf', gives an impression of the ambivalent attitude of shepherds to wolves: both of them share the same environment, and although the wolves devour some of the sheep, the shepherds nevertheless respect and to some extent admire the wolves. There is also a belief that wolves help maintain the health of the flock by taking the weak or sick animals (Isayev 1988, 62).

41. Black-eyed Ashura *(Lak)*

Introduction

This song is current in the southern *auls* of the Kuli region of Daghestan. The motif of the creation of a musical instrument from bones and hair is also encountered among other peoples of the world.

Black-eyed Ashura
Came home and spoke:
'The girls of my generation
Have all gone hunting.
The young widows
Have already gone off hunting.'
'Don't go, my beloved daughter,
They are not going hunting,
They are going to ruin you.
The widows are cunning, it is well known to all.

Rest content, daughter.'
For a long time her mother tried to persuade her.
But the daughter did not listen.
'If you go all the same,
My beloved daughter Ashura,
Let it be easy for your feet,
Put on your Cherkess *chuvyaks*.
Let it be comfortable for your body,
Put on your silk clothes.
Let it be cool for your head,
Throw over, daughter, your tulle scarf embroidered with gold.
In the mountains the shepherds are wild,
And the dogs are drunk with whey,
Be careful with them.'
So we went on and on and reached
The tops of the high mountains.
The shepherds on the high mountains
Started shouting to us:
'Girls, beauties,
Come, we will treat you.
We will slaughter a ewe that has remained barren
And put on the pot with fresh meat.
We will milk a milking ewe,
We will make a cask of cheese.'
They slaughtered a barren ewe
And threw the meat into the pot,
After milking a ewe,
They made a barrel of cheese,
They were very hospitable,
The shepherds in the mountains ...
There was no end to the laughter and jokes,
They played much.
Now they gave Suleyman
A pebble the size of a pea.
He threw it at the girls,
It landed in Ashura's kerchief.[1]

---

1   Kh. Khalilov considers this to be the echo of the custom of throwing a pebble to select a lover.

The *aul*'s girls left,
Leaving Ashura with the shepherds.
With his right hand the young man
Began pulling the girl by her kerchief.
Out of the *burka* that was on him
They made a soft bed.
From the staff that he was holding in his hands
They made a soft pillow.
From her gold-embroidered kerchief
They made a silken blanket ...
When the girls were hidden behind one of the hills,
Black-eyed Ashura
Easily caught them up.
'How light you are in your step!
Why do you proudly throw up your head?
Why have you become proud,
Black-eyed Ashura?
After all, now you have
Been with your own brother!
The master of your body was
Your own brother, Ashura!'
Ashura turned around
And went back into the mountains,
Selecting a high crag,
Ashura threw herself down.
The narrow valley was filled
With Ashura's sweet body.[1]
The big crags were covered
With her silken clothes.
The gold-embroidered tulle kerchief
Was ripped against the crag ...
The black ravens started calling.
Suleyman went to the crag,
He saw the ravens pecking
The body of the beauty, Ashura.

---

1   This is a common epithet in lyrical songs, used both for men and women. Here it emphasises
     the whiteness of her body.

From her bones he made a *chagana*,[1]
He made the strings from her hair.
Shedding bloody tears,
He started playing on it.
The shepherd was not able
Even to sing two words,
Before a crying and a begging voice
Sounded from the *chagana*.
'I ask you, my brother,
Fulfil my one request.
It will be both shameful before God
And a disgrace if anybody should hear about us.
I shared a bed with you
And my soul is now in torment.
Do not play on the *chagana*,
Do not make me weep.'
When he was convinced
That Black-eyed Ashura was his sister
Who had shared his bed with him,
He took his *kinzhal* the width of a palm
And thrust it into his belly.
Thus they finished with themselves:
Black-eyed Ashura
And the shepherd in the mountains.

This Lak song was recorded by Kh. Khalilov in 1957 in the settlement of Khosrekh of the Kuli region of Daghestan from the words of Abacharayevy Gafizat, aged sixty. It was published in Kh. Khalilov, *Lakskie epicheskie pesni*, Dagestan filial AN SSSR, Makhachkala, 1969, 193–197.

---

1   A *chagana* is an antique mountain violin. It has a gentle sound. When the *chagana* is being played, the Laks say, 'The chagana is weeping.'

42. Udaman Alil *(Lak)*

Introduction

In the mid-twentieth century the epic songs were most widely diffused among the shepherds. Being far from home in the summer and winter pastures, the shepherds shorten the long evenings and cloudy days by listening to the ancient songs, the songs of the grandfathers, as the folk call them.

'Alil is playing on his pipe at the spring,
Daughter, on the white balcony, can you hear?
Do you understand what the pipe is singing about?'
'Yes, I know what the pipe is singing about.
"I am hungry," it says, "Bring me bread,
Thirst torments me, bring me a pitcher of water."
My old mother, let me go to him with bread.
I will take him water and quench his thirst.'
'I will let you go with bread to a hungry man,
I will send you with water to a thirsty man.
If you come back unharmed, like you are now.
But do not go, my dear, into the high mountains.
There the dogs are drunk on whey.
And the shepherds behave wildly from the meat they eat.'
'What will those shepherds do to me,
After all my Udaman Alil is with them in the mountains?!'
The mother spoke to her, but the daughter did not take heed,
So as to look shapely, she put on silk,
She went down into the larder, picked out some gifts.
And Udaman Alil's beloved started off,
Ploughing up the road with the shoes on her feet,
Sweeping a trail with the ends of her kerchief.
Towards evening I reached the mountain.
At the cold spring, from where the shepherds take water,
I sat down to have a rest.
A certain shepherd came out from behind a crag
With a wooden vessel in his hands.
'*Salamum alaykum*, my young beauty!'

'*Va alaykum salam*, ey, herder of sheep!'
'Who have you come to see, young beauty,
In these high mountains that do not see beautiful girls?'
'I have come to see Udaman Alil.'
The herder of sheep began demanding for himself
The sweet sugar brought for Alil.
The herder of sheep began demanding for himself
The pitcher of sweet drink brought for Alil.
'By God, I will not give you the sweet sugar
Until Udaman Alil is close by!
By God, I will not give you the pitcher of sweet drink
Until I see Udaman Alil with my own eyes!'
Turning around, the herder of sheep went away,
Without even wetting his wooden vessel.
Time passed ... And when some time had passed,
Udaman Alil came to the shepherds' camp.
He asked where the cauldron was and why there was no water.
'How can I put on the cauldron, or pour out water,
If a demon is sitting at the spring?'
'Can that be true, ey, young shepherd?'
'It's the truth, by God, Udaman Alil.'
After hanging his Stambul pistol at his side,
Udaman Alil turned and went away.
And he went to that spring.
At the spring he spotted a silhouette in red.
'If you are a human, speak with me,
But if you are a demon, I will shoot.'
The silhouette bent down and straightened once more,[1]
But did not start speaking with me, may its house burn down.
I took the Stambul pistol from my side
And fired a bullet of blue lead.
As soon as the bullet had reached its target,
The red silhouette fell with a cry.
What could it be, I went to have a look.
In a puddle of blood I found my young lady love.
'May your house burn down, Udaman Alil.

---

1   A characteristic of Muslim prayers.

After all, I was praying, you should have waited.
By God, thank you, Udaman Alil,
You have quietened my restless heart.
By God, thank you, Udaman Alil,
My loving eyes have now closed.
My ivory legs that were coming to you
Are now broken, Udaman Alil.
My brown eyes, which used to follow you,
Have now been extinguished, Udaman Alil.
I ask you, if God is dear to you, Udaman Alil,
Lift me out of the bloody puddle.
I also ask you, if God is dear to you, Udaman Alil,
I am dying, you must recite a prayer over me.'
I thrust pieces of *kurdyuk*[1] into the wound,
I bound up the wounds with the sash that was around my waist.
And from there I returned to the sheep camp.
I cut off the heads of all seven shepherds that used to be with me,
And threw them towards the cabin.
The white sheep, which were on the pasture in the mountains,
I scattered through the mountains with shouts of 'Tstsus-Kya'.[2]
All seven hundred sheep left by my father
I bequeathed to the simple people of the mountains.
You thoroughbred dogs that were guarding them,
Now howl on the tops of the mountains!
From there I returned to that spring.
I found my young beauty barely alive.
'Do not reproach me, beautiful mountain rose,
While you are giving up your life, I will give mine first.'
I placed the handle of the tempered *kinzhal* bought for a sheep
On the ground with the blade pointed to my belly.
I pronounced a prayer and fell on the *kinzhal*.
The *kinzhal* came out of my back a whole palm width.
With the Stambul pistol that would shoot straight,
I shot myself straight in the heart.
'Let me die while you are still alive.'

---

1   The mountain men stuff pieces of *kurdyuk* (tail fat) or felt into a wound, especially a bullet
     wound.
2   This was a typical cry when driving sheep.

The powder smoke came out of my back.
The girl and the youth passed away together.

This song was recorded by Kh. Khalilov in 1956 from the words of S. Amirova of the settlement of Kuma and from the words of Alil of Karashi, aged forty. In 1962 a variant of this song with slight changes was recorded from the words of Ibrahimov Musa, aged seventy-two, from the settlement of Khanar. Published in Kh. Khalilov, *Lakskie epicheskie pesni*, Dagestan filial AN SSSR, Makhachkala, 1969, 210–213.

43. Seska Solsa and the Wolf *(Ingush)*

Formerly Seska Solsa used to pasture his father's sheep. One day a wolf came to him. 'I am old. Give me one sheep,' said the wolf. 'If weakness had not overcome me, I would not think of asking. If you give me one sheep, I will do you three good deeds.'

'I cannot give you one sheep without asking father,' said Seska Solsa.

'Go and ask your father, and meanwhile I will watch over your sheep,' said the wolf.

'How can I trust you and leave my sheep, wolf?'

'May I be the father of a family in which the father is neither obeyed nor honoured, if I devour your sheep,' swore the wolf.[1]

Seska Solsa set off home and related to his father all that the wolf had said, and he conveyed the wolf's oath. Then his father said, 'Quickly go back again, and before the wolf pronounces that vow as a curse, give him all the sheep.'

The wolf, however, took only one sheep.

This Ingush text was recorded by I. Dakhkil'gov in 1964 from the words of Fatima Adalovna Khanieva, aged fifty-seven. It was published in U. B. Dalgat, *Geroichesky epos chechentsev i ingushey*, Nauka, Moscow, 1972, 359.

---

1   This oath has the power to inspire great fear among the Ingush, even to this day.

CYCLOPS LEGENDS

In Caucasus folklore there is a whole *constellation* of legends and tales that can be classified as being of the Cyclops type. A constellation of stars consists of a loose grouping of stars, of which some are more prominent, others are less so; but it does not contain a supreme central star, as in a planetary system. There is the temptation to define the 'Cyclops' constellation of legends as if it were a planetary system that could be grouped around the Homeric tale. However, the Homeric tale itself was probably also part of a contemporary constellation of legends, of which all have been lost except the one that Homer recorded. There is no evidence that the Homeric tale was the unique central 'sun' within a planetary type of legendary system: at the time of its recording it was probably just one version among many.

However, it is still convenient to take one legend as a reference and discuss the other legends relative to this reference legend. The obvious choice of the reference legend is the earliest recorded version, namely the one that Homer recorded in the Odyssey. But it is important that the reader bears in mind that the reference legend has been selected artificially, so that those legends or variants that omit certain motifs contained in the reference legend should not be omitted from the Cyclops constellation merely for that reason.

Twenty-five versions or variants of the legend from the Caucasus were identified as fitting this definition. However, there were three variants of another interesting legend in which some of the usual Cyclops motifs were inverted, and this legend has also been included.

All of the legends, including the chosen reference one recorded by Homer, were analysed for their motifs. The Homeric legend revealed the eighteen motifs listed below and in Table 1. Although the eighteen listed motifs might be considered as a definitive list, other variants that were contemporary with Homer but now have been lost may have included other motifs but lacked some of these. As the list and the table show, some of the Caucasus legends contain additional motifs that are not in the selected Homeric reference version.

Homer's Cyclops legend contains the following eighteen motifs:

1. Giant shepherd
2. Giant lives in cave
3. Giant's dwelling blocked by large stone that only the giant can move

4. Hero and his men enter dwelling (as thieves)
5. Giant kills some of hero's men
6. Giant turns out to be cannibal
7. Giant goes to sleep
8. Giant has one eye
9. Giant is blinded (with hot stake)
10. Hero and his men are unable to escape unless giant opens exit
11. Hero and survivors escape with flock next morning
12. Hero says his name is 'nobody'
13. Giant's neighbours disperse after giant blames 'nobody'
14. Hero and his men steal giant's animals
15. Hero taunts giant shepherd
16. Giant throws huge rock at hero
17. Giant curses hero and his men
18. Hero and his men sail away

Additional motifs were found in some of the other versions from the Caucasus:

19. Giant tries trick (ring that crushes or makes noise)
20. Giant's herd led by special goat, which sometimes speaks
21. Hero wrestles with giant and beats him
22. Hero escapes simply by running quickly
23. Hero is injured by giant's flung rock
24. Giant is weakened by seduction (Enkidu motif)[1]
25. Warning message sent by music
26 Heroes pose insoluble question, giants fight, heroes escape during confusion

Table 1 lists these motifs and shows which versions of the chosen legends contain which motifs. The authors, reference numbers and titles of the legends are listed in Table 2. These are the legends that have been defined as 'Cyclops' legends according to the definition given above.

---

1   In the Gilgamesh epic, Enkidu loses his strength after being seduced.

Table 1. Motifs included in the reference legend of Homer (*); and the 'Cyclops' legends (a to z) that are listed in Table 2.

Table entries:
x – motif present;
? – motif only indirectly present.

	Motifs	*	a	b	c	d	e	f	g	h
1	Giant shepherd	x	x	x	x	x	x			x
2	Giant lives in cave	x	x	x		x	x	x	x	x
3	Huge stone blocks exit	x	x	x		x	x	x	x	
4	Hero enters dwelling (as thief?)	x	x	x		x	x	x	x	
5	Giant kills hero's companions	x	x	x	x					
6	Giant is cannibal	x	x	x		x		x	x	x
7	Giant goes to sleep	x	x	x		x	x			
8	Giant has one eye	x	x			x	x	x	x	
9	Giant is blinded (hot stake)	x	x	x		x	x		x	
10	Hero needs exit to be opened	x	x	x		x	x		x	x
11	Hero escapes in animal disguise	x	x	x		x	x			
12	Hero says name is 'nobody'	x								
13	Giant blames nobody, friends disperse	x								
14	Hero steals giant's animals	x				x				
15	Hero taunts giant shepherd	x				x	x			
16	Giant throws huge rock at hero	x	x	x						
17	Giant curses hero and his men	x								
18	Hero and his men sail away	x		x						
19	Giant tries trick (magic ring)					x	x			
20	Special goat leads giant's flock					x				
21	Hero beats giant in wrestling									
22	Hero escapes by just running away									
23	Hero is injured by rock flung by giant									
24	Enkidu motif: girl seduces giant									
25	Giant's warning sent by music									
26	Heroes pose insoluble question, escape								x	

Note that the absence of the 'giant shepherd' motif does not necessarily mean that the giants were not shepherds; only that their occupation was not specified.

i	j	k	l	m	n	o	p	q	r	s	t	u	v	w	x	y	z
				x	x	x	x	x	x	x	x	x	x	x	x	x	x
x			x	x	x		x			?		x	x	x	x	x	x
x			x		x					?				x		x	x
	x		x	x	x				x	x				x	x	x	
				x	x	x	x	x	x	x	x		x		x		
x	x	x	x	x	x		x		x	x	x	x	x		x	x	x
				x	x				x	x	x	x	x	x			x
				x			x		x	x	x				x	x	x
							x		x	x	x				x	x	x
x	x	?								x	x	x				x	x
				?			x			x	x	x			x	x	x
		?								x		x	x				x
										x		x	x	x			x
					x		x			x		x	x				
											x			x			
						x					x		x				x
		x															
			x					x									
					x	x	x	x				x					
													x				
													x				
x	x	x	x														

Table 2. Caucasus versions and variants of the Cyclops legend.

Code	Ethnic group	Author	Title	Note
a	Abaza	Colarusso	Sosruquo Brought Fire to his Troops	
b	Abkhaz	Bgazhba	Khajaja, the Son of Khaji Smyel	
c	Abkhaz	Bgazhba	Sasrykva and the Ploughman	
d	Balkar	Khajieva	Yoryuzmek and the One-eyed Emegen	
e	Balkar	Khajieva	Yoryuzmek and the One-eyed Emegen, the Goatherd	
f	Balkar	Khajieva	Debet's Sons and the Emegen Woman's Daughters	
g	Balkar	Khajieva	Three Narts and Three Emegens	
h	Balkar	Khajieva	Yoryuzmek and Sosuruk	*
i	Balkar	Khajieva	Sosuruk and Sibilchi	
j	Balkar	Khajieva	The Narts and the Giants	1
k	Balkar	Khajieva	The Emegens	1
l	Balkar	Khajieva	Who is Stronger?	1
m	Chechen	Dalgat	The Travelling of a Nart	
n	Chechen	Dalgat	Timar with the Scorched Side	
o	Chechen	Dalgat	The Legend about the Giant Govda	2
p	Chechen	Dalgat	Tinin Vyusu and Erzhi Khozha	
q	Chechen	Dalgat	Strong Solsa	
r	Chechen	Dalgat	The Tale about the Hunter and the Nart	
s	Chechen	Dalgat	Lyal-Sulta	
t	Georgian	Virsaladze	The Story of One-eye	*
u	Ingush	Dalgat	The Zarvash, or the Seven-headed Minotaur	
v	Ingush	Dalgat	Stories about Giants (*vampolozh*)	*
w	Ingush	Dalgat	Koloy Kant	*
x	Ingush	Malsagov	Parcho	*
y	Karachay	Khajieva	Sibilchi	
z	Ossete	Menzies	Urýsmäg and the One-eyed Giant	

Notes
1. It is not known whether this variant was collected in Balkaria or Karachaya, at the time the two groups were united, with one language.
2. It is not known whether this variant was collected from an Ingush or a Chechen – both speaking a similar language.
* The full texts of these legends are given below.

There are several versions of Cyclops legends that contain the theme of a boastful strong man who sets out into the world to find a man who is stronger than himself. Typically he finds stronger men, from whom he is obliged to flee, and during his flight he finds an even stronger one, often a ploughman. The hero takes refuge in this man's mouth, usually in the gap in his teeth, which had been caused by the rock that the giant had thrown at him and that had knocked out his molar tooth. This includes legends c, o and q (in Table 2), and the text of a Balkar example given here as 'Stories about Giants'. It is interesting to note that in some of these legends it is a ploughman (i.e., an agriculturalist) who had a narrow escape from the giant shepherd (a livestock breeder), suggesting a possible animosity between the two types of land-users.

There is another group in which there are several heroes trapped by a number of cannibal giants. At the crucial moment, before the first hero is about to be slaughtered, one of them poses an insoluble question to the giants (Motif 26 in Table 1). In the example given below, 'Yoryuzmek and Sosuruk', the question concerns the relative age of the blacksmith's anvil, his hammer and his tongs. More commonly the question starts with a long rambling tale about an extraordinarily large ox, eagle, goat, shepherd, fox, old woman and baby. Each figure appears to be as big or bigger than the previous one, so that by the end the listener is totally confused. The heroes then pose the question of which is bigger. This story is included in legends h, i, j, k and l of Table 2.

TEXTS OF CYCLOPS LEGENDS

44. Yoryuzmek and Sosuruk *(Balkar)*

One day, during a conversation between Yoryuzmek and Sosuruk about bravery and cowardice, Yoryuzmek said to Sosuruk, 'How can a man be afraid of anything in this world? I am very surprised at that. I am interested, what is it – fear?'

These words became deeply imprinted on Sosuruk's mind, but he did not say anything. When some time had passed, Sosuruk suggested to him: 'Yoryuzmek, let us set out on a *zhortuuul*.'

They took with them six more Narts, and the eight set off in the direction of the setting sun. After riding through many gorges and dried-up river-beds, they reached a certain river.

When Yoryuzmek jumped off his horse, went down to the water and sniffed it, he sensed the smell of *emegen* flesh. Dipping his finger into the water, he tasted it. The drop from his finger set his teeth on edge, and his tongue went yellow. Yoryuzmek informed his fellow travellers about the smell and the effect of the water. And then Sosuruk said, 'Ey, Yoryuzmek, after all the *emegens* are living in the upper reaches of the river. They always pollute the water in the river. They urinate in the river so that the Narts cannot drink from it, but if they did actually drink it they would become ill. Neither we nor our horses must drink this water. If our horses drink it they will go blind, and if we ourselves drink it, we will get sick with leprosy. The *emegens* do not only eat the meat of animals and people. They also eat poisonous snakes and frogs. If they do not add *chemeritsa*[1] to their food, then for them that food is not real food. We cannot drive the horses into the river to swim across to the other side. We will continue our journey along this bank. I know where the caves are, where the *emegens* live. We will cross the river after riding upstream from these caves.'

After a long journey, towards evening they reached a certain dark cave in which *emegens* were living. Nine *emegens* were there. 'Good day, wise, quick-witted and thrifty *emegens*,' Sosuruk greeted them.

'Thank you and welcome, crafty sons of men!' they replied.

That night the *emegens* fed the Narts with some kind of tainted meat. In the morning, after blocking up the entrance to the cave with an enormous rock so that the Narts could not go outside, they dispersed through the forest. In the evening they returned to the cave and each brought a slain wild beast. The eldest of the *emegens* addressed the Narts thus: 'Well, all right, sons of men, today you are obliged to treat us to food. According to our customs, one night we are obliged to treat you, and the next night you treat us,' he declared.

And then the Narts were obliged to slaughter one of their horses.

One night the *emegens* did the entertaining, and the next night the Narts. So it continued until the Narts only had one skewbald horse left. This skewbald horse was Yoryuzmek's horse. This horse was well known to all the land

---

1   *Chemeritsa* is a poisonous herb, Veratrum, a plant of the lily family, containing the potent alkaloid veratrine.

of the Narts as steel-hoofed, with iron jaws and ears the length of one *karysh*.[1] He was the wind-like Genzhetay, possessing human intelligence. He was the apple of Yoryuzmek's eye.

Sosuruk told Yoryuzmek, 'Why not slaughter your skewbald horse now, if we have no other horses?'

He objected: 'No, it would be better to slaughter me than him.'

The *emegens*, hearing that, said, 'Good, then we will slaughter you. We love human flesh more than horseflesh. It is already a month since we ate human flesh.'

They laid Yoryuzmek on a large flat stone and tied him up. One of the *emegens* took a bright red copper knife three *lokots* in length,[2] another took a grindstone, and they began sharpening the knife.

Sosuruk was sitting, deeply thoughtful. Then he announced to the *emegens* as follows: 'Ey, wise and thrifty fellows, don't be hasty, the night is long, we will have time both to eat and to drink. We are the messengers of the Nart land, you know. They sent us to you for a purpose. You do not ask us, "Why have you come riding to us?" – and we also have not told you why we are at your place.'

'Well, all right then, tell us, why did they send you to us?' said the *emegens*, looking at Sosuruk.

'In the land of the Narts,' began Sosuruk, 'an argument has broken out about which was made first, the anvil, the hammer or the tongs. Because of this, enmity has arisen among the Narts. The arguments and the enmity do not cease. Now, if you slaughter Yoryuzmek, then who will convey to the Narts your correct answer; after all, among us he is the most intelligent and clear-spoken.'

When Sosuruk had finished speaking, the *emegens*, clapping their hands and stamping their feet, burst out with a wild thunderous laugh, shaking the crags and the mountains. The eldest *emegen* said, 'How is it that these idiots don't know that the tongs are older?'

'Our *tamada*, you are wrong,' objected a second *emegen*, 'the hammer is older.'

Another *emegen* said, 'Are you joking, or are you saying all this from your heart? Why don't you understand that the oldest among those is the anvil?'

Their argument developed into a fight.

---

1   A *karysh* is a measure of length equal to the distance between the outstretched thumb and little finger.

2   A *lokot* is a measure of length equal to one cubit, or the length of the forearm, about 50 cm.

During the fight they brushed against and knocked down the rock covering the entrance to the cave. Tearing up by the roots the plane trees growing around the cave, they began using them to beat each other up and, continuing to fight, they descended into the gorge.

In the cave there was left only one very old *emegen* with suppurating eyes. The Narts harnessed him into the *emegens'* huge iron cart, sat in it and rode off to the land of the Narts.

When they had come back home, Sosuruk asked Yoryuzmek, 'Well, Yoryuzmek, have you now understood what fear is?'

'How could one not understand, I have experienced it myself,' replied Yoryuzmek.

'Well, in that case, in future do not say, "I don't know what terror is, there is nobody stronger than me, and nobody can beat me,"' said Sosuruk.

Recorded by S. O. Shakhmurzayev from the words of Balkar narrator Said Kudayev in 1959, village of Upper Chegem. It was published in T. M. Khajieva & R. A-K. Ortabayeva, *Narty*, Nauka, Moscow, 1994, 493–495.

45. The Story of One-eye *(Georgian)*

Introduction
Traditions about the Cyclops in Georgian folklore are examined in detail in the work of M. Chikovani, 'Questions of Greek and Georgian Mythology' (Tbilisi 1971), where he points out the existence of motif coincidences in the myths of Polyphemus compared with the Georgian tale, and also in the epos of Amirani.

Once, a certain traveller between Redut-Kale and Anaklia was taken unawares by a rainy dark night.[1] All around was a thick forest, and no kind of habitation for several *versts*. He became surrounded by a pack of wolves, who threw themselves at him, trying to pull him off his horse. The

---

1   Redut-Kale was a port on the Black Sea, and Anaklia is a village on the coast of the Black Sea.

horse did not budge, in spite of either the affectionate words or the threats of the traveller. In spite of the fact that the latter had tied some little sticks to the horse's tail, the wolves continued throwing themselves at him in a frenzy. What ought the poor man to do? Terror was overcoming him; his sword was freezing in his fingers. Only one thing was left – to shout with all his might. At that adverse time a small light appeared in the distance. The wolves ran away and the horse ran towards the light. Here the traveller saw a solitary little house whose owner was running with a light towards his shouts.

After warming himself, our wayfarer began complaining about the misfortune that had befallen him. But the householder, with moaning and lamentation, directed his attention to the people around them.

'You, my brother, consider yourself unfortunate because some wolves surrounded you in the forest ... No, if only you knew my grief, then you would consider what has happened to you as great good luck. You can see that we are all wearing mourning, from the smallest to the biggest. We were eight brothers, and we were all occupied in fishing. Sometimes for months we did not get off the boat, and only once a week we would send in the fish on dinghies. One day, after casting our fishing lines from the boat, we noticed that our boat was starting to go out from the shore and to go out to sea: some kind of force was dragging it, in spite of all our endeavours to stop it. Several weeks later we saw a rocky shore, from where a stream of honey was flowing.

'Our boat headed straight towards that place from where the honey was flowing. When we sailed up nearer to the source, we saw swimming out from under the boat a large fish whose mouth was wider than a *sazhen*.[1] It began swallowing honey with such greediness that it almost dried up the stream. This enormous fish used to swim here to drink honey, and to Anaklia to eat corn. It had turned out that unfortunately for us our fishing lines had become entangled in its fins, and that was what had dragged us. Here, while it was drinking the honey, we stole up to it and cut off all the lines. The fish, after having a good drink of honey, began swimming back, and our boat stayed there. Where we had landed we did not know: sometimes we were laughing with joy that we had seen land, and sometimes we were weeping, not knowing what to expect. After consulting together, we made up our minds that, after gathering wax and honey, we

---

1   A *sazhen* is a measure of length equal to 2.13 m.

would travel by the shore in a certain direction. For a whole week we were gathering honey and wax and loading our boat, but in the morning that we planned to travel, we saw a flock of sheep and goats approaching the stream. Walking behind the flock was a man of huge stature, and with only one eye. He was holding in his hand an enormous stick, as thick as a pillar, and was twirling it like a spindle. We were benumbed with terror. One-eye pulled our boat out on to the shore and drove us with his flock. We approached a colossal building. Around it was growing a vast forest, and the trees were so tall that our sight could not reach their tops. Even the reeds there were like our oak trees.

'The colossal tall building was formed of huge undressed stones, and inside it was divided up into compartments by stone partitions in which various animals were lodged. But especially great were the four compartments for the goats, the sheep, the lambs and the kids. Here One-eye shut us in, while he himself went away with his flock. We attempted many times to open the door somehow, but we could not, in spite of the fact that it was not closed with a lock. Here we sat from morning to evening, like mice in a mousetrap. In the evening we saw our One-eye come back with his flock and, after driving it into the stalls, he kindled a fire. After throwing whole trees on to the fire, he took a spit and, after selecting a fat ram and without dressing it, he began roasting it. The ram was turned on the spit until its eyes burst. After gobbling up the whole ram, he stretched himself out and began snoring.

'The next day he gobbled up two more rams, but in the evening, after returning with his flock and choosing the plumpest of us, he set him on the spit and began roasting him over the fire. Our brother was revolving and shouting to us, 'Save me!' But what could we, poor fellows, do?! When our brother's eyes burst, One-eye tore off one leg and threw it to us while he himself guzzled the remainder. We buried it right there. Thus that monster ate up all our brothers except me and the youngest one, and we could not do anything, finding ourselves in the situation of lambs being torn to pieces by a wolf. My brother and I lost our heads, wanting to die, but not such an agonising death.

'When One-eye had eaten his fill of human meat the last time, and he lay down by the fire according to his habit and began snoring, my brother and I quietly went up to the spit stuck in the ground at his head, and with great difficulty we drew it out of the ground. After that we laid it in the fire and waited with fear while it was heating in the flame. When the spit had become red hot, we wrapped our hands in our *arkhalukis*[1] and thrust it straight into One-eye's eye. One-eye, throwing the spit from his eye, leaped upwards with such force that we thought he would make a hole in the ceiling. But he made a hole in his own head instead. With terrible cries One-eye was running through the building, trampling the goats and sheep, but he could not find us, because we were slipping away from under his legs.

'In the morning the sheep and goats began bleating as if asking their master to let them out to the pasture. One-eye was unable to endure the suffering of his beloved animals and, standing at the door, he began to let the goats and sheep through between his legs, feeling their backbone, belly and head. He was doing this until noon. After that, having grown tired, he stopped feeling the sheep on all sides, but only stroked along their backs with his hands. Fortunately for us my brother happened to have a knife with which we took the skins off two rams and, after putting them on, we made up our minds to get through between One-eye's legs. I, hardly alive with terror, decided to be first to make my way through between One-eye's legs. He groped over me, but he did not recognise me, and I saw the world once more. My brother followed my example. At once we set off for the place where our boat was moored. Fortunately for us, it was still in the same place. When we saw it, our hopes of saving ourselves became stronger. At this time our tormentor's flock was approaching the shore. Wishing to take revenge on him in some way, we took hold of the best goats and sheep and loaded our boat with them. But we had only just managed to cut off the anchor when we saw One-eye come running to the place where our boat was moored, and trying to discover whether our boat was tied up there. After sailing a little farther out, we began shouting our names to him, being proud that we had caused him such harm. With a furious howl he flung his club at us so violently that it raised such waves that our boat was almost lost.

'After long journeying, and suffering many hardships, we made it home.'

Recorded by I. Petrov, instructor in the teaching seminary of Khoni (western Georgia) from the words of narrator F. Ashordia, of the village of Anaklia, Samegrelo. Published in SMOMPK (Sbornik materialov dlya opisaniya

---

1   An *arkhaluki* is a long shirt.

mestnostey i plemen Kavkaza), Vol. V, 1886, Part II, 101. Re-published in E. Virsaladze, *Gruzinskie narodnye predaniya i legendy*, Nauka, Moscow, 1973, 301–303.

46. Stories about Giants (*vampolozh*) (*Chechen-Ingush*)

It was a long time ago, but the old men tell it like this. In a certain settlement there was a man who, in the presence of his wife, picked up a cow by the tail, carried it over the fence, lowered it on to the ground, picked it up again and carried it back. After that he always used to hit his wife and ask: 'Tell me, who is stronger than me in the world?'

His wife was unable to point to anybody. The wife of Pez-Amiev learned about it. She came to the strong man's wife and told her, 'How is it that you don't know, when I certainly do know it, and I am the last woman in the settlement? Let him cross over the mountain. The people on that side of the mountain catch fish; let him measure his strength with them, they are stronger than he is.'

In the evening the strong man came home and, picking up the cow by the tail, he again asked his wife, 'Tell me, who is stronger than me in the world?'

His wife replied, 'Cross over the mountain. There you will find people who catch fish, and they are stronger than you.'

The strong man crossed over the mountain and saw three men fishing. He said to them, 'Let us test our strength!'

'Why should we test our strength? We do not know why you are here. You had better come later on and we will have a test of our strength.'

He went up to them. Then one of the brothers said, 'Here you are, hold the fishing rod while I go into the yard.'

The strong man took the fishing rod, and immediately a fish was hooked on it and started dragging him into the water. Then the one who was sitting near him, while still sitting down, grabbed the strong man with one hand and drew him and the fish in towards himself. 'Ah, you have come to test your strength with ours?' After saying that, he puffed on him and blew him away to the middle brother; that one puffed and blew him away to the third brother, and thus he started flying from one brother to another. 'Now God has sent us some fun, here is something to amuse ourselves a little,' they said. While returning home, they kept on blowing at him, and he was flying in front of them along the road. After stopping to have a rest, they had dinner and lay down to sleep, intending to have a game with him again when they woke up. However, the strong man ran away after they had fallen asleep.

On the road he met a certain *vampal*-man of enormous height, with one arm and one eye missing;[1] with one hand he was carrying thirteen carts of hay. The man addressed the *vampal* with the words: 'Ni dela hashus' (I am your guest and God's).[2] After those words the *vampal* could not fail to receive him, and he suggested to him that he should climb on to a cart and cover himself with matting.[3]

'No, give me a safer place.'

'Just where can I find room for you? Well, climb into my trousers.' And the strong man completely hid himself in the *vampal*'s trousers. The *vampal* went further on his way.

The three fisherman brothers ran to meet him. 'Have you seen our plaything?'

'What kind of plaything? I haven't seen anything.'

'No, you probably have seen him, you had better tell us.'

'Get away from me or I will beat you.'

'It is not easy to beat us, and there are few who can do it,' they answered.

Then he swung his arm and struck one of them on the cheek with his hand, and all three fell down from the one blow. The *vampal* turned to his guest: 'Just pull out one hair from behind me.' His guest dug both of his feet in (to his back) and, straining himself, with difficulty he tore out one hair and gave it to the *vampal*. He took the hair, tied up all three brothers and said, 'Well, now tell me, what was it that happened to you?'[4]

The brothers related how that man had come to measure his strength against them when they were fishing, how they were returning home and how he had run away when they lay down to sleep. Then the one-eyed *vampal* said to the *vampal* brothers,[5] 'Now listen to me. There were seven

---

1   As we learn from the story, this giant was not one-eyed from birth, but lost one eye (Note of B. Dalgat).

2   An Ingush expression recorded by the collector with the help of the alphabet of P. Uslar; according to contemporary orthography, '*Khan daylei khyaysha va so*'.

3   This shows the customary strength of the concept of hospitality among the Ingush; even the cannibalistic giant obeys it (Note of B. Dalgat).

4   This is a regular method of binding mighty *bogatyrs* in the legends of the Chechens and Ingush.

5   The brothers were *vampals*, giants, but weaker than the one-eyed one (Note of B. Dalgat).

of us brothers. We also went out to measure our strength, considering ourselves the strongest of all in the world. We were walking and met a shepherd of enormous height and one-eyed, driving a vast flock of sheep. At our first sight of him we became frightened and hid ourselves in the skull of a horse lying close by (and the horses were huge in those times). The huge shepherd's dog ran up to us, dragged the skull with all of us in it, and laid it at his feet. 'Thank you, my dog, for the present,' said the shepherd. He passed his stick through the hole in the skull and, putting it on his shoulder, he went on his way as if nothing had happened.

Arriving home, he roasted my six brothers on a spit, ate them up and lay down to sleep, leaving me for the morning as a snack. When he went to sleep, I took the spit, got it red-hot in the open fire and with one blow thrust it into his eye.

'Ah! You have deprived me of my eye! Just wait, you shan't get away from me anyway,' said the shepherd, and in the morning he began letting out the flock of sheep one at a time. He was passing his hand along the back of each sheep, looking for me. Seeing the inevitability of death, I slaughtered a goat and, putting on its skin, I walked through past the shepherd, thus deceiving him. On getting out of the cave, I drove away the flock and, after getting well away, I shouted to him, 'You have eaten my six brothers, but I have saved myself and deprived you of your eye, getting revenge on you at least partly, and now I am driving away your flock.'

As soon as I had said that, the shepherd threw a huge rock in the direction from which he heard my voice, and with that rock he tore off one of my arms and deprived me of one eye. So here is my advice to you: do not think of yourself as stronger than anybody in the world, but each live your own life. After saying that, he let them go, and they all dispersed to their own homes.

Recorded by B. Dalgat from the words of narrator Ganyzh Abievich Keligov-Falkhanov in 1892 from the village of Bayni of the Metskhal community. It was published in U. B. Dalgat, *Geroichesky epos chechentsev i ingushey*, Nauka, Moscow, 1972, 280–281.

47. Koloy Kant *(Chechen-Ingush)*

There lived three brothers, and the youngest of them was Koloy Kant.[1] From his early years he never worked, and spent his time building up his physical powers. For seven years he lived at the expense of his two elder brothers. When he felt himself to have significant strength, he got down to work. He had a special passion for sheep, and so he became a shepherd. At that time the brothers had between them altogether twenty sheep, and among them was one goat, who spoke in a human voice and was nicknamed with the name of his master, who was Koloy Kant.

When Koloy Kant set off to pasture his sheep for the first time, he lost his way and crossed several mountains. For twelve[2] years not a word was heard of him.During that time Koloy Kant's flock grew so much that it was impossible to count his sheep, and if one looked over the expanse of land that they occupied while grazing, it was impossible to see the end of the flock. Koloy Kant used to drive all of his sheep into an enormous cave, which had an entrance resembling gates. Instead of doors he would lean a flat stone, which only sixty men could shift; but he himself placed it there with one hand.

Soska Solsa, with sixty Orkhustoys, decided to set out for booty; but first he called in, as he always did, at Botoko Shirtga's place to seek advice about where he should set off to. 'Ride to Koloy Kant. He has an innumerable flock, but I warn you in advance that you will not cope with him. He is too strong,' said Botoko Shirtga.

'What are you talking about, Shirtga,[3] why do you shame me in front of my Orkhustoys? Is it possible that I, Solsa, who has not yet found a rival for strength, bravery and cunning, am unable to overcome a shepherd?' He set out with his comrades to Koloy Kant with the intention of driving away his flock of sheep.

When they went up to the cave where Koloy Kant was, the Orkhustoys combined to move aside the stone that was standing at its entrance. As soon

---

1   Koloy is the name of an *aul* which at the present time is in the Galgay Gorge; in the Ingush and Chechen language Kant means a successful young fellow or a youth (Note of Ch. Akhriev).

2   According to the folk beliefs of the Vaynakhs, the number twelve is considered to be positive, and symbolises virtue. The number thirteen has the opposite meaning; it is used in a curse when, for example, they say, 'May thirteen men die at your father's place!' Sometimes also the number thirteen is favourable.

3   *Shirtga* means 'little weasel', used here as a pun.

as they went in, the goat that spoke with a human voice headed towards them and began fighting with them. 'What are you doing, Koloy, can't you see that they are guests?' said Koloy Kant, who had only just woken up.[1] He began to drive the goat aside, but at that moment the sixty Orkhustoys rushed at him from all sides, and Soska Solsa himself also attacked him. Koloy Kant swung his shoulders and struck all of the Orkhustoys against the wall of the cave, and gave Solsa such a box on the ear that the latter spun around like a top. They went away barely alive from Koloy Kant.

Solsa went to Botoko Shirtga and acknowledged that in the world there existed a man stronger than he: it was Koloy Kant. 'But either he or I must die,' added Solsa. 'It is impossible for us both to live at one and the same time!' Solsa asked Botoko Shirtga to find a means somehow of diminishing Koloy Kant's strength, or to teach him how to overcome him.

'I know one means,' said Botoko Shirtga. 'Koloy Kant must be involved in a love relation with some woman. If he spends two weeks with a woman, then he will lose his former physical strength.[2] If you want to overcome your rival, Koloy Kant, then dispatch your sister to him. Let her try to entice him. After two weeks you set out with the other Orkhustoys to Koloy Kant's place, and you will be able to boldly tie him up and drive off his flock of sheep.'

Solsa did just that. He sent his sister to Koloy Kant. Koloy Kant received her and at night he slaughtered a sheep for his unknown guest. After having supper, they lay down to sleep separately, but some time later Solsa's sister got up, went over to the place where Koloy Kant was lying, and wanted to lie down with him, saying that fate itself had appointed her to be his wife.

'Go away,' said Koloy Kant. 'Know that I have given my word never to marry, and not to have dealings with any woman. Tomorrow you must leave me; if you want to ask for something, then I will willingly give you half of my flock, only leave me alone!'

But she stayed, and on the next night she again presented herself at Koloy Kant's bed. Again he drove her away. On the third night, when she approached him, he could no longer overcome his passion, and he let her lie

---

1   A common theme of the Vaynakh legends: the mighty hero initially meets his enemies with a hospitable invitation, and then later accepts battle.

2   A hero loses his power after intimacy with a woman. This idea of asceticism comes from deep antiquity. Not only does Enkidu, the hero of the Akkadian epos of Gilgamesh lose his *bogatyr's* strength, but also Samson (ancient Semitic Shammu); Samson was blinded by his enemies (Philistines) after he had fallen sound asleep, weakened after intimacy with a woman.

with him. From then on Koloy Kant gave himself up to his passion, spend-ing all of his time with Soska Solsa's sister. He had already stopped grazing his sheep; instead of him it was the goat, the one that spoke with a human voice, that looked after them and drove them into the cave. The more time that Koloy Kant spent with Solsa's sister, the more he lost his strength. He was no longer able to place the stone tightly at the cave entrance. From day to day the entrance became wider. After ten days one could freely enter the cave.

Meanwhile Solsa had not forgotten Botoko Shirtga's advice. Two weeks later he set off with Botoko Shirtga and his Orkhustoy comrades to Koloy Kant's place. Since the entrance into the cave was open, they went in there without any hindrance and caught Koloy Kant sleeping on Solsa's sister's lap. The Orkhustoys immediately tied him up with a rope made of horse hair.[1]

Koloy Kant only awoke when he had already been tied up. On waking, he began struggling so hard that the rope, which was binding him, cut him to the very bones. The Orkhustoys slaughtered his beloved goat for kebabs. Koloy Kant asked them to give him some kind of bone from his goat. The Orkhustoys refused his request.

'I will give him what he asks for,' said Solsa's sister, and she gave him a thigh-bone. Taking the bone from the hands of the woman who was guilty of his helplessness, Koloy Kant made a *zurna* from it and began playing on it dolefully.[2] That sound was heard by the wife of Koloy Kant's elder brother, in the evening when she was milking the cows in the yard. She said, 'The one who is playing is none other than my husband's youngest brother. Some misfortune has happened to him.' She went to inform her husband and her brother-in-law about it. They immediately galloped off in the direction where the Orkhustoys lived, having a presentiment that the Orkhustoys had driven off their brother, together with his flock of sheep.

They had already nearly caught up with the Orkhustoys between the Jerakhov and Darial Gorges. However, God foresaw that if Koloy Kant's brothers overtook the Orkhustoys, human blood would be shed. To avoid the bloodshed, he rerouted the River Terek so that Koloy Kant with his brothers, Solsa's sister and half of the flock of sheep remained on the right bank; while on the left bank were the Orkhustoys with the remaining half of Koloy Kant's flock of sheep. It was almost as if this were the *kalym* for Solsa's sister.

---

1   A recurring method of binding *bogatyr*s in Vaynakh heroic legends (also sometimes a woman's hair).

2   This song motif is well known among the mountain people under the name 'Koloy Kant' and is widely used among the shepherds (Note of Ch. Akhriev).

Koloy Kant, seeing that the Terek was separating him from the Orkhustoys, and wishing to show them his strength and hatred towards them, picked up a long flat stone and struck it against the ground, saying that he would hurl them against the ground too, if only they fell into his hands.[1] The Orkhustoys too, as if in answer to him, struck a similar stone against the ground. After making threats and demonstrating their strength, they parted: the Orkhustoys set off to Sanabi,[2] while Koloy Kant with his brothers and Solsa's sister, whom he took as his wife, set off for home.

On arriving in his native *aul*, Koloy Kant wished to test how much of his strength was left after his marriage. With this aim he climbed up to the summit of a mountain and placed three stones of enormous size one on top of another.[3] From that time nobody disturbed him or attempted to drive away his flock of sheep.

Text recorded and published by Ch. Akhriev in 1870. It was published in U. B. Dalgat, *Geroichesky epos chechentsev i ingushey*, Nauka, Moscow, 1972, 311–314.

48. Parcho *(Chechen)*

Introduction

In this tale is reflected the most ancient motif of the worship of stones and springs, the origin of which are connected with various epic heroes.

---

1   The stone that Koloy Kant struck, according to the tradition, used to stand on the right bank of the Terek. In 1856, when Russian troops arrived in the Jerakh Gorge, it was broken up into blocks by the soldiers. The stone thrown by the Orkhustoys still stands on the left bank of the Terek, near the Jerakh fortification (Note of Ch. Akhriev).

2   The settlement of Sanabi is in an Ossetian mountain gorge, so that the Orkhustoys are presented as newcomers, outsiders.

3   These stones together form something that resembles a reasonably tall tower. Between the second and the third stones there are small stones which evidently serve as props. It is these stones that lead the mountain people to the conviction that they were laid by a human hand (Note of Ch. Akhriev). The stones of Koloy Kant in actual fact are slightly more than five metres and remind one of phalli.

Long long ago there lived a strong man with one eye in his forehead. He was named Parcho. When he was pasturing his sheep in the forest, three brothers who were looking for a place to spend the night stumbled across him. Parcho invited them home to spend the night. He led them into a cave. He ate up one of them and said, 'Tomorrow morning I am going to eat one of you, throw lots between yourselves.'

He ate up a second brother too. After this Parcho threw a firebrand on the fire and began to rest. The firebrand flared up. Parcho fell asleep by the hearth. The third brother took the red-hot firebrand and poked out Parcho's single eye. The frantic Parcho rushed about the cave, but he could not find the third brother among the sheep. 'Where have you got to! I am now going to drive out the sheep and catch you,' shouted Parcho.

He began to drive the sheep and to stroke his hand across each one's back. The third brother clung beneath the belly of a sheep and, without being noticed, he got out of the cave. Parcho drove out his sheep and rushed about the cave. But the third brother shouted, 'Do not trouble yourself, Parcho, I am here!'

'You have beaten me by cunning. Here is a ring, as a present for you,' and Parcho threw him a ring.

The third brother put the ring on his finger and it began to emit an unimaginably loud noise through the forest. Parcho set out towards this noise. The third brother wanted to take the ring off his finger but it would not yield. Then he cut off his finger together with the ring and he ran away.

The blinded Parcho approached and, thinking that it was the man, he began to inflict blows with his sword. From these blows there arose a spring, which exists even today.

છ

Recorded in 1960 by M. Malsagov from the words of Kh. Soltagireyev, the village of Geldagan, Chechnya, and published in A. O. Malsagov, *Skazki i legendy ingushey i chechentsev*, Nauka, Moscow, 1983, 123.

VIII

Abundance

Although there are Caucasus legends about human fertility and about mul-
tiplication of flocks of animals, most of the legends that deal with abun-
dance are about agricultural crops, of which a selection is included here.
Some of them also include regrets for a lost golden age of abundance, a kind
of lost Garden of Eden.

The first legend, 'How the Ubykhs Became Gardeners', describes how
working off the land was given a sacred character. This is the second Ubykh
legend that is included in this book. The Ubykh ethnic group and the
Ubykh language have now become extinct. The Ubykhs were considered to
be some of the bravest warriors in the struggle of the Caucasus people, when
they were trying to avoid being incorporated into the Russian Empire. In
the words of Tsar Nicholas I, the purpose of the war of conquest by the
Russians was 'the suppression for all time of the mountain peoples or else the
extermination of the recalcitrant ones'. The cruel war lasted for more than
four decades, but when defeat finally came in 1864, the Ubykhs and other
ethnic groups were given the choice of being removed to other Russian-
controlled regions or of exile. They almost all chose the latter, emigrating *en
masse* to the Turkish Empire, where they settled in Anatolia. Descriptions
of the emigration are very sad: how the Ubykhs set fire to their own villages,
killed their own livestock, went down to the shore of the Black Sea and
suffered terrible hardships before and during the voyage. Many of the provi-
sions were lost, one of the ships broke down, there was no drinking water
and many drank seawater, and so on. Many of the emigrants died on the
voyage. In the middle of the twentieth century the French scholar Georges
Dumézil learned their language and managed to preserve some of the folk-
lore from the few remaining old Ubykh men who still spoke the language,
but both their language and their folklore were doomed to extinction
(Dumézil 1957). The above information was taken from Rusudan Janashia's
introduction to *Ubykh Folklore* (Gelashvili 1995, 17–24).

The lands previously occupied by the Ubykhs on the southwest-facing
Black Sea coast and mountain slopes were a kind of earthly paradise,

where the soil was so fertile, according to Klaproth (1814), that it needed no tillage, and their fruit included plums, peaches, walnuts and chestnuts, which in many places grew wild. Needless to say, the Russians were only too pleased to take over such a rich land. The Russian governor-general of the time stated that 'the indispensable conditions for the end of the war was the utter cleansing of the Black Sea region ...' About sixty Ubykh families who chose not to emigrate were deported to an area of the plains of southern Russia, where the Russian authorities could control them easily.

The next legend, 'The Murderer', also gives the crop growing on the land a sacred character, with the murderer miraculously saved from being hanged by miraculous growths from the earth itself, as a reward for his respect for a crop of corn. The next two legends, 'About the Origin of Abundance from the Earth' and 'The Little Bird of Abundance' both associate abundance with a bird. As is pointed out in the introduction to the second of these, the growing season is often associated with the arrival of the swallow. In this latter legend it mentions bad people who 'destroyed the nest' and this probably refers to the Nart-Orstkhoys, who figure in the next legend, 'How the Nart-Orstkhoys Vanished from the Earth'. In this legend it is curious that abundance existed 'at the time when there was no wind in the universe.' Other Caucasus legends also associate the end of a previous lost 'golden age' with the introduction of wind, where previously wind had not existed. 'Soska Solsa and the Pelvic Bone' also describes a lost golden age of abundance. In this case it is described by a giant who is temporarily brought back from the dead. The next legend, 'The Return of Abundance', at first appears as more of a moral tale, but reference to Chapter 11, 'Religion and Relations with the Dead', shows that in the former religion, and therefore in the local tradition, the deceased ancestors are also considered to be part of the family. Therefore family harmony is important to the ancestors too, and the dead are able to influence abundance for the family. This legend therefore also has a religious connotation. The legend 'How Lake Ritsa was Formed' shows how an incognito holy wanderer miraculously turned pebbles into food for a poor widow and her starving children, after she had shown hospitality to him. This mysterious stranger is not named, but in another legend in which poor people try to show hospitality, the mysterious stranger is Saint George in disguise. The miracle worked by Saint George, and the punishment of the inhospitable neighbours by God, show that this legend too associates abundance with religion, but in this case the abundance has been transferred from the original 'pagan' religion to that of Christianity. The same can be said for the next legend, 'Elia, Christ and Saint George', where Christ specifically orders abundance for the soil on which they had had a picnic. The final legend, 'The Meeting of Abul with the Shaytans', is the only abundance legend in this book in which abundance is not clearly associated with a religious influence. In this case the influence is provided by the *shaytans*, whose characteristics appear to be somewhat like those of our fairies, although under the influence of the mainstream religions of Islam and Christianity the *shaytans* are now considered as demons. There are nevertheless religious connotations, since the hearth and chimney, from which the mysterious characters rush, were considered to be sacred in the original Caucasus religious beliefs – they were associated with the family and the ancestors, as is described in the introduction to Chapter 11 of this book.

A further example of the holy respect of Caucasus people for agricultural crops is conveyed by the statement of a highly respected Balkar narrator (*geguako*), quoted in the appendix of this book. When asked what he considered to be the basis of religion, he said, 'In my opinion, millet grain has to serve as the basis of religion.' Two examples in the Holy Bible of the association of food abundance with religion are the feeding of the Israelites with manna from heaven (Exodus XVI), and the feeding of the five thousand with five loaves and two fishes by Christ (St Matthew XIV).

49. How the Ubykhs Became Gardeners *(Ubykh)*

There was a time when the Ubykhs did not occupy themselves with farming, and especially not with gardening. They considered that agriculture was the work of slaves and captives, and gardening was certainly no business of an Ubykh warrior. And anyway, by God's will the Ubykh land abounds in apples, pears, walnuts, cherry-plums and other edible fruits.

On one occasion a certain Ubykh man died in an unequal battle with his enemy. But in spite of his military services, God sent his soul to hell, where it fell to his lot to go hungry, although beyond a huge wattle fence he could see people in paradise cultivating gardens and savouring rosy fruits aplenty. At that time he and sinners like him were looking at these toilers and becoming envious. Time passed. The Ubykh man became terribly hungry and grew thin. The fruits that one could gather in the dense thickets and on the mountain slopes were bitter.

And then the Ubykh man swore by all the saints that if God would deign to grant him life, he would summon his people to the labour and occupation of gardening. God heard his groans and sent him back to earth. The people ranked the revived Ubykh man among the saints, and without questioning they all started fulfilling his instructions.

First of all the Ubykh man declared gardening to be a sacred business, saying that each man must plant fifty trees during his life. Only after that could he get to paradise. As for the women, they had to occupy themselves with market-gardening.

ﻉ

No narration details are available for this Ubykh legend, which was published in V. P. Pachulia, *Padenie Anakopiya*, Nauka, Moscow, 1986, 118–119.

50. The Murderer *(Georgian)*

There was a certain bad man who was always ready for a fight. Nine men were on his conscience. He began a fight with a tenth, and he wanted to kill him too.

The watch came, and he ran away. They chased him. He ran along a path leading to a cornfield. Suddenly the path came to an abrupt end. He could see that there was no way past it. He did not want to trample the corn and so he stopped. They came, bound him and threw him into prison. The judges condemned him to the gallows.

The day of the execution arrived. He was led to the gallows, and his head was inserted into the noose. As they pushed him, so as to hang him, suddenly two posts grew up out of the ground. One of them supported one foot, and the other supported the other one. They simply held him, so that he did not choke. Everybody was surprised. They sawed off those posts, but new ones came up in their place; they would not allow him to die.

Everybody was asking, 'What is this? Is it a miracle?'

The murderer said to them, 'I did not start trampling the cornfield, I spared the labour of men's hands, for which the blessing of the corn is on me.'

They forgave him all his offences and let him go in peace.

ટ♪

This Georgian legend was recorded by A. D. Machabeli in 1899 from the words of M. Zhizhniashvili in the village of Kurta, Tskinvali District, Georgia. It was published in E. B. Virsaladze, *Gruzinskie narodnye predaniya i legendy*, Nauka, Moscow, 1973, 269–270.

51. About the Origin of Abundance from the Earth *(Ingush)*

Over all the earth, on which we now live, there was at one time drought. On all the earth there was not a single drop of water, nor any plants.

A huge white bird flew in and landed on the earth. The bird covered the entire earth with its body, it was so enormous. From this bird's droppings, water and seed arose. And from these seeds, so they say, the forest, the grass, the gardens and the cereals grew on the earth. And the water spilled into the seas, the lakes and the rivers.

The water abolished the drought, and the seeds made the earth fruitful. From the water and the seeds came the abundance of the earth.

ટ♪

An Ingush legend, recorded by I. A. Dakhkilgov in 1975 from the words of L. Magiev in the village of Alkum. Published in A. O. Mal'sagov, *Skazki i legendy Ingushey i Chechentsev*, Nauka, Moscow, 1983, 299.

52. The Little Bird of Abundance *(Ingush)*

Introduction

The Metskhal Shakhar is the Metskhal community of mountain Ingushetia. The territory of the Metskhal (Jerakhov) community lies on both sides of the Malkha-Chozhe (The Sunny Gorge). One side of it is covered in forests, and the opposite side, the sunny side, is nearly treeless. According to folk memories, there were once forests on the sunny side too. They were cut down so the land could be used, then dehydration of the soil gradually took place. Sheep trampled down the grass, and landslides began. The population grew. There was not enough food for everybody. The gradual impoverishment of the land was noticed by the people, and it was possibly then that this tradition developed.

According to V. Abayev, the little bird of abundance (in Ingush *'fayra khyazilg', 'fayra'* from the Iranian *'farn'*) is 'an ancient Iranian cult term'. In greetings and good wishes a greater degree of abundance is meant (see V. Abayev, 'From the Ossete Epos. Ten Nart Legends', Moscow-Leningrad, Publisher AN SSSR, 1939, 74). The little bird of abundance reminds us very much of the swallow. Among the Ingush there is a belief that if a swallow's nest (or a dove's nest) is destroyed, then that home will suffer bad luck. One should distinguish the natural loss of abundance (as is reflected in this legend) and the loss of abundance caused by the Nart-Orstkhoys bringing the people to ruin, as described in 'How the Nart-Orstkhoys Vanished from the Earth'.

O ne day the little bird of abundance built its nest in the Metskhal Shakhar. Therefore the grain harvest never failed there. The lands on both sides of the River Armkhi were fruitful, and on them the cattle were put out to graze.

One day, some people who had no qualms about doing anything bad, destroyed the nest and drove out the little bird of abundance. It flew away from that land, from that region. While flying away from that land, the little bird of abundance touched the land of the Lyachkhoys with its wing, and the places where the towers stand in Balta.[1]

These places are plentiful to this day. The little bird spent the night in Lars, but built its nest in Georgia.[2]

ئ

An Ingush legend, recorded by D. Mal'sagov in 1920 from the words of Genarduko Pkhugievich Akhriev, aged seventy-five, inhabitant of the mountain *aul* of Furtoug. Published in U. B. Dalgat, *Geroichesky epos chechentsev i ingushey*, Nauka, Moscow, 1972, 331.

---

[1]   The Lyachkhoys live in the small town of Lyachakhe in mountain Ingushetia; and Balta is a village on the Georgian Military Highway.
[2]   Lars is a village on the Georgian Military Highway.

53. How the Nart-Orstkhoys Vanished from the Earth *(Ingush)*

Introduction

In the description of the time of abundance, the idea of lack of wind is of special interest; this same indication of the time of plenty is included in an Ingush tradition 'Magal' (SSKG, Issue VIII, 1875, 15). The same motif occurs in an Abkhaz tradition about the Atsany, a vanished race of dwarves who lived before the arrival of men, at a time when there was no wind; after the arrival of the first human baby, the Atsany noticed that the long beard of their billy goat started fluttering in the wind, and this portended the perishing of the entire tribe of the Atsany.

In those olden times all the earth was abundant. In the universe they did not know what a puff of wind was. A thread hung down from the sky, and on its end were little rags. They never stirred. And how could they have fluttered without wind? People lived in peace and plenty. What was sown, what was stored, as also what was yielded – it was all abundant. At that time the Nart-Orstkhoys appeared in our region under the leadership of Seska Solsa.

With his sixty Nart-Orstkhoys he used to ravage villages, committing violence on the people. With the appearance of the Nart-Orstkhoys, evil appeared in the universe and the winds began blowing. The winds used to carry away the grain stacked on the mountain hills, and they scattered the mown hay. The crops of grain began giving small harvests; the sheep and the cattle grew sickly. Everything created by the labour of man became meagre.

Around that time Seska Solsa arrived in a large village with his sixty horsemen, in order to rob the people and to kill those who showed resistance. Solsa's followers said, 'This is a large village, many people live here. We will suffer if they show resistance. It is better for us to divide into groups and come to them as guests, making out that we are looking for shelter.[1] After that we will steal the weapons from the dwellings, and then we will take the village without injury to ourselves.'

Seska Solsa agreed. After dividing up into groups, the Nart-Orstkhoys headed for the houses.

---

[1]   The intention of the Nart-Orstkhoys to commit robbery under the protection of hospitality was the very greatest crime in the eyes of the mountain people.

Seska Solsa turned up at Zherbaba's house with thirteen Nart-Orstkhoys as guests. Zherbaba willingly brought the guests into the room and set about getting a meal for them. Into a copper thimble she took flour for the making of bread, broke off a little piece of sheep's rib and began preparing the food.

'Ey, what is that you are doing?' asked the surprised Seska Solsa. 'Whose hunger are you planning to satisfy with such a little amount of food, with what you are cooking?'

'Eh, boy, after you have all eaten your fill, there will still be food left over. After all, this food was on the earth before the appearance of Seska Solsa and his Orstkhoys. That was at the time when there was no wind in the universe, and there was only plenty. Anybody who has not seen Seska Solsa – let them not see him; anybody who has seen him once – let them not see him again! After showing up with his Nart-Orstkhoys, he took away abundance from our land. The land has been reduced to beggary and the people have been ruined.'

After hearing what she said, Seska Solsa remained sitting in his seat, paralysed with grief.

'Ey, what has happened to you?' said Zherbaba in surprise. 'You have lost the colour in your face and become like wax. Aren't you Seska Solsa? Anybody who has not seen Seska Solsa – let them not see him; anybody who has seen him once – let them not see him again!'

'I am Seska Solsa,' he told Zherbaba, and he went away with his Orstkhoys not only from the village, but also from that region.

From that time nobody ever saw them again.

ھ

An Ingush legend, recorded by D. Mal'sagov in 1964 from the words of I. Kh. Mal'sagov, inhabitant of the village of Gamurzievo of the Nazran region. The narrator had heard this legend from Patarkhan Kutsigovich Archakov in 1920. Published in U. B. Dalgat, *Geroichesky epos chechentsev i ingushey*, Nauka, Moscow, 1972, 330–331.

54. Soska Solsa and the Pelvic Bone *(Chechen-Ingush)*

Introduction

According to Ch. Akhriev, the hero was known on the plains as Seska Solsa, as in the previous legend, while in the mountains he was known as Soska Solsa. In the Vaynakh languages, the first name was his father's name, while the second is his own name. The Vaynakhs constitute the Chechens and Ingush, who are neighbours and share a common language, with minor differences.

Long, long ago there lived a man, Solsa. At the time people lived under the ground in large underground chambers faced with masonry; these underground chambers are preserved in some places to the present day. Solsa was a very clever and honest man; he was born not from an ordinary woman, but he sprang directly from God. One day Solsa was riding through an underground passage, and on his way he came across a human pelvic bone, so large that Solsa rode through it on his horse.

Then Solsa grew upset, that he had violated the peace of a dead man. Solsa then began asking God to resurrect that man in a form such as he had been previously, and he struck the bone with his whip. At that same time the bone became a man, as big as a mountain, but he was blind and unable to see the sun. Solsa had asked this of God, so that the big man would not do him any harm.

The big man asked loudly, 'Who revived me?'

'I did, Soska Solsa!'

'Just why didn't you give me sight?' asked the big man.

Soska Solsa replied, 'If you had sight, you would eat up the whole world.'

'What kind of world is this?' said the big man. 'Formerly there was only forest here!'

'I ought not to tell you,' replied Soska Solsa. 'Tell me, what did you eat before?'

Instead of an answer, the big man groped about and, picking up a big stone, he ground it in his hands and began eating it. 'We used to eat that,' said the big man, 'and anything that turned up for us.'

'How did you do battle with one another?' Soska Solsa asked again.

Then the big man tore out a plane tree, hastily cleaned it off and threw it at Soska Solsa. But the latter, on seeing what the big man was preparing to do, jumped to one side in good time.

After the big man had thrown the tree, he said to himself, 'I have killed that ant for bringing me back to life without my sight.'

'How is it that you have killed me, when I am alive?' retorted Soska Solsa.

In reply the big man said to him, 'The ones who are born after us will be cleverer than we were. We were ashamed to save ourselves from death, and we used to kill each other with plane trees.'

'Just how were you able to battle bravely between yourselves, when you had such bad food as you showed me: sand and stone?' said Soska Solsa.

The big man told him, 'Ride along this track to the end. There stands a birch tree, and beneath it lie two loaves. Take them and bring them here.' Soska Solsa rode off as the big man had told him, found the loaves and brought them to him. Then the big man asked, 'How do they seem to you, are those loaves good?'

'They seem very good to me,' replied Soska Solsa. 'I was ravenously hungry, bit off just one piece, and now I am satisfied.'

'With those two loaves,' said the big man, 'we could travel for four months. But what do you feed yourself with?'

'We are small,' said Soska Solsa, 'but nevertheless it seems to me that there is not enough of these loaves for even one occasion.'

'Probably it is bad in the world,' said the big man, 'if the same amount of bread serves you for one time as served us for four months. You have woken me up, so give me my sight too, but if you won't give it, then make me into a bone again.'

Soska Solsa brandished his whip, and the big man became a hip bone.

ﻪ

A Chechen–Ingush legend, recorded by Ch. Akhriev. First published in Sbornik svedeniy o Kavkazskikh gortsakh, Issue VIII, 1875, 5–6; and later in U. B. Dalgat, *Geroichesky epos chechentsev i ingushey*, Nauka, Moscow, 1972, 273–274.

55. The Return of Abundance *(Chechen)*

A man woke up in the morning; he went out into his yard and saw that, across the fresh snow, some tracks led out of his house. But into his yard there were no tracks. He started thinking, what could this mean, who on earth has left my home? Having decided to find out, he set off along the trail, which led him to a cave. The man entered it and shouted, 'Leading into my house there are no tracks, but there are some coming out. What does this mean? Who left my place?'

A voice answered him, 'I am Abundance, who has become angry at you and abandoned your home. In vain you have taken the trouble to come for me.'

Then the man began to beg Abundance to return, saying that without Abundance he was done for.

Abundance answered, 'Because you have taken the trouble to come to me, I will give you just one thing. If you want it, ask for gold or a big farm; if you want it, ask for health or for something else, but do not ask me to come back to you.'

The man thought for a bit and said, 'I do not have much sense. If you let me, I will ask advice at home.' Abundance agreed. He returned home and told his people all about it. They began to give him advice: some to ask for gold, some for grain. But his wife said, 'Ask for harmony in our family. Where that is, nothing else is needed.'

He agreed with her; he went to the cave and asked that his family should be given harmony. And Abundance said, 'You have outwitted me. I give you harmony. And where there is harmony, I must be there too. Therefore I will return to you.'

Abundance is not present where there is no harmony.

A Chechen legend, recorded by R. Saydulayev in 1976 from the words of S. Saydulayev in the village of Alkhan-Kala. Published in A. O. Mal'sagov, *Skazki i legendy Ingushey i Chechentsev*, Nauka, Moscow, 1983, 299–300.

56. How Lake Ritsa was Formed *(Abkhaz)*

The old people tell a legend, heard from their great-grandfathers, that in the place where Lake Ritsa is now, there was formerly a valley.[1] In it lived the proud and miserly people of the family Apshisba. They all lived richly except for a certain widow with many children. The poor woman worked day and night in order to give her little children something to eat, but still she could not give them enough food. The only thing she heard from them was: 'Mother, give us something to eat!'

Every day, from early in the morning until late in the evening, the widow worked for her neighbours. They obtained a rich harvest of millet and wheat and did not have time to thresh the grain. The neighbours hired the widow, but they paid her by giving her the grain which did not fall into the *alakhvara*. Did she acquire much grain like this? Enough for about two or three little *lepeshki*. But however little she was paid for her work, the widow never complained, because she knew that she would gain nothing from her stingy relatives by complaining.

One day her unfortunate family found itself in an especially difficult situation. In the house there was not a single grain of food, but the children were hungry; time and again they plaintively cried, 'Mama, let's eat!' 'Mama, we are hungry!'

For the poor woman it was already the second day that food had not even passed her lips. She had given it all to her children. In despair she thought, it would be better for me to die than to hear the complaints of the hungry children. Why don't I go once more, I will try and beg from my neighbours at least a handful of grain.

The widow went around several homesteads, but all her neighbours refused her. She came home empty-handed. But the children were weeping: they were asking to eat. So what was there left for the poor woman to do? She poured little stones into a pot and put it on the stove. 'My dears, let your mother look after you, now I will cook you a dinner. Have a little patience while it is cooking.'

She was speaking like that, stroking the children on their heads and caressing them. The poor little children sat down around the hearth, above which was hanging the pot with the little stones, and they waited for dinner.

---

1   It should be noted that Lake Ritsa is in the Caucasus Mountain region, which is known for earthquakes, rerouting of rivers and so on. Nowadays the lake is a holiday resort.

But what could they be waiting for? Evening came. The children were all weeping, waiting, until sleep wore them out. The woman was sitting at the hearth and grieving.

At that time some newly-arrived old man was walking through the village, and he asked for a night's lodging. But everybody refused him both shelter and food. So he approached the widow's home. 'Eh, master!'

'Ay!' answered the widow. She went out and greeted the old man with the words: 'You are welcome!'

The old man went in and said, 'I am very hungry, there is probably no point in trying to hide it. Can't you give me something to eat?'

'Oy, right away, good man,' said she, and she looked into the pot. She was ashamed and sad that there was nothing to feed her guest.

'I see that you have little stones in the pot. If you have nothing put by, then what are you going to feed me with?' asked the guest.

'No, I have nothing put away,' answered the widow. 'But I will wait, perhaps God will send me something so that I can observe the laws of hospitality and feed you.'

After a short time, the little stones in the pot turned into meal, and the widow cooked *mamalyga*. She fed her guest, then she woke the children. She gave them something to eat and put them to bed. Then she herself ate what was left and lay down to rest.

When she got up early in the morning, the guest had already gone. She went out on to the threshold and saw that water was coming up on all sides towards her house. All around was already flooded and only her little house, like a little island, stood in the middle of a big expanse of water. From her little house a narrow unflooded path ran to the shore. The widow woke her children and said to them, 'A great misfortune has come: water has drowned the whole village. Only our home has survived, and from it runs a path, along which one can reach the shore. It means that God does not want us to perish. Let's go quickly!'

She picked up the smallest babies in her arms, telling the others to hold on to her hem, and they went along the path. The water advanced along their tracks as they walked. The widow had only just got out with the children on to the high bank when the entire expanse of the valley was completely swallowed up by water.

Thus Lake Ritsa was formed. The old people also say that anybody from the Apshisba family who appears at the lake is drawn by some kind of mysterious force to drown himself in it. This is why, of the Apshisba

family, only the descendants of the sons of the poor widow have survived
to this day.

ॐ

An Abkhaz legend. Details of its recording and narration are not known,
but it was published in Kh. S. Bgazhba, *Abkhazskie skazki*, Alashara,
Sukhumi, 1985, 32–34.

57. Elia, Christ and Saint George *(Georgian)*

Elia,[1] Christ and Saint George were walking together. They grew hungry.
On the mountain they saw a shepherd and they told Elia, 'Go and get
a sheep, so as to relieve our hunger.'

Elia went to the shepherd and asked him, 'Give me one sheep!'

'Who are you, asking me for a sheep?' asked the shepherd.

'The master of the rain and the hail, Elia.'

'Why would I dream of giving you a sheep? You cannot distinguish
between a bad man and a good man, you destroy the harvest of a poor man.'
He brought down the stick from his shoulder – and one, and two ... Elia
went back with nothing.

Now Christ set off to the shepherd: 'Give me one sheep, wise shepherd ...'

'Who are you, who is asking a sheep from me?'

'I am Christ, the son of God!'

'Why would I dream of giving you a sheep, when you don't know how to
distinguish the bad from the good!' and he drove Christ away with nothing.

Finally Saint George set off to the shepherd. 'Wise shepherd, give me one
sheep!'

'Who are you, that is asking one sheep from me?'

'I am Saint George, the protector of the people and of all the land.'

'Take the whole flock!' the shepherd told him.

'No, I don't need the flock, one sheep is enough.'

The shepherd selected a nice sheep and gave it to him. Saint George
brought the nice sheep to his friends. They slaughtered the sheep, roasted

---

1   Elia means Saint Elias or Saint Ilya.

it and ate it with gusto. After dinner, Christ shook down his hem and said, 'Whoever ploughs up this field will be replete all year!'

They set off on their way. But Saint George went to the shepherd and advised him: 'There, where we ate our meal, Christ shook out his hem. Whatever happens, plough up that place and sow wheat!'

And in truth, the shepherd bought that land, ploughed it up and sowed wheat. When it ripened, the human eye had never seen better wheat.

One day Elia looked down from heaven and, seeing that field, he said to Christ, 'Have a look: what a cornfield is standing there where you shook out your hem.'

Saint George, hearing this, said, 'That field belongs to the shepherd who gave me the sheep.'

'If that is so, look and see what I will do with it!' said Elia.

While Elia was gathering himself, Saint George ran down to the shepherd and told him, 'People will buy that field of yours. Sell it as a standing crop this very day, however much they give you.'

That very same evening the shepherd sold the field as a standing crop. And during the night Elia beat down the field with hail so that nothing was left of it.

On the next day Elia said to Saint George, 'Have a look and see what I have done with your shepherd's field!'

'That field no longer belongs to the shepherd, he sold it yesterday to a certain merchant,' Saint George answered him.

'Since that field does not belong to him any more, look and see how I will raise it up,' said Elia.

After learning this, Saint George came running once more to the shepherd and told him, 'Get that field back. The merchant will sell it with pleasure, after he has seen how it has been beaten down by the hail.'

The shepherd retrieved his field. On the next day Elia brought on a lot of rain, and the field rose up once more.

Elia happened to meet Saint George and told him, 'Look, how I have put the merchant's field right.'

'But once more it belongs to the shepherd ...'

Christ heard that, got in a rage and cursed that field: 'May the harvest from that field be not more than one *kodi*[1] on each cart.'

---

[1]   A *kodi* is a measure of weight of free-flowing materials, 4 to 5 *pood*s. A *pood* is a weight equal to 16.38 kg.

Saint George immediately went running to the shepherd and said, 'However much people laugh at you, lay only one sheaf on each cart, not more.'

The shepherd did just that, and he gathered a plentiful harvest.

ৎৡ

A Georgian legend, recorded by A. Glonti in 1938 in the village of Karagaji of the Kaspi region, from the words of D. Kvrivishvili. Published in E. B. Virsaladze, *Gruzinskie narodnye predaniya i legendy*, Nauka, Moscow, 1973, 260–262.

58. About the Meeting of Abul with the Shaytans *(Dargva)*

Introduction

This legend, and in particular the meeting of the hero with *shaytans*, who live underground and are fond of dancing (figures rather like our fairies), reminds us of some British folk tales, containing motifs F261, F348.7 and F450.[1] Moreover, the episode of conveying mysterious news about a death to some figures who rush out of the chimney is also similar to the British tale of 'The King of the Cats' (Tale Type 113A).[2]

O n one occasion Abul went to the mill. He had ground his grain and was returning. He reached the place that went under the name of 'The yard of the seven walnuts' and stopped to take a short rest. This was a narrow road between the crags, with forest and the river below (editor's note: it is a real place, not far from Kubani). From behind the crags some enormous men in white came out and invited him: 'Come to us to dance at a wedding.'

'I cannot,' he declined. 'I have to carry this sack home – there is no flour at home.'

---

1   See Stith Thompson, *Motif-Index of Folk-Literature*, 6 vols, Indiana University Press, Bloomington & Indianapolis, 1955.

2   See Antii Arne, *The Types of Folktale*, tr. Stith Thompson, FF Communications No. 184, Suomalainen Tiedeakatemia, Helsinki, 1981.

One of the men took the sack from him and said that he would carry it to his home. The rest of them led him inside the rock, after opening seven doors, and beyond the seventh the wedding was going on. They fed him with seven dishes, and when he had had enough, they began calling him to dance. They kept repeating, while clapping their hands:

'Ay, Abul, ey, Abul,
Tiny, like a little grain of millet, dear Abul!
Yet one more time, Abul, dear Abul!'

They made him dance until dawn. 'Now I need to go home,' he said, and they led him out through the seven doors to the same place.

They told him, 'Pass on the message that Utsran has killed Shupran.'

'But who should I pass it on to?' he wanted to ask. He turned around, but there was no longer anybody there.

He went home, perplexed. At home his wife met him. 'Did my sack arrive home?' asked Abul.

'I heard somebody say, "Here you are, this is the sack of your Abul." I went out, the sack was lying on the top step, but there was nobody. Where have you been until now?' asked his wife.

He told her everything. Just as he said that he did not know to whom he had to convey the message that Utsran had killed Shupran, four men in black leapt out of the chimney. Exclaiming *Khoy, khoy!* and picking up flaming brands, they rushed out of the house.

The frightened husband and wife stared at one another. 'It is a good thing I conveyed the message that I was told,' he said.

Abul's wife began preparing food from the flour, but the flour did not come to an end. All winter they were using the flour and did not go to the mill. The neighbours noticed this and became interested to know where they had got the flour from – they were not buying at the market and did not go to the mill. The wife tried to conceal it, saying that Abul had bought the flour at the market. But the neighbours kept pestering her so that she admitted what had happened. She told them about it.

In the evening she went for flour, but in the sack there remained only flour dust.

৵

A Dargva legend from Daghestan, recorded by M. Khalidova in 1979 from Pirdaz Abdullayeva, born in 1921 in the settlement of Kubachi of the Dakhadayev region, Daghestan; Manuscript Archive of IIYaL, f. 9, op. 1, d. 421. Published in F. Abakarova, *Darginskie fol'klor*, Kavkazsky Dom, Tbilisi, 1999, 144–145.

IX

Family and Personal Honour

Family honour has great importance in the Caucasus society. Any disgrace that falls on a family can never be the subject of a joke within that family. Personal honour is also closely connected with that of the family, since personal dishonour reflects on the status of the family itself. As can be seen from the legends below, the honour of men revolves much around personal bravery and honesty, and being true to one's word. The honour of the women revolves around chastity. Family honour also depends very much on hospitality to guests. A failure of any individual in any of these respects is considered to bring general disgrace on the family. All of these topics are included in the legends below.

An idea of the importance of honour in the Caucasus is conveyed by an Ingush fable, 'Lost Honour Cannot be Recovered,' which is presented here in an abridged form:

Once, The Water, The Wind, The Fire and Honour were friends. They were always together, but on one occasion it was necessary for them to separate for a while, so that each could deal with his own affairs. On parting, they started discussing how they would find each other again afterwards. Water said that it could be found where the reeds were growing. Wind said that it could always be found where the leaves were fluttering. Fire remarked that it could be found through smoke going upwards. Only Honour alone stood without saying anything. They became interested in why he did not name his own recognisable features. He said, 'You can disperse and come together again, but for me it is not allowed. Anybody who once parts from me will part forever, and will never meet me again.' (Published in the newspaper *Serdalo*, 1962; this shortened version published in M. M. Zyazykov, 'Traditsionnaya kul'tura ingushey: istoriya i sovremennost', SKNTs VSh, Rostov-on-Don, 2004.)

One of the most common themes relating to family honour in these legends is connected to feminine chastity and to the male family members' control of the marriage of the girls, and to some extent also of the boys. The parents, and especially the father, decided when and to whom the children would marry. If a boy and girl fell in love but the parents had other ideas about the marriage there was obviously the temptation to elope. But elopement was a dangerous undertaking, risking death from the outraged family. Baddeley has a description of an actual elopement and its sequel, which took place in Vedeno, Chechnya:

> [Mamadee] pointed out with a wicked twinkle in his eye a house whence he had once carried off a fourteen-year-old girl, and ridden with her to Andi. He had made things right by marriage and succeeded in effecting a reconciliation with her family ... One can hardly doubt that this method of courtship, though somewhat abrupt and coupled with much danger, must have lent a singular charm and zest to marriage. The story of young Lochinvar has been enacted with various modifications many thousands of times in the Caucasus, but woe betide the gay lover should the fleet-ness of his horse fail to place between him and his pursuers the barrier of a black night and an accomplished fact; for consummation with these strange, but after all practical, people opened the way to reconciliation, whereas if caught in the first hot pursuit, the hero of the escapade paid for his love and daring with his life, the daggers of his avengers sheathed in his heart, while the bride, if a consenting party, went back to face insult and contumely, if not worse, at home (Baddeley II 1940, 88–89).

The first two songs, 'Adyif' and 'Adiyukh', both deal with the same Adyge story, about an elopement that was followed by an unfortunate accident in which the girl died. The distraught boy does not know what to do with her body, as she now belongs to neither family – she has not yet become a member of his family by marriage, but her own family will disown her because of the elopement. The next legend, 'The Fortress of Chirks-Abaa', describes an elopement and chase in which both of the lovers were killed: the man by the enraged father, and the girl by her own suicide. The next legend describes how a young man used magic to seduce Timur's (Tamerlane's) daughter, with eventual happy results. This is followed by the description of a young man's honourable behaviour with his fiancée at her home, with a hint of the consequences if he had failed. Still on the theme of female chas-tity, there is a legend of a peasant's resistance to his feudal lord's assumption of *droit de seigneur*, which ended with the overlord's murder. The following legend, 'Beloved Albika', describes a contest between a married woman and a would-be rapist, in which both parties use ploys involving the concepts of honour, but the woman's ploy eventually wins. The woman avoids direct rape by mentioning the man's family honour. Then the man plays dead and obliges the woman to fulfil the duties of a mourner, during which he again attempts rape. The woman then offers to let the man freely have his will at a future date to be agreed. Finally the woman tricks him into becoming her adopted son, so that a sexual relation would imply that he had committed incest with his adoptive mother.

There follow two legends about the bravery of men. Said of Kumukh chooses to go to his certain death rather than be disgraced as a coward. Then the dying Murat Marshan makes sure that nobody had heard his plea to his mother for sympathy. In the next legend Shota (Rustaveli, the great Georgian writer) offers his life to rectify the disgrace of breaking his oath.

Finally, there are two legends about hospitality: the 'duty of hospitality' is shown even to transcend the duty of blood revenge: the consumption of 'bread and salt' within a home conferring on the hosts the sacred duty of protection towards a guest, regardless of other considerations. In the final legend the young hero manages to combine the obligations of hospitality, blood revenge and the protection of his fiancée from the feudal princes, with hospitality being his first priority. This legend shows that of those three obligations, hospitality takes precedence. There are also legends throughout the Caucasus in which a holy beggar, often Saint George or sometimes Christ in disguise, asks for hospitality from a household (Tale Types 750ff).[1] According to his reception, the householder is either rewarded or punished. The usual legendary punishment for inhospitality is to be turned to stone, often together with the miser's flocks and even his unsuspecting shepherds. This type of legend is used to explain curious rock formations in various places. The Caucasus, with its many crags and vast numbers of scattered lumps of stone is fruitful soil for innumerable stories that are connected with these stones. In Daghestan, near the settlement of Kayakent, for example, there is a group of stones that represent a miserly sheep-owner and his flock; the shepherd had served up a dog instead of a sheep to his heavenly guest. Near the village of Majalis, also in Daghestan, a miserly sheep-owner served up a cat to the disguised Prophet Elijah, who then turned him and his flock into stone; the local people could distinguish

---

1   See Antti Aarne, *The Types of the Folktale*, tr. by Stith Thompson.

the shepherd and his staff, the food on the plate, the cauldron and so on
(Chursin 1913, 63–80).

59. Adyif *(Adyge)*

The front door of your maiden's room is slightly open, my Adyif,
The back door of your room is not watched, my Adyif.
E-o-oy, e-o-oy, my Adyif,
The back door is not watched, my Adyif.

The pheasant flew out on to the forest road, my Adyif,
The horse shied to one side, you lost your life, my Adyif.
E-o-oy, e-o-oy, my Adyif,
The horse shied to one side, you lost your life, my Adyif.

I would bury you in the forest, my Adyif,
But the wild beasts will eat you up, my Adyif.
E-o-oy, e-o-oy, my Adyif,
The wild beasts will eat you up, my Adyif.

I would lay you in the fork of a tree, my Adyif,
But the forest birds will peck at you, my Adyif.
E-o-oy, e-o-oy, my Adyif,
The forest birds will peck at you, my Adyif.

I would lay you in my bosom, my Adyif,
But my bosom is too small for you, my Adyif.
E-o-oy, e-o-oy, my Adyif,
My bosom is too small for you, my Adyif.

I would take you to your father's house, my Adyif,
But I feel nervous before your many kinsfolk, my Adyif.
E-o-oy, e-o-oy, my Adyif,
But I feel nervous before your many kinsfolk, my Adyif.

I would take you to my home, my Adyif,

But they will tell me it is a stranger's corpse, my Adyif,
E-o-oy, e-o-oy, my Adyif,
What am I going to do with you, my Adyif.

No narration details are known about this Adyge song, which was published in J. Bardavelidze, 'Adygsky fol'klor', Kavkazsky Dom, Tbilisi, 1994, 46. A Shapsug version of this song was published in E. V. Gippius, *Narodnye pesni i instrumental'nye naigryshi Adygov*, Sovetsky Kompozitor, Moscow, 1990, 27–29.

60. Adiyukh[1] *(Adyge)*

Introduction
The story is that the love of the youth and Adiyukh was forbidden: they were not equals, he was an *uork* (of noble birth) while she was of the *karakhalks* (peasants, or 'base folk'). In the night the youth kidnapped Adiyukh. The horse stumbled and the girl fell to the ground and died. Various other versions of this song have been published.

Since childhood we have loved one another,
O, my Adiyukh,
Since childhood you have been dear to me,
O, my Adiyukh,
I have always been thinking of you,
O, my Adiyukh,
My heart has become exhausted with thoughts of you,
O, my Adiyukh,
You gave me an interval of one year,
O, my Adiyukh,
For a year I waited for you,
O, my Adiyukh,

---

1   The name means 'white hands'.

You made me wait for yet a month,
O, my Adiyukh,

In the night on Friday,
O, my Adiyukh,
I tightened the saddle girth of my black horse,
O, my Adiyukh,
I rode up to your window,
O, my Adiyukh,
You flung open your window,
O, my Adiyukh,
You jumped on the horse and we rode away,
O, my Adiyukh,
We rode out on to an unknown road,
O, my Adiyukh,
I wrapped you up in my black *burka*,
O, my Adiyukh,
You embraced me,
O, my Adiyukh,
We rode out on to an unknown road,
O, my Adiyukh,
A forest cock, a pheasant, jumped out from the forest,
O, my Adiyukh,
The horse reared up and threw you off,
O, my Adiyukh,
You fell from my arms and were badly hurt,
O, my Adiyukh,
The blood streamed over your body,
O, my Adiyukh,
In my presence your soul departed from you,
O, my Adiyukh,
I would lay you on a hummock,
O, my Adiyukh,
But the ants will eat you up,
O, my Adiyukh,
I would put you at the top of a tree,
O, my Adiyukh,
But the black ravens will carry you away,

O, my Adiyukh,
I would leave you on the earth,
O, my Adiyukh,
But the beasts will begin gnawing you,
O, my Adiyukh,
Where, then, can I take you,
O, my Adiyukh,
What am I going to do with you?
O, my Adiyukh.

❧

No narration details are known about this Adyge song, which was published in J. Bardavelidze, 'Adygsky fol'klor', *Kavkazsky Dom*, Tbilisi, 1994, 47–48. A Kabardan version of this song was published in E. V. Gippius, *Narodnye pesni i instrumental'nye naigryshi Adygov*, Sovetsky Kompositor, Moscow, 1990, 436–439.

61. The Fortress of Chirks-Abaa *(Abkhaz)*

With the Chkhaltini Fortress, or as it is still called, the Fortress of Chirks-Abaa, is connected the following absorbing legend.

In the old days, in the Dali Gorge there lived a brave hunter. One day, while pursuing a wild animal, he found himself on the Kuban. Here the first hospitality was rendered to him by a certain prince, whose daughter was famous for her beauty through all of the North Caucasus. The young newcomer at once captured the girl's heart, and indeed he knew how to recount tales very fascinatingly, and moreover he was handsome. The young people so much appealed to each other's heart that after several days they swore to love each other until death, making up their minds that no matter what happened, they would get married. The hunter's proposal was turned down by the beauty's father. The self-willed old man called the young man a playboy and an idler ...

When they received the refusal, the young lovers arranged to escape to Abkhazia. In order to avoid any kind of suspicion, the hunter had quickly to leave the house of his beloved's father and meet her in three days' time on the border of the Kuban region, near to the Dali Gorge. No sooner said than done. Our hunter, having gathered the best riders, sent them ahead to meet his bride, while he himself went to wait in the agreed place.

In the dark of night the bride rode out of her parents' home on her father's best horse, and when she saw the waiting horsemen near at hand she galloped towards them. Already they had almost reached the place where the bridegroom was waiting with a beating heart for the bold fugitive. But at this point something terrible and unforeseen happened. Completely unexpectedly, the beauty's brother turned up – he was returning home with his numerous retinue. Catching sight of the galloping horsemen led by his sister, the brother ordered his company to cut off the fugitives' way and to hold them by force. To avoid the shedding of blood the sister confessed everything to her brother and explained the reason for her flight from her parents' home.

'I will not let anybody shame my father,' declared the brother, and he ordered his sister to return home.

With his sabre he fell upon the horsemen accompanying her, telling his retinue not to spare anybody. A cruel slaughter began. Many men fell on both sides, and nobody of the beauty's retinue was left alive. At first the girl seemed rooted to the ground at the sight of the bloody fight, but then nevertheless she came to herself and, cursing her brother, she galloped ahead, hoping to meet her suitor. In her hopes she was not disappointed. However, her brother did not lag far behind. Near the River Chkhalta he killed the lovers' horses with several accurate shots.

Perhaps the bridegroom would have managed to escape from his pursuers, since in the exchange of fire he mortally wounded his bride's brother and killed three horsemen of his retinue, but the father of the fugitive girl arrived at the critical time at the place of the bloody slaughter. Without lingering to think, the bridegroom grabbed his bride and threw himself with her into the River Chkhalta. Being an outstanding swimmer, he managed to get across to the other bank with his precious burden. Only a few steps remained to the walls of the Chkhaltini Fortress. They were making incredible efforts to clamber up the steep mountain, so as to escape from the shots of the angry father.

At last they reached the fortress gates. But here a bullet caught the groom: he was mortally wounded. The young couple took cover in the fortress. Tenderly embracing her dying lover, the unhappy girl was trying to return him to life with passionate kisses. However, the father and his people surrounded the refuge of the fugitives and insistently demanded that they should give themselves up. The bridegroom was consoling the poor girl, but he could feel that his own powers were failing him. Then before the eyes of the infuriated father they threw themselves from the height of the Chkhaltini Fortress into the rushing waters of the Chkhalta.

*

Twenty kilometres from the village of Lata, in the valley of the River Kodori, where the Chkhalta falls into it, a craggy cliff can be seen in the distance. Its summit is thickly overgrown with forest. On the cliff can be seen the ruins of the early medieval fortress of Chirks-Abaa. It is located on three small platforms, washed by the waters of the rivers flowing together here. At the corners of the platforms the remains of the preserved war towers joined to the fortress wall can be seen. In the centre of the fortress are the ruins of a central tower and some buildings. The situation of the fortress made it almost inaccessible.

ೞ

The text of this Abkhaz legend is cited from the record of K. Machavariani, published in K. Machavariani, 'Sem' dney v gorakh Abkhazii', Batumi, 1906. There also exists another variant of it, recorded in 1966 in the settlement of Koapchara of the Gul'ripshi region from the centenarian narrator Kiskinja Gogua. This version was published in V. P. Pachulia, *Padenie Anakopiya*, Nauka, Moscow, 1986, 154–156.

62. The Black Candles *(Abkhaz)*

In times long ago a wise man was living in the famous town of Anapa. He was a bachelor, and so he took in an orphan boy and educated him. He grew very fond of the clever little boy and became attached to him with all his heart. And the boy returned the same feeling to his *atalyk*.[1]

Time passed, and the boy learned much. During this time he grew up into a handsome youth. But the wise man had grown old and weak. And

---

[1]   An *atalyk* is a Tatar word, meaning tutor or educator. This could refer to a temporary foster father, or a man who has adopted an orphan.

the time came for him to die. He called the young man to him and said, 'There is nothing I can leave you as a legacy, except the accomplishments which you have acquired, and besides that, this little chest. Take care of it like the apple of your eye. Some time it will be very useful to you.'

The wise man spoke thus and died.

For a long time the young man was grieving, mourning his *atalyk*. But time passed, and he decided to find out exactly what was kept in the cherished little chest. He lifted the lid and was surprised: the little chest was empty! Only in the very corner lay two black candles: one was whole, and the other was half burnt.

What good are these candles to me, thought the young man. Perhaps I should burn them in memory of my teacher?

He struck fire from his flint and lit the half of the black candle. But the red flame had hardly flared up when it produced a hot wind, and a black spirit, a giant with red eyes appeared before the young man.

'Why did you open the chest, and what do you need?' he asked the young man.

'I would like to see my *atalyk*, so that he can pass all his wisdom on to me,' replied the young man.

'The dead frequent the other world, to which I have no way in,' said the black spirit. 'But I can fulfil all of your other wishes, any time you light a candle. Only remember: it will soon burn down, and moreover the second one will not last long. And when the second candle has burnt out, I will not present myself to you any more. So choose your wishes with care.'

But who can be circumspect when young blood is boiling? So the young man lit the candle once more and expressed his most cherished wish to the black spirit: 'Get for me the most beautiful girl of the Caucasus, and bring her here for the night!'

And at the time the mighty Aksak Temir was ruling in Derbent. He had an only daughter, and she was considered the foremost beauty of the two sides of the Caucasus chain. And it was she whom the spirit selected for his master. In the night he conveyed the beauty to Anapa, and the young man exchanged caresses with her until the first cock crow. But at dawn he summoned the black spirit and told him to take the beauty back.

The next morning it all seemed to the beauty like a girlish dream. However, this same dream was also repeated on the second night, and on the third … The beauty grew sad, and became pensive.

The beauty fell completely into despair, and made up her mind to tell her parents all about it.

When Aksak Temir found out about his daughter's shameful secret, he blazed with anger and swore to punish the seducer cruelly. And for now he placed a guard at his daughter's room.

However, once again the beauty spent the night in the embraces of the young man in Anapa, and nobody noticed anything.

Then Aksak Temir told her, 'Put on your mother's necklace, and wind my rosary round your hand and, when you are in that house, leave them all surreptitiously in some corner. By these tokens we will find and establish the guilt of the culprit.'

But these tricks resulted in nothing: all the things remained on the beauty's bed. The black spirit did not take them, while she herself disappeared each night.

Aksak Temir went into a rage: 'Surely, at least you would recognise the seducer by his face?' he asked his daughter.

'Oh certainly, I would recognise him! And I will tell you something more: his house is by the sea, each night I hear the noise of the waves.'

'Then I will go through all of the coast of the Caucasus, and I will search him out!' exclaimed the father.

Aksak Temir called together all his princes and *uzdens*, gathered a large army, took his daughter with him and set off to look for the seducer.

They were going for a long time and subdued quite a few tribes on their way. But nowhere did the daughter of Aksak Temir see the familiar face of the young man whom she had managed to fall in love with. But she passed each night with him, and she came to like him more and more.

But now Aksak Temir's army reached Anapa. When they saw such a terrible force, all the inhabitants of the town went out to meet the conqueror. Only the young man alone stayed in his house in the empty town. This was because he knew: all his hopes lay with the black spirit.

And so once more he opened the special little chest, and his heart sank. The half of the first candle had burned up long ago, and only one candle-end remained of the whole second one. He had used up all the power of the candles on his love!

But all the same he lit the end of the black candle, and the spirit appeared before him. 'Fill my house with riches from top to bottom,' the young man commanded him. 'Place behind the house a racehorse of a kind the world has never seen, and prepare the richest clothes and the most precious gifts for my bride and her father.'

'Hurry, the candle is burning to the end,' the black spirit interrupted him.

'Do it!' said the young man, and he blew out the little flame. He could see that only one last wish remained from his candle.

Meanwhile all the men of Anapa passed before Temir's daughter, and she did not find her lover among them.

Then Temir ordered the whole town to be searched: to see whether somebody was left there. And in one of the houses his soldiers found the young man: he was sitting on the threshold of a poor house in modest clothes.

The soldiers seized him and brought him to Temir. 'How dare you to disobey, why didn't you come with everybody else?' exclaimed Aksak Temir angrily. 'Execute him!'

But now Temir's daughter saw the young man and recognised him. She threw herself at her father's feet and said, 'It is he, it is he, my sweetheart. Spare him!'

But Temir answered, 'Because of this commoner I have gone through the entire Caucasus with fire and sword. Am I really going to give my daughter away to a nonentity?'

Then the young man said to him, 'I am not such a nonentity as you think, great Aksak Temir. A wise *atalyk* brought me up and gave me many accomplishments and riches. I love your daughter. Permit me to appear before you in my real aspect and then make judgement on me.'

Frowning, Aksak Temir consented. He let the young man go into the town. And after a little while there stood before him a *jigit* on such a racehorse as the world had never seen, in the very best clothes and with precious gifts for his bride.

'And besides,' he said, 'I have a talisman. Here in this little chest is the end of a black candle. If I light it, a black spirit will appear and fulfil everything that I wish for.'

Aksak Temir smiled: 'If that is so, then let your spirit dig a canal from here right to Derbent, so that my horses can drink clean water to the very end of the journey. Then I will give my daughter to you.'

The young man opened the little chest he had been bequeathed, got out the stump of the black candle and lit it. And the black spirit with the red eyes presented himself and said to the young lover: 'It is your last wish.'

The young man answered him, 'Did you hear Aksak Temir's command? Do it!'

And his wish was fulfilled.

The terrible conqueror was obliged to keep his word. A wedding took place in Anapa such as had never before taken place. And after that the happy young people set off together with Temir's army to Derbent. And all the way their horses were drinking clean water from the canal that had been dug by the black spirit.

Old men relate until the present day that one can find traces here and there of that very canal, with a bank on the side towards the sea. And among the people it is called Malkhashagos, which means 'road of the son-in-law'.

And nobody saw the black spirit ever again after that.

ॐ

This Abkhaz legend was first recorded in 1864 by K. Pomyalovsky. It was published in V. P. Pachulia, *Padenie Anakopiya*, Nauka, Moscow, 1986, 184–188.

63. The Young Man and the Girl *(Abkhaz)*

A young man fell in love with a girl, and she fell in love with him. However, they never managed to meet together or speak to each other in private. Several times he sent matchmakers to her parents, but after the matchmakers had seen the beauty, they lost their heads and forgot about their mission. In the end the young man saddled his horse and went to her himself.

It was morning when he rode up to the gates of her house. The girl's father and brothers had already gone off to work. She met her guest and asked him to come into the house. 'But after all, neither your brothers nor your father are at home,' he objected. 'It would not do for me to drop in when they are not here.'

And so they chatted near the gates. The time went past quickly, and they did not notice how it was getting dark. After cooking *mamalyga*, the girl's mother came out to the gates and addressed the young man: 'Welcome, dear son! Get down off your horse and call in to the house!'

When he heard these affectionate words, the young man raised his head. 'Good evening!' he answered. 'Thank you, but now it is late already'; and he touched his horse, getting ready to ride away; but the girl caught hold of the bridle and said, 'No, come in!'

Soon the men came. After supper, the mother called the eldest son to her and said to him, 'That young man and your sister love each other!' When she had said that, she spread beds in one room for her son and their guest.

When he lay down to sleep, the girl's brother put a pistol beneath his pillow. 'When everybody is asleep,' he decided, 'my sister and this guest will obviously want to meet. I will keep an eye on them.'

And indeed, when everybody in the house was sleeping, the young man quietly got dressed. The girl also got up. He went out on to the balcony. She went to the window, and they spoke about their love and their future life.

The cocks crowed, heralding the dawn, and the young man suddenly thought: 'What shame!' he exclaimed. 'What a disgrace, that we are conversing here!'

'Why?' she asked.

'We are deceiving your parents. After all I am violating the laws of hospitality. To shoot me for it would not be enough.'

The girl's brother was observing the lovers through a chink, fearing that their meeting would not stop at mere conversation. He took the pistol with him, so as not to allow a family disgrace. When he was satisfied of the restraint and nobility of the young man, the brother went to sleep.

In the morning he saddled his guest's horse, woke him up and said to the young man, 'I do not think we could find a better brother-in-law. Ride home, and prepare everything for the wedding. Your bride will be waiting for you.'

In a week's time the wedding was celebrated, and the young people began living happily.

ॐ

No narration details are available for this Abkhaz legend, which was published in Kh. S.Bgazhba, *Abkhazskie skazki*, Alashara, Sukhumi, 1985, 303–304.

64. Solsa *(Chechen)*

In remote times, in the gorge of the River Argun, there lived a Prince Solsa. This prince spent the first night with the bride of every man of his subjects. Only after spending the night with him was the bride allowed to go to her own husband.

One day a poor man came to the prince and asked him not to disgrace him. Solsa called the poor man names, drove him away, and shouted after him, 'Why are you better than the others?'

Then the incensed poor man went to Solsa's son and asked him for his father's sword in return for a golden *abaz*.[1] Solsa was able to wind the sword around his hand, just like a thread wound on a bobbin. One only had to press the handle of the sword and it straightened itself at once.

For the golden *abaz*, Solsa's son gave the sword to the poor man. With this sword the poor man took off Solsa's head. The head of Solsa rolled three times across the Argun and shouted out, 'May the power of the princes go to the slaves, and the power of the slaves go to the princes.'

The waves of the Argun carried away Solsa's head. But the poor man brought his wife home and began living happily.

Since that time there has been no prince in that region.

This Chechen legend was recorded by A. O. Malsagov in 1971 from the words of Kh. Zhalieva, in the village of Bamut. Published in A. O. Malsagov, *Skazki i legendy Ingushey i chechentesev*, Nauka, Moscow, 1983, 311–312.

65. Beloved Albika *(Ingush)*

Seska Solsa was mighty among mighty men. He used to ride on a grey horse. Behind him there always stood sixty horsemen, Orstkhoys (Arkhustoys). His horse had a height altogether of three *lokteys*, and his horse's hoof was not larger than that of a foal.[2] He was able to ascend

---

1   An *abaz* is a small coin, named after the Shah Abbas.
2   Here the pagan patron and saint, T(kh)amazh-Erda, comes to mind. He was well known in the aboriginal religion of the Vaynakhs (Chechen-Ingush), and he used to ride on a horse the

high into the mountains, and on the next day gallop as far as Georgia by dinnertime.

Seska Solsa had a friend, Okhkarkhoy Kant. He was an equally well-known man. Okhkarkhoy Kant had a beautiful wife, who was called Beloved Albika. Seska Solsa had the idea of taking her from Okhkarkhoy Kant. Sitting on his grey horse, Seska Solsa and his sixty horsemen rode over to Okhkare. Okhkarkhoy Kant did not even suspect what Seska Solsa had planned. Beloved Albika said to Seska Solsa when he arrived in Okhkare, 'Seska Solsa! You are the chief of the land of the Galgays, as Okhkarkhoy Kant is the chief of the land of the Georgians. I am warning you: if you have taken it into your head to abduct me by force, you will not then be able to visit the land of the Georgians, and Okhkarkhoy Kant will be deprived of the possibility of frequenting the land of the Galgays. We must not let that happen. I am a woman in my body, plump and beautiful in my face; my breasts lie (find a place) on my shoulders.[1] I myself will leave Okhkarkhoy Kant and marry you.' After saying that she sent Solsa packing, but she remained on her guard against him, although she said nothing to her husband of what had happened.

Solsa spent seven months in anxious expectation. He kept on hoping that Albika would fulfil her promise. At last he realised that Albika had deceived him, and then Solsa thought up a trick. Pretending to be dying, he said, 'I am dying. When I die, send a messenger to Okhkarkhoy's wife with the news of my death. Leave my body unburied for three days and nights.'[2]

His people did what Solsa had said. On the third day Albika came. Sitting down next to Seska Solsa's body, Albika pricked him with an awl without anybody seeing. She wanted to find out whether he was actually alive. Other women were still in the house, and so Solsa did not throw himself at Albika, he did not even stir himself. Albika, convinced that he was dead, started to keen over him, saying such words as: 'El is not worthy to take you, Seska Solsa![3] You were the chief of the land of the Galgays!'

---

size of a goat. However, that did not hinder him from accomplishing distant journeys and returning quickly (according to Ch. Akhriev and B. Dalgat).

1   Such a representation of feminine beauty has to be regarded as very archaic, going back to remote epochs. The exaggeration of her feminine attributes is probably linked to a cult of motherhood.

2   The hero's pretence of death (often even decomposing as a corpse) with the aim of deceiving somebody, is a common Nart motif.

3   A distinctive idiomatic expression (the hero is too good to die, i.e., to land up in El, the kingdom of the dead).

When everybody had gone out, and Albika was left alone at the head of Solsa's bed, the latter jumped up and rushed towards her. But Albika asked him to listen first to what she had to say. 'You are a man, and you are the chief of the land. You have honour and respect, but today you want to discredit it. Even the children will say to one another, "May your honour slump, like that of Seska Solsa, who wanted to rape his guest!" I do not want you to lose your honour on account of my body. But if you do what I say, then you will become even more worthy than you have been up to now. Now I will call the people and tell them that Seska Solsa has not died and is still breathing. And at that time you wake up and start telling the people something, saying that all of it is the news from El. Then I will spread it everywhere that Seska Solsa descended into El and once more returned to the sunny world.[1] I know that you will not rest until you have familiarised yourself with the taste of my body. On the first Sunday Okhkarkhoy Kant will set out to the land of the Georgians. You come riding to Okhkar with your sixty horsemen. Then you will indeed be able to discover the taste of my body.' Solsa listened to her advice. From that time the rumour went around that he was able to go down into El and return to the sunny world.

At the appointed time Solsa arrived in Okhkar. Okhkarkhoy Kant was not at home, and Albika herself came out to meet the guests. She said to Solsa, 'Take four comrades with you to sit at the table with you, and go into the tower; and let your sixty Ortkhustoys make themselves comfortable around the tower.' For the sixty horsemen she slaughtered an ox, but for Solsa she prepared all kinds of dishes; they were of various colours (appearances), but all with the same taste. After all that she also made *kasha* of her own breast milk. When Solsa, together with his table companions, had tasted her dishes, which were of various colours but of the same taste, Albika placed before Solsa a silver bowl with the *kasha*, at the same time saying, 'I have made the *kasha* only for you, and you yourself have to eat it. You have never eaten anything tastier than this *kasha*.'

Solsa ate the *kasha* and then Albika spoke as follows: 'Seska Solsa, I have prevented the hostility which could have overtaken all the land, and I have made your friend Okhkarkhoy Kant your brother. Now he will not have to shun the land of the Galgays, as also you, Seska Solsa will not have to flee from the land of the Georgians. For your companions I cooked an ox, while

1   The case of the apparent 'revival' of Solsa in the legend testifies to the scepticism of the folk with respect to their belief in life after death.

you and your table companions I fed with dishes of various colours but the same taste. That food was also prepared for you as an example so that you should know: all women in the world have diverse forms and appearance. But when you taste them, they all have the same taste! But besides, Solsa, you have eaten *kasha* which I have prepared with the milk from my own breast.[1] Seska Solsa, since you have fed on my milk, that means that you are now my son. And a son is not permitted to do what you had intended.'

Then Solsa acknowledged and appreciated the wisdom of Albika. He felt ashamed before her. From that time he brought silver from the land of the Cherkess and gold from the land of the Georgians into her house, and made her presents of them. That is the kind of fine fellow that Seska Solsa became. He himself was a Galgay and from the family of Magat.

This Ingush legend was recorded by Kh. Osmiev in 1938 from the words of Umar Atievich Gatiev, born 1880, in the village of Angusht of the Prigorodny region. Published in U. B. Dalgat, *Geroichesky epos chechentsev i ingushey*, Nauka, Moscow, 1972, 321–322.

66. Said of Kumukh *(Lak)*

Notes from Kh. Khalilov
This song is about Saidbek, the cousin of Surkhay-Khan II. The folk do not call him a *bek*. According to the traditions, Saidbek was a fervent supporter of the conclusion of peace with Russia and acceptance of Russian citizenship. He persuaded Surkhay-Khan II of the uselessness of war with Russia, since the tsar had innumerable soldiers and weapons; that Russia was a huge country with a multi-million population, and it would overwhelm them in the end.

---

1   This refers to the custom of foster relationship, which had existed among the Vaynakhs for a long time. According to the custom, the man must spontaneously touch the woman's breast with his teeth, after which he is considered to be her foster son (see paper of A. Bazorkin, 'Gorskoye palomnichestvo', SSKG, Issue VIII, 1875, 1–12, which is a description of the ceremony of forgiving a blood enemy, including adoption as a son); in the Vaynakh tales the heroes who become brothers, usually say one to the other, 'From today we are sworn brothers and *enchiks* (i.e., milk brothers), having sucked at the one breast.'

It could be suggested that Said also convinced influential circles in the khanate about the uselessness of the war activities. He expressed his views openly and boldly. Being afraid of his influence on the masses, Surkhay-Khan II decided to deal with him. In the song Surkhay-Khan II is called mean and base and is shown as cowardly. Thus the folk express their attitude to the khan, who is well known in historical traditions as a bold and decisive man. For his wise leadership of the khanate he was nicknamed Khun-Butta (Great Father).

The Kazikumukh khan resided in Kurakh (now the regional centre of the Kurakh region) for some time. In the eighteenth century, in the days of Surkhay-Khan (Cholak Surkhae), the lands of neighbouring peoples, namely the Kyura and Agul' peoples, were forcibly joined to the Kazikumukh khanate. When Surkhay-Khan fell sick with malaria during his campaigns in the trans-Caucasus, he received treatment in the Kurakh Fortress. He settled there many families of Laks, the khan's serfs, for maintenance of the khan's court.

The khan sent a letter
Into the town of Kumukh,
Demanding that Said of Kumukh
Should ride to Kurakh.
When they were reading the khan's letter
To Said of Kumukh,
The daredevils of Kumukh
Bowed their heads.
'Why are you so upset,
You young Kumukh men,
After all, I am not worried,
Although I am summoned to a certain death.'
'Our concerns have grown,
Our hearts have become sad.
That low-down Surkhay-Khan
Will not do you any good.'
'Don't think, but listen,
Young men with lion hearts.
What is written as our fate
Will not apply to another man.'

After putting on his bright weapons
And getting ready his good horse,
Said sat on his black horse
And started on his way.
When Said shouted 'Gyayta'
The ground shook,
His black horse neighed
And the sky trembled.
The blue crags of Shovkra,
On which even grass does not grow,
Were blossoming with violets
And afterwards started shedding tears.
The elders of the Lak *auls*
Had barred the road to the Shara Plain:
'Turn back, Said,' they said.
And many times they entreated him.
Said with the lion heart
Did not heed their request:
'Big thanks to you,
Elders of Daghestan.
Say a prayer for me,
Asking God for protection.'
He struck his horse with the whip
And galloped to Kurakh.
When Said was riding
Through the Kuli and Khosrekh green fields,
Both the sun and the moon in the sky
Became frozen in admiration.
When Said approached
The town of Kurakh,
The voice of a *gazi* was heard
From the centre of the town:
'Let all of us go
To the khan to ask
Him to give us
Said with the lion's heart.'
Could this base Surkhay-Khan
Really heed our request?

He ordered his slaves
To decapitate him (Said).
Seven slaves approached,
Intending to decapitate him.
When Said was assured that they would kill him,
He swung his Egyptian blade
And laid out all seven.
When he saw with his own eyes
The skill of Said's hands,
The khan hid himself in a room
And started locking the doors.
Said climbed up
Nimbly on his horse
On to a high balcony
Of forty stairs ...
From behind the doors
The khan called his slaves.
At the khan's command, a slave
Killed bold Said.

❧

This Lak song was recorded by Ali Kayayevy in 1930 from the words of Shapi, the son of Muhammad, in the village of Khosrekh. Published in Kh. Khalilov, *Lakskie epicheski pesni*, Makhachkala, 1969, 181–183.

67. Murat Marshan *(Abkhaz)*

Esmy had only one son and his name was Murat. From his early years he became fond of hunting, and in his search for game he used to wander along the upper reaches of the turbulent Kodori.

On one occasion, Murat was returning from the hunt, a chamois that he had killed was hanging on his back. The successful hunter was striding happily as he set off for home. But suddenly he was stopped by the cries of his neighbours coming to meet him: 'Murat, Murat!' they groaned. '*Abreks* have fallen on Pskha! Woe to us!'

Murat called his brothers, but they refused to go on such a dangerous expedition. Murat set out alone to the distant Pskha. He traversed forest thickets, torrential streams, he overcame steep cliffs. Finally he walked into Pskha. Murat dashed at his enemies, who were not expecting him; he routed them and saved the inhabitants from destruction.

A year later the raid was repeated. Once more Murat turned up in Pskha, and once more he won a victory. But meanwhile Murat's enemies began thinking of revenge: they gathered a raiding party, in order to catch Murat alive and to carry him away into captivity.

It was very early: after Murat had woken up he had sat down at the hearth to find a smouldering coal in the cinders to light up his pipe. Suddenly a threatening shout sounded in the yard: 'Eh, Murat! Surrender! Lay down your arms, come out!'

'At least let me have a smoke! Wait a little!' answered Murat.

It became quiet in the yard and in Murat's *saklya*. Suddenly he jumped up. With a kick he knocked out the door, which flew off with a crash; and with a growl like a lion he threw himself on his enemies with his drawn sword. Many of his foes were laid out by Murat's well-aimed blows, until an enemy bullet hit him in the head. The blood streamed from his temple. Staggering, Murat covered the wound with his *bashlyk* and sat down, leaning his elbows on a stone. From the *saklya*, with a howl, his mother ran out and rushed towards her son. 'Murat, Murat! You are wounded, there is blood on your face!'

'It is not blood, it's not blood, but sweat!' answered her son, repeating the customary incantation with which wounded people are reassured.

Leaning his head on the stone, he directed his dying gaze steadily towards his mother. 'Nan, pity me!' he suddenly whispered.

This staggered his mother: 'My son!' she exclaimed. 'You always were a hero. So why then now, before your death, do you speak to me like that?'

Murat gathered his remaining strength and got up. His face was just as stern as before. 'Tell me, has nobody heard our conversation?' he groaned.

'Only I alone,' answered his mother.

Murat slowly sank on to the stone, and a proud smile lit up the face of the dying man.

He died, satisfied with his mother's reply.

৵

No details are available of the narration of this Abkhaz legend, which was published in Kh. S. Bgazhba, 'Abkhazskie skazki', Alashara, Sukhumi, 1985, 328–329.

68. Shota and the Lord of Tmogvi *(Georgian)*

Toma Tmogveli possessed the fortress and town of Tmogvi.[1] He had a sister by the name of Tinatin, and she was beautiful to look at. When Shota returned home, he wanted to take Tinatin as a wife.[2]

He rode from Rustavi[3] to Tmogvi to propose marriage. He was riding past the Fortress of Ormotsi.[4] It was there that the seven Abashidze brothers lived. All seven were renowned heroes, but were unmarried. They had a sister. She had a slight limp, but she was educated and knew how to speak well. When he rode up to the village, he asked that sister of the seven brothers, by the name of Kekela, to quench his thirst. Kekela answered him, 'If you want water, call in to our house.'

Shota went into the house. They started up a conversation and spoke between themselves so much that they even came to an agreement about marriage. Shota thought, I will not find a better girl. They gave each other their word: if Shota was unfaithful to his word, he had to accept death at the hands of Kekela. If Kekela was unfaithful, Shota would kill her. After giving this promise, Shota left the house and headed for Tmogvi. He climbed up to its overlord, Toma Tmogveli. It was evening. They had supper. Now he and Tinatin met, and he realised that he liked her better than Kekela.

And now they gave each other their promise: in May, Shota should come for the girl. Shota returned to Rustavi, but he did not pass along the way that led past Kekela. He avoided it by going along the other bank of the river. The time came for Shota to take Tinatin away to his home. Once more he took a roundabout route, in order not to see Kekela. Shota celebrated their wedding in Tmogvi, and started conveying Tinatin towards Rustavi.

---

1   Toma Tmogveli was the lord of the fortress of Tmogvi.
2   Refers to the return of the famous Georgian poet Rustaveli from the distant lands to which he had been sent to get an education. The poet lived during the reign of Queen Tamar (1184–1210 AD).
3   Rustavi is a village and fortress in Meskheti.
4   Ormotsi (literally, 'forty'), means the 'Fortress of the Forty'.

Kekela learned that Shota was taking Tinatin by the Tolosha Road.[1] All seven of her brothers happened to be home at that time.

Kekela was preparing dinner for her seven brothers at the same time as the wedding train was riding along the other side of the river. The brothers knew nothing about it. The brothers had a horse, and for seven years he had been at pasture without being broken in. Kekela did not even have time to serve dinner, and she left the food bowls in the kitchen without placing them on the table. She put on her eldest brother's weapons, sat on that horse and dashed with him into the water of the overflowing river.

Since the dinner was late, the brothers sent the youngest of the brothers to tell their sister that it was time to bring dinner. The youngest brother saw that the dinner was cooked, and the bowls had been taken from the shelf, so he thought that she had gone outside somewhere for a short time.

Again Kekela was not to be seen.

Then the second brother went out. He saw the same thing as the first one had, and he so informed his brothers. Once again Kekela did not appear.

The eldest brother went out. He saw that his armour was missing. He ran to the stable and he saw that the horse was not there either. At this point he called his brothers: 'Come out, somebody has kidnapped our sister, or else she has run away of her own volition.'

The brothers went out into the yard and began scanning the road. They saw the girl directing the horse into the river. Their own horses were not able to enter such fast-running waters. They watched and saw the horse that had been resting for seven years forcing his way so deeply into the water that only the head of the rider could be seen. After a short time the horse bore his rider out on to the other bank of the river. And the wedding party was riding just there. The girl blocked Shota's way and said, 'Stop the wedding train.'

She got out their agreement, written on that night. Shota flung open the clothes on his chest and said, 'I am guilty before you and must perish by your hand.'

'Show me your bride,' said Kekela.

Tinatin showed her face. 'Yes, she is better than I am,' said Kekela. She got down from her horse, blessed the young couple and, after sitting on her horse, once more forded the river.

The brothers were looking and marvelling. Her brothers asked Kekela,

---

1   The Tolosha Road is the road going past the Tolosha Fortress.

'What happened, why were you riding to the other bank?'

Their sister answered them, 'That was Shota Rustaveli. He was taking his bride from Tmogvi, and I gave my blessing to the young people.'

She did not tell her brothers the truth. She was afraid that they might kill Shota.

ॐ

This Georgian legend was recorded by A. Makharadze in 1937 from the words of F. Gogoladze in the village of Khizabavra (Meskheti). Published in E. B. Virsaladze, *Gruzinskie narodnye predaniya i legendy*, Nauka, Moscow, 1973, 172–173.

69. The Duty of Hospitality *(Ingush)*

Once some brothers captured their inveterate enemy, who had caused them much harm. Therefore the brothers decided to inflict cruel torments on him. They tied up their enemy's hands and feet with rope, and they started thinking about how to deal with him.

At this time the brothers were obliged to set off somewhere in a hurry. They said to their mother, 'We will be absent for three days and three nights, but we will come back and subject our enemy to the torments that he deserves. While we are away, do not give him anything to drink or eat, no matter how much he pleads.'

The brothers rode away. One day passed, a second; and on the third day the prisoner said, 'Do not let me die of hunger. Give me a pinch of salt with *churek* bread and a little water.'

'Our men ordered that nothing should be given to you,' answered the mother.

'May God turn his back on you, if you are going to torment me so! Tomorrow your sons will kill me, and I am prepared to accept death. But today give me a mouthful of water and allow me to touch food with the tip of my tongue,' begged the prisoner. The mother was moved to pity and she gave him something to eat and drink.

The sons came riding home. They looked at the prisoner and asked their mother, 'Did you give him anything to eat and drink?'

'I gave him some,' answered the mother.

'You made a mistake doing that. We really cannot kill a man who has eaten food in our house! We will have to capture him another time, but for now we will let him go.'

And the brothers let their worst enemy go, since he had tasted food in their home.

ટ

This Ingush legend was recorded by I. A. Dakhkilgov in 1972 from the words of A. Khamkhoyev in the town of Grozny. Published in A. O. Malsagov, *Skazki i legendy Ingushey i chechentsev*, Nauka, Moscow, 1983, 238.

70. Gazi, the Son of Aldam *(Ingush)*

To the east of the mountain region of Chechnya, not far from the famous Lake Kazena, is situated the great castle of Aldam-Gezi, with which folk memory associates the events described here.

Gazi, the son of Aldam, was three years short of fifteen years old. One day at twilight a horseman came galloping to him and reported, 'Tonight at midnight, the man who murdered your father will ride across such-and-such a bridge.'

Not even a few minutes had passed when another horseman came galloping up: 'Tonight your beautiful beloved Zaza will be forced to marry a Cherkess prince.'

Gazi had not had time to start thinking properly about which he should undertake first when yet another horseman appeared: 'Tonight your father's friends are arriving here.'

Sadly Gazi went into the *saklya*. 'What are you depressed about; what sort of thoughts are bothering you, my boy? Tell your mother about them,' said his mother. Gazi told her the cause of his grief.

Then his mother said to him, 'If our folk's enemy and your father's murderer is fated to perish at your hands, then there is no hurry. If the beautiful Zaza, the daughter of Anzor, loves you, then you will always succeed in marrying her. But if you do not receive your father's friends today with all honour, then you will be disgraced for the rest of your life.'

Gazi received his father's friends in a worthy manner. He met them warmly at the threshold of the *saklya*. He fed them, gave them drink and saw them to bed. Then he saddled his horse and arranged an ambush at the place across which his father's murderer was supposed to ride. At midnight his father's murderer approached the bridge on a black horse. On the bridge the villain's horse began to hesitate. 'May you be accursed, why are you stalling? We have nobody to fear! After all, Gazi, the son of Aldam, is three years short of fifteen years old!' The black rider landed blows with his whip.

'Gazi, the son of Aldam, is three years short of fifteen years, but he is in front of you. Prepare your weapons for battle!' shouted Gazi. And in an honourable battle, Gazi, the son of Aldam, gained the victory; and the evidence for it was the chopped-off moustache of his enemy.[1]

Then Gazi set out to the home of the beautiful Zaza, daughter of Anzor. He entered the house and greeted the Cherkess prince: 'May nothing disturb your peace, I am collecting my bride!'

'Stop joking!' said the prince.

'Jokes are the source of quarrels, but do not reproach me for being underhand,' said Gazi. He took his bride, returned home towards dawn and said, 'Here, Mother, is your daughter-in-law.' Then he pulled the moustache from his belt: 'And this is the moustache of your husband's murderer.' From her joy, Gazi's mother danced so lightly around the hearth that even a trace the size of an ant's track could not have been left on the cinders.

Some time later the Cherkess princes arrived. 'We will give you your weight in gold not to humiliate us before the other princes. Return Zaza, Anzor's daughter, to us,' they asked Gazi, the son of Aldam. 'If you do not give her willingly, we will take her by force.'

This was heard by the guests, the friends of Gazi's father. They came out and said, 'Gold and silver are the adornments of princes. The beautiful Zaza is the adornment of Gazi's home. If you have come in peace, then we will meet you as guests. If you have come in war, then we are ready for war.'

The princes realised that they would not succeed, and they scuttled off back home. Only now did the wedding feast in the yard of Gazi, the son of Aldam, really get going. Evidently it will not finish in our time.

---

1   To cut off the moustache or to seize somebody by the beard is considered by the Vaynakhs, as also by many other people of the world, as a great insult.

This Ingush legend was recorded by A.U. Malsagov in 1962 from the words of A. Yevkurov, in the village of Olgeti. A Chechen variant of this legend was recorded by I. Matsayev in 1977 from the words of A.-Kh. Dayev of the village of Shali. Published in A. O. Malsagov, *Skazki i legendy Ingushey i chechentesev*, Nauka, Moscow, 1983, 318–319.

X

Relations Within the Family

The relations within the family depended on blood connections – nowadays we would say 'shared genes'. The other important factor was that the daughters would marry into another family and leave their home and blood relations, and conversely a new wife would have come from a different family, with different blood, different genes. When newly introduced into the family, a wife would be expected to take part in the economic life of the family, doing her share of the domestic chores, but the family's chief hopes were that she should bear children, and especially male children. The main importance of male children was that they would continue the family line and enlarge (strengthen) it, whereas female children would have to be fed and then would eventually leave the family altogether: and *their* children would not be considered as a continuation of that family, but of somebody else's family. Once the young wife had borne even one child, she now automatically acquired a close blood connection with at least one member of her new family – namely her own child – and through that child a blood connection with the family in general. The more children she bore, the more members of that family would have a direct blood connection with her: her status would thus be increased. Because male children would remain inside the family, they would be expected to look after their parents and grandparents in their old age.

In general no men but only women entered a community from outside; so an expanding community would continue to exist as a single extended family. The equivalent in our society would be a community where all of the families had the same surname, not because of inherent inbreeding, but because new blood only entered in the form of females who take their husbands' names.

Generally a Caucasus mother has a close relationship with her son, as is clear from the explanation above. Besides their emotional relationship, it is her son who gives her status within the family. There is a saying in Georgia that when a French soldier goes into action he thinks about his girlfriend, when a Georgian soldier goes into action he thinks about his mother.

The family in the Caucasus was basically male-dominated. However, that male domination mainly applied in the field of external relations. Within the home, the females had considerable control. The relative status of some family members is illustrated by a typical exchange in a Lezg anecdote, 'The Khan and the Peasant'. This tale exists in various parts of the Caucasus:

It so happened that each morning when a khan set off hunting, he met a peasant chopping firewood. And although enough firewood had been cut to form quite a large hillock, he did not give up his work. The khan was surprised. Finally one day the khan could not contain himself: 'You, peasant, are clearly a very poor man with many children?'

'Be healthy, khan,' answered the woodcutter. 'One cannot say that I have such a very large family. But what I earn I divide into three parts. With the first I am paying off a debt, the second I am giving on loan, and the third I throw away into the river.'

'Somehow I do not understand you, man. Can't you disclose the meaning of those words?'

The peasant answered, 'I am repaying the debt to my very aged parents. The part I am lending is because I am raising a son. I am throwing a part into the river, because I am wasting it on my daughter.'

The legends included below generally follow the principles of the above description. Blood relations are loyal to each other, with the exception that in some legends brothers are rivals and accordingly become enemies. In the case of girls and women the situation is more complicated. As long as a girl is unmarried, her loyalty is to her blood family, i.e., her brothers and her parents. However, once a woman marries, her loyalties often are transferred to that of her husband and his family. As can be seen from the legends themselves, the relationships are sometimes complicated.

In the first legend, 'The Warrior of Shamil', Shamil' names the various members of the hero's family in turn. The warrior feels the need to return home for the death of his various *blood* relatives, namely his father, brother, mother and sister; but when it transpires that it was his wife who had died, he is not prepared to return home. In the following legend, 'Love for the Father and Love for the Son', the loyalty required between father and son is emphasised. The next four legends involve relationships between brothers. In 'The Fall of Anakopia' there is conflict between two brothers who are rivals. The real harm is done by a niece who has actually married outside her family, so has little connection with the central family, and merely performs the wishes of the ambitious brother. 'The Fortresses of Gogia and Petre' depicts a straightforward conflict between two rival brothers who kill each other, and no other relatives are involved. In 'Ali was Left on the Cliff' one brother is destroyed by his other two brothers who were rivals for the family property, but in this case their mother disgraces them for breaking up their family (the father has already died). In 'The Hunter-brothers' the situation is more complicated, since the younger of the two brothers has a positive attitude towards his elder brother, but the latter misunderstands and considers him to be a rival, and accordingly kills him. As in the previous legend, the mother shows her disapproval.

In the next legend, 'Akhkepig', the sister is loyal to her brother until her marriage outside the family, but as soon as she marries she transfers her loyalty from her brother to her new husband, the ogre who has already destroyed the rest of their family, and she helps him to destroy her brother too. After his faithful dogs have resuscitated him and killed his sister's ogre husband, the brother still retains sufficient loyalty to his family blood to refrain from killing his sister. Instead he wills that she should change into a thorn. In 'Burkhay Izazha' the girl marries outside the family, but in this case she is given away against her will (i.e., sold). Any loyalty that the family might have had towards her is now replaced by avarice for the bridegroom's gifts. In the next legend, 'Chyuerdi', the widowed mother marries her second husband and transfers her loyalty away from her own hero son to her new husband, who was an ogre. After various adventures the boy hero's stepbrother rescues him and kills the hero's stepfather; but the hero was unable to strike his own mother, who shared his blood (i.e., he had retained his loyalty to her although she had transferred her own loyalty from her first son to her new husband). After further adventures the hero is again rescued by his stepbrother. The situation in 'The Sister' is more complicated: the woman has already married and has a son, and she is given the difficult choice of saving the life of only one of her male relatives: her husband, son or brother. She chooses her brother, using the logic that she could replace the other two, but not her brother. The last legend, 'The Son Who Went Away to the Army in Azayni', reveals somewhat complicated relationships, and is perhaps not typical. As the hero lies dying, both his wife and mother show disloyalty to him, and only his unmarried sister takes him in and tries to look after him. As in the previous legend, his sister considers him to be unique, whereas both his wife and mother regard him as being replaceable.

71. The Warrior of Shamil'[1] *(Chechen)*

Shamil''s army took up a position high in the mountains. Shamil' was informed that the wife of one of his warriors had died. 'Send that warrior to me without delay,' ordered Shamil'. 'We will test him to see what sort of a man he is.' The warrior appeared immediately.

'Your father has died,' said Shamil', using cunning.

'My father has died, which means that our home is left without supervision; therefore I must ride to my birthplace,' answered the warrior.

'I made a mistake, it was not your father who died, but your brother.'

'If my brother has died, the home has lost a trustworthy support and I have to return.'

'No, it was not your brother, but your mother, it seems, who has passed away.'

'To share the grief with all the relatives and to bury her with all honours requires that I get to my birthplace urgently.'

'Not your mother, but your sister has died.'

'A flower has fallen from my heart, I will ride to my birthplace.'

Finally, when Shamil' said that his wife had died, the warrior answered, 'Then it is not worth while my returning, because with the death of my wife the whole household has gone to pieces.'

੩੭

This Chechen legend was recorded by A. O. Malsagov from the words of A. Akhriev in the town of Grozny. It was published in A. O. Malsagov, *Skazki i legendy Ingushey i chechentsev*, Nauka, Moscow, 1983, 324.

72. Love for the Father and Love for the Son *(Dargva)*

They tell that a certain man once lived in this world. He had a wife and a small son, and in addition he had an old, decrepit father. That man was no doubt one of those who do not remember their forebears, for he treated

---

1   Shamil' was an imam, the Daghestan war leader in the Murid Wars against the Russians in the nineteenth century.

his feeble father very cruelly. He always watched with a laugh when his wife made her father-in-law go from one place to another, when she drove him from the communal table but fed good-for-nothing beggars, when she gave him nothing for his bed, and the wretched old man had to make do with his fur coat. It was only because it was too old and torn that she did not take even that away as well. The man derived special pleasure from watching as his wife egged on their small son, who understood nothing, to hit his grandfather, to tug at his beard, to pour water over him and to tease him. The unfortunate old man endured all that because he had no other refuge, and he used to pray that death would take him a little more quickly.

One hot day, when the grandfather and father went to the field – that nasty man used to make his decrepit father work – the grandson attached himself to them.

During the ploughing, when the sun became scorching, the father stopped the oxen and went up to his boy. He took off his cap and put it on the boy. Then the old man hastily ran up to him and put his own cap on to his own son. The latter was very surprised and asked his father, 'What are you doing, Father?'

'After all, you are the same kind of son to me as he is to you,' replied the old man, pointing to the boy.

It was only then that the man first recalled that his father had raised him with the same love with which he was now raising his own son. He repented deeply for his behaviour, and from that day he never made his father work. He showed him all kinds of honour and respect, for he had found in his own heart kindness and love towards his father.

This Dargva legend was recorded by M.-Z. Osmanov in 1959, from the words of narrator Magomed Dibiraliev, aged sixty, in the village of Khajalmakhi, Levashi region. It was published in M.-Z. Osmanov, *Darginskie skazki*, Nauka, Moscow, 1963, 50–51.

73. The Fall of Anakopia *(Abkhaz)*

Introduction

The legend of the fall of the Anakopia Fortress contains features that are clearly reminiscent of the well-known story of the Trojan Horse.

One of the variants of this legend was recorded in 1957, during research into the Anakopia Fortress, from the words of its curator V. S. Korua, one of the most senior narrators of Abkhazia. It dates from a much later time and is attributed to the treacherous seizure of Anakopia by the Turks.

In this latter legend it is said that Nakopia-Ipkha was a distinguished woman who lived in Istanbul and, when travelling across the Black Sea, spent some time in Anakopia. She liked it very much, and she asked the Abkhazian prince, the owner of the fortress, to permit her to come here once more and stay a bit longer as a guest. The prince agreed with gladness. After some time Nakopia-Ipkha arrived on a ship with her things in large boxes, which were brought into Anakopia. The Abkhazian prince arranged a big feast in honour of his guests. When they had all become drunk, soldiers came out of the boxes, massacred all the Abkhazians and took possession of the fortress, which they later called Nakopia.

Even now the Anakopia Fortress seems unassailable, but at one time it was absolutely unconquerable. However, one day cunning and treachery inflicted defeat on its defenders. It happened a very long time ago, during the rule of Bagrat.

Bagrat ruled at a troubled time. An enemy was worrying his country. And the people were very poor, and because of it there was great unrest among them. Also Bagrat had a brother Dmitri, who greatly envied his crowned relative. His envy actually led him along the path of treachery. Through his mother, the treacherous queen, he came to an agreement with the Greeks (i.e., Byzantines). And one day the Greek ships put in to the land of Apsny,[1] and under cover of darkness and not meeting any resistance, the enemy soldiers entered the fortress. But they only held the fortress for one day. Dmitri became afraid of his brother's anger, and he fled to Constantinople, taking with him much wealth and his niece Anakopey-Ipkha, the sister of the chief of the fortress. Five or ten years

---

1   Apsny is the local name for Abkhazia.

passed, and word went around the land of Apsny that Anakopey-Ipkha wanted to come back to her native land and was allegedly carrying gifts to her uncle, for she had married a rich merchant and owned countless treasures. Joy filled the hearts of the inhabitants of Anakopia when they saw ten ships bringing Anakopey-Ipkha and her gifts. The people met her with great honours. And that day there was a big holiday with feasting and war games.

But towards evening, when the sun had dipped into the sea, Anakopey-Ipkha ordered the gifts to be taken from the ship and conveyed into the fortress. On each cart there were two enormous chests. These chests were set down by a high tower. Anakopey-Ipkha promised the people that the gifts would be shared out among them the next day. And the people dispersed, each to their own home.

Night came, and everybody went to sleep. It was only Anakopey-Ipkha and her loyal servants who did not sleep: they were getting ready to accomplish their treacherous plan, which Bagrat's cunning brother had suggested to them.

And so now they made their way under cover of night to the tower where the chests with the gifts were lying, and they opened them. And in each chest were two armed warriors; the warriors got up and took their swords and torches in their hands. And now there was indeed a legion of them. Then the fortress of Anakopia resounded with war cries, and now a great massacre began. The fortress was taken altogether in just one hour.

For many long years it was in the possession of the Byzantines, until Abkhazian and Georgian soldiers liberated it, driving out the treacherous foreigners and the traitors from their native land.

౨♥

This Abkhaz legend was recorded in 1958 in the village of Anukhva, in the Gudauta region, from the words of narrator Kansoua Tarkila. It was published in V. P. Pachulia, *Padenie Anakopia: Legendy kavkazkovo prichornomorya*, Nauka, Moscow, 1986, 151–153.

74. The Fortresses of Gogia and Petre *(Georgian)*

Introduction

The ruins of both fortresses even now tower up on both sides of the Borzhomi Gorge. Other traditions are also attached to these fortresses.

Not far from Borzhomi, on opposite sides of the Mtkvari,[1] stand two fortresses. The people call them the fortresses of Gogia and Petre. According to tradition, Gogia and Petre were brothers. They were at odds with one another and were competing between themselves. They lived by robbery and by plundering travellers, and they both grew rich. They used to fall on belated travellers or caravans, especially on merchants. More than once the soldiers of the brothers went against each other, showing at the time marvels of spirit and heroism, and surprising everybody.

Finally, after long efforts, a reconciliation was successfully brought about. Both brothers, accompanied by their armed detachments, met in the house of a mediator. The brothers embraced and took an oath of perpetual love and loyalty. However, after the oath there began a riotous feast, and the *azarpeshas*[2] and horns went round the table. The Kakheti wine was unable to cool off their long-standing embittered feelings. A disagreement arose right there at the table, the quarrel developed into blows, and the affair ended with *khanjalis*. At that point each armed supporter stood up for his own master, and it ended by both brothers and their numerous followers lying dead, to the very last one.

Since that time these fortresses have remained without owners, and they have turned into ruins.

This Georgian legend was recorded by I. Alkhazishvili around 1877. It was published in E. B. Virsaladze, *Gruzinskie narodnye predaniya i legendy*, Nauka, Moscow, 1973, 223–224.

---

1   The River Mtkvari (Mtqvari) is the same as the Kura, which flows through the towns of Gori and Tbilisi and through Azerbayjan to the Caspian Sea.
2   An *azarpesha* is a bowl for wine.

75. Ali was Left on the Cliff *(Avar)*

'Let's go Ali, let's go to the Steel Cliff –
The falcon has hatched young again this year.'
'I will not go, brothers, to the Steel Cliff –
Perhaps this is a trick or a crafty deception.'
'What kind of trick, Ali, from your own brothers?
What kind of deception, Ali, from your own brothers?'
'If that is so, my own brothers,
Take from the *aul* a good long rope –
Let it be so! Let us go to the Steel Cliff,
Cast the lots into one *papakha*!'
They threw the lots into one *papakha*:
Unfortunate Ali withdrew the shorter one.
They roped up Ali and lowered him down.
There was no falcon, a magpie lived there alone,
There was no falcon, a magpie had built its nest there.
'Just who said, "Only a falcon can be here"?
Whose words were: "A magpie cannot build its nest here"?
My own brothers, may God give you good fortune,
My five hundred sheep, father's legacy –
I will count them out in fives and share them with you.
My field at the *aul* – our mother's allotment –
I will measure off with a rope – don't leave me here!'
'Father's legacy, your five hundred sheep –
We will count out ourselves, but we will leave you.
The field before the *aul*, mother's allotment –
We ourselves will share, we will not raise you up.'
A little time passed before the brothers went away,
And the sun had not yet sunk to the west,
I saw a river raven flying from afar,
It was touching the earth, and soaring in the heavens.
'Even a bird does not touch the Steel Cliff –
Whose trick has beaten you, little Ali?
There is not even an animal track to my nest –
Whose intrigues have succeeded, you bold *jigit*?'
'Even a bird does not touch the Steel Cliff –
The trickery of my own brothers has beaten me.

There is not even an animal track to your nest –
The intrigues of the children of our own mother have succeeded.
I wish you good luck, black raven,
Can't you help to raise me up?'
'How can I help to raise you up?
My talons have become blunted, I don't have the strength,
I have become thin with caring for my offspring,
Of my former strength there is left not a trace.'
'Good luck and blessing upon you, black raven!
Only give the news to my mother,
And tell my wife where I am.'
That black raven flew off ...
He started circling above Ali's home.
'Don't circle any more, you black raven,
I know: Ali has been left in the gorge.
Why croak so much, you black raven?
I have realised: my son is hungry, isn't he?'
She took a little bag of sugar under her arm,
She took a little jug of *buza* in her hands
And went from there to the Steel Cliff.
She shouted, 'Ali!' He called back, 'I am here!'
She threw down the little bag of sugar:
Ali could not catch it – it fell on the ground.
'Happiness to you in your life, mother who bore me,
Bend forward slightly and have a look.'
She bent forward slightly and had a look there:
The mottled *beshmet* on his pearly body
Was falling and spreading over the steep cliff.
The Khorasan *kurpey*[1] on his bright forehead
Was flying and tumbling among the heaps of stones.
'Vo-ba-bay! Vo-ba-bay! May my tongue dry up!
O-kho-kho! A-kha-khay! May my flesh rot!'
One must choose a shorter way, there is no road here –
I went down by a roundabout path.
The sweet flesh on his pearly body
Had melted and was flowing down over the cliff.

---

1   Khorasan *kurpey* is a Karakul *papakha*, highly valued among the Daghestan people.

The white bones, like ivory,
Were rattling down the cliff and beating against the stones.
I gathered up his bones into the little bag for sugar,
The little jug for *buza* I filled with his blood
And went straight to Ali's home.
Father's legacy, his five hundred sheep –
The brothers were dividing five at a time between themselves.
The field at the *aul*, their mother's allotment –
The brothers were measuring out with a rope between themselves.
'Perhaps that's too little for you? Here's this in addition!'
I threw the little bag of bones at their feet.
'With that you won't quench your thirst, so drink this too!'
I poured out the blood from the jug for them.

No details are available about the narration of this Avar song. It was published in L. Chlaidze, *Avarsky fol'klor*, Kavkazsky Dom, Tbilisi, 2006, 98–100.

76. The Hunter-brothers *(Abkhaz)*

Not far from Lake Ritsa there once lived two brothers. The elder was called Sharpy-Yatsva, 'the morning star': he was born at dawn. The younger brother, however, was born in the evening, and so he was called Khulpy-Yatsva, 'the evening star'. Both brothers became celebrated hunters.

One day the brothers descended into a ravine, in order to rest at a stream in the intense heat of noon. Suddenly a deer ran across their path. Sharpy-Yatsva followed the trail of the deer, and he chased it for so long that the sun was already beginning to set. Only now did he notice that he had clambered up the highest mountain.

Night quickly descended and covered the tracks of the deer in the gloom. Taken unawares by night, on a precipitous slope, Sharpy-Yatsva firmly held on to a rock, making up his mind neither to climb higher nor to descend in the darkness. And he began to sing about his trouble, hoping that somewhere below his brother would hear him, and maybe somehow even would help.

Khulpy-Yatsva heard his brother's song; but no matter how much he thought, he could not think of any way to help him. However, he realised that if sleep overcame his brother, he would not be able to hold on to the ledge, that he would fall and be killed. 'I will not let him go to sleep before morning!' he decided, and so he started singing, 'You, Sharpy-Yatsva, are sitting lonely on the cliff. The deer outwitted you, the deer has disappeared. But I will overtake him and shoot him. Towards morning you will fall, you will not see tomorrow's dawn, and the stars will not light up for you.'

When he heard this song, the elder brother began to squirm with anguish. 'Khulpy-Yatsva,' he started shouting in anger, 'I am still alive! Morning will come, the mountains will grow red, and I will come down and settle accounts with you for your gibes!'

But Khulpy-Yatsva sang even louder, 'You will not be seeing either the sun or the mountains; you will go to sleep and break loose, like a stone, from the cliff. When she learns of your death, your wife will not shed even a little tear. She is a *chamois*, she needs a *jeyran* who is not afraid of a dark night on a high mountain. I am that *jeyran*!'

Sharpy-Yatsva held on even more strongly to the ledge of the cliff. Grinding his teeth, he yelled to his brother, 'Khulpy-Yatsva, keep quiet! If it was not so dark, I would shoot you. You have forgotten that I have a son, he will avenge me.'

Khulpy-Yatsva began to laugh loudly: 'Your son, Sharpy-Yatsva! I will make him a swineherd.'

Sharpy-Yatsva began to groan with fury. It seemed that the mountains began to tremble in answer to him. It was as if he had become rooted into the cliff, angry and full of hatred. But Khulpy-Yatsva kept on playing on his pipe, and until the very dawn he tormented his brother with songs, each one more biting than the previous one. And so Sharpy-Yatsva did not even start getting drowsy, and at dawn he safely descended from the cliff.

He decided to hold back his anger for now, and he silently followed his brother. Khulpy-Yatsva was overjoyed that he had saved his brother. Sharpy-Yatsva was morose, and evil thoughts were tormenting his heart: 'If I had fallen from the cliff, I would have been battered to death. After that, Khulpy-Yatsva would have carried out all that he sang about to me in the night. Even now he is satisfied and proud.' When they approached a stream across which a log had been thrown, Sharpy-Yatsva could no longer restrain himself; he let Khulpy-Yatsva go first, and he shot him in the head. Khulpy-Yatsva tumbled down into the seething torrent, reddening its foam with his blood. The fast current snatched up his corpse and carried it far, far away, into the sea's embrace. In front of Sharpy-Yatsva's gaze his brother's face just vaguely flashed, and a smile was frozen on it.

Sharpy-Yatsva came home, he did not glance at his wife, nor did he greet his mother. 'But where is Khulpy-Yatsva?', asked his mother.

Sharpy-Yatsva grinned: 'He is sitting there beneath the mountain, singing his jolly songs.'

His mother did not believe him: 'Tell me, Sharpy-Yatsva, where did you leave him?'

'He is there, beneath the mountain ... he is playing on his pipe.'

There was an evil glint in her son's eyes, and the mother's heart sensed misfortune. 'Where is your brother? Tell me, what has happened to him?' she asked once more.

Now Sharpy-Yatsva began to shout, 'To me he is no brother, but a traitor! I shot him dead.' Then he told his mother all about it: how night had caught him on the cliff, how he had called to his brother for help and how Khulpy-Yatsva had mocked him.

'And did you not understand why your brother sang such songs to you?' said his mother, lowering her head.

'No, I understood everything and did what my heart prompted.'

'Then you have a bad heart. And your intelligence is no better,' she replied. 'You have forgotten what the people say: the tongue is the interpreter of the heart. You did not think a little about what your brother was singing, you did not ask him ...'

Sharpy-Yatsva did not sleep all night, and in the morning, taking his flint-lock, he went to that stream where he had shot his brother. For a long time he stood on the log and looked at the seething torrent. It seemed to him that once more he saw his dead brother with the frozen smile on his face, and the current kept on carrying the corpse away, farther and farther, into the embrace of the sea. Then Sharpy-Yatsva placed the muzzle of the flint-lock to his forehead and fired – the impetuous torrent received his dead body with indifference.

Their mother sighed deeply when she learned of the death of her second son, and she said, 'Everything that people carry out of a dwelling, when the morning star is extinguished, may that be your share, Sharpy-Yatsva! And everything good, which people carry into a house when the evening star rises, may that be your share, Khulpy-Yatsva!'

ॐ

No details are available about the narration of this Abkhaz legend. It was published in Kh. S. Bgazhba, *Abkhazskie skazki*, Alashara, Sukhumi, 1985, 316–318.

77. Akhkepig[1] *(Chechen)*

In times long ago there lived a certain man named Akhkepig. He used to rob people, and he also killed them and ate them. One day he killed a father, mother and two brothers. He intended to kill also the brother and sister who remained alive, but they ran away into the forest. In the forest they met an ox who was not afraid of anything in the world. Even Akhkepig was rather afraid of that ox.

The ox asked the children in a human voice, 'What sort of people are you?'

'A man by the name of Akhkepig killed our parents and our two brothers, and now he wants to take our lives too. So we ran away into the forest,' said the boy.

Some time later the ox met them once more and again he asked, 'What sort of people are you?'

The little girl told him once more why they had landed up in the forest. Then the ox said, 'Children, sit on my long back, I will save you.' The children sat on the back of the ox.

Far beyond the forest was a big sea. The ox walked with the children across the surface of the sea, so that not only did their feet not get wet, but not even a drop of water landed on them.

Akhkepig saw through his telescope that the ox was rescuing the children. He began to suck in the sea and stopped the ox in the middle. Then the ox said, 'I have grown weak, so now I will transfer to my feet all of the strength that is left in my body. Then I will have sufficient strength to cross the sea.'

Akhkepig could not do anything; they crossed the sea, but he could not cross the sea, and he sat on the opposite shore.

'Now I shall die,' said the ox to the boy. 'You have to slaughter me. Do you have a knife?'

---

1   *Akhkepig* means literally 'half-kopek'.

'There is a knife in our bag,' said the sister.

The ox said, 'Then quickly slaughter me. Put my skin in the place where you select your dwelling place. Lay my skin with the inside on the ground and the hairy side upwards and you will have a huge farm. Scatter my intestines around the skin, and there will appear high gates with two doors for coming in and going out. Place my legs with the hoofs downwards in the four corners: out of them will grow four towers. Throw my ears into the sea; people will appear, together with everything that they need. Throw my eyes and say, 'May two brave and pugnacious hounds appear. May all who see the hounds grow fond of us.' Throw my liver and heart into the sea and you will have the weapons and powder that you need. All the weapons will be of gold and silver. If you have need of gold, throw my liver into the sea and say, "Let it be gold." Throw my gall bladder between the two hounds and say, "May your hatred towards our enemies be just as bitter."

'In a certain tower there lives a girl about whom people know nothing; but if they did know, they would not leave her in peace. Boy, if you wish to go near this tower, she will make an approach to you. The girl will notice you when you go out with the hounds. She will fall in love with you and she will send her servant to you with an invitation saying that on such-and-such a day she will expect you. And you answer that you are willing to come on that day.

'When you have got ready to go to her as a guest, throw my kidneys on the ground and a horse that can keep pace with the morning dawn will appear. He will gallop and stop, according to your wish. His saddle will be of pure gold and silver.

'May my words be prophetic, and there will be no need to repeat them; it is enough to pronounce them only once. All that I have said will come true. And when you sit on the splendid horse, you say, "May I always recognise an enemy. May I have enough intelligence and bravery to punish him."'

The young man got the knife from his bag. He slaughtered the ox and performed all that the ox had told him. He founded a big farm: you could not take it in with a glance. He saddled the splendid steed and set out to the girl.

He came riding to her, and the girl fell in love with him. The young man and his two hounds climbed up to her in the tower. And the girl, taking the hounds as witnesses, said, 'I give my word that, beneath this sky, I will marry only you. If you will take me, I am willing to be your wife.'

'I also give my word that, while we are both alive, I will marry only you,' answered the young man. And he returned home with the girl.

As soon as the young man got back home, he threw the liver of his ox into the sea, and the sea threw out to him an incalculable amount of gold. He filled up some bags with gold, and he took many other things and came to the girl.

Meanwhile the young man's sister was riding in a boat on the sea and enjoying herself. And on the seashore stood Akhkepig. 'Girl, bring your boat nearer to the shore,' shouted Akhkepig.

'What do you want to talk to me about?' asked the girl.

'We will live together and I will become your father,' said Akhkepig.

'I had a father, but you killed him.'

'I would replace your mother!'

'I also had a mother, but you killed her.'

'I would be a brother to you!'

'I also had brothers, only you killed them.'

'If you are willing, I will become your husband,' said Akhkepig. The girl brought the boat to the shore at once.

Then Akhkepig said to her, 'Hide me until your brother comes.' She hid Akhkepig in her large tower.

Her brother came back and went to his sister with the two hounds. Scenting a stranger, the hounds began pawing the ground. The sister said to her brother, 'Why did you bring these hounds? They only paw the ground. Drive them away from here!' Her brother drove the hounds away, but they would not settle down.

The brother sent the hounds to his bride as gifts from his sister. And the sister said to Akhkepig, 'The hounds are not at home, if you kill my brother, then we can start living happily.' After sending off the hounds, the brother once again went in to his sister.

At that same moment Akhkepig ambushed him with a big *kinzhal* in his hand; and the sister egged him on. The brother begged, 'Do not take off my head, do not mutilate my body. Kill me by some other means!'

Akhkepig had a bear's claw. If this claw was thrust into the heart, the person died. Akhkepig threw down the young man, squeezed his throat, thrust the claw into his heart and killed him. 'We must quickly bury him,' said his sister. The boy's bride knew nothing about the death of her bridegroom.

Fearing that the hounds would come back, the sister and Akhkepig dug a hole and buried the young man. The hounds returned, and the sister began lamenting to them: 'My dear brother fell ill and by the will of God he abandoned this sunlit world.'

The bride had said to the hounds, 'He was not sick in any way, and when he left home he was well.' The hounds dug up their master. They saw the claw in his heart. One of the hounds pulled out the claw and there and then he died, but the young man revived. The second hound rushed and pulled the claw from the first one. The first hound came to life but the second one died at once.

The hound remembered how he had pulled this claw out the first time, and he realised that it penetrated the body of the one who pulled it out. The hound used cunning. He pulled out the claw with a stick, and the second hound revived. One hound ran off for the young man's things and imparted the joyful news to the bride. The bride brought some clothes; the young man got dressed and went to his sister, with the two hounds.

'Va, sister,' said her brother, 'if I had known that you would marry the murderer of our parents and brothers, I would have given you away in marriage. I have not the power to kill you, since you and I are brother and sister from the same womb. Change yourself into a thorn that can lodge in the hand: not in an empty field, but only in desolate places.'

The hounds tore Akhkepig to pieces, and the brother and his wife began to live happily.

ॐ

This Chechen legend was recorded by M. Z. Chakhiev in 1977 in Grozny from his daughter, A. Chakhieva. It was pulished in A. O. Malsagov, *Skazki i legendy ingushey i chechentsev*, Nauka, Moscow, 1983, 156–159.

78. Burkhay Izazha *(Lak)*

Introduction
Not far from Kumukh on a hillside in the locality of Burkhayalu is a grave which is called the grave of Burkhay Izazha. Here in the old days they would light ritual fires, and here the traces of the fire can be seen on the gravestones. According to Lak tradition, here was buried a girl who had been forced into marriage with a foreigner (in some traditions she was sold into Georgia, in others into Azerbayjan). Because she loved her native land and her people so strongly, she did not want to remain in a foreign land and she ran away in the

night. By day she hid from pursuers, and by night she continued her journey. Hungry and exhausted, she reached the locality of Burkhayalu, and with the words 'Praise be to God, I have reached my native land!' she fell down lifeless.

The story of a mountain woman being sold into a foreign country is widespread also among the Avars and Dargvas.

In the Avar song 'Bakhtika' the Avar khan Umakhan sells his sister to the Shushin khan (the Khan of Shusha, in the Nagorno-Karabakh region of Azerbayjan, settled by Armenians). In the Dargva song 'Mesedu was Sold' Umakhan sells his daughter Mesedu to the Karabakh khan.

In this song, 'Burkhay Izazha', the girl is forced to marry into the Tatar Horde (in another variant the Horde is not called Tatar). Evidently this song refers to the Golden Horde, which was formed in the thirteenth century. By giving the mountain girl in marriage to an influential man in the Golden Horde, the mountain elders probably wanted to have blood relations with the powerful neighbouring state, to have a means of defence in case of any conflict.

The song was recorded in two variants.

I was weeding in the middle of a green field
When a voice sounded from my native *aul*.
What could it be, I thought.
'Ey, dear Izazha, come home,' they shouted to me.
I picked up an armful of flowers and went home –
The yard was full of short-legged white horses.
'What is it?' I asked, climbing on to the balcony.
Here the bows and arrows were hanging in rows.
Steel weapons were gleaming on the balcony.
'What kind of spectacle is this?' I said, and went into the house –
In the big room there was much silver and gold.
'Please tell me, my old mother,
Those short-legged white horses in the yard,
What were they sent for, what has been promised?
The gold-embroidered cloths in the rooms,
What were they sent for, what has been promised?'
'Those short-legged white horses were sent
For the promise to give you in marriage.
The gold-embroidered cloths were sent

For your old father's promise to give you in marriage.
That silver and gold, which we did not have,
The *aul's* elders received it,
After promising to give you away,
It all was received from that Horde.'
'Let those short-legged white horses be slaughtered
For the funeral banquets of their owners.
Let that gold and silver be distributed
On the graves of their owners.
The steel weapons gleaming on the balcony,
Let them be covered with rust after their owners' deaths.
Don't give me away, Mother, into the Tatar Horde,
I don't know their language.
I ask you, I ask you, my old dear mother,
Do everything to stop them giving me into the Tatar Horde.'
'Oy, what can I do, your mother's favourite daughter,
"I shall give her," said your old father,
"Agreed," said the Lak elders.
How can you not be given into the Horde:
The Kumukh *magals*[1] have already received the wealth.'
'Shame to you, you Lak elders,
Letting foreigners pluck a flower grown up in the *aul*,
Shame to you, brave Lak men (heroes),
Letting go a flower that has grown up in the *aul*.
May typhus carry off the Lak girls
Who threw out a flower grown up in the *aul*.
"Silver, silver!" you Lak elders say,
I was dearer than silver to our young men.
"Gold, gold!" says my old father,
The girls respected me more than gold.
"Silver, silver!" you Lak elders say,
Build a fortified wall of that silver around the town.
"Gold, gold!" you say, my old father,
Now gild the surface of that wall.
Let the silver and gold obtained for me
Be distributed on the graves of the elders.

---

1   A *magal* is a local district.

Let them use the large robes taken for me
To cover the corpses of the old women.
May the wooden troughs filled with silver and gold
Pass to strangers, after the death of my old father.'
In grief I went out on to the street.
Those who had come for me had gathered in the yard.
'Oy, father!' I said, and rushed to my father,
Father pushed me away rudely.
'Oy, brother!' I said, and rushed to him.
But my brother grabbed me and set me in the saddle.
'Let me burn up in the fire,' I said, and threw myself into the fire.
Like fiery sparks these Tatar youths rushed.
The muslin had not even yellowed before they dragged me from the fire.
'Let the river carry me away,' I said, and threw myself in the river.
Are they drakes or something, these Tatar youths?
My shoes were not even wet before they dragged me from the water.
And then I said, if you give me into the Tatar Horde,
Let them make a silver bridge across the Koysu,
Let them gild the posts on the bridge,
And let them take with them a bush of the mountain rose
With turf and with green grass at its roots.
Let them send with me a certain girl singer
With a bag of songs at her belt.
Rather than me eating sugar and dates in the Horde,
It would be better for me to live and eat millet bread in Lakia.
Rather than me wearing gold and silk and living in the Horde,
It would be better for me to wear simple coarse calico in Lakia.
A violet that has not been plucked by anybody
Is riding to a foreign land, may her journey be good!
'They did not give me to you, my young falcon,[1]
Now I have to follow another man's will.
You did not manage to buy me a big diamond,
There will be no thanks to one who let me slip from his hands.
The *aul's* brave heroes ought not to wear *papakhas*,
After agreeing to let me go to a foreign land!
The young girls ought not to wear kerchiefs,

---

1   That is, her own boyfriend.

After letting me go to a foreign land!
In the mountains the wolf eats the deer,
The violet dies when left under the ice,
If it breaks its wing, the falcon falls into the gorge,
An unhappy dog whines all night in the yard.
How can I convey in words the pain, and what can I do
With my tortured heart when riding to a foreign land?
I have only grown up a little and begun to realise the joy of life,
All my life will now be spent in suffering.
In the shade of the clouds my heart has grown cold in springtime,
Where shall I find coolness in the steppe under the scorching sun?
Can I forget the water of my native spring,
When quenching my thirst with the water from the Itil'?[1]
My eyes have turned into inexhaustible springs,
And are shedding tears like a river.
My heart is torn out upwards towards the clouds,
To settle on the peaks of the high mountains.'
The Tatars had a good name, may their tribe vanish.
They turned out to be worthy of that name.
In Lakia they bought the famous beauty,
Burkhay Izazha, for great and appropriate wealth.

This Lak song was recorded by Kh. Khalilov in 1962 from the words of Bibizhamalov Bibi, aged ninety, a female inhabitant of the *aul* of Ulluchara of the Akusha region. It was published in Kh. Khalilov, *Lakskie epichesnye pesni*, Makhachkala, 1969, 197–201.

79. Chyuerdi *(Karachay)*

In ancient times one of the *auls*, where the Nart-Gurts[2] were living, was overtaken by misfortune, and the people abandoned it. In the *aul* there

---

1   The Itil is the River Volga.
2   The Nart-Gurts is an archaic name for the Nart folk.

was a pregnant woman, and she was unable to escape. The Narts dug out a large hole for her, put food and drink into it, hid her there and left.

Before leaving, they also left arms for the woman, saying, 'If you bear a son, give them to him!' Some time after they had abandoned the *aul*, the woman bore a son, and she named him Chyuerdi. When the boy had grown a little, his mother gave him the weapons left by the Narts.

Chyuerdi grew up and became an outstanding hunter. He used to go hunting and kill wild animals. By this, he and his mother lived.

One day, when returning from hunting, he saw a castle in a certain big and dense forest, and he looked it over. He had the thought: if I was to move here with my mother, it would be closer for me to go hunting from here ...

He had only just thought it, when an *emegen* ran up to him and started choking him. They wrestled for a long time. Chyuerdi beat the *emegen*, threw him into a large deep hole and covered it from above with a big stone. After several days he took his mother with him and settled in that castle.

Afterwards, Chyuerdi would go hunting as before. His mother busied herself at home and did all that was needed for her son. That is how they lived.

One day the woman heard somebody muttering. She went up close to the place from where this noise could be heard, had a good look all around and saw the hole covered with a large stone, and in the hole an *emegen*. When the *emegen* noticed her, he asked, 'Pull me out of here, I will be your father!'

'May you be a sacrifice instead of my father!'

'I will be your mother!'

'May you be a sacrifice instead of my mother!'

'I will be your brother!'

'May you be a sacrifice instead of my brother!'

'I will be the head of your house, your husband!'

The woman kept silent, and then she asked, 'But how can I pull you out?'

'In the black chest there is a rope, bring it, make an opening at the edge of the stone, and let the rope down to me.'

The woman did as he had told her. The *emegen* dislodged the stone with his head and climbed out. For a long time they lived together secretly. When Chyuerdi was expected to return from hunting, the mother hid the *emegen*; but when he left, the *emegen* could be free in the house.

After some time Chyuerdi guessed what was going on, but he said nothing. When about a year had passed the woman gave birth to a child, and she called him Allah-berdi.

Chyuerdi was very upset, and he even wanted to abandon his mother and go away, but he could not do so. What can I do: whatever I say, however I curse, she is still my mother, she fed me with her milk, he was thinking, and he carried on living at home.

One day the *emegen* said to his wife, 'If you do not kill your son, I will not live with you!'

'But how shall I kill him?'

'Put poison in his food and feed it to him, then he will die.'

By this time the boy had grown a little. He heard their conversation and secretly related it to Chyuerdi.

The woman cooked *khychyns* after putting poison in them, and placed them before Chyuerdi. 'Eat. You are probably hungry, after all you came back from the road tired,' she said.

'No, Mother, I am not hungry, my dogs are hungry!' he said, and threw the *khychyns* to his dogs. They sniffed the *khychyns* and did not even begin eating them.

'Mother, how can a man eat what dogs will not eat?'

When it did not turn out as they had planned, the woman asked the *emegen*, 'And what shall we do now?'

'Sew him tight clothes and put them on him, and also make him a pair of leather *charyks*. When he puts all this on, I will throw myself at him and strangle him. At this time you sprinkle millet on the floor,' said the *emegen*.

When the woman had got it all ready and put it on her son, the *emegen* rushed at him and began choking him. He had only just begun choking the young man when the woman sprinkled millet on the floor. Chyuerdi slipped and fell.

'Run and get the knife, which is in the black chest!' said the *emegen* to the woman. When the woman brought the knife, Allah-berdi said that he himself would strike. He took the knife from his mother's hands, thrust it into the neck of the *emegen* and took off his head. Chyuerdi got up, took the knife out of the boy's hands and had only just raised it threateningly at his mother when her younger son stood up in front of his mother. Chyuerdi held back, he was unable to strike his mother.

After that the elder brother gave the younger one a lead bullet and said, 'If I die, blood will begin flowing from this bullet. If milk is flowing, be with your mother; but if blood appears, set out to look for me ... I can no longer look into the eyes of such a mother.'

After saying that, Chyuerdi left. After a long journey he stopped at a certain high plateau and carefully had a look in all four directions. A faint sound came from far away. After listening, he went in the direction from where the sound came. He reached it and saw that beneath the plateau was a large cave, and in it a girl was sitting next to a corpse and weeping.

'Why are you weeping, what has happened?' asked Chyuerdi.

'I have seven brothers, they are waging war with the *emegens*, and with this one you can see what they have done!' answered the girl.

'Where are they fighting?'

The girl explained. Chyuerdi headed towards them. 'Leave it, they can do a lot of harm to you too,' said the girl. But the young man did not stop. He went on and on, and saw two groups of people in the distance. One group was a bit bigger than the other. Chyuerdi went and joined the smaller group. He greeted them and sat down. When the time came, they all got up and set out on their way. On that day they did away with quite a large number of *emegens*. The young man was a skilful warrior. On the second day, after clearing the neighbourhood of *emegens*, they went back to that girl. The young man wanted to leave without staying there too long.

'Marry our sister!' the girl's brothers insisted. Chyuerdi did not say no to that.

After the wedding his wife began sighing in bed in the night. 'Why are you sighing, what has happened?'

The woman did not want to answer. Her husband insisted, and in the end he made her speak: 'Now there is only one place where one of the *emegens* remains. If only he was gone, it would be peaceful for us ...'

'Where is he?'

The woman tried to explain it as she knew. In the morning the young man sat on his horse and set out on his way. He rode for a long time and reached the end of a certain gorge. Above this gorge he saw a castle. It was the castle about which the girl had spoken. He headed towards that castle. He had not yet had time to reach the castle when the *emegen* caught him.

'Shooting or wrestling?'

'Wrestling,' Chyuerdi answered.

The *emegen* struck and drove the young man into the ground up to where his *nogovitsas* were tied. Chyuerdi struck and drove the *emegen* into the ground a little higher than the ankles. The *emegen* struck and drove him in up to his knees, the young man struck and drove him in to the straps of his *nogovitsas*. Thus the *emegen* drove the young man into the ground up to his neck. Just as he was about to take off his head, the *emegen's* daughter pleaded with him not to do so.

Allah-berdi squeezed the bullet that his brother had left, and blood came out together with the milk. He told his mother that he was leaving to look for his brother. He rode along many roads and came out on to a certain plateau. Beneath this plateau he heard somebody talking. When he went down to the cave he saw a beautiful girl, who was weeping one minute and resting content the next.

'Why are you distressed?' he asked.

The girl related how her brothers had been fighting with the *emegens*, how a certain dare-devil young man had turned up, joined her brothers and finished off the *emegens*. But one *emegen* was left, and the young man had gone away to fight with him and had not returned for a long time. 'My brothers gave me to him as a wife,' she related it all to him in detail.

'Then, it seems that you are my sister-in-law, if that is my brother!' said the lad.

After that, not lingering long, he set out to where Chyuerdi had gone. As the girl had told him, he headed towards the gorge where his brother had gone. When he saw the *emegen's* castle, he thought that it was probably here that his brother was to be found, either dead or alive, and he hurried there. At this point the *emegen* jumped out and rushed at him. They began throwing each other on to the ground. The *emegen* lifted him and threw him on the ground, and he sunk into the ground below the knees. Allah-berdi drove the *emegen* into the ground above the knees. Fighting thus with the *emegen*, he drove him into the ground up to his neck.

'Tell me, where have you put my brother? If you don't tell me, I will cut off your head,' after saying which, he stood up over him.

'Don't take off my head,' asked the *emegen*, and he pointed to the place where his brother was.

Allah-berdi ran quickly and pulled his brother out, and afterwards went back and took off the *emegen's* head. When the joyful brothers were getting ready to leave, the *emegen's* daughter shouted, 'Why are you leaving me here?'

Chyuerdi went back to her and said, 'I shall never forget your kindness to me. But you are the daughter of an *emegen*, how can I take you to the people?'

'No, I am not the *emegen's* daughter! He kidnapped me as a child and brought me into this castle. Today I have reached the age of sixteen, and today he wanted to marry me. Now I am free, the *emegen* is dead, and this castle is now yours,' she said.

Allah-berdi went back home and married the girl, while Chyuerdi rode off and brought his wife to that place.

ॐ

This Karachay legend was recorded by R. A-K. Ortabayeva in 1979 from the words of Yusup Bayramukov, born in 1911. It was published in T. M. Khajieva & R. A-K. Ortabayeva, *Narty*, Nauka, Moscow, 1994, 542–545.

80. The Sister *(Georgian)*

Introduction
There is some confusion here about who the 'infidels' actually were. The name Tatar usually refers to people of Turkish or Mongolian origin, whereas the shah was specifically the King of the Persians; in this legend it is probably the latter who were the infidels. The Georgians were of course Christians.

One day an infidel army surrounded Georgia. There were very many of the infidels. But there were few Georgians. The Georgian king realised that all of his army would be killed in the battle, while at the same time Georgia would not escape destruction. What could the king do? He sent an ambassador to the Tatar king. He wanted to make peace. The infidel king ordered the message to be conveyed to him: 'If you do not want a battle, then send me three picked warriors as a sign of submissiveness. I will execute them in front of my troops.'

Such a humiliation insulted our king. Angry, he was already getting ready to give the signal for the start of the battle, when suddenly three soldiers stood before him, saying, 'O king, do not expose our soldiers to a massacre. Let us fall as a sacrifice for them.'

For a long time the king refused: it was hard for him to send brave warriors to their slaughter, but what could he do? Force ploughs mountains! Peace was dear to the king, and he let the three heroes go to their death. The three chosen ones were standing before the Tatar king, waiting for death. Suddenly a Georgian woman threw herself at the feet of the shah. She was weeping and she asked him not to kill the heroes, but to give them their lives. The woman's tears softened the heart of the savage shah, and he said to her, 'I will not give you all three, but just one of them. Whichever one you want, take him.'

The Georgian woman became paralysed. Just which one should she take? One was her husband, the second was her son, and the third her brother. What should she do? Time was getting short: she had to save at least one, otherwise he would kill all three. All of a sudden she came to a decision: I will find a husband yet, thought she, and I will bear another son, but I will certainly never have another brother.

She seized hold of the hem of his *chokha* and dragged him away by force, saving him from death.

Such is the strength of the love of a sister.

₴

This Georgian legend was recorded by L. Trelashvili in 1959 in Tusheti from the narrator D. Bachulashvili. It was published in E. B. Virsaladze, *Gruzinskie narodnye predaniya i legendy*, Nauka, Moscow, 1973, 197.

81. The Son Who Went Away to the Army in Azayni *(Avar)*

My son, my little one, went out to the *godekan*
But at once he returned – even his tracks had not become dusty.
'What happened to you, my son, my little one,
You came back so soon – even your tracks have not grown dusty?
Did you start a fight with your fellows?
Did you get into a quarrel with the lads?'
'Why should I start a fight with my fellows?
Why should I get into a quarrel with the lads?'
'Mother, the *jigits* are going to the *bo* in Azayni.[1]
The one whose horse prevails among the troops in Azayni,

---

1   Azayni is the old name of the settlement of Tarki.

He will be given the first place in the *aul*.'
'Don't go, my son, to the army in Azayni:
A puppy is not a sheepdog, it is not for him to catch a wolf,
You have not grown enough to be a *jigit* – it is not for you to bring down
    a *jigit*.'
'Then give me a spindle and send me to the girls.
If I have not grown enough to bring down a *jigit*,
Then give me some dough and tell me to bake a *churek*.'
'Since I am unable to hold you back, and you will give me no peace,
Saddle the thoroughbred horse,
Take the gun with the thicker barrel,
Fasten on the sabre with the finer blade.'
I saddled the thoroughbred horse,
I took the gun with the thicker barrel,
I fastened on the sabre with the finer blade,
I set off from there to the army in Azayni ...
Among the army in Azayni my horse actually prevailed,
Although not grown up, I felled a *jigit* in the battle,
But I too received a mortal wound,
And the horse, alas, did not escape a serious wound.
My guts were hanging, I held them back with the saddle,
The horse's guts were hanging, I tied them back with the harness,
And from there I set off with difficulty to my wife.
'Dear wife, unlock the doors into the sacred house,[1]
A mortal wound is gaping open on me,
The horse is seriously wounded too, I feel sorry for him.'
'By God, I will not open the door into this sacred house –
I have seen many such lads,
I don't want to interrupt my pre-morning dream.'
With difficulty I dragged myself from my wife to my mother:
'My mother, unlock the doors into the sacred house,
A mortal wound is gaping open on me,
The horse is seriously wounded too, I feel sorry for him.'
'I swear, I will not open the door into the sacred house –
I will give birth to a hundred such sons,

---

1   The hearth and home have a sacred character in the former religion of the Caucasus people,
    as described in the next chapter.

I will not spoil my pre-morning dream.'
From my mother I went to my own sister.
'Sister, unlock the doors into the sacred house,
A mortal wound is gaping open on me,
The horse is seriously wounded too, I feel sorry for him.'
In the dark she put on her trousers inside out,
Hurriedly she pulled on her dress in the same way.
Just what had happened? She went to open the door
He was standing at the door, her own brother!
She laid him on a downy bed ...
The golden soul of her unlucky brother
Flew off to the sky, by the will of Allah ...
His mother demanded her share, for her milk,
His wife asked for a share, for her marriage portion.
His mother took his belt and led away the horse.
His wife took away his clothes and *cherkeska*,
For the poor sister – only a bitter tear.

No information is available about the narration of this Avar song. It was published in L. Chlaidze, *Avarsky fol'klor*, Kavkazsky Dom, Tbilisi, 2006, 93–95.

XI

Religion and Relations with the Dead

Naturally, religion is an important part of people's lives, but as we shall see, religion is closely associated with deceased ancestors, who in turn are bound up with the family, the home and family honour.

Officially the religious views of the Caucasus groups are clearly defined: Georgia is officially an Orthodox Christian nation, while most of the other Caucasus ethnic groups are officially Muslim. There is also a small Jewish group, the Mountain Jews. However, the real situation is much more complicated, even if one ignores the strong Russian Orthodox Christian communities. Many of the groups that are now Muslim were Christian in the past. But before the introduction of Christianity and Islam the people had their own religion. Although this religion did not worship a single God, one hesitates to label this original religion as 'pagan' since it had many aspects in common with the mainstream religions. In fact it developed by an evolutionary process starting from the inhabitants' view of the universe. The present religious view of the indigenous peoples of the Caucasus now generally consists of a mixture of all three, in proportions that vary from one locality to another. As everywhere, the religious beliefs and rituals are overlaid with tradition.

Since the concepts of Islam and Christianity are well known, a summary of the 'original' religion is given here, so that some of its characteristics that appear in the legends can be recognised. This religion was studied in depth among the Chechens and Ingush[1] by Bashir Dalgat, and his various published works were compiled and published by his daughter, U. B. Dalgat (B. Dalgat 2004). B. Dalgat did his research in the 1890s, gathering information from some very elderly men who were familiar with the beliefs, stories and legends of the past. One of his informants had actually been a priest of the original religion. B. Dalgat's study was made about thirty years before writing was introduced for the local language, so that the traditions were

---

1   The Chechens and Ingush are neighbouring groups who speak a common language, and their common name is 'Vaynakhs'.

still being handed down from master to pupil by word of mouth. The traditions conveyed by these old men therefore really had been handed down from 'time immemorial', for nobody knew how old the traditions were.

B. Dalgat concluded that the original religion was based on respect for ancestors. Combined with this was the belief that the death of a person really meant that their soul was conveyed to another place: i.e., that the real person did not die, only their earthly body. This was a real literal belief in life after death. The soul went to another place that was vaguely located in a lower world. For the relocated soul, life went on in the same way as before: husband and wife would live together, they were both involved in the same farm and house work, earthly feuds and friendships continued, and so on.

But the relations between the living and the dead were very important for the living. The dead relied on the living to provide them with food, clothing and other essentials, some of which was given to the dead during the required memorial feasts. Clearly there is some inconsistency here, since the dead also owned farms, collected harvests and so on, and so ought to have been self-sufficient. Since the living could not see the dead, but it was assumed that the dead could see the living, the dead clearly had certain powers that we would consider to be supernatural. Simple logic therefore shows that the dead were in a position to reward or punish their living progeny if they wanted to show gratitude or displeasure. Such rewards or punishments were especially likely to be used in connection with the way the living progeny provided food during the memorial feasts. In this way, the concept of the sacrifice creeps in: in order to show special respect for the ancestors, some of the choicest bits of meat and other foods could be put aside for them as a sacrifice. In return for this respect, the living might ask their dead relatives to use their supernatural influence to do them favours. This effectively meant saying *prayers* to them.

The ancestors were also concerned with the general behaviour of their progeny. After all, they were still considered to be part of the family, and any stain on the family honour would affect their status among the other dead souls. For instance, the perceived cowardice of, or adultery by, a living family member, would bring shame upon them among their dead neighbours. This made the living take care of his or her image not only among the living but also among the dead, for fear of disapproval and the consequent danger of supernatural punishment. Moreover, the living member would eventually die and join his dead ancestors, including those whom he respected and perhaps feared such as his own father and grandfather; and he hoped to be welcomed by them.

As a family became more extended, it might encompass a whole community. Moreover, there would often be an especially important ancestor – perhaps he was considered to have been the primogenitor of the family, or perhaps his brave exploits in the past saved the family from annihilation by enemies. The supernatural ability of this special ancestor to reward or punish could then apply to the whole community, so that when really important communal matters such as the success or failure of the harvest, or the danger of epidemics were considered, it was especially important to make good sacrifices and say prayers to that special ancestor. This ancestor thus gradually acquired the status of a local saint. To facilitate the bringing of sacrifices by the whole community, a sanctuary would probably be set up for the local saint. As some communities thrived while others suffered, the evolutionary process accordingly elevated the local saints of a thriving community at the expense of the saints of a less successful community, so that some local saints were gradually elevated to the status of regional saints. This regional saint would have his or her regional sanctuary, which would then become a site for pilgrims.

By a similar evolutionary process a local saint might acquire the status of being a specialist in a certain field, such as the fertility of barren women or protection from disease.

Some of these concepts are included in the legends below. The first legend, 'Batoko Shertuko', from the Vaynakh group, deals with the importance of the provision of food for the dead and epitomises the local beliefs. The Balkar legend 'Karashauay's Revenge' relates how a living hero performed blood revenge for a dead hero as well as for his own horse-herd. It also portrays the importance of food for the dead. In this case the living hero does not visit the dead in person, but by means of a dream. It also mentions how important it was to the dead souls that the food sacrificed by the living was given with good intent. The Georgian 'Lega and Kopala' describes how a man accidentally strays into the world of the dead. The dead are working in their fields, and he can see the dead although they cannot see him. This Georgian legend is overlaid with Christian concepts, since the hero is finally rescued by a Christian 'saint', Kopala. As a result of his adventures the hero is smitten by a kind of madness, and ends his days as a functionary of the Church. 'The Resurrection of the Narts' describes how the souls of the dead take on an animal form when they

308   LEGENDS OF THE CAUCASUS

want to warn the local population of impending misfortune. 'The Horse of Zezva Gaprindauli' shows that the soul of a heroic horse also lives on and benefits from sacrifices, and presumably those who make the sacrifices also benefit. 'Orshamar Arsh' describes how snakes, which crawl on the earth, on the border region between the world of the living and the dead, have the ability to transfer souls through that border from the dead to the living.[1] These snakes therefore know the secret of revival of the dead, and in this case it is by means of a little golden ball. In other legends with a similar motif there is a special magical revivifying herb. 'Seska Solsa and Byatar' describes a journey to the world of the dead, which evidently lies below the earthly world since it is reached by descending a long ladder. The concept of punishment for sins is included in this legend, indicating that it has been influenced by one of the major religions, presumably Islam. However, in this legend the sins of the dead are evidently judged by a special deity who is in charge of the dead and of the Other World, i.e., not by the one Supreme God, as in the monotheistic religions. The last two legends are from Georgia and clearly include Christian concepts. 'Mikel-Gabriel' is a figure who combines the two archangels as one Angel of Death (the equivalent among the Muslim population is called Azrail). This angel is subject to the one God. 'About Paleostomi' also includes God and the preservation of an icon of the Virgin Mary. In this legend God decides to punish the entire community except for the lone righteous man. This legend is clearly Christian.

82. Batoko Shertuko[2] *(Chechen-Ingush)*

It is well known that Batoko Shertuko used to rescue the Orkhustoys from all calamities and was the chief in all of their undertakings. Batoko Shertuko was also able to set off to the other world any time he wanted, and then to come back from there.

---

1   Most living creatures, and certainly people, all live above the surface of the earth; whereas after death they are buried beneath the surface. This makes the surface of the earth the border between the living and the dead. Any creatures, such as snakes, that live in this border region, have a special symbolic significance; as do creatures that live simultaneously in both regions, such as trees, frogs and mermaids.

2   The name in other transcriptions is Botky Shirtka, Botoko Shirtga or Batyg Shertga.

The mother of one of the Orkhustoys died. The latter was grieving terribly about his mother. 'If you love your mother so dearly,' said Batoko Shertuko, 'you know how you can comfort yourself and her too?'

'How?' asked the Orkhustoy man.

'Slaughter some of your animals, and what is slaughtered will be for your mother.'

'Are you speaking the truth, Batoko Shertuko?' asked the Orkhustoy man, as if not believing him.

'If you don't believe me, then send a trusted agent with me to the other world, while you slaughter something here as a consolation to your mother.'

That is what the Orkhustoy man did. He slaughtered a cock and a hen, and distributed them to the poor together with a basket of *churek* bread. Meanwhile Batoko Shertuko and a trusted agent set out to the other world. They walked and saw some mountains. At their foot sat the dead mother of the Orkhustoy man, and on its very summit were the cock and the hen, and next to them was a basket of *churek* bread. After returning from the other world, Batoko Shertuko told the Orkhustoy man, 'We saw some mountains where your mother was sitting, and on the summit were a slaughtered cock and hen, and next to them stood a basket.'

'No, I did not slaughter anything for my mother!' the Orkhustoy began saying, in order to test him.

'How are we to know?' said Batoko Shertuko and his companion. 'Only we saw in the other world your mother, a cock and a hen!'

The Orkhustoy man was then convinced that the animals slaughtered in memory of the deceased reached them. They say that it was from that time that they introduced the custom of having a memorial meal for the dead.

This Vaynakh (Chechen-Ingush) legend was recorded by Ch. Akhriev and first published in 1875. It was published in U. B. Dalgat, *Geroichesky epos chechentsev i ingushey*, Nauka, Moscow, 1972, 296.

83. Karashauay's Revenge *(Balkar)*

Introduction

In the Nart epos of the Balkars and Karachays the Narts traditionally worship and pray to the Turkish pagan gods (basically Teyri). Teyri was the supreme god in the pagan pantheon of the Balkars and Karachays. But in this legend the mention of the Muslim *namaz* (prayer) is probably a later development.

In the time of the Narts there was no man in the Caucasus stronger than Rachikau. And he was living somewhere in these regions. With time another one like him appeared in the Caucasus, a strong mighty man. He used to hear much about Rachikau, and one day he decided to kill him, so he set out on the road to do so. Knowing that he could not beat Rachikau in an honourable fight, he laid in wait for him, and at the moment when Rachikau was performing *namaz* he crept up to him from behind and killed him with a blow of his *kinzhal*. He rode off home saying, 'Well then, now I am the strongest one in the Caucasus.'[1]

Some time passed, and he heard that a very strong man by the name of Karashauay had appeared in the Caucasus. Why, now I need to kill him too, he thought, and he got ready and set off to Karashauay. He did not find him at home. When he questioned the people, they said, 'He has ridden off somewhere for two months, he will not come back sooner than that.'

'Well, all right, if he is a real man, if he is in fact as manly as they say he is, then he will search for his own man without fail,' he said to himself. He seized Karashauay's horse-herd, threw him across the withers of his horse, carried him away, killed him, and threw the corpse into the water.

Whether Karashauay was away for a short time or a long time, who knows. When he returned, he asked, 'But where is my horse-herd?'

The people answered, 'A certain man threw him across the withers of his own horse and took him away with him.'

'I am not a man if I do not find him!' said Karashauay, and he rode away to look for him. He was riding for a long time, but nowhere did he find that man.

One day he came riding and spent the night right here, where the funeral

---

1   In the original text it was literally: 'Aha, now the Caucasus is left for me!'

monuments stood. On lying down to sleep, he turned to one of the graves and said, 'Tonight Teyri and I are your guests.'

When he had fallen asleep, he dreamed that somebody shouted, 'Ey, Rachikau!' and at this call another voice asked, 'What do you need?' 'The Narts have invited you, they are waiting for you,' replied the first voice. 'Today Teyri and a guest are spending the night at my place, I cannot go to them tonight,' said the second voice. When they called him the third time, they said, 'Come there with your guest.'

And so they went there. When they arrived, all of the Narts were sitting in one room. The elder Narts were sitting at a table, eating and drinking. They did not even attempt to invite them to the table, but each man at the table merely separated out part of his own share of food, and the guests ate it on the threshold of the room.

After they had eaten their fill and the diners dispersed, they went back. 'Did you see?' the former voice asked him in his dream. 'Such is the custom here. Now you search for your horse-herd. A certain man killed him in such-and-such a place and, after chopping him up, threw him into the lake. If you celebrate his funeral feast and place a gravestone for him, as custom expects, then on your next visit I will tell you the name of the murderer and instruct you how to take revenge on him. But until then I will tell you nothing. Moreover, it would be very good if you were to celebrate a funeral feast for Rachikau too: would you slaughter one more sheep, with your whole heart and without begrudging, and distribute the meat and one basket of *lokums* to the people?'

When he awoke, Karashauay rode off to the place about which the voice had spoken in his dream. He found the lake and pulled from it the chopped-up corpse of his horse-herd. After burying him according to custom, he arranged the funeral feast for him and made a tombstone. Afterwards he slaughtered a sheep for Rachikau too, prepared the food and distributed it to the people.

He returned to the cemetery and again lay down to sleep at the same grave, saying, 'Teyri and I are your guests.' In his dream he again heard the voice: 'Come, the Narts are waiting for you.' He was not willing to go. The third time the voice said, 'Take the guest with you too.' And they went.

On the previous night, when they had greeted the Narts, not one of them had even attempted to stand up. But this time, as they said their greetings, all of these old men received them standing, and then seated them in the most honoured seats. If on the previous night they had each shared with them part of their own portion of food, this night Rachikau treated them all.

When they both went back the voice said, 'Did you see? Until today I was fed by their charity. But that funeral food, which you distributed to the people after arranging my wake, will be quite enough for me in this world, because you have done it from your whole heart, without begrudging it. Such is the custom here.'

'Now you ride off to that *aul* where this man lives. Sell your horse and instead of your own clothes put on some old rags. In the morning go out on to the street and stand there in public. When this man comes out on to the street in the morning with his hands behind his back, all the people, both men and women, will run away from him with a shout. But everyone that he overtakes, he will knock off their feet with a blow of his heel. When he runs up to you and asks, "And what are you standing here for?" you answer, "I have come to get a job as a workman." To his question: "But what are you good for?" you answer, "I will be a horse-herd!" And he will appoint you to look after his herd. If he likes you, he will make you his partner. Well, and what to do afterwards, you will work out for yourself. Kill him only with his own sword, but do not inflict more than one blow on him.'[1]

Karashauay went and stood on the street, as the voice had told him in his dream. The man appeared, with his hands behind his back. When the people began running away, he ran after them and began knocking them off their feet, all of those he caught up with. Running up to Karashauay, he asked, 'Why have you come here? What are you good for?'

'I want to get fixed up as a horse-herd or a groom,' replied Karashauay.

He took him and appointed him to look after his herd. And Karashauay worked for him about a month. The man began thinking, I swear by Teyri, he could be my partner, if I take him with me, and he took him home, having decided that Karashauay should wait on him on his journeys and perform all of his little commissions.

One day they stocked up with provisions, mounted their horses and rode off. When they reached a certain *aul*, the man left Karashauay in a shed on the edge of the village while he himself set out into the *aul*. From the *aul* could be heard noise and people's shouts. After some time the man returned. A girl was sitting before him on his horse. He rode up and took

---

1   A common motif in Caucasus tales is that a second blow can revive an enemy; in other words, the first blow must be decisive.

her from his horse. The girl shouted, 'You have massacred all of our family. May Allah, in return, destroy all of your family!' and she began sobbing loudly. Paying no attention to her, he told Karashauay: 'Get our provisions, and let us have something to eat.' They both ate. Then the man said, 'I am going to have a little nap. Meanwhile, you do not trust this girl, keep an eye on her.'

'All right,' Karashauay answered.

The girl happened to be near the man. And Karashauay was standing a little way away. When the man went to sleep, the girl indicated to Karashauay that she would give him the sleeping man's sword, if Karashauay would kill him. Karashauay, also silently, expressed his agreement.

When Karashauay struck the man with his sword, the man jumped up instantly and shouted, 'May all your family become extinct by the will of Allah! Strike once more, let me die without pangs!'

Karashauay answered this: 'My father willed me not to inflict more than one blow on an enemy.'

'Och, you damned fellow, it looks as if you were at Rachikau's grave and saw him!' the man shouted and died.

And Karashauay led the girl back to her *aul*.

ॐ

This Balkar legend was recorded by M. Zhurtubayev from the words of A. Bekkiev in the village of Kenzhe in 1985. It was published in T. M. Khajieva and R. A-K. Ortabayeva, *Narty*, Nauka, Moscow, 1994, 522–524.

84. Lega and Kopala *(Georgian)*

Thirty years ago in Tianeti, so they say, there was a certain old man, Lega Tegerashvili. One day he lost his mare and foal. He only realised it towards the evening, at the time when the herds were returning home. The herdsmen told him they had seen the mare and foal grazing on the bank of the river, not far from the village.

Lega went at once to drive the mare home: he was afraid in case wolves might cause her some harm. As he began to approach the place indicated by the herdsmen, he looked and saw: standing right there next to the riverbank, so he thought, was the wife of his relative. The woman shouted to him, 'Batono, what are you looking for here?'

The old man answered, 'They were saying that my mare and foal were grazing here, and I am looking for them.'

'That's right, Batono, your mare and foal are grazing a little lower down. Let's go, I will take you to them,' his neighbour said to him.

The old man followed her. However much he asked her where they were, she always answered, 'Here we are, we are already there.' She led him on and on, and took him into a certain house and locked the door. The old man looked and saw that she was not his neighbour but an entirely different, unknown woman. Then he realised that he had been tricked. The cap on his head rose in terror. He tried to get out, but he was unable to find the door. For a long time he was distressed. He saw that he was achieving nothing, and he said to the woman, 'If you believe in God, show me where the door is and let me leave here.'

The woman answered him, 'If you will lie down with me tonight, I will open the door to you and you shall go home in peace. If not, you shall not leave here alive.'

The old man said to her, 'Do not talk nonsense. I do not engage in things like that. And besides, do you really think at my age it is my business to do that kind of thing? You could serve as my daughter.'

After that the woman got up, opened the door, showed him a straight road and said, 'Start along this high road and walk.'

The man started walking. He was walking along the road and no way could he make out whether it was day or night: the sun was not visible, but it was as light as day. He was walking and saw that in one place they were ploughing, in another they were reaping the cornfield, in another they were digging with spades, but they were all working silently, nobody said to him 'Gamarjoba'[1] nor did they thank him in answer to his greeting. Among these people he recognised many neighbours, and also some livestock. All of them were people who had previously drowned, and all of the livestock were those that had been slaughtered. He also recognised the lame goat that had been slaughtered at the funeral banquet of his neighbour, who had been drowned in the river. He saw the goat next to the drowned man.

The old man walked for some way and arrived at a crossroads. His way was crossed by a wide highroad like the one on which he was walking. He

---

[1]   Gamarjoba (literally, 'victory') is a greeting on meeting somebody.

was standing at the crossroads and thinking. He did not know which road to go along. He could not come to any decision, so he decided to go back and ask the same woman which way to go next.

The old man smoked *tseko*. He got out his tobacco pouch, sat down and began to smoke. He was looking, and suddenly he saw a marvellous young man tearing along on a horse, like a bird going through the air. The young man came bounding up to the old man and asked him, 'Where are you going and where do you come from?'

The old man told him everything: how the woman had pretended to be a neighbour, how she had enticed him into her house, locked the door, and then brought him out on to this road. He also told how he had come to this crossroads and not known which way to go, and that he was thinking of going back to the woman for advice.

Then the young man said to him, 'I am your hero Kopala, to whom you pray, and you are my faithful servant. What accursed one have you followed? Who set you on this enchanted road and directed you to your father? There you would be strangled and eaten. Get up quickly, sit with me on my horse and let us go.'

The old man lost no time in getting up and sitting with him on the horse. Kopala took him with him. He rode to the very middle of the Bazaleti Lake,[1] rode through it on his horse and took him towards the Dusheti Gorge. He had only just carried him through the Gorge when it grew daylight. The young man said to him, 'Do not be afraid now, go! This is no time for jokes, do not go to sleep anywhere, but go straight home.'

After that the old man became ill; he was taken over by a *kadagi*. From that time Kopala made him his *dekanozi* until his very demise.

This Georgian legend was recorded by E. G. Godziashvili in 1882 from the words of G. Chanadiri in the village of Etvalisi in the Dusheti region. It was published in E. B. Virsaladze, *Gruzinskie narodnye predaniya i legendy*, Nauka, Moscow, 94–95.

---

1   The Bazaleti Lake is located in the mountains of eastern Georgia not far from the town of Dusheti. A series of traditions are connected with the lake.

85. The Resurrection of the Narts *(Balkar)*

Judging by the *khapars* that have reached us, the resurrection of the Narts starts at night, when the *auls* and the people are asleep. It is a sign of trouble. It happens when the people are anticipating some kind of misfortune or disaster.

These are the souls of the *deu* Narts, who lived in ancient times. They led a continual conflict with the wild aggressors, the *emegens*. I heard that the tribe of Narts perished from a pestilence, which spread from the decomposing corpses of the *emegens*. And now they look at us from the world of the dead and, when we are expecting some kind of misfortune, their souls turn into eagles, ravens and various wild animals:

> Shouting and howling, they fly through the *auls* at night
> And so warn the people about the impending calamity.
> These are the sacred souls of the courageous Narts.

This Balkar legend was recorded by S. O. Shakhmurzayev from the words of Zhashyu Aytekov in the village of Upper Chegem in 1960. It was published in T. M. Khajieva and R. A-K. Ortabayeva, *Narty*, Nauka, Moscow, 1994, 592.

86. The Horse of Zezva Gaprindauli *(Georgian)*

After the capture of the Bakhtrioni Fortress the king wanted to reward the mountain men who had won this war. To the Pshavs, so they say, he granted Shiraki,[1] and the Tushis, by the advice of Zezva, wanted to get those lands which his horse was able to ride around in one circuit. The horse took too wide a sweep: he rode around much, but he could not endure it, got tired and fell at the end of his journey. He was buried with great honour. Ever since that time the people honour his grave. Anybody who wants a long life for his horse or is seeking success in horses, to this day still brings a sacrifice to the tomb of Zezva's horse, especially the Tushis, Pshavs and

---

1   Shiraki is a steppe in eastern Georgia.

Khevsurs. Not one of them passes this tomb without getting off his horse and drinking to the peace of the soul of that horse, and of his master, the hero Zezva.

ॐ

There is no data on the collection of this Georgian legend. It was published in E. B. Virsaladze, *Gruzinskie narodnye predaniya i legendy*, Nauka, Moscow, 1973, 178.

87. Orshamar Arsh *(Ingush)*

Introduction
The name Orshamar Arsh (Arsh, son of Orshamar) is encountered only in this legend. When Fatima Khanieva recounted this legend, her sister Shishkha remarked that she remembered her mother mentioning the name as Ozdamar Ayrsh (Ayrsh, son of Ozdamar) (Note of I. Dakhkilgov).

O nce there lived three friends: Seska Solsa, Batar Shirtka and Orshamar Arsh. They were good friends.

Orshamar Arsh fell in love, more than his own soul, with a certain girl who was 'dying of beauty'. No matter what he did, they would not give that girl to him. He swore that he would not marry anybody but her.

All of a sudden the girl died. Orshamar Arsh told the *garbash*[1] of this girl, 'When you dress the girl in her shroud, do not let anybody know about this, but wrap me in the shroud with her.' Saying this, he gave her a gift.

The *garbash* did as Orshamar Arsh had told her. They laid him in the grave with the girl. When they closed the burial ground, he cut through the shroud with his diamond *kinzhal*[2] and sat next to his beloved girl. He was sitting miserable and thoughtful. At that time a flint snake crawled in.[3] Orshamar Arsh chopped it up into several pieces. A little while later

---

1   A servant-girl, a slave.
2   In Ingush, a 'diamond *shalta*'. This epithet is rarely encountered; it signifies the beauty and great hardness of the *kinzhal*.
3   In Ingush, '*moakkhaza tekkharg*', a flint-coloured snake.

another flint snake appeared. When it saw the slain snake, its friend, it crawled back the way it had come. After some time it came crawling in once more, holding in its mouth a little golden ball. After laying together all of the parts of the slain snake, each one to the next, it began rubbing with the little golden ball all of the places that the *kinzhal* had touched, and revived its friend.

On seeing this, Orshamar Arsh killed both snakes, took the little golden ball and lightly touched the girl with it. He passed it over her lips and she began breathing, he passed it across her eyes and she opened them, he passed it over her arms and legs, and she revived and stood up. They dug through the burial ground and came out. Then they became husband and wife.[1]

ಎಲ

This Ingush legend was recorded by I. Dakhkilgov in 1964 from the words of Fatima Khanieva, aged fifty-seven, in the town of Grozny. Khanieva was born in the village of Nasyr-Kort of the Nazran region; she heard the legend from her mother. It was published in U. B. Dalgat, *Geroichesky epos chechentsev i ingushey*, Nauka, Moscow, 1972, 295–296.

88. Seska Solsa and Byatar *(Chechen-Ingush)*

Introduction

Byatar is the hero's personal name; probably of Turko-Mongolian origin, from the word '*batyr*' (*bogatyr*). This name is rarely met in folklore. Possibly it has something in common with the name Botky Shirtka (Byatar Shirtka). Byatar has some analogy with Botky Shirtka, since he can also descend into El, the land of the dead. In the legend Byatar is portrayed both as an epic warrior-hero and as a tiller of the soil, a mower and a cattle-breeder, which is not typical for the Nart-Orstkhoy warrior-heroes.

---

1   The Khanieva sisters emphasised that this was only part of a grand legend, in which the actions of two other heroes mentioned are described, Batar Shirtka and Seska Solsa (Note of I. Dakhkilgov).

Listen. Many years have passed since those times, much water has flowed since those times. The water that has passed will not flow backwards, the lost time will not return. And nobody knows when it was.

They say that once there lived a young hero by the name of Byatar. Except for his old mother, he had nobody. Byatar used to feed his mother and himself, and that was how he lived. His plough land was long, his scythe mowed widely, and he grazed his sheep and cows – and thus day after day passed in work. And towards night, when darkness had only just fallen, he would play on his *pandyra*,[1] entertaining himself and his mother with his playing. He shunned craftiness and baseness, and lived peacefully by his work. If it became necessary anywhere, then he was able to show his martial skill, but never did he seek out wealth through war. People respected him for his intelligence and manliness, for his strength and kind thoughts.

At that time there also lived a man by the name of Seska Solsa. He led an armed force, and he was robust, both in strength and courage. For that reason people called him 'Seska Solsa of forged steel'.[2] And his fame spread around, because with his horsemen he was always making war and performing raids. Byatar and Seska Solsa did not know one another. Seska Solsa was always the victor, he would overcome any obstacles and, confident of his strength, one day he asked his seven-*arshin* high and omniscient horse, 'Is there a man in the world stronger than I am and more manly than I am?'

His omniscient and truth-speaking horse answered him, 'I have known you for a long time, Seska Solsa, and we have travelled plenty of roads and paths in this world. You have both strength and manliness in abundance but, without meaning any offence to you, there is in the world a certain young hero by the name of Byatar. I will not say that he has more strength and manliness than you have, but nor is he weaker than you are.'

Seska Solsa knew that his horse never told a lie. He was greatly saddened on learning about the obscure young hero who, although not surpassing Seska Solsa, was not inferior to him in any way. A desire to show his mettle crept into his heart, he was gripped by arrogance, and he asked his horse, 'Old belly-band, foot-shuffling animal, how do you know this?'

His horse calmly replied, 'That young man has a little nag that I know well. I actually learned it from him, who knows his master well.'

---

1   At that time Ingush men also played on the *pandyra*, which is a stringed musical instrument of the mountain people. They did not consider it to be shameful or humiliating (note of the narrator).

2   This testifies to the steel tempering of the legendary hero.

'You, who would not say even a pleasing word, then let us go, take me to that Byatar. We shall find out whether he really is like you say.'

After accomplishing the journey in seven days and nights, they reached Byatar. '*Salam-aleykum*. Do you receive guests?'

'*Va-aleykum salam*. Come in peace. One who does not love a guest is unloved by God. Come in.'

Having heard much about Seska Solsa, Byatar received his guest with respect. When they had eaten and drunk, the host even played on his *pandyra*, in order to entertain his guest. Observing Byatar's noble behaviour, Seska Solsa spent three days with him.[1] At last, Solsa disclosed the purpose of his coming. 'Which of us is stronger and more manly?' the guest asked.

They argued this way and that, they asked people, who all answered in different ways: some said that Byatar excelled, other said Seska Solsa. The young fellows became thoughtful but did not know how to resolve the argument. And now Byatar's old mother excused herself and gave them the following advice: 'Beneath the earth, in the other world there is Elda, the sovereign or master of the dead, who watches over their souls.[2] He knows everything that happens both in the sunny world and in the underground one. It is only from him that you can find out which of you is the stronger and more manly.'

The old woman taught them how to reach El, into which no living person had yet entered. Both Seska Solsa on his steed and Byatar on his little horse set off on the indicated road. Thus they rode as far as the Terek, which was rushing headlong and rolling its rough waters. It was only by getting across the river that they could continue their journey. At that time the Terek was more swollen and swifter than it is now. But from the rain it had become absolutely black and, picking up the stones, it whirled them headlong in the current. Everything that fell into it was carried away like a bullet by the swift water. It was dangerous to cross it. Byatar said, 'That water is dangerous, we had better look for a ford.'

But wishing to show his courage, Seska Solsa replied, 'We will cross, it is not dangerous at all!'

---

1   According to an *adat* of the Ingush, a guest is considered to be a guest for three days, including the day of arrival, and for all that time the host has to attend to him as a guest. During this period it is considered improper to ask the guest the purpose of his coming. After three days the guest can remain in the house however much he wants, but they will already address him as a member of the household.

2   Elda means literally 'the master of El', the god of the underground kingdom of the dead. Ch. Akhriev calls him 'Eter' or 'Eshpor', B. Dalgat calls him 'Eshtr'.

With that, he lashed his horse with a whip, and directed it towards the raging river. Although he lashed it with the whip and shouted so that the horse cowered, nevertheless the horse snorted and tossed but would not go into the water. Seeing his discomposure, Byatar softly squeezed his knees and directed his little nag into the river. The horse sniffed the wind, sized up the situation, and, choosing a ford, began calmly and confidently cutting through the water. After him went Seska Solsa's horse too. But in the middle of the river, where it was faster and deeper, Seska Solsa's heavy horse began being carried away by the swift current.

Then Seska Solsa addressed the Terek with the request: 'Diminish your waters, and I will make you a present of my golden belt.' He threw his golden belt, manufactured by skilled craftsmen, into the water as he spoke. The Terek was satisfied with the gift. Admiring the belt, playing with it and bathing it in its waves, the Terek quietened down and diminished its waters.

As the people relate, from that time the water in the Terek decreased.[1] Even today the Terek is high, so how must it have been then? Crossing the river, they went on further. They crossed seven mountains and seven seas. And at last they came to the edge of the world. The land here came to a completely abrupt end, and there was nowhere to go. As Byatar's old mother had actually related, they saw a ladder going away downwards from the edge of the world. After releasing their horses to graze, they began climbing down. In front went Seska Solsa, thirsting to display his courage, and after him Byatar, who did not have excessive pride (he was not a braggart).

However far they went, no end could be seen, and there was nothing except for black steam coming from below. Thus, forging ahead, they came to El. Sitting at the copper gates leading into El was a nine-eyed, tusked, terrible *yeshap* with nine arms and legs.[2] Huge in stature, and overgrown like a bear, with a long mane and covered all over with lice, he was ceaselessly scratching himself with his nails. Would that a man did not see him, and would that he did not even dream about him! When they related why they had come here, the *yeshap* burst out laughing and said, 'Until this day no living man has presented himself before me, wishing to enter here. A

---

1   The epic concept of increasing or diminishing the Terek was evidently connected with the people's observations on the river at various times of year. The interference in the flow of the River Terek also features in the legend of Koloy-Kant.

2   *Yeshap* is the common name of an anthropomorphic creature hostile to man encountered in Vaynakh folklore. This sexless creature sometimes appears to have feminine characteristics, as in this legend, where it stands guard at the entrance to the underground world.

living man does not enter these gates, he can only come in after his death; and those who come in never return. For that reason they have placed me on guard, and I perform my service meticulously. When you die, you can freely pass through here.'

'If you do not let us in, I will chop you in two with my sword, you *yeshap* without a man's appearance,' said Seska Solsa, and he drew his sword.

The *yeshap* clapped his hands, mimicking Seska Solsa, and he burst into laughter. Not to fulfil one's spoken word, and not to strike with a drawn sword, is a great disgrace! Gathering all of his available strength, he struck the *yeshap* with his great sword. There was a ringing sound, as if the sword had struck against a hard stone, giving out a 'zou' noise. It broke, without cutting a single little hair on the *yeshap*'s body. Seeing the funny side of it, the *yeshap* burst out laughing even more. 'If I had been so weak, they would not have set me here. Thank you, my boy, you have killed on my body one of the insects that give me no peace.'

Byatar had the thought: although it is actually a *yeshap*, it is nevertheless like a woman, and turning to him, he said, 'If only you would permit us to enter, I will bring you something good from there.'

The *yeshap* became amiable, but he still did not let them pass. Noticing that he was uncertain, Byatar continued: 'And truly, let us in. As we promised, we will bring you something good. Have a look at yourself, you are so pleasant and attractive to look at. After all, it does not become a creature as beautiful as you to answer no.'

Everyone always used to tell the *yeshap* that he was ugly, as he actually was. But after all it was very offensive, since the *yeshap* considered that there was nothing in the world more beautiful than he. The crafty words of Byatar, like oil softening the sole of a dried-out slipper, loosened the *yeshap*'s heart. Very pleased, he suddenly said, 'May you live long and pass through.'

He moved to the side slightly as he spoke. They quickly went in the slightly opened gates. There and then the *yeshap* repented of his sudden soft-heartedness, but it was already too late.

In El it was dark and cold. Everywhere were the souls of the deceased, lamenting 'akhy-vakhy'. The souls of old mothers were weeping, remembering their children left in the sunny world. The souls of children were weeping, recalling their fathers and mothers. The amazed Byatar and Seska Solsa observed these souls attentively. They were dressed only in their shrouds. The souls were not like people living in the sunny world. The majority of them were the souls of old men and women. The souls of the young reminded them of people infected with plague, or maimed and slain warriors. The travellers kept going on further. Souls began approaching them, cursing Seska Solsa. They were all either without arms, or without feet, or without heads, or with their bodies chopped up or riddled with holes, and none of them had forgotten anything bad that he had done to them. These souls kept on threatening him with reprisals after his death, when he descended into the underground world forever. But the travellers kept on going. Now other souls approached them; those whom Byatar had helped during their lives and done kindness to. All of them were thanking him.

In the midst of the dwelling place of the dead they saw a tall tower, built of human bones. In it sat the sovereign of the underground world, Elda, and he was dealing out impartial judgement on the deceased. He was sending the righteous to paradise, and lodging the sinners in hell. On seeing living people, Elda was very surprised. 'What are you doing roaming in the underground world, what brought you here? After all, nobody presents themselves to me by their own will, and all are ready to escape from here!'

'We cannot resolve the dispute, which of us is the better. Only you can answer that question.'

The sovereign of the underground world began pondering deeply and said, 'Nobody knows better than I do about all that happens in the sunny world. After all, there are no immortal people, and after death everything that has been done by a man is presented before my judgement. It is hard to say which of you is better, but I will try to give you an answer. I will relate something to you, and each of you will tell me your opinion.'

'In olden times there lived two friends. Everybody knew about them, as true and devoted friends. One of them fell in love with a girl, and the girl gave her agreement to throw in her lot with him. The second one also fell in love with that girl, not knowing that his friend loved her, and he sent matchmakers to her, through whom he actually received the consent of her parents. But the first one did not know about this and, as always, he wanted to carry on sweet conversation with his beloved girl. She related her trouble to him and said that she was prepared to elope with him. Returning home, that young man met the man who had murdered his father in a desert place. His blood enemy was weak, hungry, dying of thirst and unarmed. Tell me, how would you have acted in that young man's position?'

Seska Solsa said, 'If you ask me, in that young man's place I would have taken away the girl, because he had fallen in love with her before the other man. And with the blood enemy I would have acted as one ought.[1] However he was, all the same he was my blood enemy! But if he had no weapon, I would have given him my spare one.'

Byatar then replied, 'Friendship is needed, not to pass the time after a substantial dinner, and not for the sake of a witty word. It manifests itself in important matters and in misfortune. Two difficult problems had befallen the young man. It seems to me that I would have left the girl to the comrade who had fallen in love with her, no matter how difficult that would be, but it is precisely how a true friend should act. It is difficult to pass by a blood enemy. But nevertheless, after meeting him in such a pitiful state I would have let him go, after sharing bread and salt with him. Moreover, there is little honour in killing a helpless man! But at another time I would have taken my blood debt without fail. So much the more because when he is healthy, it is harder for him to part with life!'

After listening to both answers, Elda said, 'Cheer up, Seska Solsa. If one judged manliness your way, then there is nobody more manly than you. According to your replies I realise that Byatar understands the word "manliness" more correctly. It does not consist of bravery alone, and includes many things. Manliness includes common sense.'

Then Seska Solsa realised that he was inferior to Byatar in manliness.

'Now we shall see which of you is the stronger,' said Elda. After saying this, he lifted over his head the staff that he was holding in his hand, swung his arm and thrust it halfway into a sturdy cast stone lying before him.[2] 'The one who pulls the staff out of the stone is the stronger one.'

At this point Seska Solsa really thought to himself, now at least I shall show my strength, otherwise I will be disgraced! Seska Solsa had much strength in his body, and he was confident of victory. 'I will pull out that staff,' said he.

But Byatar was in no hurry. Seska Solsa collected all the strength in his body and tugged at the staff with both hands. He dug his feet into the stone so strongly that he turned it into stone chippings. After expending

1   He would have killed him as his blood enemy.
2   Stone occupies a special place in the epos connected to the life and places of habitation of the heroic characters. According to the folk ideas, there is special beauty and wonderful properties reserved for the 'blue stone' (*siyna kkhmera*, in Ingush). It was specifically in a blue stone, according to the tradition, that the foetus of Seska Solsa was formed. The specification 'cast stone' is most likely a substitute word, which has the same meaning as 'blue stone'. In folk divinations of the Vaynakhs they distinguish further, between a round stone, a black stone and a white stone as having sacred meanings (note from U. B. Dalgat).

all his strength, Seska Solsa did not pull out the staff, and he was hardly standing on his feet from tiredness.

After that Byatar approached. With one hand he calmly pulled the staff out of the debris and held it out to the sovereign of the dead. Elda realised why Byatar had not been first to pull the staff, and now he said, 'Seska Solsa, concealed in your body is great strength, but when strength is combined with intelligence, a man becomes even mightier. Byatar has beaten you in the dispute. Until now I have not spoken with living people from the sunny world, although I judge the souls of the deceased for their earthly acts. Thus I have judged you too. Do you need anything more from me?'

Byatar replied, 'Thank you for your words. We cannot ask you for much, but we have yet one more request. By speaking fine words to the *yeshap* guarding the entrance to El, we got through into here; by promising to make him a gift. It is now that we need your help. Apart from you, nobody can help us to get out of here!'

'There is nothing easier than that,' said the sovereign of the dead, and he gave Byatar a comb with thick teeth measuring two *loktey*. 'For a long time the *yeshap* has been troubled by lice, and if you present him with this comb, then you cannot do him a greater kindness!'

After expressing their gratitude to Elda, they set off on the return journey. The *yeshap* saw them and immediately stood in the gateway. Smiling, he asked the travellers, 'Where is the gift you promised, my little children? Now you will not manage to get out of here so easily. It is much more difficult than getting in!'

And then Byatar replied, 'Thank you for calling us your children, and here is our gift,' and he gave him the comb.

Grabbing the comb, the *yeshap* viciously set about combing his locks with all his might. With his joy he went into ecstasy and choked with laughter, while the lice, the size of a thumb, were falling on the ground, knocking like stones: tokh, tokh.

After saying to themselves, 'God save us from being your children,' and running out through the gates, they set off on their way. And once more clambering up the ladder leading out of the darkness of El, they came out into this sunny world and, sitting on their horses, they returned home.

Although Byatar had really won the argument, Seska Solsa, without concealing the black envy in his heart, entered into friendship with him. And after that he gave Byatar his sister, dying of beauty, and thus sealed the ties of kinship with him.

Byatar began living with his beautiful wife. They had children, and those children also had children, and from them children came, and their family line has reached the present day. If you see a noble, intelligent and courageous man, you should know that he originated from them.

This Chechen-Ingush legend was recorded by B. Dalgat from the words of the narrator Ganyzh and was first published in 1901. It was published in U. B. Dalgat, *Geroichesky epos chechentsev i ingushey*, Nauka, Moscow, 1972, 304–309.

89. Mikel-Gabriel[1] *(Georgian)*

God told Mikel-Gabriel, 'Go down on to the earth. In such-and-such a house lives a mother. Take out her soul and bring it to me.'

Mikel-Gabriel, the Lord's slave, descended to the earth. He travelled about the world a great deal until he found his victim: the woman was in a hovel, lying in childbirth, destitute, unhappy, naked. She was giving birth to twins. The first one pressed itself to one breast, and the second one to the other. Near them could be seen neither fire nor food, and there was nothing for her to drink. Instead of a blanket, her knees were covered with rags. The woman herself was hungry and sick, and the children were mewing like weak kittens. There was neither a husband nor any close friend or relative to look after them.

Mikel-Gabriel, the Extinguisher, went in and had a look. His heart was filled, not with pity but with horror. He turned and went, closing the door of woven twigs behind him so as not to see this dreadful picture. He went without looking around, so as not to see once again how, like little worms, the naked babies were wriggling.

'Have you brought her soul?' asked the Lord.

'Great God, Creator of heaven and earth! I saw such misfortune, such need, such hunger and cold, such helpless infants having to be left without

---

1   Mikel-Gabriel is a combination of the archangels Michael and Gabriel. Among the folk he is considered as a single angel of death, who comes for the souls of those who have died.

their mother that I preferred to incur your wrath, if only not to deprive them of their mother. There is nobody in that world to care for them besides their mother. Who could I leave these innocent creatures with? If their mother has committed some offence, at least the infants are still like angels. I could not bring myself to do it. For the sake of the children I gave the mother her life.'

The Lord grew angry. 'You good-for-nothing, how dare you fail to carry out my order?! Who are you to know worldly affairs better than I do? Will you teach me? Are you the one to comprehend inscrutable Providence?!' the furious Ruler of the World roared.

The Lord gave Mikel-Gabriel a stick and told him, 'Descend once more to the earth, and strike the rod against the Black Sea. The sea will open wide, and you will behold a black rock. Strike that rock with the rod, and the rock will gape open too. Report to me all that you see there!'

Mikel-Gabriel took the stick and descended to the earth. He struck the sea with the rod, the sea opened wide and he saw the rock in the middle of the sea. He struck the rock with the rod, and the rock split. Mikel-Gabriel looked, hoping to see something surprising, but he saw nothing apart from ants. There were only black ants crawling and bustling about.

Mikel-Gabriel returned to the Lord.

'Did you carry out my order or not?' God asked him.

'I carried it out, Lord.'

'Well, and what did you see in that rock?'

'Nothing, Lord. There were only ants crawling.'

'It was just those ants you were supposed to see, you useless fellow,' pronounced the Lord. 'If I, the Heavenly Father, concern myself about black ants at the bottom of the sea and in the heart of the black rock, and give them food, is it likely that I would not concern myself about those children?! Go immediately and bring me the soul of that woman.'

Mikel-Gabriel plodded off. By then he was really convinced that he had acted badly by not taking the poor mother's soul. He came to the hovel and saw that the mother was feeling better, she was sitting on the bed, and both of her infants were cooing on her knees, luxuriating in their mother's affection. The Extinguisher stood and gazed at all this; he gazed and turned around and went. He went on and on. The Ruler of all the World had grown tired of waiting for Mikel-Gabriel. Mikel-Gabriel was not to be seen. The Lord sent Saint Elia: 'Go and find where Mikel-Gabriel has got to.'

Elia descended to the earth, he searched and searched and finally found him. 'Where were you? After all, the Lord has been waiting such a long time for you!'

'No, I cannot look on at God's injustice,' Mikel-Gabriel said to him. 'I am in no hurry to go there.'

With great difficulty Elia just managed to persuade Mikel-Gabriel, and conducted him to the Lord.

'Well, what have you done with the soul? Did you bring it?' the Lord asked him.

'No, Creator of Heaven and Earth. I saw how the mother was caressing her little ones, how on earth could I take her soul? I could not even think of it ... After all, that mother is both an earthly mother and a heavenly father to them. How can you substitute for their mother? You are a long way from the people, you are unable to take the place of a father to them.'

'Take him and tear out his heart!' ordered God.

Mikel-Gabriel was taken out, his chest was cut open, and his heart and liver were taken out. Since that time he does not pity anybody, he extinguishes poor and rich alike, regardless of whether they are solitary or surrounded by their family.

This Georgian legend was recorded by T. Razikashvili in Pshavi, Georgia, and was first published in 1909. It was published in E. B. Virsaladze, *Gruzinskie narodnye predaniya i legendy*, Nauka, Moscow, 1973, 262–264.

90. About Paliastomi *(Georgian)*

The following tradition has been preserved about the origin of Lake Paliastomi.

At one time the town of Paliastomi was on the site of this lake. In this town was a church in which was located an icon of the Mother of God.

The inhabitants of the town had become so depraved that, in spite of the holiness of the church, they began riding into it on their horses. So as to hamper them in this, God lowered the doors of the church so much that it was impossible to ride into it on a horse. After that the town's inhabitants began climbing down off their horses by the entrance to the church, but all the same they led them into the church by the reins. God, wanting them to enter the church without their horses, and moreover stooping as if bowing to him, lowered the doors yet more. The inhabitants of the town certainly began leaving their horses in the courtyard, but they did not stoop at the entrance into the church; instead they first poked their legs through and after that their whole body. Then, seeing the incorrigibility of the inhabitants, God decided to drown Paliastomi.

Only one man by the name of Kiko preserved his piety. The Lord came to him in a dream and said, 'Take the icon of the Mother of God and carry it to the settlement of Shemokmedi,[1] because the town of Paliastomi has to perish.'

Kiko quickly sat on his mule; in front of him he placed the holy icon, and behind him he sat a woman whom he respected, whose death he did not want, and he rode off to the place named. As soon as Kiko had ridden out of Paliastomi, God let forth a cloud-burst from above and drowned the town. Kiko was riding, but the deluge was overtaking him: the back legs of the mule were already in water. Then the Lord appeared to him and said, 'Abandon your woman and save yourself, if you do not throw her off, then you will perish!'

Kiko threw off the woman, and the tidal wave stopped.

Three months after Kiko had come to Shemokmedi, God came to him in a dream and told him, 'Take the icon to Bakhvi.'[2]

Then Kiko moved to Bakhvi and brought the icon there.

No details are available about the recording of this Georgian legend. It was published in E. B. Virsaladze, *Gruzinskie narodnye predaniya i legendy*, Nauka, Moscow, 1973, 276–277.

---

1   Shemokmedi is a settlement in Guria.
2   Bakhvi is a settlement in Guria.

XII

Prometheus Legends

As the subjects of the previous eleven chapters of this book are clearly of importance to the mountain people, and therefore may be expected to be the subjects of legends, the question might arise: why are 'Prometheus legends' locally prominent? One possible answer could be that the theomachy motif (conflict with the gods) might have been associated with a change of religion in the past. With so many different ethnic and linguistic groups living in the Caucasus, there have inevitably been religious conflicts and changes of religion. Another possible reason for the prominence of the legend may be connected with the motif of the theft of fire. As described in the previous chapter, the hearth with its fire has a religious connotation, and is very important in the local culture. If the fire in the hearth is so important to a family, then the theft of fire would clearly be an inexcusable outrage on the family. How much bigger outrage would it then be for the gods if their fire was stolen?[1]

The importance of Prometheus legends in the Caucasus can be gauged by the forty-four different versions that have been identified. Many of these may appear to differ somewhat from the original Greek Prometheus legend. Moreover, it is not easy to decide what constitutes a Prometheus legend: it is the same problem we encountered with the Cyclops legends in Chapter 7, only here it is more complicated. One basic difficulty is that the story in the original Greek version of the Prometheus legend in Hesiod is somewhat vague (Hesiod 1966, 314ff). Nine motifs have been identified that are common, both to some of the Caucasus legends and to the Hesiod version. In this analysis, those motifs marked with * will be considered as key motifs, although the choice is open to debate.

1. Theomachy: disrespect to, or conflict with God, a god or the gods; sometimes the gods being given poor parts of the food, and people getting the best parts.*

---

1   It should also be noted that fire is a key element of what was once the prevailing Persian religion of Zoroastrianism.

2. God commandeers fire, and withholds it from men.
3. Giant hero steals (back) fire and gives it to men.*
4. Fire associated with the blacksmith (Hephaestos among the Greeks).
5. Giant hero punished by God.
6. Giant hero chained to rock, post, mountain or cave.*
7. Giant hero chained up for eternity.
8. Giant bird (eagle) torments giant hero.
9. Bird pecks hero's liver (or heart).

In order to consider whether a Caucasus legend can be considered to be a Prometheus legend it would be useful to try to elucidate possible underlying meanings or themes.

The first key motif of theomachy suggests that the conflict might have involved a change of religion. During the changeover, any unexpected natural disasters, such as food shortages or epidemics, are likely to be blamed on the loss of the old 'gods' and on their consequent anger. The unequal distribution of food suggests sacrifice to the gods. In ritual sacrifice, after the animal has been killed, a few small or inedible parts may be offered to the gods, either by burning and letting the smoke go upwards towards 'heaven' or by direct donation, in such cases as horns and antlers (B. Dalgat 2004, 110). In other cases edible material would be given to the saint or god through the officiating priest, who then presumably kept it for his own use. The remaining edible parts would be eaten by the sacrificer and the people attending the ceremony (ibid, 139).

The second key motif (No. 3) involves the acquisition of fire by men. But what does fire signify in its basic sense? Firstly, fire is necessary for cooking: whereas an animal eats its meat in a raw state, man eats it after cooking. Therefore fire can signify the difference between animal and man. Secondly, the essential central item in a home is the hearth, the place of fire. This applies even if home is a cave; i.e., it is not walls that make a home, but the permanent hearth with a fire. Although nomads and travellers might light a fire, it is only a temporary fire. The permanent fire signifies the difference between home and 'no home' (see Chapter 11 on the sacred importance of the fire and the hearth). A third possibility is that fire is essential for certain basic manufacturing processes that could be considered as necessary for culture: pottery, the smelting of metals, the forging of iron, as included in motif No. 4 above. Fire therefore could be considered as an essential difference between culture and 'no culture'. The problem here is in deciding which, if any, of these three essential differences are the bases of the theft of fire by the hero of Prometheus legends. A fourth possibility could be suggested: that fire is important because of its possible connection with sacrifices. However, in the Caucasus region sacrifices were often made without fire, except for the fire that was used for cooking the meat consumed by the people involved. In addition to the slaughter of livestock, many of the items sacrificed were unconnected with fire, including such things as bread, beer, money and bullets (B. Dalgat 2004, 131).

The third key motif (No. 6), together with the last motif (No. 9), could suggest that the struggles of the chained giant might explain the occasional sudden earth tremors in mountainous regions, causing avalanches and earthquakes. In some Caucasus legends about chained giants this effect is specifically mentioned, the Caucasus being an earthquake zone. A slightly different slant on the hero chained to the crag is given by Elena Virsaladze (Virsaladze 1976, 108). She mentions that in the Kabardan tradition Mount Elbrus is the habitation of a god: a certain one-eyed man attempted to climb to its summit. The goddess of hunting and fertility punished him by chaining him forever to a crag. In some traditions the one-eyed hero represents one of the heavenly luminaries such as a star or the sun or moon.

The first two legends feature the Georgian Prometheus figure, Amirani. The main feature of Amirani is the conflict with the Christian God, in this case Christ, for which he is chained for all eternity within a cave. The next legend also features Amirani, who is already chained in the cave. Tradition says that the cave occasionally opens and allows an ordinary mortal to enter and converse with the hero for a short time. This legend is one of the many that describe how Amirani almost escapes but is always frustrated. The next legend, of the return of fire, contains a possible underlying suggestion of a change of religion: the eternal flame in the sacred hearth has been extinguished, and the abundance of the land has been threatened. But then abundance is returned to the land by the obtaining of fire with a little piece of the sun. The next legend, 'Pkharmat', is particularly interesting for two reasons. Firstly, because it is the only Caucasus legend identified that contains all nine of the motifs listed above, and secondly because it specifically states that the hero allowed himself to be sacrificed for the benefit of mankind, including being exposed to the elements and even having his right side (containing his liver) wounded – a notable parallel with Christ's own sacrifice. The legend of how Sosuruk obtained fire for the Narts is one of many Caucasus variants that describe how the hero saves his people from cold and hunger by stealing fire from an exceptionally strong man or sometimes a dragon. In each case the superior intelligence of the man overcomes the superior strength of the guardian of the fire. The next legend, of Abrskil, is the Abkhazian parallel to the Georgian Amirani, but has its own distinguishing features, many of which have great poetic quality. Abrskil's furious shaking of the iron post to which he is chained can of course be connected with the frequent earth tremors in the Caucasus mountains. The legend of Amiran is the most traditional version of the Georgian Prometheus legend, but here has been drastically abridged, in order to include some of the most interesting motifs. This version has more than a hint of Amirani's hunting background, his father having been a hunter, and his mother having been Dali, the mistress of the beasts; and so it is interesting to compare this with the legend in Chapter 6, 'Dali and Amirani. Why Khazhoie Birds Have Little Moustaches'. In this legend the goddess's hair is also an important feature. This legend also describes the legendary hunting dog Kursha, which features in many Caucasus legends. The next legend, 'Nasran', is one variant of the many Adyge versions of the Prometheus story. In some of these there is a specific mention of the overthrow of the former god, possibly hinting at a change of religion, and in at least one version the hero is eventually rescued. The final legend from the Lezg people of southern Daghestan and northern Azerbayjan, 'How Sharvili Found Fire', is too short to search for significant motifs, but it contains hints of underlying interesting themes.

91. The Chained Amirani *(Georgian)*

There lived a man, Zhadal. This Zhadal was very strong. There was no man in the world capable of beating him in wrestling. At the same time he was also in control of land and people. Zhadal bore a son whom they called Amirani. Zhadal was very pleased at the birth of his son; in his joy he went out on the road and began shouting, 'I am strong, but my son will be even more so!'

He took some stones of weight two to three hundred *poods* and threw them, just like balls, in various directions: 'Who is there who dares,' he said, 'even to fight with me, let alone with my son. Who dares to dispute our supremacy!'

They said to Zhadal, 'There is a man who is stronger than you. He is called Christ. After twelve days he will wrestle with you, and he has forty assistants.'

Zhadal grew upset and, wishing to terrify Christ completely, he began throwing still heavier stones and shouting yet louder. He wanted to frighten Christ with his shouting.

Now Christ arrived too. He told Zhadal that both he and his son would have to relinquish their mastery of the world. Zhadal answered, 'We will have a contest. The one who turns out to be stronger, he will be the master.' Christ agreed.

Zhadal took an enormous stone and threw it upwards, just like a ball. After two hours that stone fell down again and half buried itself in the earth.

Christ threw up that same stone and said to Zhadal, 'Tomorrow at this time that stone will fall down. Then you will see.'

And that is what happened. Only on the next day did that stone fall, and it almost entirely disappeared into the ground.

Zhadal realised that he was not going to overcome Christ, and he said to him, 'I have a son Amirani. Well then, have a contest with him!'

Zhadal brought Amirani. Amirani proudly approached Christ and said to him, 'Do you want to measure your strength against me?'

He seized a stone almost the size of a mountain and threw it beyond forty *versts*. Christ picked up that stone and told it not to come back at all. He threw the stone, and it disappeared beyond nine mountains and went way into the ground. It went so deep into the ground that it could hardly be seen.

Then Christ said to Amirani, 'Well then, if you are a capable fellow, fetch that stone.'

Amirani rushed to that stone and laboured over it for a long time, but he was unable even to move it from its place. He was simply exhausting himself with the stone, until Christ ordered him to be chained to it. He chained him, and covered him over with a mountain. Every day he was given one *shoti*-bread, and a certain little pet dog was given to him. The little dog licks the chain, he licks it until he has made the chain extremely thin. It seems that with just a little more, Amirani will tear the chain apart and get free. But on the morning of Great Thursday all the blacksmiths get up and strike their anvils with their hammers, and the chain once again returns to its former thickness.[1] How Amirani would like to break those

---

1   The custom of striking the anvil with a hammer on Great Thursday (or Maundy Thursday, the

chains! Then it would be a bad look-out for those blacksmiths; he would tear off all their heads!

This Georgian legend was recorded by Yu. Dzamashvili in 1937 from S. I. Dzamashvili, inhabitant of the village of Sakobo, in the village of Shroma. It was published in E. B. Virsaladze, *Gruzinskie narodnye predaniya i legendy*, Nauka, Moscow, 1973, 100–101.

92. The Dragon Turned to Stone *(Georgian)*

Having a false idea of his own importance, Amirani decided to measure his strength with Christ-God himself. For this, God chained him to the slope of Mkinvartsveri.[1] A dragon, the unremitting enemy of Amirani, decided to take advantage of this. He crawled down from the summit of Mkinvari and got ready to swallow the chained Amirani. But Saint George found out about it and appeared there right away. After making threatening gestures at the dragon with his finger, the saint said, 'Stop! We chained Amirani so that he would repent of his sins, not to satisfy your hunger. Become a stone at once!'

The dragon turned to stone there and then.[2]

This Georgian legend was recorded by S. Makalatia in the village of Khevi, in the Kazbek region. It was published in E. B. Virsaladze, *Gruzinskie narodnye predaniya i legendy*, Nauka, Moscow, 1973, 102.

---

day before Good Friday) is observed by all the blacksmiths in Georgia.

1   *Mkinvartsveri* means literally 'the peak of the ice-houses', the local name of Mount Kazbek (Georgian Kazbegi).

2   Note that on the left bank of the River Terek, on the eastern slope of Mount Kazbek, there is a crag which from a distance resembles a dragon in its outline.

93. Amirani and the Herdsman *(Georgian)*

There was a certain herdsman who approached Amirani's mountain and saw that the entrance into the mountain was open. Amirani called the herdsman to come to him. The man became frightened: 'I cannot,' he said. (Amirani's eyes were large).

'Do not be afraid, come near,' said Amirani.

The herdsman became bolder and approached. Amirani said to him, 'Let's have a look at your bread, what sort do you have?' He squeezed the bread with his hand, and blood ran out of that bread. Then Amirani said, 'You eat bloody bread,' and he added, 'Would you hand me my bread that is lying there.' When he squeezed his own bread in his hand, milk ran out of it. 'I live on milk bread,' said Amirani. 'Well then, now move my sword up to me. My sword is lying there, but I am fastened with a chain here.'

The herdsman could not find anything to tie to the sword to drag it to Amirani.

'You grasp it yourself.'

The herdsman took hold of the sword and Amirani began to pull the herdsman. The herdsman's arms started hurting. Then Amirani said to him, 'All right, go home and bring me some straps of ox-hide. If a woman starts speaking with you, do not say a single word to her, otherwise the doors of my dungeon will close.'

The herdsman went for the straps. He took them off the wall of his own house. He did not want to speak with anybody, but his wife ran after him, 'Where are you going? What are you carrying that for? Why aren't you saying anything?'

'What are you bothering me for, woman!' the herdsman finally lost his patience.

And that mountain closed up at once. When he approached it he could see that the mountain had closed up. And so Amirani remained chained up. They say that if he tears apart his chains he will walk through the world and kill off all the women. He is angry at them, so they say. But who knows who he is angry at! He is simply chained up beneath the mountain.

ॐ

This Georgian legend was recorded by M. Chikovani in 1937 from A. I. Baliashvili, in the town of Akhaltsikhe. It was published in E. B.

Virsaladze, *Gruzinskie narodnye predaniya i legendy*, Nauka, Moscow, 1973, 102–103.

94. The Legend of the Return of Fire *(Abkhaz)*

Introduction

Amra was the ancient Abkhazian pagan deity of the sun. So strong was the worship of this deity that even at the time of construction of the Orthodox Pskal Church in the early Middle Ages on the conical summit of Mount Pskal, a craftsman drew his image in the altar barrier.

Mount Ertsakhu, mentioned in the legend, is named as the biggest, although in reality Ertsakhu is lower than Mount Dombay-Ulgen, which is also within the boundaries of the Abkhazian Alps.

In times long, long ago, when the lands of Abkhazia were completely covered with thick forests, and the mountains showed green under the rays of the hot sun, good-looking and strong people were living here. They lived in harmony and without cares. Nature endowed them generously with fruits and the meat of wild animals. The clean rivers bore their cool waters to these people. In a word, they were living carefree lives, for it did not take a lot of work to obtain food or to find shelter: Abkhazia was then a land of abundance. And one thing which these people valued, which they guarded more than their own eyes, was the fire, which had already burned hundreds of years on the summit of a hill. The people did not let it go out, for among them existed the superstition: if they did not have fire they would not have a happy life.

But one day it happened that a downpour extinguished the eternal flame. A careless fellow tribesman had not looked after it. The people came to the hill and saw with horror that instead of the hot flame in the sacred hearth, a pitiful puff of smoke was coming from it. And then a great lament began among the people. The hearth had gone out for ever. And the people? As in the old days, they gave way to weeping and wailing, for they piously believed in the prediction of their ancestors. Then the oldest and most experienced man among them got up and asked the people whether anybody knew the secret of obtaining fire. Their answer to him was silence.

'Then we are going to perish,' said the old man. 'But isn't there a dare-devil among us who would get a small piece of the burning hot sun from the sky?'

The people looked at one another in bewilderment. 'No, such a person can't be found amongst us, he can't be found,' they were whispering.

But suddenly the crowd stirred and made way, and a very handsome youth appeared.

'It is Amra, he is called Amra,' they began saying all around. They knew Amra well. The young man was the embodiment of beauty and courage. 'I will get a little piece of the sun!' said he firmly. 'We have lost the fire once, but we can acquire it yet again. But a little piece of the sun – isn't this too much for a small people?'

'No, no!' the people began shouting. 'Use our hands, Amra, to help you, only get what you promised for us as quickly as you can.'

'All right,' said the young man.

Three days and three nights the people spent making a gigantic bow under Amra's guidance. This bow was hundreds and hundreds of *loktey* in height. And they twisted the string for it from the tendons of a thousand oxen. At last, on the expiry of the third night, the people raised the gigantic bow with an arrow, on the summit of the highest mountain, Ertsakhu. And when the sun was already standing at the zenith, thousands of people stretched the string. Amra carefully aimed. And a miracle happened: the arrow directly hit the centre of the sun. The sun began trembling with the pain, dropping a little tear. Very soon the little tear reached the ground, and a thousand-year-old forest burst into hot flame. The valleys of our land were covered with smoke for three months. There were many fires, and the forests vanished, the prey animals were burned alive, and the rivers became shallow.

'You have got back our fire, but you have deprived us of food,' the people reproached Amra. 'Now we cannot live comfortably. Leave us, young man who has brought us bad luck.'

'All right,' said Amra, 'I will leave. And may the sorrow that has settled in your hearts vanish together with me.'

Amra spoke thus and instantly changed into a sunray which began playing on a baby's face.

Since that time the forests grow plentifully in our land only in the foot-hills. But on the other hand the land at the foot of the mountains is rich and fertile. And here various fruits spring up, and the people dwell happily under the sun, which in Abkhazian is called 'Amra'.

ॐ

This legend belongs to the most ancient layer of Abkhazian folk poetic works. It was published in V. P. Pachulia, *Padenie Anakopia*, Nauka, Moscow, 1986, 78–80.

95. Pkharmat[1] *(Chechen)*

May God bless you, may he prolong good in your life and remove bad from it. I have many stories for you, which one should I tell you? I will relate one tale. Let your ears be as keen as a fallow deer's, and your eyes as sharp as a wolf's.

I shall tell you from what time the eternal snows have been lying on the summit of Bashlam,[2] from what time the wide plains and the slopes of the mountains have been covered with sweet-smelling herbs and multi-coloured flowers.

Long, long ago, in ancient times, the high mountains that you see were even higher.

In past times there was neither snow nor ice on these peaks, as there is now, but beautiful herbs and flowers were growing; whereas the eternal snow and ice were lying in the deep gorges, on the slopes of the mountains and on the wide plains.

In those times our ancestors, the Nart-Orstkhoys, were living in the gorges, in caves and in high towers. They were tall, like those mountains, and their horses were likewise enormous. The Nart-Orstkhoys were strong like bears, brave like wolves, agile like tigers and crafty like foxes. They would easily break off whole crags and throw them at one another. The mountains and the sky would shake at their cries. But nevertheless they were weak because they did not have fire.

Mighty Sela was merciless.[3] He was the sovereign of the sky and was in control of fire. What is the use of power if it is of no use to people? What is the use of power if it brings the people only suffering and misfortune. In order to show his mightiness, Sela used to seat himself on a flaming staff

---

1   Pkharmat was a mythological hero, similar to the Georgian Amirani.
2   Bashlam is the snow-covered peak of Kazbek.
3   The mighty Sela was the deity of rain and hail.

and raise such a terrible crash that it was as if the sky was splitting into pieces and falling down, and lighting up as during a thunderstorm.

The sky in that place where Sela lived was always covered with clouds. Sela used to fill the clouds with rain and tip it down on to the earth. The hail brought the people the most misfortune of all, during the thunderstorms. Often Sela would take in his hands a rainbow, woven of light and fire, and would throw it on to the earth and burn up all around.

Good and evil were in Sela's hands. He used to scatter evil generously, but he spread good only sparingly. The people received good with great difficulty, but Sela distributed evil without stint. Between the sky and the earth there was permanent enmity!

Between Sela and the people there was a continual cruel struggle! The more the adversities and misfortunes increased for the Nart-Orstkhoys, the more Sela was pleased. The more Sela was pleased, the more miserable Sata became. Sata very much wanted to help the Nart-Orstkhoys, but she was afraid of Sela.

Living in the mountains at that time was the mighty Nart Pkharmat. He used to labour in his smithy and serve the people. He was a skilful craftsman.

Pkharmat was modest, generous and hard-working. He used to think much about how to lighten people's lives. He used to think about how to take fire from Sela and give it to the people. It was Sela's will not to give fire to the people.

From his very birth, Pkharmat used to learn from people everything of the very kindest and best, their knowledge and wisdom. His horse Turpal would wander freely over the mountain slopes. The Narts used to tell Pkharmat, 'A horse ought to be tempered in the hands of its owner, but be a young hero in battle. Why does your horse walk free?'

'My horse has been tempered. The time will come when he will bring you fire from the sky.'

One day Pkharmat called up his horse. The gorge of the Argun and the mountains trembled at his call. This call woke up the sleeping Sela and made him turn over. The horse, pasturing in the mountains, heard his master's voice and answered with a neighing. Swift as lightning, the horse came galloping at Pkharmat's call. Pkharmat took a cudgel in his hands, dressed in a chain-mail shirt, fastened on his belt a quiver with arrows, put on his arm a shield of bison skin, hung a bow on his neck, armed himself with a sabre and took in his hand a spear with a copper tip.

Pkharmat saddled his horse Turpal, drained a full *tur*'s horn of beer with the wish: 'Let my legs hold themselves firmly as in tar, and my hands as in dough.' He sat on his horse and headed along that road along which nobody went, and if anybody did go, he did not return.

The Nart-Orstkhoys scattered millet behind Pkharmat so that his journey would be successful, they filled a mortar with barley so that he would be able to ride there easily and freely, and return with what he had gone for!

Pkharmat was riding for a long time. He spent seven days and seven nights journeying. He passed seven gorges and mountains. Finally he rode up to the Bashlam Gorge. Bashlam was resting its summit against the sky in which Sela lived. Bashlam's summit was covered with fragrant herbs and abounded with flowers.

The sun-faced Sata had descended on to that summit for a rest. Sela-Sata, the sweetheart of Sela, was the mother of the Nart-Orstkhoys. She turned into a white bird, met Pkharmat and said in a human voice, 'Ey, mighty Nart! Evidently you have climbed to the summit of Bashlam for a good reason!'

'Surely, good bird, I have climbed to the summit of Bashlam for a good reason. I have come to take, for the people, a hot firebrand kindled from the heavenly hearth. I will not go back without it,' said Pkharmat.

'To the one who goes out with good intentions the road has to be lucky,' said Sela-Sata. Then she asked, 'Is your horse good?'

'My horse is swifter than the wind,' replied Pkharmat.

'And is your horse strong?'

'Where his hoof strikes, a spring gushes forth.'

'And are you strong yourself?'

'In my hands cold bronze becomes softer than pitch and wax.'

Sela-Sata instructed Pkharmat how to get near to Sela's hearth and how to grab a hot firebrand from it. 'Now Sela will be sleeping. Drive away his swift-as-wind horse. Jump over Sela's hearth. When you are above the hearth, bend down and pick up a hot firebrand. Then direct your horse towards Bashlam. If Sela wakes up, he will not leave either you or your horse alive, and you will be unable to take the firebrand to the earth.'

As Sela-Sata had instructed him, so Pkharmat actually did.

At a full gallop Pkharmat's horse jumped over Sela's hearth. Pkharmat bent down, seized a hot firebrand and directed his horse to the summit of Bashlam.

Pkharmat's horse was galloping so fast that the firebrand scattered sparks all around, and behind him stretched a tail of smoke and sparks.

Some sparks, landing in Sela's nose, woke him up. Sela saw that the coura-geous Nart had stolen a flaming brand from his hearth. He grasped the fact that man, after taking control of fire, would become mighty and bold and would be able to rise up against Sela himself.

Man had taken possession of a great force. Sela became frightened and sent a host in pursuit of the Nart. At first Sela opened a *burdyuk*, into which dark night had been driven. It suddenly grew so dark that Pkharmat could no longer see the fingers on his hands, nor the ears of his horse. It was as if Pkharmat and his horse had gone blind. They were just on the point of falling over a precipice when the beautiful bird Sela-Sata flew in front and showed them the road with her marvellous voice.

It was beyond the powers of the dark night to stop the Nart and his horse. Sela opened his *burdyuk* filled with the hurricane and sent the hurricane in pursuit of Pkharmat. The dark night and the hurricane exhausted Pkharmat and his horse. And then the beautiful bird Sela-Sata sheltered them from the wind with her wings and showed them the road with her singing.

Pkharmat saw that the hurricane was extinguishing the flaming brand in his hands. And without fire he could not return to earth. Then he hid the firebrand in his bosom. The terrible hurricane was whirling around the brave Nart in a deadly dance, the unlit night was blinding him, and the hidden firebrand was burning his chest. The earth began trembling, the waters of the Argun came out of their craggy channel, and mighty oaks, torn out by the roots, were flying in the air like grass stalks.

Sela realised that neither the dark night nor the wild hurricane had the power to stop the Nart and his horse. The Nart was escaping unharmed from the heavenly chase. Then Sela opened a third *burdyuk*, filled with cruel frost. The cruel frost split the crags and gripped the mountains, but Pkharmat on his horse kept on galloping forward.

Sela was not frightened for nothing. He saw how the mighty Nart was getting near the foot of Bashlam. Now he was already approaching a safe place. Sela grew angry, seized his fiery rainbow and began flinging lightning at the Nart.

The mountains began trembling at the lightning strikes. Springs began gushing forth from the frozen earth. The waves of the Argun, like a fright-ened flock of sheep, surged on to the slopes of the mountains. Enormous crags rocked as if they were alive.

Neither the cruel frost nor the mighty hurricane nor the dark night nor the lightning were able to stop the Nart Pkharmat. He rode up to the cave where the Narts were waiting for him. 'Here is fire for you!' he said to the amazed Narts. 'In every tower, in every cave, in every fortress, kindle a fire! Let a great flame arise! There has to be fire in every home! Let there be warmth! Let there be light! May the fire never go out! Good fortune to us Narts!'

At this time a terrible crash sounded. Sela was raging ... Heaven was declaring eternal war against the earth! Man was declaring eternal struggle with Sela! The angry Sela was threatening the people!

And then Pkharmat told the people, 'Be happy, I have to go to Sela for punishment instead of you. Be happy! Do not grieve for me!'

The brave Nart Pkharmat rode off to Bashlam to meet the lightning, the frost, the hurricane and the black night. Over his head the lightning flashed, the hurricane buffeted him in various directions, the frost froze his hands and feet. There was no lull in Sela's raging.

When Sela, on the cloudy summit of Bashlam, saw the Nart coming to him, he gradually began driving back the hurricane, the frost and the night into his *burdyuks*. From the plains and the gorges and from the slopes of the mountains, the cold, the eternal snow and the ice slowly ascended Bashlam following Pkharmat. The summit of Bashlam found itself imprisoned by the snows and the ice. It muffled itself in a *bashlyk* for all time.

Sela shouted, 'May you spend all eternity wishing for the fire and warmth that you stole from heaven!'

Sela sent his faithful servant, the one-eyed Uzhu, with iron chains to Pkharmat. With these chains Uzhu chained Pkharmat to the summit of Bashlam.

The cold, the snow and the frost, which Sela had summoned to torment Pkharmat, began freezing and gripping the summit of Bashlam for all time.

The fire brought by Pkharmat warmed all the earth; the plains, the mountain slopes and the deep gorges became thickly covered with fragrant herbs and multi-coloured flowers.

Each morning the king of birds, Ida, comes flying in, sits on Pkharmat's knees and repeats one and the same thing: 'Oy, unfortunate Pkharmat! Oy, sinful Pkharmat! Don't you regret your action? If you regret it, I shall not touch you, but if not, I shall eat up your liver!'

In spite of the terrible torments awaiting him, Pkharmat answers one and the same thing: 'No, I don't regret it! I gave the people happiness, I gave the people warmth and light! You cannot regret the good you have done!'

Then the king of birds, Ida, after sharpening his steely beak against a flint, begins pecking at Pkharmat's liver.

Pkharmat does not emit a single groan, and tears never show in his eyes. He endures the terrible torments and sufferings steadfastly and bravely.

From those times our Nart-Orstkhoy men never cry. Since those times the snow and eternal ice lie on the summits of the mountains, and the hurricane rages. After Sela chained Pkharmat to the summit of Bashlam he gathered there the ice, the snow and the hurricane, so that they would not cease tormenting Pkharmat, so that Pkharmat would not stop yearning for the warmth and light.

Since those times on the vast plains, in the deep gorges, and on the slopes of the mountains, the sweet-smelling herbs grow and the beautiful flowers abound. Since those times there is warmth, abundance and light on the earth. It was Pkharmat who gave warmth to the people! Pkharmat is chained to the summit of Bashlam. He endures eternal torments, but he is immortal! The hero does not die! The hero lives forever!

ॐ

This Chechen legend was published in N. Gelashvili, *Chechensky fol'klor*, Kavkazsky Dom, Tbilisi, 1996, 128–133.

96. How Sosuruk Obtained Fire for the Narts *(Balkar)*

In ancient times the Narts used to kindle a fire thus: they would tear out a huge dry tree by the roots and would set it on fire by presenting it to the sun, or they would start a fire by knocking down a star from the sky with an arrow.

Now in those times, in one of the severe winters, all the men of the Nart land set off on a campaign.

When the *emegens* found out that in the land of the Narts only the helpless old men, women and children were left, they attacked the Nart *auls*. After eating up many people and animals, they destroyed the Narts' dwellings and left, after extinguishing the fires in their hearths.

When the Nart *batyrs* returned from their campaign, they saw that in the Nart land there was no fire, and the Narts left alive were dying of cold.

The *emegens* knew that the Narts had no fire left. And so that the Narts should not kindle a fire from the sun or a star, they raised such a snowstorm with their *zhel kyoryuk*[1] that it seemed that it would wipe the land of the Narts from the face of the earth.

So then the Narts gathered for a council. 'We have no other way out than to steal fire from the *emegens*,' said Satanay-Biyche, 'and apart from young Sosuruk, nobody can do that.'

Then the Nart Sosuruk set off on his way. When he had galloped as far as the Kuf Mountains, where the *emegens* lived, he saw smoke belching from a cave where one of them was living.

Sosuruk fearlessly rode into this *emegen*'s cave. He rode in and saw the *emegen*, who was sleeping, coiled in a circle around a large fire. Sosuruk decided to steal the fire without waking the *emegen*. But when Sosuruk grabbed a burning brand out of the fire and was just about to jump outside, a little coal fell from the brand and landed in the *emegen*'s only eye. The *emegen* woke up and seized Sosuruk and his horse.

'Who are you, and what are you doing here?' he asked.

'I am from the land of the Narts, and I have come for fire,' replied Sosuruk.

'And do you know the Nart Sosuruk?' asked the *emegen*.

'I know him,' answered Sosuruk.

'And do you know his games?' asked the *emegen*.

'Certainly I know them,' answered Sosuruk.

'Well then, teach me his games.'

Then Sosuruk made up his mind to kill the *emegen* and so obtain the fire for the Narts. Sosuruk said to the *emegen*, 'Give me a big crow-bar. Then stand beneath the crag and beat off with your head the stones that I will rain down on you from the crag. This is actually one of Sosuruk's games.'

Sosuruk took the iron crow-bar, climbed up the crag and began raining huge stones down from there. As for the *emegen* standing below, he was beating off these stones with his head, and with such force that they were flying over the crag. This even frightened Sosuruk.

When Sosuruk realised that he would not overpower the *emegen* like that, he thought up another game and said, 'The second game is the freezing of the lake.'

---

1   *Zhel kyoryuk* means literally 'wind-bellows' – one of the magic things of the Nart epos; with its help the *emegens* send hurricane winds down on the land of the Narts.

The *emegen* got into the lake. At Sosuruk's supplication, Teyri froze the lake so hard that the *emegen* was unable to break its ice. When Sosuruk was aware that the *emegen* could not get out of there, he asked, 'Now what, should I cut off your head? The Nart Sosuruk, it is I.'

The *emegen* answered, 'As it happens, when you took my crow-bar and climbed to the top of the crag to rain stones down on me, I watched you going and suspected that you were Sosuruk. It is because I have heard that your legs are crooked below the knees. Your sword will not take my speaking head.[1] Go into my cave, take my sword, bring it and cut it off with that.'

Sosuruk went into the *emegen's* cave and saw the sword. But perhaps some kind of *emegen's* craftiness is contained in this sword, thought Sosuruk, and he did not set about taking the sword in his hands, but touched it with a stick. At that very second the sword tinkled loudly, jumped away and, after cutting through the iron support post, fell on the floor. Then Sosuruk took the sword in his hands and went and cut off the *emegen's* head.

Before Sosuruk cut off his head, the *emegen* said, 'Well, now of course you will kill me. However, after you have taken off my head, pull out my spinal cord: it will be useful to you everywhere and in all your affairs.'

Sosuruk pulled out the *emegen's* spinal cord, but thought, why did he advise me to do that? Perhaps it is the next one of his crafty tricks? He hung it on the branch of an enormous tree. This spinal cord wound itself around the tree and, like the sword, cut through it. It was obvious that the *emegen*, knowing about this, wanted to kill Sosuruk.

After taking possession of the *emegen's* cave, Sosuruk took the fire, brought it to the land of the Narts and saved the freezing Narts from death.

After several days he and four Narts rode to the *emegen's* cave, took all his wealth and brought it to the Narts.

The Narts arranged a big *toy* at which they presented Sosuruk with the hero's cup – the *aguna*[2] – and in his honour they began singing this song:

Oyra, oyra, the son of Narts, Sosuruk!
Oyra, oyra, the Nart hero, Sosuruk!

---

1   For a multi-headed *emegen*, the other non-speaking heads are easily cut off, but the single speaking head can only be removed by the *emegen's* own sword.

2   Whereas in the Balkaro-Karachay epos in the cycle of Rachikau, and in other national versions in the cycle of Batraz, the hero receives the magic cup (*keg*) of the Narts only after relating his exploits, in this case the Narts themselves present the cup of the Narts to the hero.

He tricked the *emegen* and took away his fire, Sosuruk,
He delivered the Nart *auls* from their troubles, Sosuruk.

Oyra, oyra, the son of Narts, Sosuruk!
Oyra, oyra, the Nart hero, Sosuruk!

He did not leave the land of the Narts without fire, Sosuruk!
Among the Narts he is the most brave, Sosuruk.

Oyra, oyra, the son of Narts, Sosuruk!
Oyra, oyra, the Nart hero, Sosuruk!

He brought fire and warmed the Nart *auls*, Sosuruk,
He saved the Nart *auls* from many calamities, Sosuruk.

Oyra, oyra, the son of Narts, Sosuruk!
Oyra, oyra, the Nart hero, Sosuruk!

ف

This Balkar legend was recorded by S. O. Shakhmurzayev in 1965 from
the words of Amiy Bashiev, born 1873, from the village of Kichmalka. It
was published in T. M. Khajieva & R. A-K. Ortabayeva, *Narty*, Nauka,
Moscow, 1994, 367–369.

97. Abrskil *(Abkhaz)*

Wonderful was the childhood of Abrskil. He grew not by the days but by the hours. By the age of ten he was already fully grown. Equally quickly his intelligence matured, his strength increased and his skills developed.

At that time Apsny[1] – the Land of my Heart – was often attacked and ravaged by foreigners. Abrskil gathered his brave fellow countrymen and in heated battles he overcame their enemies. The raids ceased, and it became

---

1   The land of Apsny is Abkhazia.

peaceful in Apsny. The mere name of Abrskil inspired fear in their foes; their enemies were afraid to display their arms, their swords and *kinzhals* rusted in their sheaths. And the people loved their friend and protector Abrskil. The reports of him were carried from land to land, from region to region.

When the bandits and robbers had disappeared, Abrskil set about exterminating the ferns, which suck out from the earth its life-giving juices. He cut down the thorny creepers, he hacked down lianas hanging across the roads. The fields began to give unheard-of harvests; lush grasses grew green on the meadows, the udders of cows and goats were full of milk.

Abrskil was merciless towards oppressors and wicked people, but he did not want to make peace even with God. He would dash high into the sky on his warhorse, his *arash*. He would cut the clouds with his sword and hew lightning from them. On the ground, if his way was blocked by an obstinate liana that had crossed over from tree to tree, he would cleave through it, so that he would not need to stoop and so that people would not start thinking, now Abrskil is bowing his head before God.

But Abrskil had a rival in strength – a wicked *adau*. He lived on a high inaccessible mountain, and from there he would stretch out his long arms towards the sea and would swamp the boats on a whim. Having grown hungry, he would seize a fish from the deep, hold it up towards the sun, bake it and eat it with the bones and the entrails.

One day, Abrskil entered the domains of the *adau*. He went close to the giant and hailed him, 'Eh, what are you doing here?'

'Don't you see? I am eating fish.'

'And are you capable of anything more than that?'

'See how I will jump into the sea now, and I will splash out so much water that it will drown all the coastal inhabitants, and also you with them. Watch out!' shouted the *adau* and he prepared to jump.

But Abrskil forestalled the scoundrel. He shot an arrow at him, it pierced him in the leg, and the *adau* crashed down on to the ground. And the blood flowed in such a brown torrent that it almost carried Abrskil away into the sea. The *adau* pulled at his wounded leg, and with his ankle-bone he knocked down an ancient grove of oak trees.

Now, finally, God could no longer endure Abrskil's ways, he called his servants and said, 'Go and seize this arrogant man, throw him into the abyss and let him suffer there until he sees reason.'

But Abrskil chose for himself as refuges the peak of Mount Ertsakhu and the seashore. Hardly had God's servants reached the peak of Ertsakhu when

Abrskil leapt up on to his faithful *arash*, who instantly carried him away to the seashore. There Abrskil lay down on his *burka* in the shade of a rock and rested. Then when God's servants descended to the shore, he once more sat on his *arash* and dashed up to the summit of Ertsakhu.

Thus Abrskil saved himself from his enemies. God's servants could do nothing with him. At last, they set off to a certain old sorceress, who had given her word to Abrskil that she would give up her vile trade, and he had spared her. But she, in the depths of her heart, hated him. 'Come to our aid!' begged God's envoys. 'Without your help we cannot cope.'

'Slaughter a herd of oxen and cows,' said the old woman. 'Remove their skins and spread them with their hairy side downwards on the summit of Ertsakhu and sprinkle them with millet. When the *arash* steps on to the animal skins, he will slip and fall. When that happens, just seize Abrskil.'

Having done everything as the sorceress had ordered, a party of God's servants set off towards the seashore where Abrskil was resting, and the remainder began lying in wait for him at the summit. As always, the keen *arash*, by neighing, warned his master of the danger. Abrskil jumped on him and in an instant found himself at the grey-headed peak of Ertsakhu. But the *arash* slipped on the skins; Abrskil did not manage to jump off him, and they both crashed down into a deep gorge. There the messengers of God seized and bound the hero.

God ordered his servants to imprison Abrskil in chains in the most inaccessible cave. The old sorceress pointed out to them the Chlousky Cave. In it were imprisoned both Abrskil, bound in chains, and his horse. The chains were fastened to an iron post, hammered deep into the ground. God charged the sorceress with watching the cave, so that nobody would penetrate it. Abrskil was supposed to die of hunger.

But the old woman, having quenched her thirst for revenge, all the same pitied Abrskil; she gave him milk and boiled pumpkin; and she gave his *arash* ground steel.

God found out about this and he became furious. He turned the sorceress into a dog and laid on her the curse – to keep eternal watch over Abrskil and his *arash*. Then the dog began licking the chain with which Abrskil was fettered. Soon the chain became thin; it became like a silken thread. But hardly had the dog squatted down to rest than the chain became as it was before. Once more the dog would set to licking, the chain would become thin, and once more the chain would recover itself as soon as the dog became tired. So it was repeated, without end.

And nor did Abrskil sleep; with ever-increasing fury he would shake loose the iron post. Now the post was already loosening: one more little push, and now it seems that Abrskil would bring it down and get free. But suddenly some little black bird alights on the top of the post, and the prisoner notices that the post has stopped giving way to his efforts. Abrskil chases the bird from it. He tries again to shake the post loose, but once again it sits on the top of the post ... In annoyance the hero strikes with a hammer in the place where the little bird was sitting, but he only knocks the post all the more deeply into the ground.

Once again the hero toils – day after day, night after night, but his efforts are in vain: hardly is the post shaken loose when in flies the mysterious little bird ...

One day some brave people with flaming torches penetrated into the depths of the cave; they loudly called to Abrskil, they wanted to free him. For a long time they walked up to their waists in water, exhausted with the cold. It was not easy for them to walk in the low cave with its uneven vault. At that time Abrskil, having clenched his teeth, shook the post loose. Now he heard the human voices, the chained *arash* also began to neigh joyfully. In the darkness there shone a ray of light.

Out of the darkness of the cave sounded the voice of Abrskil: 'You will not be able to reach me, good people; the closer you get to me, the more the evil powers are moving me away from you. Go back again! Only tell me: do ferns and weeds still grow on the earth? Are there still thorn bushes and thorn trees? Are wicked people oppressing the weak?'

'Yes, they are growing,' sorrowfully answered Abrskil's followers, who had penetrated into the cave. 'Yes, there are thorns ... Yes, there are oppressors!'

Abrskil tore at the post with renewed force and the chains began to ring. The hero uttered a groan: 'Ech, there is still not happiness in my native land. There is still not peace for man on earth!' With that the cave fell silent and for centuries no voice spoke there.

Now and then, people tell different versions of the capture of Abrskil. They say that he was always rescued by his mountain staff, an *alabasha*, with a sharp iron tip. At a moment of danger, Abrskil thrust his *alabasha* into the ground and, leaning on it, made such a leap that he vanished from the sight of his enemies.

But God's servants turned to the black woodpecker to damage Abrskil's *alabasha*, and in exchange they promised him a little red cap. The woodpecker searched out Abrskil, and while he was sleeping, he began to peck his *alabasha*. He pecked it halfway through, and then informed God's servants about it. They rushed towards Abrskil. The hero woke up in time. He saw his enemies, jumped up and, leaning on his *alabasha*, was about to leap across the gorge. But the *alabasha* broke under him and he fell. There and then his enemies came and seized him ...

In this manner or otherwise, Abrskil remained a prisoner in the cave. But his memory is alive amongst the people. His exploits remain an example for brave and noble people; they inspire them in their struggle with their enemies and with the ungovernable forces of nature.

ॐ

This Abkhaz legend was published in Kh. S. Bgazhba, *Abkhazskie skazki*, Alashara, Sukhumi, 1985, 38–43.

98. Amiran *(Georgian)*

In a certain dark dense forest, where the tops of the trees rested against the very sky, stood a high steep cliff. Not far from that forest lived a certain hunter, Darjelan. He often went hunting in the forest.

One day the hunter approached that cliff and it sounded to him as if somewhere a woman was calling. The hunter had a look at the cliff. He kept on looking higher and higher, but yet he could not see the top; it was lost somewhere high, high in the distance. The hunter wanted to climb up to the top of the cliff, but he could not manage it; it was so steep and impregnable. The hunter returned home.

Meanwhile, at home he had a wife who was very nasty and also lame. The hunter told his wife to prepare food for him for the road the next day. He himself went to the blacksmith and ordered from him a large number of sharp pegs and an iron hammer.

Towards morning everything was ready for him. He took food for the day, he picked up the iron pegs and hammer at the blacksmith's and set off towards the cliff. He started to drive the pegs into the cliff. The hunter was driving the pegs into the cliff with the iron hammer and climbing up them like steps. His pegs were finished, the iron hammer was worn out, but the hunter had reached the very top. He looked around and saw that an entrance had been cut out of the cliff, just like a door. He went through and made his way into a cave. In the cave Dali was lying.

There lay Dali: a woman with an unearthly beauty. Around her head were wound heavy golden plaits. Dali saw Darjelan the hunter and they loved one another at first sight. The hunter remained with Dali. Dali did not want to let him stay, but love conquered her and she gave in.

In the morning Dali began begging the hunter to return home, but he would not agree and again he stayed with her. Now Dali still more strongly urged him to return home. 'Go,' said Dali, 'your wife has second sight. She is accustomed to your returning home every evening and she will not wait for you. She will pay a visit to us; she will follow your trail; she will find us and destroy us.'

'No,' said Darjelan, 'my wife is lame, and she hardly walks around home. How could she get here?'

And Darjelan's wife was truly very surprised that her husband did not return home. She waited for two days, but on the third day she got up, took food for the road and followed her husband's trail. The trail led her to the cliff. She scrambled up the little steps to the top of the cliff and went in to the cave. She saw Dali and her own husband, sleeping soundly. The hunter's wife searched out Dali's golden scissors and used them to cut off her golden plaits. She took both the scissors and the plaits and went away with them.

Dali and Darjelan awoke. She slightly raised her head, but somehow it seemed light to her. She passed her hand over her hair and her golden plaits were not there. She got up and looked for the scissors: no scissors. Dali grew miserable, turned to the hunter and said, 'You are the cause of my misfortune. I told you that your wife would destroy us. I cannot live any more on this earth. Take your knife, cut open my womb, for I am pregnant, and get my baby. If it is a daughter, then name her as you wish, but if it is a son, then call him Amiran. My son will be a hero. If he had been allowed to live the whole term in his mother's womb, he would even have overcome God; but now he will be weaker. Listen, and fulfil everything that I tell you. When you get the son out of my womb, keep him for three months in calf's entrails, so that he matures and keeps warm, since he is not able to mature in his mother's womb. Then lay him in a cradle, carry him in the cradle to the river of Iaman and leave him on the bank. There, the one who ought to do so will find him and christen him. He will tell our son all that he needs to do.'

The hunter did not want to cut into his beloved. He was sad and distraught. But Dali would have her own way, and he was obliged to do all that she had told him. With trembling hands he cut open Dali's belly and removed the baby, beautiful, like the sun. The hunter fulfilled everything according to Dali's orders, and then he carried away the baby in the cradle to the river of Iaman; he left the cradle on the bank and returned home.

Some travellers were passing along the bank of the river of Iaman, and they saw a baby lying in a cradle. They asked, 'Who are your father and mother, or who ought to christen you?'

'I do not know who my father and mother are, but an angel himself should christen me,' answered the baby.

Now an angel came, and he also asked the baby. The baby answered him the same way as he did all the others. Three times the angel asked, and three times the baby answered him. The angel declared himself to him, christened him and named him Amiran. He gave him a *khanjali* and ordered him to hide it in his *paichi* and not to get it out except when in great difficulties. He blessed Amiran, told him that nobody on earth would overcome him, and left him.

*

The precocious child grew fast. He and his foster brothers had many adventures, they fought with *devs* and monsters, and Amiran obtained a wife after killing her father, who lived in the sky. During his life he violated three oaths that he had made 'in the name of Christ'.

*

After this Amiran went alone on heroic exploits. There was nobody in the world who could withstand combat with him; Amiran overcame all his enemies and exterminated them. There remained in the whole world only three *devs*, three wild boars and three oak trees. Amiran even fought with God, three times he betrayed his oath to Christ and he committed many other bad things. For that God punished Amiran: he fastened him with an iron chain and chained him to an iron post buried deep in the earth. Together with Amiran God chained up the dog Kursha, who had killed off many of God's beloved ibex.

Throughout the whole year Amiran and Kursha tug at the chain and drag the heavy iron post upwards. They just about drag the post out of the ground and free themselves when God sends a bird, and it sits on the post. Amiran gets angry; he swings the chain at it and hits the post. The bird flies away, but once again the post is driven back into the earth. The same thing happens every year.

Kursha is the puppy of an eagle. Every spring the hen-eagle Orbi gives birth to one puppy, together with its own chicks. When she sees the puppy, the hen-eagle takes it, carries it up high and throws it to the ground, so that people will not find it and tame it. All the same a certain hunter found and raised this Kursha, who was chained together with Amiran. Along Kursha's sides grow eagle's wings. And he is so swift and clever that with two jumps he catches an antelope. Indeed he considers three jumps shameful for him.

As a punishment for killing many of the ibex, God chained him with Amiran. About Kursha, the Svans composed a hunter's lament for the lost Kursha:

Kursha, my Kursha,
My lost Kursha, Kursha!
I have lost you
At midnight, exactly at midnight!
Woe to me. What if a merchant
Takes you, a merchant takes you?
Woe to me! What if a Kaji
Steals you from me?
Kursha's mouth and ears
Are like gold, like gold.
Kursha's eyes, his eyes
Are like the moon, like the moon.
Kursha's bark is like the thunder of heaven,
Kursha's paws are like a threshing floor,
Kursha's leap is as long as a field.
Kursha's food, his food –
Is soft bread, and fresh.
Woe to me! What if they feed you
With chaff, with chaff!
Kursha's drink, his drink –
Is fresh wine, and sweet.
Woe to me! What if they give you

Muddy water to drink!
Kursha's bed, his bed –
Is a featherbed and a blanket.
Woe to me! What if they put you
On wood chips, on wood chips!
Kursha, my Kursha,
From above you are like a lion,
From below – like a pheasant,
On dry land you are a hero,
On the sea – a boat!
Kursha, my Kursha,
I cry for you, I cry,
I am grieving, I am grieving
A whole year, a whole year!

This is an abbreviated version of one of the most ancient variants of the Georgian legend of Amirani, and was recorded by B. Nizharadze in the nineteenth century in Upper Svaneti, and published in M. Ya. Chikovani, *Gruzinskie narodnye skazki*, Merani, Tbilisi, 1971, 133–139.

99. Bound Nasran *(Adyge)*

O Nart Nasran!
Bearded Nasran!
Your acts have caused great harm.
You have ignored God's words.
You have thwarted his deeds.
O you, accursed by God!
O the one who was brought up on to the mountain,
The eagle flies above you.
Your dog lies by your side.
Roaring and thundering he dashes against his chains.
He is bending the pillar to which he is bound.
A bird flies over you.

She alights on the pillar.
Your heart fills with malice.
You yell, making a great noise.
You aim at the bird with a stone
And try to throw it at her,
But your chains wind more tightly,
And your pillar sinks deeper into the earth.
The dog, lying near you,
Gnaws at your chains,
Making them thinner.
They become as thin as gossamer.
They will soon be gnawed away!
All the early-rising blacksmiths
Down in the smithies are good men.
They strike upon their anvils,
And all your chains are restored,
Exactly as they were before,
Until we unshackle you.
May God keep you bound!
May God kill you at the pillar!

This Adyge legend was translated and published by John Colarusso, 'Nart sagas from the Caucasus', Princeton University Press, Princeton, 2002, 168–169; from the book by A. M. Gadagatl', 'Geroichesky epos Narty i evo genesis', Krasnodar Knizhnoye Isdatel'stvo, Krasnodar, 1967, 258–261.

100. How Sharvili Found Fire *(Lezg)*

One day, when the people were working in the field, a spark fell from the sky into a haystack and set it alight. The people were afraid of fire and they scattered, because they had never seen fire before.

A *dev* saw the fire and approached it. For a little while he stood at the fire, feeling how warmth and light was radiating from it. Then he took the fire and went off to his home.

The people clutched their heads. Only now did they realise that this spark had been sent to them by God. They started thinking: what could they do now to get the fire back from the *dev*.

They all gathered together, set off to Akhti to the *bogatyr* Sharvili and told him of their trouble. 'I will bring you the fire,' said the hero. He collected the strongest men and came with them to the house of the *devs*. Not a single *dev* was left in their house, they were all annihilated! Rivers of blood flowed across the meadows, and all of the *devs* perished. After that Sharvili took the fire and gave it out to the people.

They say that since that time the Lezgs have worshipped fire. From that day the fires in their hearths never go out.

This Lezg legend was published in L. Chlaidze, *Lezginsky fol'klor*, Kavkazsky Dom, Tbilisi, 2006, 112.

Appendix

LEGENDS ABOUT THE NART BOGATYRS AMONG THE MOUNTAIN
TATARS OF THE PYATIGORSK REGION OF THE TEREK PROVINCE

S. A. Urusbiev

In the mountains of the Pyatigorsk Region of the Terek Province there lives a tribe of Tatar or Mongol origin, populating several *auls*; they speak the Tatar language. On the plains of this region live Kabardan people, whose language has no similarity with the language of the aforesaid Tatar tribe.

Having spent a long time in the surroundings of the latter and belonging to it myself by my origin, I made up my mind to record the oral traditions preserved among these people from deep antiquity. Among such traditions the prime place belongs to the legends about the Nart *bogatyrs*; this is the *bogatyr* epos of the mountain Tatars, preserved in their songs, sung by them to the present time. Similar legends are preserved among all of the mountain tribes living in the Caucasus, constituting their common heritage from times of deepest antiquity. Of course, when passing from the mouths of one generation to the next, they undergo some alterations in details, but in none of the tribes are there preserved traditions dating back to more distant times than these.

To the present day, both the very name of 'Narts', and also the meaning of these deeply poetic legends about them, remain unexplained. Nonetheless some sayings that are used at the present time by the mountain Tatars and the Kabardans, although few, mark the image of the Nart with vivid traits. 'He is brave, cunning, strong – he is successful, like a Nart,' they say about some noble *uzden*. 'He is well-proportioned and stately, like a Nart,' the mountain people say about a man who is distinguished among the others by a majestic and attractive appearance, and who is renowned for his feats of nobility, fearlessness and strength. Thus, the name Nart in the mouths of the folk has become a noun and is used as a synonym for 'a daring, good, kind, successful young man'. Likewise also, the legends recorded by me: they say that the Narts were a people of enormous size and unbounded strength, a people tempered in the endurance of hardships and deprivations. They spent their life chiefly in the search for dangers and adventures, in raids for the purpose of booty, and also in special wanderings, named *jortuuls*. When setting out on exploits, they used to say, 'Ach, if only we should happen to get hungry and meet with difficulties and dangers!' Everything that came to them without special difficulty, and was not connected with dangers, was offensive to them; they used to search for such adventures in which they would be able to demonstrate their daring and strength to their full extent.

Alongside the Nart traditions they refer to the *emegen*-giants, who were distinguished, like them too, by enormous physical strength and gigantic size, but at the same time by stupidity, and among them there was absolutely no quick-wittedness and cunning. According to some legends, they had many heads and one eye in their forehead. Between the Narts and the *emegens* a perpetual struggle was carried on, in which thanks to their mental superiority the Narts were always left as the victors, in spite of the *emegens* possessing a far greater size and physical strength. The Narts continually nurtured their hatred for the *emegens* because they used to eat human flesh, and because when one of the Narts landed up with them, the *emegens* would try not to let him get away alive from their hands.

In their spare time from *jortuuls* (correctly *jortuuuls*), the Narts would arrange fun gatherings, at which they would indulge in *bogatyr* games and dances. Their gatherings always took place in the home of the Aligovs, where a large cauldron containing the meat of forty bulls permanently hung above the fire.

The location of the activities of the Narts was chiefly the Kuban Province and in general all of the North Caucasus as far as the River Volga, which is very often mentioned in these legends under the name of Edil', and across which the Narts sometimes took themselves for the purpose of raids on their enemies and the rustling of their herds of horses. In the Kuban Province there are very many mementoes bearing witness to the existence of the Narts. Eye-witnesses have told me that where the River Teberda falls into the Kuban, near to the Khumarin Fortress, there is a big castle on a certain high crag which even today carries the name of 'Chuan'. According to tradition, the Nart, Evil-Tongued Gilyakhsyrtan, once lived in it. On the left bank of the Teberda there is also another castle, 'Synty', exceeding Chuan in beauty.

Near to Chuan there lies a large stone, named as the stone of the Nart Sosruko. According to one legend, Sosruko rode up on to this stone on his horse, which left the traces of its hoofs on the stone. At the same place there can be seen the tracks of a dog, which also climbed up on the stone, and even the urine of Sosruko's horse. All of this confirms that the main area of residence of the Narts was in the Kuban Province, in the North Caucasus, from where during their military wanderings they would get even to the Edil'.

Here are the names of those Narts about whom the mountain people have composed songs: Uryzmek, Sosruko, Shauay, Shirdan, Khmych, Batrez, Rachikau, Sibilchi, Evil-Tongued Gilyakhsyrtan, Deuet and Alaugan. To each of these Narts there is devoted a special song; the tunes of the songs are quite unchanging. But with the course of time these songs are gradually going into decline, and at the present time there are very few singers singing them with skill; one might say that there are almost none at all. They used to sing chiefly as wandering poet-singers, celebrated in their time in Kabarda and called *geguakos* (see Glossary).

These *geguakos* were men who had no property, and were not definitely employed by any household; they did not carry arms, and used to travel about Kabarda exclusively for the purpose of being present at folk gatherings, battles, various entertainments and dances, funerals and other proceedings, in general always looking for some kind of folk assembly. It was here that they actually sang their songs about times long past, or else they would sing of some important contemporary events and would glorify contemporary heroes. Thus the *geguakos* were minstrels of their native tribe, and in their time their repertoire substituted for written literature. As wandering singers, they themselves carried their works throughout Kabarda. Thus, the folk would gather at a *pon* (a folk assembly) for the decision of some social questions on an open elevated place behind an *aul*; here the young men would show their skill in trick riding, wrestling and various games, while the older men would occupy themselves in debates about communal affairs: without fail the *geguakos* would turn up here too. They would discerningly follow all that was going on here, and if they spotted among the young men any who were outstanding with their daring and adroitness in trick riding, then they tried to provide an incentive with their praise, carrying the news of them around all of the *auls*, near and far, and glorifying their prowess with their songs. If anybody attracted general attention to themselves with their wise counsels and speeches in the folk assembly, the *geguako* would immediately compose a song, which he actually sang there and then in the presence of those gathered. But woe betide those who besmirched themselves with bad behaviour or displayed harmful intentions: the incorruptible song of the *geguako*, like a conscience, drew on to them disgrace and general condemnation.

If a man died, and he was respected for his wisdom and bravery, the people would collect at his grave, invite several *geguakos* and ask them to compose a song about the deceased, for the memory of his successors, and so that the future generations would also praise his name and valorous life.

In such cases one of the *geguakos* would undertake to sing of one aspect of the activities of the deceased, another would take another aspect, and so on. After this the *geguakos* would withdraw from the world for some time into secluded and solitary places and, leading a most quiet life there, they would compose their songs. After some time they would announce their work was finished, and then the folk would throng from all directions to an appointed place, where the *geguakos* would also appear. Usually, in that place where *geguakos* were passing through, some movement would be noticed: one would straighten his *papakha*, another his *kinzhal*, a third his *gazyre* – in a word, each one was showing their fear in case the *geguako* would notice some shortcoming in him and would ridicule him in a harsh joke. One of the *geguakos* would mount an elevated place in the middle of the crowd and would at first sing for a while only the vocal motif of the song, at the same time striking the *khars*; everybody would wait impatiently for the moment when he would start to sing the song itself. After catching the rhythm of the *khars*, the first *geguako* would sing through his composition, after him another would sing, and so on to the last one.

The crowd would pay close attention, holding its collective breath; only in the pauses could one catch the whisper: 'Where do they get such marvellous words?' At the conclusion of the singing there would resound an outburst of enthusiastic cheers and the feast would begin; treating the folk to food and drink and rewarding the singer-poets. The relatives of the deceased would confer on them clothes, a horse, arms, and so on. The *geguakos* lived exclusively on such charity.

They would also accompany warriors on campaigns and sing of their feats on the field of battle, with their songs serving as dispensers of rewards to the brave heroes and chastisers of cowards. During battles they would settle down in some concealed place from which it was convenient to observe not only the general progress of the business, but also the actions of separate warriors, and they would observe attentively: the one who goes before everybody else, who fights most bravely, how that or another defeated warrior dies; and their songs soon notified all those who stayed at home about the outcome of the battle and the prowess of the brave warriors.

It is clear from what has been said that the *geguakos* in their time had an enormous importance among their people and brought great benefit. In their free songs, like ancient prophets, they would praise virtue and chastise vice, and they would pour light on the deepest questions of the life of the folk. Understanding, or better sensing, the benefit brought by the *geguakos*, the folk respected and loved them and guaranteed them inviolability and full freedom; they were able to speak boldly in public about everybody and about everything, to commit to national censure and ridicule all that they deemed worthy of it. Whether the speech turned to an exalted prince or a lowly pauper, the *geguako* would speak the truth with strict impartiality. Evidence of what love and respect the *geguako* enjoyed among the folk is shown by the fact that the parents, even of important princes, on noticing in their children special spiritual talents, would send them for education to the *geguakos*, with whom the young people would spend several years.

Not one festivity, not one folk gathering would pass without a *geguako*, and with them each person would try to hold himself decorously, as if fearing to land in his bad books; they all would get into the habit of imparting great importance to their voices.

But with the general spread of the Muslim religion, the *geguakos* fell into disgrace with the mullas. The imams began persecuting them, finding their business sinful and contrary to the new religion. I will cite here one conversation, which characterises the relationship between the *geguakos* and the mullas:

Addressing the *geguako*, the mulla says, 'You are a man who is outside of religion; you are harmful to the community; men such as you should be hunted and killed.'

'No, it is not me who should be persecuted, but it is really you. It is you who is outside of all religion, outside of everything honourable and good. Your business is only to plunder and rob the people. You wait eagerly for the moment when we lose any man, especially anybody important and rich, in order to take possession, after his death, of any of his valuable things. You are the most harmful man, you are a plunderer and a deceiver. However, I live by honest work and bring what benefit I can to the people. With one word of mine I make a brave man out of a coward, a defender of his people's freedom; I turn a thief into an honest man. A scoundrel does not dare to show himself before my eyes; I am an opponent of everything dishonourable and bad.'

'Tell me, what do you consider is the basis of religion?' asks the mulla.

'I? In my opinion, millet grain has to serve as the basis of religion ...'

The idea behind the *geguako*'s last words will be understood if we take into consideration that millet, in that neighbourhood, was one of the most widespread plants for making bread flour, and until now it is used in food in the form of *kasha*, and in the old days it predominated, since at that time they did not sow any bread-flour plants other than millet and *nartukh* (food of the Narts). Because of the persecution from representatives of the Muslim religion, as well as for many other reasons, the *geguako*s gradually began to leave the stage, and in the end they completely disappeared. The last of them, by the name of Tayair, who won universal fame, died in Little Kabarda in the 1850s. The *geguako*'s songs, which included the legends of the Narts, seem at first glance not to have a common theme; but on closer examination it is impossible not to notice an internal link between them, as if between parts of a single epic poem. The time is no longer far away, in fact it is already setting in, when even this old poem will be blotted out of the folk memory. Everything comes to an end.

Urusbievo village (1879)

Glossary

Abaz – a small coin, named from the Persian Shah Abbas.

Abrek – a partisan, or member of a Caucasian mountain band who fought the Russians in the nineteenth century. Also an escaped serf or an outlaw.

Adau – a race of giants in Abkhazia.

Aed – an angel.

Aguna – the custom of Aguna takes place in Georgia on the first evening of the New Year: the peasants go out to the wine press, knock on it with axes and repeat: 'Aguna, Aguna, come here, call into [name of our own vineyard] – to our vines, grapes; to those of others, only leaves; to our own wives, the silkworm and silk; to those of others, a stick and a spindle', etc.

Akhartsvy – *matsoni* or soured milk.

Aksakal – literally 'a white-bearded man', an elder, a headman.

Alabasha – a staff or pole that is used for carrying an animal carcass.

Alakhvara – a hollowed-out stone slab for threshing millet.

Albasly – a demonic creature of the female sex in eastern demonology.

Ambre-stone – a large stone.

Ane – a portable round table with three legs.

Arash – a legendary horse or steed; a heroic horse.

Argamak – a breed of racehorses from Central Asia.

Arkhaluki – a long shirt worn inside.

Assalam aleykum – a Muslim greeting meaning 'peace to you', with the answer '*Va aley-kum-salam*', 'And peace to you'.

Asura – an annexe to a house for household necessities.

Atalyk – a Tatar word meaning a tutor or educator. This could refer to a foster father, or to a man who has adopted an orphan.

Aul – a village.

Azarpesha – a bowl for wine.

Azhdakha – a dragon.

Bashlyk – a traditional hood worn in the Caucasus.

Batono – means lord, a form of polite address.

Batyr – a strong and brave hero, the same as a *bogatyr*.

Bay, bey, biy, beg – a Turkish feudal lord.

Beshmet – a shorter-sleeved under-robe, possibly of silk.

Beytulla – the 'House of Allah', the Kaaba in Mecca.

Bo – means the people, the army, an armed detachment.

Bogatyr – a mythical hero.

Burdyuk – a wineskin, a skin vessel from a whole goat or ox-skin: used for the storage and transport of wine or other liquids.

Burka – a traditional Caucasian black cape of felt, of goat's or sheep's wool.

Buza – an intoxicating drink not unlike beer, brewed from millet and sweetened with honey in wealthier houses.

Chabyr – a slipper of rawhide.

Chagana – an ancient mountain bowed musical instrument.

Charyks – galoshes (overshoes) of rawhide, put on to *chabyrs*; or slippers.

Chchantiaku – a pole for feeding sheaves of the harvest to a stack.

Chelti – a stretcher woven from twigs.

Chemeritsa – Veratrum, a plant of the lily family; a poisonous herb containing the potent alkaloid veratrine.

Cherkeska – an outer robe with no collar, cut with a long narrow V-shaped opening from the neck to below the breastbone; thence to below the waist it is fastened by tiny woven buttons.

Chiri – a charitable act, with absolution and forgiveness of sins.

Chokha – Georgian national men's costume of home-woven wool.

Churek – a type of Georgian bread.

Chuvyak – slippers, worn mainly in the Caucasus and Crimea.

Cossack – often means a wanderer on the steppe.

Dachu – a wooden measure for flowing material, taking about 14 to 16 kg of grain.

Dekanozi – servant at a sanctuary.

Dev – a fantastic creature, half man and half beast, of unusual strength, personifying the evil forces of nature.

Dibir – a member of the clergy whose obligations are to read the Koran in the mosque, to proclaim the call to prayer, and the observation of arrangements and furniture in the mosque.

Drofa – a large steppe bird with a long neck and strong legs.

El – the world of the dead.

Emegen – a multi-headed monster, a traditional enemy of the Balkar and Karachay Narts.

Fust – a lord.

Gamarjoba – a greeting on meeting somebody, meaning 'victory'.

Garbash – a slave-woman; witch, sorceress, Baba-Yaga.

Gazi – a fighter for the Faith.

Geguako – literally, a strolling player. He was a specialist singer, composer of songs, guardian of folklore and folk history.

Ghazavat – a holy war against non-Muslims.

Giaour – a name used by Muslims to refer to a person of another faith; a scornful name for all non-Muslims.

Godekan – the place in an *aul* where the men gather for leisure and where news is shared; the village square, a place of meeting, games, contests and so on; around its periphery are usually placed logs or stones for sitting on.

Goliati – a Goliath, see *bogatyr*.

Inyzh – a race of giants.

Jamaat – the village community; an assembly, sometimes used in the sense of 'the crowd'.

Jeyran – a gazelle or an ibex.

Jigit – a daring Caucasian horseman who can perform all kinds of tricks on horseback.

Jikhvi – the Georgian name for the mountain ibex, see *tur*.

Jinn – a spirit, somewhat akin to a traditional fairy.

Kadagi – a soothsayer chosen by a deity or dead spirit.

Kadi – a religious person among the Muslims, a judge.

Kajar – member of a Turkish-speaking tribe in Southern Iran.

Kaji – fantastic creatures, magician-people, usually hostile to man.

Kalamany – country footwear of tanned leather, fastened with small leather straps.

Kalym – the bride price.

Karakhalk – a scornful Arabo-Tatar nickname (literally 'black folk') used by gentlemen to denote peasants.

Karysh – a measure of length equal to the distance between the outstretched thumb and little finger.

Kasha – cooked grain in the form of gruel of various consistencies.

Ketkho – a storage loft.

Khachapuri – a kind of pie, of fresh cheese or curd with eggs.

Khanjali – the same as a *kinzhal*.

Khapar, khabar – an anecdote, a story or news.

Khipkhola – a field plant whose roots are used in food.

Khychauman – the month of May in the folk calendar of the Balkars and Karachays.

Khychin – a pie.

Khvtishvili – communal tribal deities.

Kibitka – a circular nomadic dwelling consisting of a frame covered with skins.

Kinzhal – a long dagger traditionally worn by men in the Caucasus.

Kizilbashi – literally 'red-headed', a Turkish nickname for Persians. The expression 'red heads' is derived from their distinctive crimson headgear.

Kizyaki – pressed dung used as fuel.

Kodi – a volume measure of free-flowing substances, equal to around 70 kg.

Kopeyek – a prematurely-born lamb.

Kumys – a fermented beverage prepared from mare's milk, used as a drink by the Tatars.

Kuralay – the female of one of the varieties of antelope.

Kuraysh – the native tribe of the Prophet Mohammed.

Kurdyuk – the tail of a fat-tailed sheep.

Kurgan – a tumulus, a burial mound; generally its height denoted the respect that the deceased had during his lifetime.

Kyzyl – means red flower, but in the ancient Nogay language it refers to the South.

Lepeshki – flat cakes.

Lokot' (plural loktey) – an obsolete measure of length, equal to one cubit, or the length of the forearm.

Lokum – a piece of dough fried on both sides in oil.

Machcha – a drink made from honey – mead.

Magal – a district or region, often of a town.

Mamalyga – a kind of porridge.

Maydan – a large open space, normally in a town, but could also be used in the sense of a field of battle.

Murid – a Muslim lay brother, bound to cultivate a fanatical hatred of the infidel, and blindly obeying his instructor, a sheikh or imam. The name became famous in connection with the Murid Wars, between Russia and the mountain people of Daghestan in the nineteenth century.

Murza – the son of a khan, a prince or leader.

Naib – selected officers of Shamil's army in the Murid Wars.

Namaz – a Muslim prayer performed five times a day at appointed times.

Nar – a male camel.

Narts – a legendary heroic race of warriors; legends of the Narts are found among all ethnic groups of the North Caucasus.

Nazir – a minister.

Nogovitsa – a footless sock.

Nukyer – was the original name of the Mongol khan's armed forces. After the Mongol conquest the name began to mean a servant or underling, often armed, of the khans and *beks*.

Nutsal – the title of a feudal overlord.

Orbi – a strong breed of mountain eagles.

Orkhustkhoys, Orstkhoys – the Ingush name of a tribe who obtained legendary prominence as the Nart-Orstkhoys.

Padchakh, padishah – a king, a sovereign among oriental peoples.

Paichi – see *nogovitsa*.

Palavan – a famous warrior, a strong hero.

Pandyra, pandura – a stringed musical instrument of the mountain people.

Papakha – a Caucasian cap of black or white sheepskin.

Paste – thick *kasha* or polenta, used by the Adyges in the same way as bread.

Peliuan – the same as *palavan*, a famous warrior, a strong hero.

Pood – a measure of weight equal to 16.38 kg.

Pranguli – the name of a good sword, literally a 'Frankish sword'.

Prostokvasha – soured milk, a kind of yoghurt.

Pshi – a prince among the Adyges.

Pyasi-Lach – a special kind of gun.

Rakhi – a strong alcoholic drink.

Sabantoy – a traditional spring festival among the Nogays.

Saklya – a dwelling in the Caucasus mountains.

Samani – a memorial or boundary stone.

Sapalne – a measure of wine.

Savrasy – a light brown horse with a black mane and tail.

Sazhen – a measure of length equal to 2.13 m.

Shahkhirman – the shah's threshing.

Shakhar – a settled area, a town.

Shamkhal – a traditional feudal title in Daghestan.

Shaytan – a devil, demon, a character resembling the traditional English or Irish fairy.

Shoti – bread baked in the form of a moon with two horns.

Stanitsa – a large Cossack village.

Tamada – a word that occurs throughout the Caucasus that means a 'leader'. It is commonly used for the master of ceremonies at a banquet.

Tavro – a brand, a distinguishing mark on the body of farm animals to denote ownership.

Tebyonki – a covering for the back and crupper of a horse, for decoration.

Tostakay – a wooden bowl.

Toy – a feast or celebration.

Tseko – a strong dark coarse tobacco.

Tukhum – a greater family or clan.

Tulpar – the same as a *turpal*.

Tur – a Caucasian mountain ibex, *Capra pallasii* or *Capra caucasica*.

Turpal, Turpul – a heroic horse, a *bogatyr*-horse, sometimes winged.

Uljay – looted goods.

Uork – a nobleman in a feudal community of the Adyges.

Uzden – an associate or comrade-in-arms; someone who has obligations of military service to a prince; also means leader or chief.

Vampal – literally a giant.

Vampolozh (singular vampal) – an Ingush word meaning 'giants'.

Vargi – minor nobility in Svaneti.

Verst – a measure of distance equal to about 1.06 km.

Vodyanoy – a water spirit or deity that occurs widely in Russian folklore, sometimes named Donbettyr or Donbyotar.

Yeshap – an anthropoid monster, usually an evil creature; may be male or female.

Yuyrau – a singer who performs Nogay heroic poetry.

Zakat – a tax on property, the proceeds of which go towards helping poor people

Zhazail – a gun with a long barrel.

Zhortuuul – an expedition or raid for the purpose of obtaining loot.

Zhummak – a lump, or little ball.

Zurna – a musical wind instrument of the whistle or trumpet type.

GLOSSARY OF GODS AND HEROES

Azhveypsh – the Abkhaz lord of the forests, protector of the beasts and birds and protector of the hunt.

Azrail – the angel of death.

Dali – the mistress of the beasts in Georgian (Svanetian) mythology.

Elia – a pagan deity of thunder and lightning. The name is also applied to the Old Testament Prophet Elijah, also known as Saint Elias.

Khydyr-Ilyas – in the folklore of the Nogay and other Turkish peoples he was an ancient wanderer who would come to the aid of lost travellers and people who had found themselves in difficult situations.

Kuday – a name for God.

Nart – one of a lost race of heroes, the embodiment of heroism and manliness. The Nart legends are distributed throughout the North Caucasus, and there are even traces of them in Georgia. The origin of the legends is much disputed, and several ethnic groups lay claim to them.

Sela-Sata – the same as Setenay, but the Chechen–Ingush variant.

Seli, Sela – the pagan god who commanded the thunder and lightning.

Seska Solsa – the Chechen–Ingush variant of Sosruko.

Setenay – the foster mother of the hero Sosruko and the wife of the hero Yoruzmek.

Shamil' – imam and Daghestan war leader in the Murid Wars against the Russians in the nineteenth century.

Shota Rustaveli – the famous twelfth-century Georgian poet who composed *The Knight in the Panther's Skin*. He lived during the reign of Queen Tamar (1184–1213 AD).

Sosruko, Sosuruk – the Adyge and Balkar–Karachay variant of one of the main Nart heroes who was supposed to have been born from a stone.

Teyri – the supreme god in the pagan pantheon of the Balkars and Karachays.

Tkha – the supreme god in the pagan pantheon of the Adyge people.

Tlepsh – the divine blacksmith in the pagan pantheon of the Adyges.

Yoryuzmek – a hero of the Narts.

Zal – the Laks call God Zal, although they also use the word 'Allah'.

GLOSSARY OF PLACE-NAMES

Anapa, town – a port on the Black Sea coast, not far from the Taman Peninsula.

Apsny – the Abkhaz name for the land of Abkhazia.

Aragvi, River – flows south from the mountains and joins the Kura (Mtqvari) at Mtskheta, near Tbilisi.

Argun, River – flows north from the mountains and joins the River Sunzha and then the River Terek.

Assa, River – flows north from the mountains and joins the River Sunzha and then the River Terek.

Bukhara, town – in Uzbekistan.

Cherek, River – a river flowing north from the mountains into the River Terek.

Darial Pass – over the mountains, linking Tbilisi and Vladikavkaz, following the courses of the Aragvi and the Terek.

Derbent – ancient town on the shore of the Caspian Sea.

Edil', River – the same as River Idil'.

Elbrus, Mount – the highest mountain in the Caucasus, and in Europe, height 5642 m. It has twin peaks, which feature in many legends. The mountain people believe that Noah's Ark stopped on Elbrus.

Gori – a town on the River Kura (Mtqvari), west of Tbilisi.

Grozny – the capital of Chechnya.

Idil', River – another name for the River Volga, although the word is used to signify 'a large river'.

Itil', River – the River Volga.

Iori, River – flows southeast through Georgia into Azerbayjan.

Irtysh, River – a Central-Asian river that flows northwards towards the Arctic.

Kakheti, region – was one of the most ancient provinces of Georgia; divided off at the time of the feudal break-up of Georgia into an independent unit and once more united with Kartli in the eighteenth century by Irakli II.

Kartli – was the most ancient province of eastern Georgia; in antique sources it was called Iberia.

Khiva – capital of the former khanate, on a tributary of the Amu-Darya River, south of the Aral Sea.

Kodor, River – flows south from the mountains into the Black Sea.

Makhachkala – the capital of Daghestan, on the Caspian Sea coast.

Mineral'nye vody – a town near Pyatigorsk in south Russia; literally means 'mineral waters'.

Nal'chik – the main town of the Kabardo–Balkarian Republic, in the North Caucasus.

Paliastomi, Lake – near the port of Poti on the Black Sea.

Ritsa, Lake – a mountain lake in Abkhazia, now a resort.

Saraychuk – the capital of the Nogay Horde on the lower course of the River Volga.

Sekerli, Lake – this lake could not be located.

Stambul – Istanbul.

Sulak, River – one of the chief rivers of Daghestan, flowing east into the Caspian Sea.

Sunzha, River – flows north from the mountains and joins the Terek.

Tbilisi – the capital of Georgia.

Ten, River – the Nogay name of the River Don.

Terek, River – one of the two main rivers flowing from the north face of the Caucasus; it then turns east and flows into the Caspian Sea. The other main river is the Kuban, which flows west towards the Black Sea.

Yartashi – the Lak name for Khunzakh in Daghestan.

References

Aarne, Antti, *The Types of Folktale*, tr. Thompson, Stith, FF Communications No. 184, Suomalainen Tiedeakatemia, Helsinki, 1981.

Abakarova, F., *Darginskie fol'klor*, Kavkazsky Dom, Tbilisi, 1999.

Anon, *Gilgamesh*, ed. Sanders, N. K., Penguin, London, 1964.

Baddeley, J. F., *The Rugged Flanks of Caucasus*, OUP, Oxford, 2 vols, 1940.

Bardavelidze, J., *Adygsky fol'klor*, Kavkazsky Dom, Tbilisi, 1994.

Bardavelidze, V. V., *Drevneyshie religioznye verovaniya i obryadovoye graficheskoye isskustvo gruzinskikh plemen*, Akad. Nauk GSSR, Tbilisi, 1957.

Bezhanov, M., *Skazaniya gorskikh yevreyev Kavkaza*, Tan, Kazan, 1993.

Bgazhba, Kh. S., *Abkhazskie skazki*, Alashara, Sukhumi, 1985.

Blanch, L., *The Sabres of Paradise*, Murray, London, 1960.

Briggs, K. M., *A Dictionary of British Folk-tales*, Part A, Folk narratives, Vol. 1, Routledge & Kegan Paul, London, 1970.

—*A Dictionary of British Folk-tales*, Part B, Folk legends, Vol. 1, Routledge & Kegan Paul, London, 1971.

Byhan, A., *La civilisation caucasienne*, Payot, Paris, 1936.

Chikovani, M. Ya., *Gruzinskie narodnye skazki*, Merani, Tbilisi, 1971.

Chlaidze, L., *Avarsky fol'klor*, Kavkazsky Dom, Tbilisi, 2006.

—*Lezginsky fol'klor*, Kavkazsky Dom, Tbilisi, 2006.

Chursin, G. F., *Ocherki po etnologii Kavkaza*, Tiflis, 1913.

Colarusso, J., *Nart Sagas from the Caucasus*, Princeton University Press, Princeton, 2002.

Dalgat, B, *Pervobytnaya religiya chechentsev i ingushey*, compiled by Dalgat, U. B., Nauka, Moscow, 2004.

Dalgat U. B., *Geroichesky epos chechentsev i ingushey*, Nauka, Moscow, 1972.

Dumézil, G., *Contes et légendes des Oubykhs*, University of Paris, Paris, 1957.

Gadagatl', A. M., *Geroichesky epos Narty i evo genesis*, Krasnodar Knizhnoye Isdatel'stvo, Krasnodar, 1967.

—*Samoupravlyayemaya strela Narta Tlepsha*, Ripo, Maykop, 2000.

Gelashvili, N., *Ubykhsky Fol'klor*, Kavkazsky Dom, Tbilisi, 1995.

—*Chechensky Fol'klor*, Kavkazsky Dom, Tbilisi, 1996.

Hesiod, *Theogony*, ed. West, M. L., Clarendon, Oxford, 1966.

Isayev, M. Sh., 'Zoonim betsi "volk" kak component struktury fraseologicheskoy edinitsy darginskovo yazyka', *Otrislevaya leksika dagestanskikh yazykov; nazvaniya zhivotnikh i ptits*, ed. Talibov, B. B., Dagestansky filial Akad, Nauk SSSR, Makhachkala, 1988.

Jousse, M., *Études de psychologie linguistique. Le style et mnémotechnique chez les verbo-moteurs*, Paris, 1925.

Khajieva, T. M. & Ortabayeva, R.-A-K., *Narty*, Nauka, Moscow, 1994.

Khajieva, T. M., 'Karachayevtsy i Balkartsy: Yasyk, Etnografia, Arkheologia, Folklor', Seria Kavkaz: Narody i Kultury, Part 1, Moscow, 2001.

Khajieva, T. M., private communication, 2003.

Khalilov, Kh., *Lakskie epicheskie pesni*, Dagestan Filial AN SSSR, Makhachkala, 1983.

Klaproth, J. von, *Travels in the Caucasus and Georgia, Performed in the Years 1807 and 1808*, tr. from German by Shoberl, F., Colburn, London, 1814.

Kukullu, A., *Zolotoy sunduk – skazki tatov Dagestana*, Nauka, Moscow, 1974.

Lord, A., *The Singer of Tales*, Harvard University Press, Cambridge, Mass., 1981.

Mal'sagov, A. O., *Skazki i legendy Ingushey i Chechentsev*, Nauka, Moscow, 1983.

Mufti, S., *Heroes and Emperors in Circassian History*, Librairie du Liban, Beirut, 1972.

Nauka, *Narody Kavkaza*, ed. Tolstoy, S. P., Izdatelstvo, Nauka, Moscow, 1960.

Neihardt, J. G., *Black Elk Speaks*, University of Nebraska Press, Lincoln, Neb., 1961.

Osmanov, M.-Z., *Darginskie skazki*, Nauka, Moscow, 1963.

Pachulia, V. P., *Padenie Anakopiya*, Nauka, Moscow, 1986.

Reichl, K., *Edige: A Karakalpak Heroic Epic*, FFC No. 293, Academia Scientiarum Fennica, Helsinki, 2007.

Shanidze, A., *Gruzinskaya narodnaya poeziya: I. Khevsurskaya*, Tbilisi, 1933.

Sikaliev, A. I.-M., *Nogaysky geroichesky epos*, Karachayevsky Institut Gumanitarnykh Issledovaniy, Cherkessk, 1994.

Sokolov, Yu. M., *Kabardinsky fol'klor*, Academia, Moscow-Leningrad, 1936.

Thompson, Stith, *Motif-Index of Folk-Literature*, 6 vols, Indiana University Press, Bloomington & Indianapolis, 1955.

Virsaladze, E. B., *Gruzinskie narodnye predaniya i legendy*, Nauka, Moscow, 1973.

—*Gruzinskie okhotnichy mif i poeziya*, Nauka, Moscow, 1976.

Zyazykov, M. M., *Traditsionnaya Kul'tura ingushey: istoriya i sovremennost*, SKNT VSh, Rostov-on-Don, 2004.